D0852998

The Shaping of the Modern Mind

Other books by Jacob S. Minkin

The Romance of Hassidism

Herod : A Biography

Abarbanel and the Expulsion of the Jews from Spain

The World of Moses Maimonides

The Shaping of the Modern Mind

The Life and Thought of the Great Jewish Philosophers

by

Jacob S. Minkin

With an Introductory Appreciation by

FANNY R. MINKIN

New York · THOMAS YOSELOFF · London

© 1963 by A. S. Barnes and Company, Inc.
Library of Congress Catalog Card Number: 63-18240

Thomas Yoseloff, *Publisher*
8 East 36th Street
New York 16, N.Y.

Thomas Yoseloff Ltd.
18 Charing Cross Road
London W.C.2, England

8928
Printed in the United States of America

Preface

SEVENTEEN OF THE twenty-one chapters of this volume were written years ago and appeared in a number of Jewish publications. When it was suggested that they be given a more permanent form, the articles were revised and enlarged and four new ones were added.

The personalities presented in this volume cover a long stretch of history—from Ezra, the scribe, one of the builders of the Second Jewish Commonwealth, to Chaim Weitzmann, one of the architects of the Third Jewish Commonwealth; and from Hillel, one of the first of the Pharisees, to the contemporary exponents and interpreters of the rabbinic tradition. The book, therefore, presents diversified portraits of Jewish heroes of the spirit—men who differed from one another in language, culture, and approach to Judaism. The resemblance between them that makes for unity and cohesion of the over-all story lies in the fact that they were all Jews, militant Jews, frontiersmen of the Jewish spirit, who zealously fought and labored for the preservation of their faith and people.

The choice of subjects was governed by consideration of space. But for this limitation several other outstanding Jewish characters would have been included. Perhaps the most obvious omission is that of Dr. Isaac Mayer Wise of our own time, a creative American Jewish spirit if there ever was one. A man of fabulous energy and organizing genius, he founded the Hebrew Union College, the Central Conference of American Rabbis, and the Union of American Hebrew Congregations. He left the imprint of his personality upon the development of Reform Judaism in this country.

The author acknowledges his deep gratitude to the Jewish Publication Society of America for permission to use their excellent publications; to Harper and Brothers for their publication, *Trial and Error;* to Dr. Irving Agus for his *Rabbi Mayer of Rothenburg;*

to Prof. Salo W. Baron for his outstanding work, *A Social and Religious History of the Jews;* to Dr. Meyer Waxman for his monumental *History of Jewish Literature;* and to Dr. Solomon Grayzel, who read several chapters in their original form and made constructive suggestions. Mention must be made of the usefulness to the author of the *Jewish Encyclopedia* and Graetz's *History of the Jews.* The author is grateful to the libraries of the Jewish Theological Seminary of America and of the Yeshiva University for their cooperation and courtesy.

The writer's heaviest indebtedness is to his wife for her valuable assistance in every phase of this book. With unwearying patience she read and reread the manuscript and was especially helpful with her sound judgment and keen critical sense. This book is therefore dedicated to Fanny R. Minkin, on the occasion of our fiftieth wedding anniversary, in love and gratitude.

JACOB S. MINKIN

Contents

Jacob Minkin: An Appreciation

AMONG THE CHINESE it appears to be customary for the husband to publish an evaluation of his departed wife. There is no such known custom among Jews. However, a life's companion possesses facts and impressions more revealing than most biographers have. It was my privilege to share more than fifty years of trials and triumphs with Jacob Minkin. I consider this relationship my credential for writing about him. Twenty years elapsed before I managed to give utterance to reminiscences that welled up within me about my father. But now time may be running out. I dare not postpone my narration about my husband, a scholar, rabbi and author.

It was not hard to know him. He was an outgoing person, frank to a fault, with few inhibitions, giving at times the impression of naivete. In reality he was an open book to those interested, yet he suffered from an innate shyness which prevented a close friendship with many he admired but to whom he could not communicate his feelings.

Jacob S. Minkin was known as a rabbi but in the words of a distinguished colleague, "by his writings he had made a contribution that transcends far beyond his congregations and particular communities." His works can be found in the leading libraries of the world. He often heard from friends who saw his books in the distant countries they visited. His peers judged his works and agreed that he had made "a significant contribution for a deeper understanding of Judaism by his articles and books."

A true son of his people, Jacob Minkin followed the Jewish pattern of setting Torah above all else. But he added academic knowledge as an equal "must" for him. Culture was the be-all and end-all of his life. From early childhood he had been exposed to

9

respect, admiration and devotion to learning in the home of his parents Leib Ariah and Rachel Leah Minkin. In his native town of Swenziani, Poland, he, like all sons of good Jewish families, was set on the path of study in the *heder* at a very young age. The importance of preparing a boy for the Yeshivah prompted an early start despite the very tender age and the frail body. Boys were sent to Yeshivoth away from home with no assurance of comfort for the student. Privation and hardships were the accepted lot of the *Yeshivah Bochur* (Talmudic student). In fact it was considered a special *mitzvah* (merit) for the student to suffer want and discomfort while dedicating himself to the study of Torah. Sacrifices in the process of acquiring knowledge of the Torah were taken for granted not only by the Minkin parents but by all Jews interested in Jewish education. There were no dormitories, nor was there any opportunity for gracious living for the students. The good women in the neighborhood of the Yeshivah, eager to earn a mitzvah for helping support Torah, provided humble board and lodging for these boys.

Leib Minkin was a gentle, refined scholarly man of a rabbinic family who knew and appreciated the value of Torah. He encouraged his son to devote himself to study in order to become wise and learned in the Jewish Lore. The first Yeshivah he chose for Jacob was in the Greva near Vilna, over which his brother, Rabbi Boruch Velvel, presided. The young student took great pride in being the nephew of this venerable scholar. He considered himself fortunate in having his uncle's interest and guidance and was profoundly influenced by his master. There he was first exposed to the contact with outstanding scholars for whom he conceived admiration and respect. This atmosphere inspired a sincere appreciation and love for scholarship. It left an indelible impression on him and served as a staff upon which he enjoyed leaning. When he was referred to as of the "old school" Minkin was not embarrassed but was rather flattered by this appellation. He was especially pleased that no less a personage than the late, highly distinguished Chief Rabbi Isaac Kook of Jerusalem and his brothers, in their early youth, also studied under this great master and teacher. Jacob Minkin subsequently attended Yeshivoth more popular and of wider repute, but his first experience left the deepest impression on him.

While immersed in study at a Yeshivah, he became aware of Haskalah, the movement of enlightenment, introduced to Germany by Moses Mendelssohn at the end of the eighteenth century. It strove to open a window into the outer world. The rabbis opposed it because the sponsors emphasized secular knowledge instead of Torah and sought to counteract the influence of the rabbinic interpretation of the Scriptures. Vigorous in its approach, its efforts were far reaching, managing to penetrate even into the citadel of old honored values in the Torah Institutions. The religious leaders' opposition to these alien ideas was due to their refusal to permit Torah to be mixed with secular knowledge. They looked askance at the imputation that Torah was insufficient to cover every aspect of knowledge essential for the Jew. The Rabbis deemed them alien ideas not fit companions to Torah study to be barred as extraneous and harmful. The students were therefore forced to choose between complete absorption in the Torah to the exclusion of any other culture, or the abandonment of this interest in favor of a wider scope of general knowledge. Many a Yeshivah Bochur found the attraction of academic study so tempting that they chose to follow the trend of the times. Jacob Minkin too was smitten. Although lured by the new vistas opening a door to the world which offered wisdom and important knowledge, he did not consider abandoning the old. He aimed to combine both cultures, thus gaining greater enlightenment. He began dreaming of horizons beyond his limited environment. New interests now beckoned and he felt impelled to heed the urgent call.

It required a definite break but he decided upon a drastic step. It demanded courage and will power to leave his home and his family to embark on an uncertain, even hazardous venture. His mother, following a natural maternal instinct to keep her offspring near her, found it hard to reconcile herself to the idea of parting from her youngest son, even though it was prompted by a pure and noble motive. But his father appreciated learning too much to oppose his son's determination to take advantage of an opportunity to become wise and learned by drinking from the fountain of knowledge in distant lands. It was therefore with the blessing of his saddened but proud parents that he decided to embark on this great adventure. Germany was the goal, the Mecca for the Jewish youth of Russia and Poland, where Jews were prohibited from attending schools of higher learning. He succeeded in crossing over to the coveted country which offered greater opportunities to those who were interested. He reached Berlin about which he had heard much. His ambition was to enter the Hildersheimer University. He appeared to be eligible but lacked the language. To qualify he applied himself most assiduously to the study of German. He sought to master the language and make it his own. His overpowering desire was to become a *Rabbinat Candidat*. The Hildersheimer Schule was primarily a seminary for the preparation of predigers— rabbis and preachers. Jacob Minkin considered the rabbinate a sacred and scholarly profession. He appreciated the privilege of being admitted to this worthy institution known for such outstanding scholars as Dr. David Hoffman, its head. Dr. Hoffman was recognized as leader, teacher and profound scholar by his colleagues and contemporaries. The student little knew that he would subsequently be privileged to continue a close friendship with this great man's daughter Hannah and her illustrious husband, Dr. Alexander Marx.

Later he spent some time in Prague and there too enjoyed an atmosphere of scholarship and rich influence which he prized highly. Here too he met with kindness and interest. He required not only guidance but financial means to devote himself to study and he never forgot his benefactors who helped him obtain scholarships, advised him in his scholastic interests, and provided him with medical aid. He was very happy to meet Dr. Guido Kisch whom he learned to respect and admire. Rabbi Alexander Kisch, his father, and Dr. Enoch Heinrich Kisch, his uncle, both helped him.

For a time Jacob Minkin planned to settle in Germany, but found it unfeasible and inadvisable. Eastern Jews were not acceptable to their German brethren. Most Russian and Polish immigrants had fled from persecution and discrimination. They had suffered destitution and were denied the opportunity to qualify for professions or trades in which they might advance themselves. They hoped to establish themselves in Germany where there seemed to be a chance to succeed. But they annoyed their German brethren by their lack of social amenities. They had had little opportunity to learn proper manners and gracious ways. He felt their plight too keenly to try to adjust himself where his people were unwanted. Being sensitive, he ceased to feel at ease in this environment which suggested an alien atmosphere. Despite his deep appreciation and attachment to those who befriended him and provided him with coveted opportunities, he nevertheless was impelled again to pick up the wanderer's staff. He decided to set out to find a haven that would offer both safety of body and peace of mind. He sought intellectual and spiritual comfort.

America beckoned the lonely youth and off he went. There was no difficulty of admittance. The doors were open to all in search of opportunities to help develop the land founded and established by immigrants who themselves had fled from intolerance. There was no quota to block one's entrance. He landed in New York City, where his brother and other members of his family had settled. He found most Jews congregated in one section. All in the neighborhood shared in an intimate community life. Their native *shtetel* was transplanted and they adjusted themselves in their family groups and *landsmanshaften*. He failed to recognize the melting pot.

The Minkins too formed a family circle or clan. They had not discovered the streets that were reputed to be paved with gold. They were engaged in petty business affairs, struggling to eke out a modest living. They welcomed the newcomer to their midst and were eager to advise and guide him to adjust properly in this new home. But Jacob's resolve did not change. Neither the new country nor clime dampened his ardor for learning. He recognized the need to work as a means towards an end. But he was determined to begin to study with little delay. His relatives knew the importance of learning. They, too, were imbued with the value of this Jewish ideal. But they were already beset with problems and looked upon study as a luxury for those who could afford it. They urged the necessity of practicality. They advised against frittering away valuable time essential in forging ahead on the road to financial stability. They cautioned him to cease dreaming and to abandon his lofty fancies and nebulous ambition. They counselled postponing his educational program for the future after he had scored economic success. He did not dispute the necessity to be practical. He was determined to become self-supporting, self-reliant and independent. To meet his frugal needs until he found a job he disposed of his few belongings. A tie-pin and such trinkets given him as keepsakes he sold to relatives and used the proceeds. He tried his hand at odd jobs. Among his first attempts was a position in a shirt factory.

Many unskilled immigrants took to peddling notions and some graduated to handling other merchandise. A number of outstanding successful merchants trace their beginnings to such ventures. But this enterprise had no attraction for Jacob Minkin. He was interested in finding a position to afford him a living and spare time enough to devote himself to study. He succeeded in being appointed as teacher in a Talmud Torah (Hebrew Free School). The salary was small but the hours were short and he found his opportunity to attend courses. He enjoyed the connections he thus made and found many rewarding experiences, which helped his adjustment in his new homeland. He taught in a New York City Hebrew School which was under the supervision of the late eminent Rabbi Dr. Philip Klein, with whom he formed a very friendly relationship. Dr. Klein, who was a friend of my father, called when he heard about our engagement to congratulate us on the fine choice of a young man he highly commended.

Jacob Minkin applied himself to the task of learning English even as he had done to acquire German when he expected to settle in that land. Hopefully intending the United States to be his permanent home he was eager to make the language his own. To acquire the correct pronunciation and proper enunciation he considered it advisable to divest himself of the previous languages which he feared were detrimental to the spoken English. He refrained from using his hard-earned German which he had mastered so well that when, in later years, we visited Germany and

Austria, he was often taken for a German. And this language proved very helpful subsequently in his research. But for the time, he put it out of his mind and away from his tongue. That also was why he stopped speaking his "mother-tongue" Yiddish. Foreigners often found that to perfect themselves accent-wise, they had to overcome the impediment created by the use of their formerly practiced languages. He made a sincere effort to learn the new tongue by becoming an avid reader of the classics, though he required the constant use of a dictionary. He listened to as many lectures as he could crowd in to hear and absorb the spoken words. He attended classes in the preparatory school entirely for the study of English. He had acquired the subjects necessary for college admission abroad, but to be fully eligible he had to learn English well. He worked diligently and earnestly to prepare himself for the Regents Examination which was a prerequisite for admission to a college by foreign-born students who did not attend elementary and high school in the United States. He qualified and matriculated at Columbia College where he subsequently was awarded the degrees of B.A. and M.A. It was a proud moment for the penniless immigrant youth.

His interest was still in the rabbinate as a calling. He was recommended to Temple Emanuel of New York City for a scholarship at Hebrew Union College in Cincinnati, Ohio. It was, as it still is, the Seminary for the preparation of reform rabbis for the more liberal congregations. He matriculated and spent a year there but he was very unhappy because, at that time, the school followed an ultra reform policy. Again he felt himself out of his environment. It was for him an alien religious climate. He could not adjust to watching practices that differed so greatly from the orthodox way of life he knew. He was disappointed and suffered from a nostalgic feeling for his accustomed atmosphere. He left Hebrew Union College and Cincinnati, and returned to New York. He applied to the Jewish Theological Seminary of America or, as it was then known and is even now remembered, the "Schechter Seminary." Admitted, he applied himself and completed the required course of study which entitled him to become "rabbi, teacher and preacher in Israel."

Dr. Solomon Schechter had recently come to America from London to reorganize the Jewish Theological Seminary. He introduced the Conservative Movement to this country, thus giving a new turn to American Judaism. He initiated a new status for the Seminary and lent prestige to the institution. Jacob Minkin fell under the spell of this great scholar and thinker. He admired and regarded with deep respect this illustrious teacher, who in turn, evidenced to his student an interest and fondness which was most touching and gratifying. Their relationship amounted to a beautiful friendship with true understanding.

Tuition at the Seminary was always free but there were no dormitories to house and board students. To maintain themselves they were obliged to find means of support. Jacob Minkin was fortunate in being awarded a scholarship which could cover his expenses. It was a mark of distinction he appreciated highly and found most useful. But he learned that a friend, a fellow student, needed the financial aid even more than he did, so he consulted Dr. Schechter and with his permission transferred the prized award. He subsequently was recommended to a position as house tutor to two sons of a friend of the Seminary Faculty, where he found a comfortable home and pleasant atmosphere for almost the entire term of his studies at the Seminary. Dr. Schechter indicated partiality to his favored student by selecting him valedictorian of his class albeit there were better orators among his fellow-students. Dr. Schechter's interest in Minkin proved a great influence. The confidence in his student's abilities became a challenge to be met. Dr. Schechter advised that Minkin begin his career in a small city with less responsibilities for the Rabbi, thus affording a better opportunity to continue the pursuit of learning. He foretold a scholarly career for his favorite student.

Dr. Schechter surrounded himself with carefully chosen associates whose scholarship and personalities added prestige and standing to the reorganized institution of higher Jewish learning. Dr. Louis Ginzberg and Dr. Alexander Marx rapidly gained international acclaim while they won the respect and admiration of both their colleagues and their students. Jacob Minkin was one of their ardent admirers, who not only respected but loved them. He proudly referred to them as modern "giants in Jewish history" for, with Dr. Schechter, they formed a triumvirate whose scholarship, in his estimation, could not easily be matched.

Fortunately he was able to continue this prized association with Dr. Ginzberg, Dr. Marx and also Dr. Israel Davidson until their death. His beloved teachers made Rabbi Minkin feel that he was one of the Seminary Family, as Dr. Marx so kindly expressed it. He appreciated them not only for their profound scholarship but equally for their noble, humane characteristics. Their passing was a grievous loss to Jacob Minkin. Minkin idolized true learning but recoiled from pretense and sham. Nor did scholarship devoid of the human touch appeal to him. Those who secluded themselves in ivory towers while their fellow men clamored for their advice, guidance and inspiration, he considered unworthy of respect and admiration.

Minkin admired Dr. Stephen S. Wise for his human qualities, even more than for his God-given gifts. He appreciated the leader who concerned himself not only with every worthwhile Jewish cause but dedicated himself to the service of all who were in need of sympathy, understanding and help. Dr. Wise was among the first to lend a helping hand to the dispossessed German scholars, the victims of the madness and barbarism of the Hitler outrages. He saved numerous sufferers from the holocaust which engulfed Europe, and helped rehabilitate them by creating posts in the Institute of Jewish Religion. Dr. Minkin joined the numerous admirers of this noble man, and Dr. Wise frequently voiced his admiration for Minkin's works and spoke of him in most flattering terms. Realizing that the author required a part time position to devote himself to his absorbing interest—writing—he considered a chaplaincy the best solution. And it was Dr. Wise who was greatly responsible for Mayor La Guardia's appointment of Minkin as Chaplain at Fordham Hospital. This friendly feeling continued until the untimely death of Dr. Stephen S. Wise. They were unlike in their religious views and practices, but were at one in their high ideals.

Jacob Minkin was already an ordained rabbi and a college graduate when we met and after a brief courtship were married. He easily met my father's standard of eligibility with his Hebraic background and knowledge. He required few more credentials to be heartily accepted by my parents. His academic achievements met the fancy of a young girl reared in an atmosphere where learning was considered an essential quality. Many young immigrants among our acquaintances were struggling students aiming to qualify for a learned profession, but their circumstances prevented them from enjoying the luxury of an academic college degree. It was a unique and unexpected attainment and added gratification for my dear ones.

We were a small family, few in numbers but devoted to each other, and one and all welcomed the new member whole-heartedly. There was, however, for a brief time, an embarrassment due to linguistic difficulties. My father did not speak English and Jacob knew little Yiddish. Both knew Hebrew but did not consider it an adequate medium for colloquial purpose. It irked father that the son of a fine Jewish family of Sivenziani, a Yeshivah student who could join in a learned Talmudic discussion, should not speak the "mother tongue" as Yiddish was called by most East European Jews. Although rabbis of different schools, they had much in common if only they could communicate with each other. Jacob quickly recognized the incongruity of the situation and set himself to correct it. In a short time he recaptured the language he was born to, but which he deliberately sought to forget while in the process of mastering new and strange tongues. All obstacles to a mutual appreciation of each other being removed, a high regard for one another was forged. My husband admired and loved his father-in-law, and my father very much appreciated his son-in-law.

There were no in-laws in the Rabinowitz family. Reuben Colman, my sister's husband, Jacob Minkin and Harris Rabinowitz, my brother, were all sons to my parents, and Ida Bernstein Rabinowitz, my brother's wife, my sister, Bessie Colman, and I were equally precious daughters to our parents. There was loyalty, love and devotion among all. But the Colman-Minkin relationship presents a saga unique in even the closest family circles. The two brothers-in-law developed a friendship and interest based on genuine affection and esteem which lasted until death untimely snatched Reuben W. Colman from us.

Recognizing Jacob's fondness for children, my sister and her husband unselfishly tried to share their youngsters with Minkin. They exposed Jacob and Leah to him, inspiring respect and affection for their "Uncle Jacob" who became their idol. They were like children to him. "Kelly" (Yankelle) was a pet name by which Minkin expressed the sincere affection for his namesake nephew. Realizing the tender and sentimental implication of the nick name, all friends accepted and used the misnomer "Kelly." Young as Miriam Greenblatt was when she became Mrs. Jacob Colman, she quickly discerned qualities attracting her to her husband's "Uncle Jacob." It was mutual and a bond was forged between them developing into a relationship which extended far beyond the usual understanding intellectual appreciation. She like Leah became a loving daughter who provided him with the experience of a proud and happy father, an intimacy and devotion which lasted to the end of his life and sweetened the last years for him. Not only Miriam but all their relatives and friends joined the circle and adopted "Uncle Jacob."

Jacob and Miriam followed the Colman tradition, and in turn created a close tie betweeen their precious offspring and their "Uncle Jacob." This introduced a very special episode. It was a relationship that by far transcended the usual uncle-nephew tie. The third generation, Robert and Arthur Colman, were exposed to the influence of "Uncle Jacob" from infancy. While babies they learned to know him as an intimate figure. They loved to hear him read to them and especially delighted were they when he told them stories. Perched on his knees, they raptly drank in every word of the tales of mystical lore he spun for them. They were never bored, nor was he tired from their delightful sessions. He felt amply rewarded by the sight of their glowing faces and shining eyes full of pleasure and anticipation. They subsequently claimed him to be their first teacher to inspire them with a love for the Bible and an appreciation of the great Jewish personalities who adorn the pages of our history.

What proved most gratifying was that this close feeling, far from lessening when these youngsters grew, matured and attained outstanding scholastic recognition, was intensified. He was proud and happy to follow the numerous triumphs they scored in their chosen distinguished fields and they, in turn, were increasingly appreciative of him. Since their intimate relationship was now based on an intellectual exchange, they continued to enjoy a true intimacy with him and claimed a fuller enrichment from the contact. They followed his writings with intelligent appreciation and were duly proud of him. Their wives too joined this charmed circle of love and admiration and together with their dear parents they succeeded in dispelling any sense of loneliness due to childlessness. The gracious acts of love shown him gave additional luster to the final days of their uncle's life. Their touching tribute after his death would have raised his spirits even higher.

He loved all children and all our nephews and nieces gave him much pleasure and delight, although this connection probably followed the usual relationship between an uncle and nephews and nieces. His fondness for children seemed to be sensed by most youngsters. Even babies usually responded to his attentions. Readily they came to him when they shied away from other outstretched arms. A mutual rapport existed between him and all the children who knew him.

Actually it may be said, Jacob Minkin loved people, young and old. He admired the great but appreciated most human beings. He often quoted, "God must love the common people since He created so many of them." He saw good qualities in practically everyone. No one, he maintained, is devoid of fine traits; it behoves us to uncover them. Friendship he regarded the outstanding relationship in life. He instinctively followed an ethical behavior prompted by the "Jewish Categorical Imperative." He found great satisfaction in proving himself helpful. A kindness done him was never forgotten and was rewarded by his eternal gratitude. All the reciprocity desired on his part was a feeling of friendship. Of ingratitude he was intolerant.

He was exceedingly sensitive not only for himself, but sympathetically shared the pain with anyone hurt. He was deeply affected by the tale of misfortune or tragedy even when he knew it to be a fictitious story, dramatized. He was apt to weep copiously during a performance that touched him emotionally.

Kindness and gentleness were the most visible traits of Jacob Minkin's personality. He was impulsive yet never offensive to anyone; even in self defense he could not utter an unkind retort. Always sympathetic, he never turned down a request for a favor in his power to perform. When an emissary (a *meshulach*) from a reputable institution came to his city to appeal for funds, the Rabbi never refused his assistance or sponsorship even when it was necessary for him to accompany the "messenger of mercy" and thus lend him prestige. While yet a struggling student he proved of help to fellow-students who for some reason were unable to meet their needs.

Active and energetic, he found it hard to understand the lacadaisical. He drove himself without realizing it. He enjoyed and was enthusiastic about everything he undertook. His sense of humor helped him meet the exigencies life managed to toss up for him. It was natural for him to meet a challenge and he rose to the occasion without a perceptible effort on his part.

Jacob Minkin was graduated from the Jewish Theological Seminary of America in 1910, and began his service in the calling he chose. He received the degree of Doctor of Hebrew Literature in 1935 when Dr. Cyrus Adler was President of the Jewish Theological Seminary of America, in recognition of his book *The Romance of Hassidism*, and was again honored by this Institution under the leadership of Dr. Louis Finkelstein in 1956 when the degree of Doctor of Hebrew Letters was conferred upon him.

Conscientiously and whole heartedly he dedicated himself to the rabbinate. For over twenty five years he sought to render the service he considered most suitable to do justice to the dignified calling. In his opinion learning and scholarship were essential attributes of a rabbi. But he neither deprecated nor minimized the popular aptitudes necessary adequately to minister to a modern congregation. His greatest interest was education. He concerned himself not only with the congregational religious schools, but took an active part in the Jewish educational program of the community. Adult education was his pet interest long before it became popular. He was among the pioneers to introduce this project to the congregational family.

He held the pulpit in high esteem and sought to maintain a high standard of Jewish ideals and teachings. But more than the religious and educational programs evoked his interest. The members, their families and friends, were always his sincere concern. He shared their joys and sorrows and was ever ready to help them with their problems and sympathized with their perplexities. They were an integral part of his life.

His first position, except for a senior year student's assignment, was in Hamilton, Ontario, a progressive modern city, which viewed in the light of a metropolitan community was small and limited. He rapidly threw himself into the community's interests, which became his. Our home was a clearing house for all troubled souls. The needy applied for relief, which the sisterhood helped to provide. The confused and perplexed sought guidance in the solution of their problems. No one was refused a hearing and everyone was assured of sympathy and understanding.

In a sense Rabbi Minkin was a novice feeling his way in the work he loved. He won the esteem and appreciation not only of his congregation but also of the community. He lent his aid to the Talmud Torah, the Hebrew Free School, under the community supervision, and to all their Jewish intellectual pursuits and activities. He also participated in many of the civic undertakings. He enjoyed the friendship of the orthodox rabbi as well as of the lay intellectual leaders of the city. The editors of the daily press came to recognize him as the authority in their city for authentic information on all Jewish topics. The Ministers Association considered him a valuable member and he counted a number of outstanding Church dignitaries among his close friends.

When the Bayliss trial (for ritual murder) shocked and aroused the world against this barbaric and vicious anti-semitic outrage, the rabbi was encouraged by his colleagues to present the matter to the Ministers Association. A few "backwoods" ministers naively inquired whether the rabbi could enlighten them as to "when actually did the Jewish ritual of using human blood for the Passover service cease?" Not only the rabbi but the intelligent members of the clergy were shocked. It was an opportunity for the rabbi to enlighten them. Unanimously they called for a resolution condemning the outrageous, libelous attack on Jews and Judaism.

Minkin was an accepted participant in all city events. At formal receptions to British visitors of importance, including members of the royal family, the rabbi represented the Jewish Community. On one occasion the chairman of a civic event, embracing his dear friend, introduced him as "Father Rabbi Minkin." All recognized it as an expression of endearment.

A special innovation by the rabbi was the introduction of adult education studies. It was still a practically unknown interest in Hamilton. During the early days of this century it was an unpopular movement and required pioneering effort. But he succeeded in interesting a number of women eager for intellectual information. Non-Jews joined the program too. They met in the rabbi's study and helped establish this new project by their appreciation and enthusiasm.

Night schools for foreigners were already well established in most large cities but not in Hamilton. It was brought to the attention of the rabbi that a number of indigent immigrant Jews were eager for an opportunity to learn the English language.

Recognizing that these newcomers were in need of sympathetic and understanding assistance for adequate adjustment in their new environment, Rabbi Minkin undertook to help them. For those in need of financial support he obtained the help of our philanthropic committee. To help those hungry to learn the language of their newly adopted country, he procured the use of the vestry rooms of the synagogue to open classes. He interested his religious school teachers and his wife to volunteer to teach English to the foreigners. This proved a successful and effective undertaking. The City Board of Education learned of it. They called upon Rabbi Minkin to extend his successful efforts to the general immigrant public, most of whom were Catholics. The Priests came to plead with the rabbi for their parishioners, promising to cooperate with him by influencing them to take advantage of this educational opportunity.

Classes were opened under the auspices of the City Board of Education and under the supervision of Rabbi Minkin. It was a hazardous undertaking but it fortunately proved a success and continued to function for a considerable time in this manner. Rabbi Minkin was very much appreciated for his having established a successful night school for foreigners without any cost to the city's educational system.

Rochester was the next community Rabbi Minkin served. He was called to a newly established congregation eager to participate in the Conservative Movement. Rochester was a well known Orthodox stronghold, and the Reform Synagogue was equally well established there. The latter represented the ultra radical policies and platform of the Reform Movement and attracted the younger generation, more fully Americanized and financially and socially successful.

There was, however, a growing interest on the part of a number of the strictly orthodox younger group to divorce themselves from their synagogue which ceased to attract or influence them. They wanted a synagogue to appeal to their children and to offer more interest to themselves. Some of the older generation, the parents of members of this group, recognized the justice of their children's arguments and agreed to join them in founding a synagogue to meet their needs. Their first rabbi was with them for a brief period. Rabbi Minkin following closely found that Conservative Judaism was little understood by the members. Much work was necessary to present adequately to them this novel although realistic phase of Judaism. He sought to convey that the Conservative Movement represented the middle path between Orthodox and Reform. He emphasized that it did not mean a complete severance from the old. It merely implied a modern interpretation of the concepts and meaningful traditions worthy of being conserved and practiced intelligently.

Some had already cut their ties with the orthodox way of life and thought. They seemed to be drifting aimlessly. There was danger of their abandonment of faith while in search of the unknown. A new garb for the fundamental values was necessary to reassure the wavering. To save those who otherwise might prove a lost generation was worthwhile, no matter the effort required.

The rabbi wholeheartedly espoused the cause that spelled progress for Judaism by means of a religious influence on the adults and an appropriate educational program for the children. He spared no effort in his sincere devotion to the task of establishing a model conservative congregation to inspire its adherents with understanding of the ideals, teachings and practices of the Jewish faith. He was especially concerned with the establishment of a religious school to appeal to and interest the children who had not been exposed to Jewish education. He realized that the parents should be provided with educational facilities which would help influence them better to recognize their children's needs. He sought to introduce an adult program for the intelligent parents who had been denied in their youth an opportunity to learn about their faith and people. He also sought to integrate different groups and types in the congregational family. He formed a Beth El council seeking to unite all the elements into a consolidated and uniform organization. Duly appointed representatives from the congregation, the sisterhood, men's club, Religious School Committee, the Ritual Committee and also the leaders of the various youth groups, all met to consider, to discuss and decide upon matters of interest to each group and to all forming the organization.

The rabbi took a personal interest in every part of the Temple's organized life but the youth groups held a very special attraction for him. He felt a particular responsibility for the young people. He guided them through the religious school, helped them through their Bar Mitzvoth, meeting the members of the Bar Mitzvah class frequently during the last year, assumed responsibility for their confirmation, which he never permitted to pass as merely a beautiful program. He made a meaningful occasion of it giving a full course of study to the applicants. The fine relationship between them continued. The boys who were Bar Mitzvah were organized and followed a program of extension studies and interests under the rabbi's guidance and leadership. In appreciation this group dedicated to him an issue of their magazine. Perhaps the best demonstration of how they felt is this quotation from an article of the leader of this group who expressed his satisfaction in meeting their erstwhile rabbi some years after he had left Rochester: "The joy which Hassidim had felt in the past when they were ushered into the presence of their Rebbe, I experienced in meeting Rabbi Minkin again. I had not seen him for a long time. There was something so warm and touching in his hand-clasp, something that brought back memories of old. The Rabbi's leaving Temple Beth El was my first real regret in my young life, for what an inspiration he had been to me in religion and faith. I felt a surge of happiness now passing through me as he was shaking my hand looking at me with his kind mild eyes."

For that matter, adults, too, proved that neither the passage of time nor the distance that separated them completely eradicated the memory of one they recognized as their sincere friend and dedicated leader of long ago. Although more than thirty years have passed since he left Rochester, there are those who still remember "their Rabbi Minkin" and the touching tributes in honoring his memory should delight his soul. The seeds he sowed took root and blossomed into beautiful plants. He did not labor in vain.

A rabbi's life is not always a bed of roses. A conscientious rabbi may on occasion find himself in difficult situations in the line of duty. He was perhaps rigid in his determination to act in the true spirit of Conservative Judaism when members required "accommodations" which were in conflict with religious dicta. Members were disgruntled when the rabbi objected to the use of the organ (which was part of the reconditioned church) in the synagogue during sacred services. A secular New Year celebration on Friday evening was criticised by the rabbi to the chagrin of some of the members. But especially upset were very important members who set the date for their daughter's wedding on a day forbidden by Jewish law, and the rabbi felt compelled to refuse to officiate. When a child of an outstanding family married out of the faith in the spouse's church, the distraught parents were outraged for a time, but subsequently decided to forgive, forget and have a public ceremony performed which actually amounted to a mock marriage. The rabbi explained his refusal to officiate under the circumstances. Such "lack of cooperation" was taken in poor grace. There were those who argued that even as a lawyer owes it to his client to find a way out, a rabbi too should realize that a "customer" should receive first consideration. A mother's heart, some said, should be given preference to a religious dictum. Forgotten were all the interest, consideration and devotion they experienced from the rabbi. He was termed unsympathetic. They failed to recognize that it hurt the rabbi to deny his friends the aid they sought. But he considered himself bound by his pledge to act in accordance with the Law and to follow his conscience. The rabbi could only hope that God was on his side while he was endeavoring to carry out His precepts.

For twenty five years Rabbi Minkin served as Chaplain in Fordham Hospital. He gave himself as sincerely and devotedly to this responsibility as he had to anything he undertook. Every patient was of real concern to him. The non-Jews had Chaplains of their own faith to minister to them but always looked forward to the cheery greeting, the friendly salutations from the Rabbi. His sympathetic interest made him a favorite in all the wards he visited. He loved his work and felt denied if for good reason he was forced to absent himself from the hospital. He missed the friendly smiles, the eager faces, that met him when he entered the wards. His association with the medical staff gave him untold satisfaction. He looked upon his work as a pleasant interest, never a chore. He was happy in the knowledge that he brought some degree of comfort to the sufferers. When the condition was so pathetic that the patient could accept no consolation, he tried to prove helpful by carrying messages to friends or family.

Jacob Minkin had many interests. He managed to find time to

answer the numerous demands made on him. Throughout his adult life he was an ardent Zionist. He supported the movement in every manner possible. He preached from the pulpit, spoke from the platform, wrote articles, expressing his enthusiastic loyalty to the cause he termed sacred. In the days when this idea was unpopular, not having as yet touched the imagination of the average person, he exerted himself towards influencing people to join, to contribute, to help the movement. During his rabbinate he stressed Zionism as a most important ideal in Judaism. He invited leaders of the Zionist movement whose presence would help stimulate interest among the masses. Among the outstanding personalities who answered his call and visited the communities he served were Nahum Sokolov, Dr. Schmarya Levin, Dr. Chayim Weizman, Dr. Judah Magnes, Vladimir Jabotinsky and many other leaders who helped spread the word. Always the great hope was for the realization of the dream of a Jewish homeland in Palestine.

When it reached the state of discussion and debate in the United Nations Assembly, Minkin was no longer active in any Zionist Group, but his ardor had not cooled, nor had his interest abated. His enthusiasm expressed itself in tension, excitement, hopes and fears. He responded to the appeals of the active leaders and helped in this way. Eagerly he awaited the decision, praying fervently for the successful outcome. His joy was unsurpassed when Ben Gurion declared the establishment of Israel as the Jewish State. Ben Gurion became an exalted leader about whom he would brook no criticism. Emotionally spent, he nevertheless was among the truly happy celebrants of the event he considered the greatest achievement in two thousand years of Jewish history. He was among the most enthusiastic demonstrators of genuine joy at the reception tendered the first Jewish Prime Minister of the reborn Jewish State. He was thrilled to have the privilege of meeting, seeing and hearing Ben Gurion at what was the supreme moment in modern Jewish history.

He considered an act of helpfulness to Israel a privilege to be grateful for, not a duty to perform. He regretted that he was limited in his capacity to help. He was pained at his inability to express more adequately his joy in terms of a greater contribution.

Endowed with an artistic temperament Jacob Minkin appreciated everything beautiful and inspiring. He loved music which he regarded as the "language of the angels." When all he could afford was standing room in the gallery it did not keep him from attending great musical performances.

Many proclaimed him an artist in his field—writing—his first love, which he never abandoned. He began to express himself in writing when he was in his teens. He recalled having rallied a few friends, youngsters like himself and living in his native town Sevenziani, to join in editing a news sheet in Hebrew. They distributed this daily among their elders, who must have favored this youthful enterprize since they paid a kopek for each issue. Poetry then was his favorite. For a long time he retained copy books filled with Hebrew poems to which he referred as follies of his early youth. Unfortunately he disposed of all his manuscripts as well as interesting and valuable correspondence. One short poem did survive. It was published in the *Hamelez* about sixty years ago. A native of Sivenziani searching for material to prepare a volume commemorating the victims of the Nazi holocaust found a short Hebrew poem bearing the signature of Yaacov Shmuel Minkin.

Poetry apparently did not prove an appropriate medium of expression for him. He probably did not feel adequate to it and turned to writing in English prose, which was, however, poetic in style. From his early days in the rabbinate he wrote for Anglo-Jewish magazines. Later he also contributed to a number of non-Jewish periodicals, including *Isis, Saturday Review of Literature* and others. Long before he thought of authoring a book he published numerous brief studies of important and interesting personalities and discussions of vital issues of the times. Many of these were subsequently absorbed in his books.

Before Jewish news penetrated the pages of the daily press Jacob Minkin published a weekly feature covering the happenings in the Jewish World with comments and clarifications. It first appeared in a number of Canadian dailies. Subsequently he syndicated this feature and it appeared in more than fifty leading newspapers in

the United States. It met with great success and proved both inform-
ative and interesting.

Minkin's interests went beyond reportorial writing. He continued
his articles for various publications but was already thinking of
larger studies about his favorite subjects. A monograph on Disraeli
was published during that period.

Though it appeared a spontaneous decision to retire from the
active rabbinate while in full vigor and vitality and at a comparatively young age, it was really not an impulsive act. Rabbi Minkin's
interest in writing became more and more compelling. He wanted
to devote himself completely to this task and not treat it as an
occasional avocation appended to his rabbinical vocation. Friends
who knew him to be active and energetic feared that a lack of
definite routine of duties and obligations would result in restlessness and discontent. Aware of the fact that creative writing
depended considerably on the writer's state of mind and temperament, some foresaw a possible disillusionment during a non-
productive period. He soon proved these fears groundless.

He allowed little time to pass before he plunged into the task he
set himself. A subject which had captured his imagination had for
sometime been growing in his mind. He became absorbed in the
theme and was quickly immersed in the subject. He was attracted
by Hassidism, a subject which had received little attention at that
time, in America. Recognizing it as a religious ecstacy which succeeded in crystalizing itself into a great movement, he was enthusiastic about this subject. He attended the play *The Dybbuk* and was
thrilled with the Hebrew and also the English productions. He also
saw *Yoshe Kalb* on the stage. He devoured the writings on the
subject of Hassidism by scholars of the past two hundred years.

Indefatigably he worked on the development of the theme tracing
the evolvement of the movement to its roots, to the Bible, the
Talmud and throughout Jewish history. Time ceased to be of
essence, he knew little rest, except the daily hours he spent with my
father, who was suffering from an eye ailment and could not follow
his usual pursuit of study. Regularly he went to read to my father,
whom he admired and whose "learning, wisdom and saintliness"

provided him, he claimed in his brief introduction, "with a model" on which he patterned many pages of his book. Father was not a Hassid, he was mentally related to the Mithnagdim; but the author referred to his purity of life and generosity of soul as Hassidic qualities. Never did father express his disapproval of the dissenting sect, for which he had little liking, to the enthusiastic author. He did not discourage his son-in-law, honoring his sincere interest in the movement he wished to present to the public. Neither Rabbi Minkin nor his forebears belonged to the movement he extolled. He was not motivated by any sense of loyalty. He became enthusiastically intrigued by the qualities he found in the leaders and decided to present this unfamiliar sect. It was purely an intellectual interest.

When he completed the manuscript he followed the advice of friends to submit it to the house of Macmillan. Unlike the angels who fear to tread on uncertain ground, he, not boldly, but naively, went to the publishing house and asked to see Mr. Macmillan. Astonished, the receptionist explained that there was no Mr. Macmillan with the American firm. Undaunted he asked to see the president. He saw and conquered. Mr. Brett, the president, was interested and promised to have the manuscript carefully studied by qualified readers to determine whether it was suitable for the firm. A few weeks passed when one morning, Mr. Lathrop, vice-president of the company, telephoned and asked for Dr. Minkin. The opinion of the company's editor was that the work was promising and would prove a permanent contribution to Jewish literature. *The Romance of Hassidism* was published in 1935.

The reception of his first effort was highly favorable, in fact far beyond the author's fondest hopes. Leading newspapers and magazines in this country and abroad carried full, glowing and flattering reviews. Not only was the content and approach to the development of the interesting subject lauded, but his style was compared to Carlyle. Many asserted that even as Martin Buber introduced Hassidism in Germany, Jacob Minkin brought this movement to the attention of the people in the United States. Practically all those who subsequently wrote on mysticism or related subjects acknowledged and referred to *The Romance of Hassidism.*

Minkin defined mysticism as "poetry touched with the sense of God." In explaining the revolt of the founders of Hassidism he described the discontent of the Jews with the realities of life which caused them to turn to mysticism as an outlet for their sensitive imagination. "Mysticism is the primitive hunger of the soul for God when the world has denied it everything else. . . . To the mysteries of life and death must be added the mystery of human character."

Dr. J. H. Hertz, Chief Rabbi of Great Britain called the book a distinct contribution to the history of Jewish culture. Dr. Rufus Jones described it as "A unique book profoundly interesting. "The author," he said, "writes with a vast background knowledge of the movement, with impartial spirit and in attractive style. It is a peculiarly valuable study of a long-time, widespread mystical movement." Dr. Stephen S. Wise spoke of it as "a superb achievement." Dr. John Haynes Holmes, Dr. Louis I. Newman, and many others hailed it as a vivid and graphic chronicle of the Hassidic movement.

Public acclaim helped to vindicate Minkin's choice of a new vocation. Writing no longer represented merely a temporary interest. He was encouraged to devote his full time and attention to writing. Fascinated by what he termed the dual personality of Herod, he applied himself to a psychological study of this complex character. Without minimizing the savage, brutal traits of this inhuman king who had been thrust upon the Jews, the author pointed to certain circumstances which could shed light on the innumerable irrational actions. Posterity condemns him for all his terrible acts, but Minkin endeavored to psychoanalyze him, studying all details connected with the barbarous deeds he committed. He did not appeal for sympathy for this depraved individual but invited an understanding consideration of this period. This was thought a novel treatment of a character universally censured throughout the ages. It evoked much interest but met with considerable controversy. Here too the critics were greatly impressed and expressed admiration for the author's interesting study. Published by Macmillan, "Herod" has been translated into French, Swedish and Spanish. A dramatization was broadcast in Stockholm, on a Christmas program. Both these works are now published by Thomas Yoseloff.

His next book was a treatment of another interesting personality. This time he was fascinated by an entirely different type. He chose a great favorite of the Jewish people. Abarbanel is acclaimed not only as a great Jew, but an outstanding prototype of Judaism. Minkin presented a scholar, diplomat, sage, financier, hero and martyr—all in one unusual person. He traced Abarbanel's life, influence and powers in country after country where he experienced the greatest honor and glory only to end his life in ruin and degradation. But whether fortune smiled upon him or evil befell him he was always true to his people and his faith. At the peril of his own safety, security and comfort he spurned personal favorable advantages when his brethren were denied the same. Picturing Abarbanel as one of the worst victims of the Expulsion of the Jews from Spain, the author described all the tragic experiences which helped illumine the subject. Abarbanel was not a controversial character. Here was a noble man sorely tried because of his loyalty to his faith and people whose troubles he always put above his own suffering. There was no dissenting voice about the merits of this interesting character, and the concensus was that the presentation was highly commendable.

For a time Jacob Minkin devoted himself to writing about men and issues that captured his imagination. Temperamental, he interested himself only in subjects that had a special appeal for him, in order to do justice to the theme. The sages who left an imprint and influence upon Jewish life and thought, transcending time, appealed to him and he wrote about them. He expressed his admiration for some of his teachers and also wrote about other important individuals whom he respected. Fired with enthusiasm and applying his gift of imagination, his writings appeared in many current periodicals, and met with general approval. He treated issues of popular interest, as well as books and authors he admired. Writing was always a stimulating and satisfying interest, never a forced activity.

No matter how strenuous the research or how exhausting composing proved, he was happy in his work. "The *Rebenesholam* owes me nothing," he would say. "I have every reason to be eternally grateful to Him and no cause to complain." If, as the doctors claim, he was living on borrowed time, he did not prove a debtor. He used his time to a good purpose. He wrote to the last. Unfortunately, copious notes remain wasted; a new book he planned will never take form.

There is however another unpublished manuscript, written some time ago. This is a semi-fictional presentation of Uriel Acosta, the tragic figure who paid the highest penalty for his religious nonconformity. His heretic views were neither forgotten nor forgiven. Minkin offers an analytical portrait of a tortured soul, sensitive, weak, yet determined. He introduces a romantic episode which throws light on the much condemned figure. In unfolding the tale of this frustrated, rebellious personality, Minkin displays a deep insight into the thinking and feelings of his subject. It is a fascinating psychological study of the world of Uriel Acosta.

But while busy producing short articles, he was contemplating doing something more substantial. He gathered and assembled material for a work he approached with reverence and humility. He had written a number of essays on Moses Maimonides for magazines. His health was poor and at times he despaired of doing more creative work. But the spirit was stronger than the flesh. Summoning every ounce of strength in applying himself to the task and by working assiduously he produced *The World of Moses Maimonides*. Not only did he present a vivid picture of the unusual personality but gave a full description and an analysis of the period this great scholar graced. The biographical portion introduces an anthology of meaningful and timely quotations from the writings of Maimonides. He arranged the material according to subjects with such chapter headings as "Good and Evil"—"War and Peace"—"Love"—"Relationship of Man to Man"—"Man to God" and many others. Exhausting though it was, he considered it a labor of love, and he was amply rewarded by the wide acclaim that the book received when published by the firm of Thomas Yoseloff.

Reviewers considered it "a sheer delight to read the pithy words which afford an insight to and an acquaintance with an outstanding personality—Moses Maimonides." He was commended for covering so well the immense wingspread of the "great eagle" as this scholar was called. It was often repeated that Dr. Minkin was endowed with the gift of popularizing difficult themes. All agreed that *The World of Moses Maimonides* is an important contribution.

But this was not to be Minkin's last work. He could not reconcile himself to inactivity. He yearned to continue expressing himself creatively. His will again proved stronger than his physical condition. Doctors had advised cessation of work, fearing that he was spending himself too rapidly, but they soon realized that to deprive him of this interest would be to rob him of all satisfaction in life. They therefore did not interfere when he summoned his strength to take up his pen for the last time. Mercilessly he drove himself and conquered what seemed a superficial apathy. He succeeded in finishing the present work. He changed, added, and improved the manuscript, thus delaying publication.

Here he undertook to present a galaxy of figures whose works have woven the tapestry of Jewish history from the time of the Bible to the present day. Covering the wide range from Ezra to Weizmann, from Hillel to Ginzberg, he offers a vivid panorama of Jewish concepts, values and principles.

For years a trip to Israel, a life's hope and ambition, seemed an impossibility, being considered too strenuous an undertaking for him. When Miriam and Jacob Colman, continuing their chosen role of beloved and devoted children, celebrated our Golden Wedding Anniversary, it seemed a turning point for their appreciative and grateful uncle. Unexpectedly, as though specifically ordained by the Almighty, Jacob Minkin gained new vigor. His geniality and cheerfulness, which had so endeared him to all in the past, now returned. His former enthusiasm and buoyancy came back. Without contemplating or planning, but with inspiration while under the spell of spiritual elation, he decided to visit Israel, "before it is too late." The idea caught fire, and all applauded his determination. The thought of being privileged to visit Israel, to stand on the sacred soil where prophets and sages trod and wrought, where Jewish martyrs enriched the spiritual world by their idealism, where the modern heroes by their sacrifices succeeded in achieving the impossible—the State of Israel—stimulated and strengthened him.

Certainly he recognized that he was on a risky venture for which he might be called upon to pay the highest price. But happy over the prospect of going, he refused to give thought to the danger. As soon as we embarked on the Israeli steamship he felt he had one foot in Israel. The official language on the ship was Hebrew. The passengers were in the main Israelis returning from a visit abroad. He was thrilled that not only the captain and mates, but practically all of the crew, in fact the entire personnel of the ship, spoke Hebrew. Upon meeting with the captain and mate, he pronounced the blessing of Shehecheyonu expressing his gratitude that he was privileged to be sailing on a Hebrew ship commanded by a Hebrew crew, going to "our" Hebrew state. He enjoyed every minute of the voyage, conversing, discussing and obtaining information about Israel. He appeared to be experiencing the same ecstacy he had described in writing about famous travellers who were overcome with delight when they beheld the land as they approached the port.

Our ship the S.S. *Israel* reached Haifa on Saturday afternoon. Not permitted to land on the Sabbath, it approached the harbor slowly. For a while we were anchored waiting for the setting of the sun when it would be time to make port. This gave us ample time and opportunity to view the Promised Land. Anxiety and impatience caused restlessness but the beauty of the outline of this famous city coupled with the enthusiasm of the approaching landing in this charming section of the Holy Land enthralled him. He landed exhausted but delighted.

The realization that his dream had at last come true, that he had actually reached Israel, to see with his own eyes the miracle that had been wrought in the Promised Land, filled his heart with unspeakable joy. Even the ordeal of passing through customs was less arduous because Israel's officials seemed more considerate, more respectful and understanding than they usually are elsewhere. The impression that Jews in Israel appeared to have taken a more benevolent attitude, a friendlier and kinder interest in visitors than is usual, was confirmed and intensified as time passed. He became convinced that most Israelis were dedicated, loyal and devoted supporters of the land they selflessly helped to reclaim and the state they defended with love and enthusiasm. They were happy to show their accomplishments and share the joy of achievement.

They were still busily engaged in building as well as defending their land. He recognized the miraculous accomplishments as results not merely of physical strength or financial aid but primarily of superhuman qualities of dedication to an ideal. Everyone he met, no matter what the status or category, enchanted him, since he found most of them intelligent and well informed.

The Israeli children had a special attraction for him. He found them beautiful, alert and bright. He was impressed by the fact that all youngsters reflected very special attention lavished upon them. Their parents had suffered all manner of hardships and deprivations and were therefore determined to spare their children any such experiences. Wholesome, nutritious food, sleeping comforts and good appropriate clothes were provided the youngsters even when there was not enough of those commodities for all to enjoy. Jewish education is of course a *must* in Israel. It includes general education too and is provided and controlled by the government, but is an expense to most parents even in the face of financial difficulties.

Most Israelis seem to be exceedingly kind and thoughtful of the tourists. They apparently know from personal experience how difficult it is for the stranger to get about. They are ever ready to be of service. Minkin recognized that all these niceties were not special consideration shown him but that they followed a pattern for all strangers and everything provided interest and evoked his admiration and appreciation. He was so happy with what he saw and experienced that he hardly recognized his increasing exhaustion.

Haifa is an enchanting city. Physically it is beautiful to behold. The view coming up or down the three levels, the beauty of the scenery especially when the electric lights add glow to the shining stars above, gave Minkin the impression of a fairy land. Visiting the institutions near and in Haifa gave him great satisfaction. He was enthusiastic and delighted with every detail.

While in Haifa we took a trip to the upper Galilee. What probably impressed him most was the visit to the ancient synagogue in Safed. The thought that he stood on the very spot where Rashi prayed and studied thrilled him. He was emotionally spent by the impressive and charming sights. We visited Tiberius but found that the exquisitely beautiful terrain was too rigorous for him. His most ardent wish was to stay in Jerusalem long enough to have the real feel of the Holy City and from there visit and view all points and sights of interest.

From Haifa we went to Tel Aviv, where we spent several weeks. We were afforded the opportunity to become well acquainted with the city and its environs. We visited the universities and Yeshivoth of the city and region as well as the noted libraries and institutions of interest, especially the Weizmann Institute. He was deeply impressed by the modern buildings, blending with antiquity and sanctity.

The trip to Beer Sheba had a two-fold attraction. Rabbi Minkin was eager to see this historically important city in its present transformed condition, and to view a plaque in memory of my father, Rabbi Moshe Chayim Rabinowitz, for which he had composed the inscription, which hangs in the Chapel of the Hias Hostel in the Negev. This was much too difficult for him; it was his last trip. It was a joyous experience while it lasted. He loved every minute of it, recognizing that there was constant change and improvement wherever he turned.

He was denied the fulfillment of his great hope to get to know Jerusalem. But fortunately he had the delightful experience of at least getting a view of the Hebrew University. We spent a day in the city, which meant much to him. The evening of the Jubilee conference of Hadassah celebrating fifty years of outstanding service was a great experience. The afternoon we spent in the University. Merely to see the beautiful scenic location, the exquisitely fine buildings, was a delightful privilege. He was impressed with the fact that this new land, beset with every hardship, had yet succeeded in establishing a Hebrew institution of higher learning which compares favorably with the finest old universities in prosperous countries. The guides were exceedingly kind and considerate especially in the Library building, pointing out every department of interest to him including the catalogue room where he had the pleasure of finding his works indexed. This visit actually proved the climax of the realization of his life-long dream.

On March thirteenth, nineteen hundred and sixty-two (Adar, 7, 5722) Jacob Samuel Minkin was summoned to the Great Beyond, while he was visiting in Tel Aviv. It was the unanimous opinion that this was a special merit that his feet had unwittingly led him to where his heart always had been, so that he could find his resting place among his sainted ancestors in the Holy Land. Friends subsequently recalled that before our departure he expressed the thought that should his time come while in Israel, he should be put to rest there. It was hard leaving the better part of myself far away, but the reminder that "he who is left in Zion is considered holy and has the assurance that he will not revert to dust but will endure forever" proved a helpful and consoling thought for one bereft and lonely.

Practically to the last Jacob Minkin's cheerfulness and geniality endeared him to all. He no longer possessed his vigor and agility but his enthusiasm for worthwhile interests never waned. His high spirits won friends for him wherever he went. He died as he had lived—at peace with the world. He will be remembered for his kindness, consideration and gentility, for his genial personality, even as he will be known for his literary contributions.

Jacob S. Minkin breathed his last in Israel, a land close to his heart, cherished as his people's homeland, but in terms of distance, far from home, relatives and friends. It seemed as though he were all alone. This illusion was quickly dispelled. A number of distinguished friends in Israel gathered to express their sense of loss and to pay their final respects to a worthy member of their circle. Headed by the eminent scholar, Dr. Meyer Waxman of New York, whom Minkin greatly admired and held in high esteem, they solemnized the funeral rites according to the laws and customs of Israel, and in a spirit of understanding, friendship and devotion. In accordance with the custom in Israel, memorial services were held after the traditional thirty days of mourning. His *landsleute* of the Swenziani organization in Israel joined the group of friends, and participated in the tribute paid to one they proudly claimed as their own. Thus his strong belief in Klal Israel Havarim was justified.

—MRS. FANNY R. MINKIN

The Shaping of the Modern Mind

Ezra

THERE ARE FEW episodes in history more dramatic and significant than the coming of Ezra to Jerusalem from Babylon about the year 458 B.C.E. To one looking back upon it through the perspective of the centuries and evaluating its importance to history, literature, and religion, the significance of the event becomes even more striking and impressive. For upon it depended not only the survival of the Jews as a people and Judaism as a religion but, in a large measure, the succeeding centuries of civilization. Had Ezra remained in Babylon, as did many of his brethren, and not gone up to Jerusalem and done his historic work, Judaism would have lapsed into paganism, its epic struggle for moral and spiritual greatness would have been lost, and Judea would have sunk to the level of the surrounding heathen tribes.

Ezra is the central figure of the Second Jewish Commonwealth. Together with Nehemiah, he kindled a fresh wave of enthusiasm for the revived homeland among the depressed and dispirited returned exiles. He brought about a religious-national unification of the Jews when the high-minded universalism preached by the prophets was not adequate to the need of the time. He originated ordinances and reforms in the religious structure of the people which gave the Jews their distinctive character and personality among the nations of the world. In all these things Ezra was not alone. He was supported in the great movement he set on foot by a brilliant galaxy of priests, prophets, and men of political insight and influence. But it is Ezra who is singled out by Jewish tradition for special honor and distinction as restorer of the Law. Ezra, indeed, say the rabbis, was qualified to have given the Torah to Israel if it had not already been bestowed by Moses, who preceded him.

43

Ezra was the teacher, expounder, and interpreter of the Torah. He was the creator of a new cultural current in Judaism which persisted for thousands of years. If Ezra was not directly responsible for them, the development of the Oral Law, the ordinances and enactments of the Men of the Great Assembly, the institutions of the scribes with their generations of students, saints, and scholars were due to the impact of his personality and influence. The Mishnah and the Talmud were still centuries in the future and many of the things which grateful posterity associated with his name were as yet unborn; but they were already present in his mind. They were the destined outcome of his conception of Judaism and its preservation.

Ezra is one of the better-known figures of the Bible. We know a good deal about him, both through his own book and through that of his contemporary and fellow worker, Nehemiah. The Bible speaks of him sometimes as a priest, which he was by descent, and sometimes as a scribe, which means that he was a student and teacher of Judaism and Jewish literature. But we know little about his position among the Babylonian Jews before he settled in Judea except that he was among the most pious and honored of the exiles and a favorite at the royal court. He was a disciple of Baruch, son of Neriah, himself a disciple, colleague, and secretary of the prophet Jeremiah. But the character and personality of Ezra and his impact on Judaism, and through Judaism on civilization, are best explained by a survey of the extraordinarily dramatic time in which he lived and worked.

Ezra lived in one of the most crucial periods of Jewish history. After more than five hundred years of existence, the Jewish State and Temple were destroyed by Nebuchadnezzar 586 years before the present era. When, eleven years earlier, Nebuchadnezzar descended upon Jerusalem and subdued her, he neither destroyed the city nor massacred her population. All he did was to reduce Jerusalem to impotence and prevent the possibility of rebellion. He transported to Babylon the young King Jehoiachin, his family, the ministers and officers, and all men capable of bearing arms, little realizing the incendiary potential remaining in the city. To pacify the community and establish law and order, Nebuchadnezzar appointed Gedaliah, a just and moderate man, admirably suited for the position, as governor of the country. Nebuchadnezzar could have made no better choice, but it far from pleased the irreconcilable patriots who fought the Chaldeans and regarded Gedaliah a traitor inimicable to the interests of his country. Secretly they left their hiding places and came to Mizpah, Gedaliah's headquarters, where they murdered him, his associates, and the Chaldean garrison.

It was not to be expected that Nebuchadnezzar would take the murder of Gedaliah and his Chaldean garrison lightly. He was furious, and his vengeance was swift and terrible. He was convinced that the rebellious city could not be pacified and was determined upon its destruction. He had his army proceed against the Judean capital with all its mighty engines of war. Jerusalem was not helpless against an attack. She was protected on three sides by deep declivities, and was dangerously open only on the north. The defenders fought with almost incredible heroism, throwing in everything they had in defense of the city. They fought to the death, young and old alike. It took the Chaldeans, with all their superior manpower, siege towers, battering rams, and varied equipment, close to two years to break their resistance, and then they succeeded only after famine and pestilence had done their ghoulish work among the defenders. When the inevitable end came and a breach was made in the north wall on the seventeenth of Tamuz—still observed by Jews as a fast day—the victory-drunk and battle-weary Chaldean soldiers poured into the city, spreading death and devastation in Jerusalem, and, indeed, over the whole country. The City of David was totally destroyed. The Temple was put to the torch, and thousands, irrespective of age or sex, were slain by the sword. King Zedekiah, the last scion of the House of David, while attempting to escape, was captured, together with his household, and brought before Nebuchadnezzar for judgment. Mercilessly Nebuchadnezzar doled out to him the lot he assigned to most of his rebel vassals. He had Zedekiah's sons slain in the presence of their father, and plunged Zedekiah into eternal darkness with his own hand.

When the Chaldean army retired Judea was almost completely depopulated. Only the poorest—the farmers and unskilled workingmen—were permitted to remain in the province. To prevent future uprisings, Nebuchadnezzar had almost the entire Jewish population transported to Babylon.

The doleful story left its record in Jewish history and literature. Lines trembling with wrath and anguish dominate scores of Hebrew prayers and poems. Their stirring lament flowed over thousands of years. On the ninth of Ab, Jews the world over sit low in their houses of worship, dismally repeating Jeremiah's mournful lament: "How doth the city sit solitary that was full of people! How is she become widowed, she that was great among nations and princess among the provinces, how is she become tributary!"

Judah fell, but not Judaism and the Jewish nation; they continued to exist, and even to thrive and flourish in captivity. A people commissioned with a divine idea cannot die. The buffeting of adverse fortune only hardened its power of resistance to death and annihilation. Thebes fell and did not rise again and the glories of Nineveh and Babylon are today difficult to remember; but Jerusalem became synonymous with a spiritual greatness that blots out the names of her erstwhile captors. Judah was always conscious of her divine charge, conscious that she was the standard-bearer of a religious idea that was destined to encompass all the world. When the long travail came and her children were led into captivity, the exiles did not depart from their homeland empty-handed. Together with their scant belongings they carried with them from the wreckage of their homes and land their most precious possession and the essential organ of their nation—the sacred volume of the Scriptures. It was their elixir of life.

The higher power manifested everywhere in Jewish history did not desert them in their sorest trial. The captives were treated in their exile far more leniently than they had expected. Although as destroyer of the Jewish State and Temple, Nebuchadnezzar is understandably spoken of in Jewish history as *harasha*, the "wicked one," he took no delight in wreaking vengeance upon his war captives. Once in Babylon, the Jewish exiles enjoyed a comparatively normal existence. Whereas when Sargon descended upon Samaria 133 years earlier and led its population away, the Ten Tribes became but a memory, Nebuchadnezzar's captives were given every opportunity to maintain their identity, to practice their religion, engage in professions and trades of their own choice, and, generally, to carry on their own affairs undisturbed. They were granted tracts of land upon which to build houses and plant gardens. Famous for his great building project—dikes, irrigation systems, hanging gardens, and temples to his deities, Nebuchadnezzar, unlike the Egyptian Pharaohs, is not known to have employed his captives for slave labor. While some of the older exiles remembered with affection the little blue hills of Zion and longed to return to them, there was little sentimental longing for Jerusalem among their sons and daughters, who had adjusted themselves to their new environment and were glad to be secure against the hazards and ravages of war.

"It was at this moment in their existence," writes Joseph Kastein, "that the problem of assimilation may be said to have made its appearance in Jewish history, and in the form in which it survived through the centuries." For large masses of the Judean captives the lure of Babylon was too great to withstand. From a country with which nature had not dealt too lavishly they were suddenly catapulted into a glittering civilization of hanging gardens and magnificent palaces, with a mixture of races and cultures Nebuchadnezzar had transported from almost all parts of the world. At the time the Jews were transferred there, Babylon was thriving brilliantly under the man who was determined to make his capital the pride and envy of all the world. Her stalls were filled with the wares of all nations; through her ports rolled the commerce and industry of all the lands and cities Nebuchadnezzar conquered. Nineveh had no wealth, Thebes no treasures, and Tyre no luxury but were made to contribute to the greater glory and splendor of Babylon.

There were, however, Jews who refused to be swept off their feet by the glory and splendor of Babylon, who would not be at ease in a strange land and never ceased to long for the land of their birth and the graves of their forebears. The prosperity and comfort they enjoyed in Babylon gave them small satisfaction when they remembered their destroyed Temple, their devastated country, and the thousands of Jews who were slain by the enemy. Desperately they warmed their hearts with the glories of Zion, with the stories of her proud past, the vision of her great future. They communicated these hopes and longings to their children and to the weak and faltering among the exiles in order to strengthen their faith and keep them from drifting utterly away. Prophets arose among the exiles whose inspiring words and work acted as a life-giving fountain to the discouraged and dispirited Jews. In clear, sonorous tones they announced that God would break the rod which He used for the chastisement of their sins. We hear the comforting message of Ezekiel, one of the greatest of the Prophets of the captivity: "Thus saith the Lord God, I will gather you from the peoples and assemble you out of the countries where you have been scattered, and I will give you the land of Israel." And we read the prophetic clarion call of the man who was contented to conceal his identity in the brightness of the Prophet-Poet Deutero Isaiah, the Second Isaiah: "Comfort ye, comfort ye, my people, saith your God. Bid Jerusalem take heart, and proclaim unto her that the time of her service is accomplished, that her guilt is paid off, that she has received at the hand of the Lord double for all her sins." So incredibly firm and persistent was Ezekiel in his dream of the Holy Land recovered and of the Temple restored that in his fervent imagination he drew up a plan of the future edifice with all the minute details of its sacerdotal service.

There is a legend in the Book of Daniel that in the declining years of his life Nebuchadnezzar went mad, was driven from the company of men, and, like the beasts of the field and forest, his body was wet with the dew of heaven till his hairs were grown like those of eagles and his nails like the claws of birds. This is likely Daniel's imaginary punishment of the man who overthrew Jerusalem, destroyed the Temple of Solomon, and led the Jews captive to Babylon. But is it not possible that, in fact, Nebuchadnezzar in his declining days, his health failing, his melancholy spirit brooding, did begin to doubt the value of the material wealth and glory he had amassed? Deep down in his being his soul repented his former insatiable lust for power, and in his depressed state of mind he saw the avenging fingers of Zedekiah, Jehoiachin, and yet others he kept in chains for many long years. Raving, he accused them of causing the gods to allow the evil spirits to do their work of tormenting his body and soul. And what was far worse, he dimly saw arise on the distant horizon a new empire which would destroy his power, his conquests, his very throne, to the security of which he had devoted his life.

Nebuchadnezzar died, and his successors lacked the genius which made Babylon the hub and mistress of the world. Weaklings sat on the throne which the great conqueror made feared and dreaded. Evil Merodach, Nebuchadnezzar's heir and successor, had a brief reign. His infant child was murdered; palace intrigues and conspiracies made the country ripe for the plucking. Babylonia rapidly declined and a new Asiatic power, Persia, which Nebuchadnezzar's iron hand had long held in check, came upon the scene, challenging the might and power that was Babylon. In 539 Babylon fell before Nabonad, the last of the Chaldean kings, realized that the bell had tolled for his empire.

If great historic personalities are but instruments in the hands of God for the accomplishment of His purpose, then Cyrus, founder of the great Persian empire and new master of Babylonia, was His most perfect tool. Cyrus' entry into Babylon and his accession to Nebuchadnezzar's throne was greeted by the pious and enthusiastic Babylonian Judeans as God's own maneuver for the accomplishment of His end—the recovery of the Holy Land and the restoration of the Temple. The rod which He had used for the chastisement of the Jews was broken. Nebuchadnezzar was dead, and the way was open for their liberation. Everything we know about Cyrus bespeaks that he was a kind and generous man and a just ruler, conscious of his world-civilizing mission. The ancient historians refer flatteringly to him as a noble, high-minded man, and the Prophets, especially the great anonymous Isaiah, credit him with being the "anointed" one, the man sent by God, one of His counsel.

There was a spiritual affinity between the Jews and the Persians which made for a friendly, sympathetic understanding between the two peoples. Although Parseeism had not risen to the full and lofty conception of Jewish monotheism, it was free of the absurd and repellent practices of the idolatrous Babylonian religion. The Prophets protested against the Parsees' dualism, which recognised two antagonistic spirits in light and darkness, in good and evil—a protest which found its way into the Hebrew prayer book; but, all in all, the Persian religion at the time of Cyrus was not so far removed from the pure conception of Judaism that it did not contain an essence of monotheism.

Paradoxically, the boldest stroke in the religious-national re-generation of the Jews came by the hand of the man who, to found his empire, had destroyed many kingdoms and subdued many nations. To be sure, it was not wholly disinterested generosity that prompted Cyrus' historic gesture to the Jews. Although Palestine was a tiny segment of the Persian Empire, Cyrus was not blind to her strategic importance. Astute statesman that he was, he no doubt realized the advantages of having a friendly and grateful community on the road to Egypt—a road which, sooner or later, he would pass.

Be this as it may, in the very first year of his reign as King of Babylon, Cyrus issued from his summer residence, Ecbatana, the historic order for the return of the Jews to their homeland and the rebuilding of their Temple. More dramatic than any paraphrase of the famous document is the actual wording of the text in the first chapter of the Book of Ezra, whose authenticity there is no reason to doubt! "Thus saith Cyrus, king of Persia. All the kingdoms of the earth hath the Lord, the God of heaven, given me; and He hath charged me to build Him a house in Jerusalem, which is in Judah. Whosoever there is among you, of all His peoples—his God be with him—let him go to Jerusalem, which is in Judah, and build the House of the Lord, the God of Israel. He is the God who is in Jerusalem. And whosoever is left, in any place where he sojourneth, let the men of his place help him with silver and with gold, and with goods, and with beasts, besides the freewill offering for the House of God, which is in Jerusalem . . . Also Cyrus the king brought forth the vessels of the House of the Lord, which Nebuchadnezzar had brought forth out of Jerusalem, and had put them in the house of his gods; even these did Cyrus, king of Persia, bring forth by the hand of Mithredath the treasurer, and numbered them into Sheshbazzar, the prince of Judah."

There were hymns of deliverance in Zion to celebrate the event; a new canticle was added to the Book of Psalms:

> When the Lord brought back those who returned to Zion
> We were like unto them who dream.
> Then was our mouth filled with laughter,
> And our tongue with singing;
> Then said they among the nations,
> The Lord hath done great things with these.
> The Lord hath done great things with us;
> We are rejoiced.

The exodus of the Jews from Babylon in the year 537 was unlike the departure of their ancestors from Egypt eight or nine hundred years before. While the first exodus was a liberation after centuries of oppression and enslavement under cruel and despotic kings, their second deliverance was after a captivity of less than two generations in a foreign land and was accompanied by singing priests and Levites marching triumphantly to their beloved Jerusalem. It was not, however, a complete exodus, for of the many thousands Nebuchadnezzar had transplanted only a minority returned to the homeland during the first Restoration under Zerubbabel. The less enthusiastic Jews who lacked the great passion for Zion, the rich merchants and property owners who preferred to remain in Babylonia with their homes and families, loaded their patriotic co-religionists with rich gifts and donations for the building of the house of God.

Between Babylon and Jerusalem lay a stretch of six hundred miles full of hardships and perils to travelers. Water was scarce, food was only what one could pluck from a corroded, unyielding earth, and there was no Moses to coax water out of the rocks or provide manna for the starving. To protect the pilgrims against marauding bands, Cyrus sent an escort of a thousand mounted soldiers. To encourage the weary wanderers and goad them on their way, Haggai and Malachi held out to them visions of the plenty which awaited them in the land of their fathers.

With singing hearts the returning exiles pushed forward steadily over the sandy miles under a scorching sun. Twice before, as unhappy captives, they had traversed the road under the lash of Nebuchadnezzar. The great Unknown Prophet, put into ringing words the feelings that were in the hearts of the pilgrims:

> How beautiful upon the mountains
> Are the feet of the messenger of good tidings. . . . .
> Hark, thy watchmen, they lift up the voice,
> Together do they sing. . . . .
> Break forth into joy, sing together,
> Ye, waste places of Jerusalem;
> For the Lord hath comforteth His people;
> He had redeemed Jerusalem.

However, it was one thing to dream, to hope and sentimentalize, and quite another to confront the stark realities which faced the returning patriots. As caravan after caravan of the pious immigrants approached the city of their dreams, their joy was turned to grief by the sight of the waste and desolation which met their eyes. Where was the beauty, the splendor of the city David built, of the Temple of King Solomon, and of the hill of Zion so passionately loved for hundreds of years? Of the buildings nothing remained but charred walls, heaps of ruins, and stones of ancient foundations. The country around Jerusalem was still inhabited by the population Nebuchadnezzar spared because it was too harmless to be destroyed or deported. The inhabitants that remained eked out a miserable subsistence from the hard, stony land far from sufficient for themselves, to say nothing of the thousands of the new arrivals. It was a sorry home-coming, indeed, for the returning exiles—a honeymoon that ended in disappointment and frustration.

Then there was the animosity the arrivals experienced at the hands of the surrounding tribes. During their captivity, Jewish towns and villages had been settled by foreigners, who introduced their pagan customs and usages. In the absence of priests and prophets, many Jews joined in the idolatrous practices of the pagan religion. Intermarriage with the sons and daughters of the gentiles was rampant, with the result that the faithful Jews returning from captivity found themselves almost strangers among their former co-religionists. Half a century was a long time in which to complete the physical and moral degradation of the Jewish community. The returning Judeans were shocked by the religious laxity of their Palestine brethren and they inwardly doubted the wisdom of the change they had made. A symbol of the cohesion of all the Jews was necessary, and there was, of course, none better than the restoration of the Temple, to which every segment of the community looked forward with the greatest enthusiasm.

It was Zerubbabel to whose happy lot fell the laying of the foundation of the restored House of God, and there was no man more ideally fitted for the sacred task. He was an aristocrat of royal ancestry on whom the hopes of the people were centered not only as restorer of the sanctuary but of the Davidic dynasty as well. He was a favorite of the court of Darius, the third Persian king since Cyrus, who commissioned him to go to Jerusalem and rebuild the Temple at the king's own expense. Thousands of Judeans accompanied Zerubbabel, bearing with them rich gifts from their Babylonian brethren, who, although they had not joined them, were eager to have a part in the building of the spiritual center of the new commonwealth. Rarely had a man approached the execution of a historic task with greater hope and joy in his heart than did Zerubbabel. There was want and poverty in the land, drought in the fields, and the cisterns were empty of water; but there was no limit to the enthusiasm with which the work began. As in the days of Solomon, cedar trees were procured from Lebanon, stone was quarried from the mountains, and building materials not found in Palestine were supplied by Tyre and Sidon. It was a happy day in the land when the Temple was restored. It was a modest performance, but it was as good as their reduced circumstances permitted. There was perhaps more pewter used than gold, and the workmanship compared poorly with Solomon's Temple. The old men who remembered the first Temple wept. But it was a Temple just the same, and it was a happy day in the land when the priests and Levites appeared in their impressive vestments singing *halleluyah* hymns unto the Lord.

Their rejoicing, however, was short-lived. When the work on the Temple was begun the Samaritans had come to Zerubbabel, asking to be allowed to take part in the rebuilding of the wall of Jerusalem and the House of God, claiming that they, too, worshiped the God of Israel and obeyed His commandments. Their offer was rejected. The rejection brought about a deep and lasting division in the two almost identical groups, for the Samaritans were almost as Hebraic as the Jews themselves. They were remnants of the Israelitish Kingdom destroyed in 719. They had survived massacre and deportation but had permitted their religion to become adulterated by contact with the heathen practices of the foreign settlers in the land. The break was serious and far-reaching. The Samaritans felt the hurt deeply, and a cleavage developed between them and their kindred Jews which was never healed. To this day the Samaritans, pathetically reduced in numbers, stubbornly cling to their religious custom of sacrificing a Paschal lamb on Passover on Mount Gerizim. Their hostility to the Jews became so keeen and tense that, unable to play a part in the restoration of the Temple, they were determined to block its progress by denouncing the "disloyalty" of the Judeans at the Persian court. Not only the Samaritans but the Ammonites and Moabites, their neighbors on the north, who were anxious to enter into friendly relations with the Jews but were repulsed by them, entered the list of the enemies of the new community working for its destruction. To aggravate the situation, Zerubbabel had suddenly and mysteriously disappeared. Had he, discouraged and dispirited, returned to Babylon, or was he quietly murdered by the Persian authorities who had no wish to encourage semiroyalties in the Persian empire?

It was fortunate that synonymous with the disappearance of

Zerubbabel two men appeared who not only saved the little Jewish community of Jerusalem from utter destruction but may be said to have been pioneers of postexilic Judaism in its essential characteristics. They were Nehemiah and Ezra. They were both Babylonians, both deeply religious and fanatically devoted to their people, and were both equally distressed by the alarming reports of their Palestine brethren. Both also occupied prominent positions at the Persian court, which, described in the Bible as the "king's cup-bearers," probably meant that they held positions of trust with Artaxerxes I, the Persian monarch. During the middle ages and afterward Jews often either supplied funds to royal houses or negotiated loans to them. But in antiquity, writes Kittel, they gained positions of importance by their skill, versatility, and mental agility. Such must have been the positions filled by Zerubbabel, Ezra, and Nehemiah at the courts of the Persian monarchs.

While Ezra was the greater scholar, idealist, and literary man *(safer mahir),* to whom we are probably indebted for the preservation of the biblical literature up to that time, Nehemiah was the more practical man and was an administrator who knew how to govern the affairs of a nation in the throes of a crisis. He was also an extremely clever man and knew how to fit the moment to his purpose. When Nehemiah begged Artaxerxes for permission to visit the graves of his ancestors in Jerusalem, as well as to repair the city's walls, the king not only granted his request but provided him with letters of protection and material for the work. For ninety years Jerusalem was a defenseless city, open to the jeers and attack of the neighboring nations. To fortify Jerusalem and make her impregnable against assault was no less in the interests of the Jews than of the Persians. Artaxerxes was hard pressed by the Greeks, who, under his father, Xerxes, had destroyed the Persian fleet, conquered Cyprus, and pressed on toward Egypt. It was, therefore, an astute thing for Artaxerxes to encourage the little Judean principality and strengthen its defenses, so that it might serve as a bastion against the Athenians.

In his memoirs Nehemiah himself describes in great detail the manner in which he accomplished his great enterprise. Upon arriving in Jerusalem he made a careful survey of conditions in the city but kept his own counsel, without disclosing to any man his identity and "what God had put into my heart to do for Jerusalem." When the situation became absolutely clear in his own mind, he assembled the elders of the Jews and told them that he had been appointed by royal decree to act as governor of the country and to repair the walls of Jerusalem. The enthusiasm was unanimous and unbounded. But the news of what was happening could not but irritate the repudiated Samaritans and instigated by their resourceful and crafty Sanballat, they did their utmost to discourage and hinder the Jews in their tasks. From that moment every man was on his guard. Nehemiah took precautionary measures to prevent an open attack. The Jews worked, as Nehemiah's memoirs metaphorically tell us, with one hand while they fought with the other. Their swords were girded to their sides as they built or carried burdens. Nehemiah, who always had a trumpet besides him, commanded them to give instant warning of any sign of attack and half the population was kept under arms from morning to starlight. Nehemiah and his men never undressed to sleep and always kept their weapons within reach.

When the wall was completed and dedicated with great cere- mony, Nehemiah, wise administrator that he was, set himself to correct the religious and social abuses in the city. When there was a housing shortage due to the influx of Jews from the country communities, he met the need at his own expense. When, in order to pay their taxes to the king or provide food for themselves and their families, the poor borrowed from the rich landowners and pledged their fields, their homes, even their children, as security, which was clearly against the law, Nehemiah made the landlords return the pledges. He set the example himself by renouncing all debts due to him. Among Nehemiah's religious reforms was the strict observance of the Sabbath, which was being violated by almost all sections of the community. On his walks he saw Jews engaging in their usual mundane occupations on the day of rest. Nehemiah reproached and reprimanded them and, to prevent the abuse, he closed the market on the Sabbath and posted watchmen to keep merchants from entering the city.

But even more than the desecration of the Sabbath inter-marriage with members of foreign tribes threatened to sap the vitality of the Jewish religion and endanger its future. Purity of race unquestionably was one of the purposes of the Jewish opposi-tion to mixed marriages; but above that objective was the anxiety to maintain the purity of the Jewish religion. In the prevail-ing chaos, much to the horror of the Jews faithful to the teachings of the Torah, marriage with the foreign Moabite, Ammonite, and Philistine peoples was proceeding at a frightful pace. To cap the evil, one of the sons of a high priest, who afterward succeeded his father, married his son to the daughter of the Samaritan Sanballat. Nehemiah spoke out furiously on the subject and had him driven from the city. But punishing one man did not remedy the situation; what was needed was to completely uproot and destroy the evil.

It was at this time that Ezra emerged from his self-imposed obscurity. He had kept himself strictly in the background while Nehemiah was carrying on his great historic work. Their lives paralleled each other, except that Nehemiah was a layman, while Ezra was of the hereditary Aaronite priesthood. They were at one in their resolution to combat the evil of mixed marriages, which, like a cancerous growth, had eaten its way into the body of the entire Jewish nation—the upper classes, most of all. For years Ezra was brooding over the problem and the method of attacking it. He was not one of those who returned early to Jerusalem. But, while he stayed behind, his heart and mind were fixed on Jerusalem. When the reports proved so distressing that his heart nearly broke he obtained permission to go up to Jerusalem from the king, who invested him with extraordinary powers to appoint magistrates, to administer justice, to teach and enforce the law, "by death, by exile, by fines or by imprisonment."

Ezra left Babylon with a caravan of about fifteen hundred people, who, fired by his religious zeal, were ready to follow him in every-thing. Before setting out, they united on the bank of the Ahava

River in a solemn fast and prayer for a successful journey. The uneventful journey was accomplished in less than four months. His arrival in Jerusalem attracted considerable attention, both because of his distinguished ancestry and because of his reputation as a master and expounder of the Law. But to Ezra these things did not count; he had his own goal—the eradication of mixed marriages, which to him spelled the dissolution of Judaism and the Jewish people.

He held conferences with the leaders and representatives of the people, and what he heard dismayed and terrified him. The defection was wide and deep, down to the sworn servants of the Jewish religion itself. Ezra had his own conception of Judaism—one perhaps differing from that expressed in the Bible. The Jews were to him a holy people in a literal sense, and its holiness was not to be contaminated by intermarriage with foreign tribes under any conditions. Proselytes who abjured idolatory and the heathen practices were to be accepted and treated with cordiality, but religiously they were not to be considered on the same plane with racially born Jews—certainly not to the extent of justifying their intermarriage with Israelites. They were to live apart, as did the Gibeonites who had accepted the Israelitish doctrine centuries before. It is interesting to note that Judah Halevi adopted the same attitude toward proselytes in the *Kuzari,* a view, however, which Maimonides warmly contested in a famous letter to a proselyte.

Powerfully affected by what he had heard, the aged sage then gave vent to the emotions which wracked his soul. He tore his garments, plucked the hair from his head and beard, refused all nourishment, and lay motionless, prostrated in the court of the Temple confessing amid passionate sobs the sins of his people.

It was a profoundly moving scene and it sent a tremor of fear and terror through the bystanders. Men, women, and children wept with him. Then, as if by prearrangement and certainly guessing what was in Ezra's mind, one of the bystanders approached him and said: "We have trespassed against our God and have married strange women of the people of the land. Now let us make a covenant with God and put away the wives and such as are born of them." This was what Ezra wanted and what he had expected. He did not want violence he contemplated to come from him but from the people themselves. He responded with alacrity. He rose and demanded from the heads of families who were present that they repudiate their foreign wives and the children born of them.

The zealot had won the first skirmish, but not without a show of resistance on the part of those whose family feelings proved stronger than the impassioned oratory of the priest. The priests and Levites and the elders of the people submitted and offered a sacrifice of expiation, however their hearts ached, and they sent away their wives and the children begotten of them. But the mass of the people, especially those living in the province, either ignored the order entirely or practiced deception by separating themselves from their wives but keeping their children. Some others debated and haggled, stalling for time in the hope that Ezra would realize the harshness of his measure and soften it or abolish it altogether.

Ezra was disappointed; he had temporarily failed in his mission. In the face of strong opposition at home, and probably at the court, where he was charged with overstepping his authority, another man would have given up all hope. But Ezra's tenacity did not permit him to become discouraged. To save the nation and its faith was to him a goal so lofty and glorious that he sought new means to attain it. Fortunately at this time, Nehemiah, the twin spirit of Ezra, came again to the fore, and together they convoked a grand assembly of all the inhabitants of Judea on the open space before the Temple. There was hesitation on the part of the Jews of the province. They probably sensed what was going to be demanded of them, and they pleaded the rainy season and the work in the fields. But they were compelled to attend on threat of heavy punishment.

It was as impressive an assembly as the combined genius of Ezra and Nehemiah could devise. Everything was calculated to produce a solemn and moving effect. The assembly was large; almost all Judea had turned out. It was held on the first day of the month of Tishri in 445 B.C.E. On a wooden platform the white-haired priest stood and read with a solemn voice from the Book of the Law in his hand. What the people heard made so deep an impression that on the following day he was asked to read again. Then Ezra determined to take the last step to bring about the reform that was in his mind. He read and expounded the portion of the Law forbidding intermarriage with the Ammonites and Moabites and ordered the men to put away the wives with whom such marriages had been contracted.

The desired effect was attained and the great restriction which so violently suppressed many natural emotions was imposed and faithfully observed—but with what immeasurable heartbreak! Families were divided, women long and happily married returned with their children to the old Ammonite, Moabite, and Samaritan homes they had left years ago. It was at this time, when the question of intermarriage was being heatedly debated, that the charming and graceful story of Ruth is conjectured to have appeared. Although the biblical idyll is set in the wild and rough days of the Judges about the year 1100 B.C.E., its application to the time we are writing about is too pointed to be missed. In the story we have the Moabite Ruth entreating Naomi, ". . . thy people shall be my people, and thy God, my God; where thou diest, will I die, and there will I be buried . . ."—an entreaty many a foreign-born woman may have made to the husbands they were compelled to leave. Not only was Ruth accepted into the Jewish fold but a son born to her became an ancestor of David, the great king of Israel. But if Ezra knew of the story of Ruth, which as likely as not was written for his benefit, it was of little avail. For not only did he not retract or modify his hard and harsh measure but he appointed officers to see to it that it was sternly carried out.

What, then, was Ezra? Was he a fanatic, a bigot, or was he the savior of his people and their religion? Certainly no other Bible character was as severely abused and criticized as he. Even so conservative a historian as Graetz seems to doubt the wisdom of an enactment which brought such grief and pain to wives who, through no fault of their own, found themselves deserted by their husbands and their children abandoned by their fathers. To quote Graetz: "But this exclusiveness was not strictly in agreement with the letter of the Law, for Ezra himself, with all his knowledge, was not able to point to any passage in the Torah, implying that mixed marriages are forbidden when contracted with those who acknowledge the God of Israel."

On the other hand it must be remembered that the measure Ezra adopted for the preservation of Judaism and the Jewish people was no more harsh and extraordinary than was the time in which it was taken. Nor was the "exclusiveness" regretted by Graetz a strange and novel invention of Ezra and his group. Racial integrity was zealously watched over in ancient times by nations other than the Jews. The late Professor George Foot Moore points to the fact that, in Athens, Pericles, a contemporary of Ezra, put through a law that only those both of whose parents were Athenian citizens should be reckoned Athenians. When nearly five thousand residents proved to be the offspring of such illegitimate alliances they were not only deprived of their citizenship but were sold into slavery. In Rome, intermarriage between patricians and plebeians was likewise violently opposed. "The motive of such legislation," concludes Professor Moore, "was to perpetuate a pure-bred race, especially to keep unmixed the blood of the citizen body; it was a measure of self-preservation and nothing more."

The Jews had a stronger reason to maintain the purity of their national life than either the Greeks or the Romans. Their religion provided the only means the Jews had of preserving their racial and national existence. They were a tiny nation in a tiny country. Notwithstanding the prohibition against intermarriage in the Torah and the prophets, the books of Ezra and Nehemiah are replete with instances of marital relationships of Jews with the offspring of the surrounding peoples. Had the condition been allowed to continue and no drastic measure taken to stem the evil, it would have led to the extinction of the Jews and their religion. Ezra was a stern patriot; he was also a man of deep human feelings and sympathies. He was deeply conscious of the pain the enforcement of his radical reform implied. But patriot and pious Jew that he was, he set the preservation of the Jews and their religion above the suffering of individual men and women. Had Ezra and his group failed, had they not succeeded in stemming the tide of paganism which resulted from intermarriage with the surrounding nations, the loss to Judaism and to the world would have been incalculable.

Hillel

HILLEL, ONE OF the greatest of Jewish scholars, was the best loved and most revered of them. His liberal spirit and his interpretation of the scriptures in terms of the social and economic conditions of the time constituted an epoch in Jewish history. He was a kind and warmhearted man who loved his people and all mankind. The Jews have adored his memory and repeated his sayings for nearly two thousand years. He left a greater heritage of wise and brilliant maxims and aphorisms than did any other Jewish sage. He was a contemporary of Jesus, although the two never met, nor would they have approved of each other. Hillel was the author of the Golden Rule which, with slight variation, the Christian church took over as her own.

His winning personality equaled his learning. He was modest and patient, gentle and forbearing. In his meekness he was likened to Moses and his modesty became a model and pattern for all men. "Be ever as modest as Hillel," was the saying. Wise and understanding, and knowing how difficult it is to fathom the deeper motivations that tempt man to evil doing, his rule was, "Judge not thy neighbor until thou standest in his place"—another maxim of our sage that Paul appropriated for Christianity. He loved peace and pursued it. His favorite principle was: "Be of the disciples of Aaron, loving peace and pursuing peace and drawing men near to the Torah." He knew difficulties and hardships, struggles and poverty; they never embittered him but, rather, made him serene and gentle, calm and considerate toward all men.

Although the greatest scholars of his time paid him the tribute of their reverence, he himself sought no honor and coveted no titles, his motto being, "He who seeks to make his name great destroys it." The great storehouse of the Talmud is full of his wisdom and learning, but he is usually spoken of simply as "Hillel the Elder," to distinguish him from another Hillel who lived about two hundred years later, or as "Hillel the Babylonian," to denote the country from which he came. He is also sometimes referred to as "Hillel ha-Nasi" (the "Patriarch"). He was the presiding officer of the great Sanhedrin and established a dynasty that stood at the head of the religious affairs of the Jews for nearly five hundred years. Yet less is known about him prior to his coming to Palestine than about most other masters of the Law.

His youth is obscure, his ancestors are unknown—he never as much as refers to his parents. There is a tradition that his mother was descended from a distinguished family of the Babylonian Jewish exiles and from the royal house of King David, but not even the name of his father is known. Hillel had a brother named Shebna, who was successful in a mercantile career and was among the richest men in Jerusalem. He invited his brother to join him as a business partner, but Hillel refused because of his love of the Torah and his ambition to become the most learned man in Israel. That Hillel lived one hundred and twenty years, as Moses did, is probably more legend than history, signifying the love and admiration in which he was held by linking his life to that of Israel's great prophet and law giver. Hillel's wife was no less noted for her piety and generosity than was her famous scholar-husband. A dinner she one day prepared for a distinguished guest she gave away to a poor man who was marrying off a daughter, and hastily prepared another meal. When she excused herself for the delay and explained the cause, Hillel praised her profusely for what she did. No further details are known about the family history of the man who stimulated the love and imagination of his people as did few other men. Hillel's youth was spent in Babylonia, where probably his ancestors lived for generations. He had his education in his own country, although nothing definite is known of the city in which he was born or who his teachers were. When, therefore, in the prime of his life he left his country and emigrated to Jerusalem to sit at the feet of the two most eminent teachers, Shemaiah and Abtalion, to advance himself in the knowledge of Jewish tradition, he came not as an ignorant beginner but as one well versed in the study of the Law. Babylonia in Hillel's time and, indeed, long before his time, was not an intellectual and spiritual desert as far as the Jews were concerned. There were schools of Law there as in other great centers of Jewish population.

Not all the exiled Jews took advantage of the Persian monarch's permission to go up to Jerusalem and rebuild the House of the Lord. The majority of the Jewish population, including the most prosperous, remained behind and continued to make Babylon their home. They were not entirely assimilated, although they adopted the Chaldean language and gave their names a Chaldean form, for the Torah was highly prized in their midst and they spared no effort to promote it. Jewish education stood high among the Jewish captives in Babylonia and there was an active participation in the interpretation of the Law. There was also a continuous intercourse between them and their brethren in Palestine, who kept them informed about the progress of the Jerusalem schools of learning. Although Hillel was unquestionably the greatest of the Babylonian scholars who went to Jerusalem for completion of his advanced training in Jewish tradition, he was not the only one. His contemporaries, the Elders of Batyra *(Benai Betyra)* are known to have been of Babylonian Jewish descent. Shemiah and Abtalion, Hillel's slightly older contemporaries and the most loved and influential teachers of their time and heads of the Jerusalem Supreme Council were in all likelihood also of Babylonian origin. Hananel, likewise a Babylonian, although recorded in history as of low priestly rank, cannot have been undistinguished in his knowledge of the Law or Herod, with all his contempt for the religious feelings of the Jews, would not have dared to raise him to the high priesthood. The hermeneutics, or rules of interpretation, which won for Hillel his spurs when he argued before the Jerusalem Supreme Council the case of the Paschal sacrificial offering, seems to have been the accepted norm in the Babylonian schools for deriving new laws from the ancient Scriptures. While, therefore, Jerusalem continued in her position as guardian of the Law and keeper of the old traditions, it was the breath of life that was infused by Hillel, the Babylonian, which kept the law from becoming fossilized and which made possible its further development.

It was a deeply disturbed and turbulent city that Hillel found upon his arrival in Jerusalem. The Judean capital, which never lacked for tensions and excitement, was experiencing its severest crisis. It is one of the paradoxes of history that the two men, Hillel and Herod, so different from each other, should be contemporaries, live together in the same city, and in their respective capacities even have relations with one another. For while Hillel is remembered as the humble and tender sage and saint, knowing no law but that of loving kindness, Herod is written down in history as a cruel and monstrous ruler knowing no law but that of ruthless aggression. King of Judea by the grace of Rome, his unwilling subjects had never regarded him as any more than a foreign usurper.

It was a tragic circumstance that led the Idumean Herod to usurp the Judean throne, and Tragedy dressed in royal purple followed every step of his unhappy career. Everything considered, Herod was but a plaything in the hands of an implacable fate. Although he was a Jew by adoption, neither of Herod's parents was of the Jewish race, having belonged to an Idumean tribe which under Hyrcanus' unfortunate expansionist policy was forcibly converted to Judaism. Under the circumstances Herod had no sympathy for Judaism as a religion nor for the Jews as a people. But the high tide of political development which swept over Judea—the Roman mastery of the country, on the one hand, and the fratricidal warfare of the members of the Hasmonean family, on the other— could not fail to play into the hands of so shrewd and astute a man as Herod and pave the way, however bloody, for his ascent to the throne.

Hillel came to Jerusalem about 40 B.C.E., almost simultaneously with Herod's accession to power. Members of the Hasmonean family were still in possession of the throne but at best exercised a mere shadow rule. The real mastery of the country lay in the hands of Rome. But Judea was a small country—too small a land for Rome's mounting ambition to bother about. Therefore, when

Herod, a young man, brave, courageous, and personable, presented himself, he had no difficulty in persuading the Senate of his fitness for the job of ruling the country, restoring peace and quelling rebellion wherever it arose. He was as hard and ruthless as was any Roman, cunning and crafty in his ambition and passionately vengeful toward anybody who stood in his way. When resistance to Rome broke out among a patriotic Jewish group in the hills of Galilee, Herod broke the uprising with unwonted cruelty which set all Judea against him.

Herod, called the "Great," was great in but one respect—that by cunning, bribery, and the use of mercenary troops he managed to hold on to his throne against a people that bore no other relationship to him than that of cold, implacable hatred. Herod was no Jew; he was at best a half-Jew, an Idumean who had been forcibly converted to Judaism, and he spent the thirty-three years of his demi-Jewishness to avenge the wrong Hyrcanus committed on his tribe. Although he knew he could not hope for the voluntary love of the Jews, he nevertheless tried to compel it—by deceit and subtlety, if possible—by torture and the execution block, if there was no other way. Herod's greatest obstacle was the presence of the Hasmoneans, on whose restoration to the throne, the heart of the Jews was nostalgically centered. He could not dispose of them offhand, after the manner of Eastern monarchs who executed the members of a dethroned dynasty. Herod was too shrewd and astute a man for such a drastic step, which he knew would rouse the Jews to bloody rebellion. He realized the depth of the love and devotion of the Jews to the Hasmoneans, descendants of the Maccabees who had fought their battles and won for them their freedom. Herod thought that by allying himself in marriage with a daughter of the ancient Hasmonean family he would reinforce his claim to the throne and finally win the friendship and devotion of the Jews. He married the beautiful Mariamne, the granddaughter of the aged Hyrcanus. In time he might have succeeded, for he was passionately in love with Mariamne and she returned his affection. But his hopes were vain. Alexandra, the queen's mother, did not for a moment relax her implacable opposition to her son-in-law and did not allow the Jews to forget that he was nothing but a usurper not even of their race and blood. The king's marriage had not only not helped matters but had even aggravated them, for now he was not only accused of being a brigand in seizing a throne that did not belong to him but also of contaminating the Hasmonean blood.

Herod's disappointment made the desert blood in his veins run wild. A pitiful victim of fear, frustration, and suspicion, he now lost every semblance of a human being. He knew he could not win the love of the Jews, not even the trust and devotion of his own family, and he determined to avenge the universal ill-will toward him by shocking acts of terror and murder. He was now no longer a Jew even by pretense, but became a raging wounded animal at bay, striking right and left, and not sparing even those closest and dearest to him. His mad instinct of brutality extended not only to his common political enemies but to the very members of his household. His palace became a charnel house. His fear of rivalry caused him to have Aristobulus, the seventeen-year-old High Priest and Mariamne's brother, drowned by "accident." On the mere suspicion of infidelity Herod had a sort of privy council condemn and execute the woman he adored. Her mother, grandfather Hyrcanus, and her two sons followed the ill-fated queen's lot. Augustus, repelled by the stories he heard, remarked: "It were better to be such a man's pig than his son."

Strange and paradoxical as it may seem, the man who did not love Judaism and may even have hated it, who all but laughed at Jewish learning and culture and was inflexibly unforgiving of anyone who stood in his coarse and brutal way, found the Pharisees tractable and comparatively easy to get along with. Indeed, while there was terror in the country and Jerusalem was numb with fear at what the next day might bring, Shemaiah and Abtalion—the two great men of the generation, the Talmud designates them— presided over their academy in Jerusalem, teaching, expounding, and interpreting the Law undisturbed, as did Shammai and Hillel after them. During Herod's long reign they were hardly conscious of the storm and fury around the throne, so occupied were they with the study and teaching of the Law. Their loyalty was to God, their devotion to the Torah. They little cared for the temporal power for which greedy men spent so much of their life. They sensed prophetically that their work would last and posterity would honor their labors while all the power and glory achieved by brute violence would turn into dust and ashes.

There are no serious clashes reported between Herod and the Pharisaic teachers. In the list of victims Herod dispatched to the execution block there is not the name of a single Jewish scholar. Indeed, Herod not only found the Pharisaic masters of the Law tractable but they opposed him and his reign less actively than they had their national sovereigns, John Hyrcanus and Alexander Janaeus. It is quite extraordinary that it was during his rule, a time of storm and stress for the Jews in Palestine, that there existed that remarkable coterie of scholars celebrated in history as the "Pairs" *(Zugot)*, Shemaiah and Abtalion, and Hillel and Shammai. In Herod's sane moments, which unfortunately were few, he conferred upon the first two the exceptional distinction of dispensing with their oath of allegiance, and this despite the fact that at one time Sameas (Shemaiah) had resisted him with great firmness.

This, however, does not mean that the Pharisees were partial to Herod and condoned the cruelty and inhumanity of his reign. Quite the contrary. They were intensely and fervently religious, and in their hearts they painfully resented his many violations of the Jewish religious and moral law. They were rigorists and they could not but regard with the utmost disfavor his tampering with the high priesthood, his association with the Greek and Roman heathens and with their pagan games and sports, and his having the Roman eagle placed over the principal gate of the Temple, and they gave expression to words of protest which, though in veiled form, carried a meaning and purport which cannot be mistaken. In that singular book, the *Pirke Abot*, which forms part of the compilation of the Mishnah, there are a number of maxims by celebrated teachers, contemporaries of Herod, which point to their reaction to his reign. Thus we read in the name of Shemaiah: "Love work and hate mastery, and make not thyself known to the government"—a counsel of prudence when the government is not sympathetic toward one's ideas and ideals. Abtalion said: "Ye wise, take heed to your words, lest ye incur the penalty of exile, and ye be exiled to a place of evil waters, and the disciples that come after you drink and die and the name of Heaven be profaned." Abtalion could have meant but one thing—a warning to scholars to be discreet in the perilous Herodian regime lest their indiscretion involve them in exile, if not in worse penalties. As a matter of fact, there were scholars who, unable to reconcile themselves to the Idumean dictator's policy, fled their country and found refuge, some in Babylon and some in Egypt. Another saying with oblique reference to the time in which he lived and which at the same time is an epigram on moral retribution is the following by Hillel: ". . . he saw a skull which floated on the face of the water, and he said, because thou drowndest, they drowned thee, and in the end, they that drowned thee shall be drowned." In general, it may be said that while the Pharisaic teachers were certainly not sympathetic to Herod's obnoxious life and rule they did not actively agitate against him because they saw in his victory the finger of God and counseled submission.

Hillel was a Pharisee and belonged to that group of Jews who, zealous for the Torah and its normal development under the changing social and economic conditions of the time, adhered not alone to the Divine Law of Sinai but also to the precepts and regulations of the Rabbis of later generations. The Pharisees were neither a sect nor a party in the ordinary sense of those words. They were the masters and molders of Judaism. Indeed, they *were* Judaism—the learned body of the nation whose devotion and idealism made possible its preservation to this day. They made laws, issued ordinances, and put up a hedge around the Law. They were a democratic fraternity of men who mingled with the crowd, taught in the synagogues, visited the market place, and on rare occasions even conducted the affairs of the nation. Josephus writes that during the reign of Queen Alexandra (139–67 B.C.E.) they wielded considerable power and influence and were consulted by her in matters of government. Their principal occupation, however, was with the Torah, its study and dissemination, its precise and minute interpretation. Herein lies the historic significance of the Pharisees which made them so extraordinary a force in the creation and development of the Jewish tradition.

When Hillel came to Jerusalem he found a store of traditions developed in the schools of Shemaiah and Abtalion which left little room for anyone else ambitious to contribute his share. He also found Shammai, a well-to-do native Palestinian. All of these were great masters of the Law, but they were not very favorably disposed toward foreign scholars. Hillel, however, was not easily discouraged. He had come under considerable hardship all the way from Babylonia to acquire from the great expositors a discipline in the method and interpretation of the Law. But how could he afford the small fee which, to keep out unworthy intruders, the academy imposed? Many entertaining stories are told in the Talmud of Hillel's coming to Jerusalem, about his student days and the difficulties he overcame in his desire for learning. But the most widely circulated story about Hillel—one that occurs with little variation in numerous talmudic sources—concerns his determination to gain admission to the academy then presided over by the Benai Betyra (the Elders of Betyra), whom Herod had appointed as successors to Shemaiah and Abtalion.

Bent on becoming a scholar but without any means of support, he took to woodcutting for a livelihood. His earnings were meager, but of the little he made he put aside a few coins for the daily entrance fee to the school. One day, during the winter season Hillel, however, did not earn enough for the admission fee. Determined not to miss the discussions of the masters, he climbed up and sat by the skylight, where he could hear their discourse. It was cold and snowing, but the zealous student did not desert his post. When it turned dark in the academy the scholars looked up to the skylight and saw someone lying there. They quickly brought down the half-frozen Hillel and resuscitated him. When his devotion to study was recognized it was rewarded by his being permitted to attend the lectures gratis. The moral of the story or legend, no doubt, is that poverty is no excuse for neglect of the Torah, and that the knowledge of the Torah is enduring only to them who sacrifice themselves for it. While the lesson of the tale is evident, there never was a time in the talmudic period—indeed, at any period—when a poor scholar was denied an opportunity to learn for lack of funds. The rule was that the Torah, which was given by God free without claim or charge, must be taught without material reward. It was not until late in the Middle Ages that rabbis allowed themselves to accept remuneration for teaching.

Hillel won his spurs in a discussion in which he took part upon coming to Jerusalem. The question, which aroused much debate among the scholars, was whether the Paschal lamb may be sacrificed when the eve of the festival happens to fall on the Sabbath, or whether the prohibition of labor on the Sabbath applies also to the Passover offering. The discussion was long and heated and it covered every point and angle of the question. The opinion of an outstanding authority was looked for, but there was no precedent anyone could remember regarding so rare a case. The Benai Betyra were in the seat of the Sanhedrin, but they, too, were perplexed. Hillel alone knew the tradition; he had heard it repeated in the name of Shemaiah and Abtalion that the Paschal sacrifice, like the *karban tamid,* which is offered daily, supersedes the Sabbath. His decision, on the authority of Shemaiah and Abtalion, was immediately accepted.

Hillel was victorious, but it was not the triumph that he had wished. What he wanted was to regenerate the operation of law by deriving its authority directly from the Bible by a rational method of interpretation and exposition *(derash)* instead of by appealing to authority and precedent. It was a new philosophy of law that Hillel had brought with him from Babylonia—one that breathed a new spirit into Judaism and rendered it fertile for further growth and development. Hillel's great historic significance in the realm of law lies in the fact that he belonged to the realm of sages, writes Judah Goldin, "whose vision went beyond past and present. They did not reject what had come from earlier ages; but they insisted that in each generation scholars were entitled to search the Torah thoroughly, and with the assistance of reason and logic, derive new meaning and new legal prescriptions." To normalize the juristic deductions and analogies and harmonize them with the Divine Law, every word of which was regarded as significant and authoritative, Hillel devised the Seven Rules *(midot),* which were extended in a later generation by Rabbi Ishmael to thirteen, and still later, by Rabbi Jose ha-Gellili, to thirty-two.

What was Hillel's position after his historic victory over the Benai Betyra? According to tradition, the Elders of Betyra voluntarily resigned their position and Hillel became head of the Sanhedrin with the title of Nasi. But this, Wilhelm Bacher thinks, is hardly historical. "All that can be said," Bacher avers, "is that after the resignation of the Benai Betyra, Hillel was recognized as the highest authority among the Pharisees and the Scribes of Jerusalem. He was head of the great school, at first associated with Menahem, a scholar mentioned in other connections, afterwards with Shammai, Hillel's peer in the study of the law." "But whatever Hillel's position," Bacher adds, "his authority was sufficient to introduce the decrees which were handed down in his name."

Hillel was no sooner invested with authority, as head of the Sanhedrin, than he devoted his interest to the modification of such laws of the scriptures as, although intended for the good and welfare of the people, created under the changed conditions of the time excessive hardships. Thus, according to the scriptural legislation, the redemption of a house sold or mortgaged in a "walled city" is limited to one year. If for any reason the seller or mortgagor fails to redeem the property in stated time it remains in possession of the present owner. If, however, the former owner is away and cannot return in time, or if the present owner locks his door and makes it impossible for the former owner to return the purchase money, the conservative says, "Too bad, but the law is the law; the property remains in possession of the purchaser." "No," says Hillel; "of course the law is the law, but the law must be amended, modified, interpreted. The lawful owner must not lose his property. If he is not at home or the purchaser locks the door, the door may be forced open and the purchase money deposited in the Temple treasury."

Another much more far-reaching example of Hillel's liberal spirit, characteristic of both the man and the jurist, is the reform he introduced with regard to the sabbatical cancellation of debts. (Deut. 15, 1–2.) The economy of Palestine in Hillel's time was no longer exclusively agricultural. Businessmen could not carry on their trade if borrowing and lending was to be discouraged. What inducement would there be to capitalists to lend their money when they knew that with the approach of the seventh year they could never collect what was due them? The letter of the law was plainly preventing the achievement of the very ideal for which it was intended. Hillel counteracted the evil by his device of the *prosbol*, a Greek term for a document by the delivery of which debts remained in force on and after the arrival of the seventh year *(shemitah)*. It was a radical innovation—one that practically destroyed the literal meaning of the biblical provision but which expressed the larger meaning of the Holy Writ rather than its literal wording. The rabbis correctly designated Hillel's enactment as *takannat ha-Olam* (for the amelioration of society), although less liberal scholars than Hillel were shocked by and denounced the liberties he took with the biblical law. The people, however, for whose benefit the innovation was intended, accepted it and abided by it for generations.

Such, then, was the man Hillel and the impact of his spirit. He was the greatest of the Tannaitic teachers of Judaism and his influence was felt for generations. The Rabbis of the Talmud paid him the full measure of tribute when they said: "The Torah was forgotten and Ezra came and restored it, and when there was danger of the Torah to be forgotten again, Hillel came and re-established it." He was a builder and restorer, an innovator and reformer who did not permit the Torah to become fixed and static but made it free and responsive to every need of Pharisaic Judaism —the most perfect blending of the qualities of heart and mind, which made him a hero and a gallant figure in Jewish folklore. The mild and tolerant spirit he infused into the study and interpretation of the Torah was taken up by a loyal and faithful following, of whom tradition says there were eighty, who carried on the master's teaching to the further enrichment and expansion of the law and who became known as *Bet Hillel*. No higher tribute has been paid to any man than tradition ascribes to Hillel. One day, so the story goes, when he and the sages were assembled at Jericho, a heavenly voice was heard exclaiming, "Among those assembled is one man upon whom the holy spirit is worthy to rest if his time were deserving of it." They all knew of whom the voice spoke, and their eyes were fixed on Hillel.

Hillel was a philosopher who did not write books on philosophy; he was an ethical teacher whose observations on life and the world were delivered in crisp and concise epigrammatic sentences. His view of life is perhaps best summarized in his reported sayings: "The more flesh, the more worms; the more property, the more anxiety; the more women, the more witchcraft; the more women servants, the more lewdness; the more men servants, the more robbery; the more Torah, the more life; the more schooling, the more wisdom; the more counsel, the more understanding; the more charity, the more peace." (Abot 2: 4.) Hillel's philosophy was social, his goal the community life. Man must by all means be self-reliant; none but himself can work out his destiny. But being only for himself, of what account is he? Thus Hillel's saying: "If I am not for myself, who will be for me? But being [only] for my own self, what am I?" And he concludes the saying with the words, "and if not now, when?" (Abot 1:13)—meaning, "Do not put off until tomorrow what you can do today."

The study of Torah was Hillel's overmastering passion, and to this end his choicest proverbs and maxims are directed. That he might perfect himself in the knowledge of the Law he freely chose a life of poverty. The wisdom of Torah cannot be acquired by overindulgence in business. Torah postponed is Torah lost. Therefore, Hillel said: "Say not, when I have leisure, I will study; perchance thou wilt have no leisure." (Abot 2:4.) With all his love and sympathy for the common man, Hillel did not hold that piety and ignorance can dwell together. Hence his adage: "The boor cannot be religious, the ignorant cannot be truly pious. Whoso is ashamed to ask will not be able to learn." (Abot 2:5.) Amplifying Hillel's saying, "Bring men to the Torah," (Abot 1:12) tradition relates that he stood one day at the gate of Jerusalem and saw the people on their way to work. "How much," he asked, "wilt thou earn today?" One said, "A dinarius"; the second, "Two dinarii." "What will you do with the money?" Hillel inquired. "We will provide for the necessities of life." Then he said to them: "Would you not rather come and make the Torah your possession, that you may possess both this and the future world?" (A.R.N., Schechter, 2:26.)

His love for Torah was equaled only by his love of man. *Ahabat ha-briot,* the love for human beings, is a frequently recurring note in Hillel's social outlook. It was considered by him as the kernel of Judaism, the fundamental principle of Jewish faith and conduct. Hillel had a mystic faith in God, yet when a heathen came to him to be made a Jew while he stood on one leg Hillel did not discourage him nor drive him away, as did the quick-tempered Shammai; nor did he teach him the love of God. Instead, he said, "Do not do to others what is hateful to you; this is the sum of religion; the rest is but commentary upon it," (Shab. 31a.) He simply paraphrased in Aramaic what is taught as an injunction in the Bible: "Thou shalt love thy neighbor as thyself." (Lev.19:18.) From his teaching of love for mankind flowed his principle of man's duty toward himself—not only his inward but his outward self. When Hillel was seen one day rushing for the bathhouse he explained that he was running to perform a *mitzvah,* and when his astonished disciples asked what *mitzvah* there was in bathing, he said: "As in theatre and circus the statutes of the king must be kept clean by him to whom they have been entrusted, so the bathing of the body is a duty of man who has been created in the image of the almighty king of the world." (Lev.R.30:3.) Hillel's love for man is illustrated, likewise, in his exhortation: "Judge not thy neighbor till thou art in his place." (Abot 11:4.)

Hillel was wont to commune with his soul. When it was noticed by his disciples that he repeatedly left them, they asked him the reason. He said, "I must hurry home to attend on an honored guest I have been rather neglecting of late." "But have you such guests every day?" his pupils pressed him. "Yes," answered Hillel, "he is a guest who is here today and gone tomorrow." And he explained: "The guest is the soul, which has her lordly place in the body, but often has very little attention given her beyond the lodging." (Lev.R.34:3.) This savors somewhat of mysticism, but Hillel was anything but a mystic. There is little of other-worldliness in his teaching and he is almost completely silent on the messianic era and life after death. What ideas he had on retribution and reward and punishment he expressed not in eschatological terms but in the plain and simple language of human experience. Thus, when he saw a human skull floating on the surface of the water (possibly during Herod's reign of violence), he was moved to observe: "Because thou hast drowned others, they have drowned thee, and eventually they that drowned thee will themselves be drowned." (Abot 11:7.)

Enlarging upon his brief dictum, "Thou shalt not separate thyself from the community." Hillel laid as a rule for human conduct that man should not appear different from others in his outward deportment; he should always regard himself as a part of the whole; or, paraphrasing his words, one should not appear naked among those who are fully dressed nor be clothed when all the others are naked. If the custom is to stand one should not be seated, nor should one stand alone. There is a time for merry-making and a time for weeping, and one should share in the mood of the people. His benevolent spirit, which extended to all men but particularly to those in reduced circumstances who had seen better times, is illustrated by his high-minded suggestion that charity should be commensurate with the needs of him to be helped. Thus to a man of good family who had become impoverished Hillel gave a riding horse, so that he might not be deprived of his customary physical exercise, and a slave, so that he might be served properly. (Ket. 67b.)

In addition to these examples, which reflect the very soul and character of Hillel, to complete the picture there are many other anecdotes with which tradition surrounds the life of its favorite saint and hero. Hillel's meekness and patience having become common knowledge, two men entered into a wager, one of them boasting that he could tempt Hillel to anger. One Friday, as Hillel was preparing for the Sabbath, the better went three times to him with the most trivial questions. But Hillel answered them all calmly and quietly without showing the slightest irritation. When the man, upon his third attempt, saw that he had failed, he exclaimed angrily, "May there not be many like thee in Israel!" "Why?" asked Hillel. "Why?" replied the questioner, "because through thee, I have lost a large bet." "Well," said Hillel, "if that be the case, it is far better that thou shouldst lose thy bet than I my temper." (Shab. 30–30.)

It would serve no purpose to continue with further examples of the stories and anecdotes with which Hillel's disciples adorned his memory. Some of the legends may be apocryphal, but they never-theless illustrate the love and affection with which the disciples surrounded their teacher. We are not informed of Hillel's relation-ship to women, but it can only have been one of respect and high regard. The man who loved peace and sought to establish a friendly relationship between men was particularly anxious, for instance, about the bridegroom's tenderness toward his bride. Thus, the great saint and scholar would forget his dignity at weddings and exhaust himself in dancing with the bride. In contrast to Shammai, who was sparing in his praise of the bride and who said, "Every bride according to her virtues," Hillel was extravagant in his eulogies of her. (Ketubot 17a.)

Legendary is a story which illustrates Hillel's serene and tranquil state of mind—a serenity that flowed from his implicit faith and trust in God's protective care. It is told that on one occasion when the scholar was returning to his native town he saw a crowd of people massed in the market place, greatly disturbed and agitated. His disciples were alarmed and feared for the safety of the master's family. Hillel, however, maintained his composure and assured his pupils with perfect equanimity, "I know that there is nothing wrong in my home," and with that assurance he proceeded into the city to inquire after the cause of the commotion, which he found to be unimportant. (Ber.60a.)

Mention has been made of Shammai, Hillel's contemporary who contrasted so sharply in personality and interpretation of the Law. While the Palestinian scholar was his Babylonian colleague's equal in the study and knowledge of the Law, they differed from one another in temperament and disposition. Where Shammai was harsh and stern, Hillel was mild and tolerant; one was rigorous and unyielding, the other lenient and gentle. Strict religious scrupulosity was Shammai's rule of the Law; Hillel tried to make the Torah a joyous acceptance. Shammai was a conservative of the patrician families of Jerusalem and would not tamper with the literal meaning of the scriptures, while Hillel, having known poverty, was friend of the common men and did not hesitate to adapt the Law to the prevailing conditions of life. Shammai disdained proselytes and discouraged their admission to Judaism; Hillel welcomed them and taught them and brought them nearer to God. When a heathen one day came to Hillel's colleague and demanded to be taught the entire Sacred Law while "he stood on one foot," Shammai, angered by his presumption, drove him away. When the man came to Hillel and repeated his desire, the gentle teacher granted his request, as already mentioned, with the famous exhortation: "That which is hateful to thee, do not do to thy neighbor. All the rest is commentary. Now go forth and study." Probably as an oblique reference to Shammai's rash disposition, Hillel coined his oft-repeated maxim, "He who is quick-tempered cannot be a teacher."

The differences between Hillel and Shammai and between the schools and followings they established, known respectively as "Bet Hillel" and "Bet Shammai," make up a considerable part of the Talmud and have affected the religious, moral, and legal life of the Jews. Indeed, in the course of time, from about the beginning of the Christian era to the destruction of the Temple, the conflicting views and differences of opinion of the two schools on matters of law and observance became so great that the saying, "The Law became two laws," was coined. In general, Shammai and his "House" took the hard and severe line, and Hillel and his followers represented the more moderate and lenient point of view. In spite of Shammai's uncompromising zeal for the Law, however, one of the most beautiful maxims in the Talmud is reported in his name. He said: "Fix a time for the study of the Torah; say little and do much and receive all men with a cheerful countenance."

Hillel is the greatest teacher Judaism ever produced. In the history of Jewish tradition his name ranks first, with that of Rabbi Akiba as a distant second, not alone because of the greatness of his wisdom and learning but because of the purity and gentleness of his life. He enriched the body of tradition and paved the way to a rational interpretation of Judaism by establishing a harmony between law and reason. He taught that authority in Judaism is not to be sought in the dead letter of the Law but in its underlying meaning. When he won his test against the Benai Betyra and was raised to the presidency of the Sanhedrin, he said to them, "Why is it that I, an insignificant Babylonian, attained to such honor? Only because you have been too indolent to heed the teachings of Shemaiah and Abtalion." Hillel loved the Torah and insisted on constant study of and occupation with it. His motto was: "He who does not progress in Torah, retrogades." But the Torah was not to him a fixed and sealed doctrine but a living organism that develops and progresses with time. Shammai taught that a law is only valid when found in the words of the Torah; Hillel derived it from the general spirit and intention of the Holy Writ. It is this liberal spirit of Hillel and his philosophic conception of law which made him one of the best-loved and most progressive Jewish teachers.

According to tradition, Hillel presided over the Supreme Council for forty years, during which time he introduced laws and ordinances for the improvement and betterment of society. His disciples remained faithful to his memory and to his liberal spirit. As did their master, the Hillelites continued their opposition to the religious austerity of Shammai and his followers. Hillel lived through the horrors of the Herodian terror, but fortunately he was spared the agony of witnessing the national catastrophe that befell Palestine when it became a Roman province. (70–72 B.C.E.) After his death he was mourned by all Israel as "O pious, O gentle, O worthy follower of Ezra."

Philo

Philo Judaeus, the Alexandrian philosopher and the greatest Jew Egypt produced after Moses, is one of the most controversial figures in Jewish history. He is one of the most written-about Jewish scholars; yet the nearly two thousand years that have passed over him have not sufficed to solve the problems surrounding his life and work. Was he Jew or was he Greek; or was he a combination of the two, speaking, as it were, with two voices—one of Hellas and one of Jerusalem? The question is still being debated by scholars, with little agreement among them.

Philo was an exemplary character, a pure and exalted spirit in a spiritually disturbed and confused age. He kept his light steady when all around him was doubt and uncertainty. And that light was Jewish—the inherited light of generations of Jewish thought and conviction. He seemed to live only to glorify Judaism and the Jewish people in the pagan world in which they were little understood and respected. He was saturated with the learning and culture of his age and environment and he wrote in the style and diction of Plato; but his works were richly embroidered with phrases and quotations from the Bible. He was a prolific writer—the ten volumes surviving today do not nearly exhaust his entire literary output. He was one of the most popular literary men of his time and cultivated heathen readers, no less than Jews, fell under the spell of the glow and warmth of the thought and style of his writings.

The Alexandrian sage was an advocate and champion of his people. The philosopher who loved his books and the contemplative life did not shrink from the din and turmoil of the life about him. He championed the cause of Judaism among his own people no less than he did before its traducers in the pagan world. The man who was dominated by love of the Bible and its high moral and ethical teachings was hurt to see it ignored and neglected by the very people who created it. With almost prophetic outrage he lashed his lukewarm co-religionists who allowed themselves to be seduced by the catchwords of alien philosophies while disregarding the abiding truths of their own religion. Time and again he reminded them of the unique quality of their heritage: they were a chosen people come into the world with a mission—to be a light unto the nations.

Yet, paradoxically, the man who wrote and acted in the style and spirit of the rabbis and who, like them, imbued with the deepest love for Judaism, labored for its preservation, was taken no notice of by the contemporary Palestine authorities. His name is not even mentioned by them. Philo could not have been a stranger to the Jews of the Holy Land. He visited Jerusalem during the reign of King Agrippa. In his writings he gave a detailed description of the Temple service. He mingled with the people in the celebration of the revocation of Caligula's megalomaniac edict. The Egyptian Jewish sage was a Pharisee of the Pharisees and demanded of his brethren the strict obedience to their religious enactments. In beauty of style, depth of thought, and fervent eloquence, Philo is easily the equal of Hillel, who came up from Babylon and became the presiding head of the Sanhedrin, whereas his Alexandrian counterpart was wholly neglected by his people.

The Jews did not take kindly to Philo. Taking their cue from the Palestine rabbis, they all but ignored his existence. They were suspicious of the man who wrote in the Greek language, notwithstanding his personal piety and the fact that he was a member of the Alexandrian Sanhedrin. Not long after his death he passed out of the memory of the people he did so much to honor and glorify. Only Josephus remembered him and referred to his struggle against the calumnies of Apion, the foul-mouthed Alexandrian arch anti-Semite. There is also a vague intimation in Saadia's principal philosophical work, *Emunot v'Deot* that he knew of Philo through translation, as might have been expected of the man who, an Egyptian himself, was a compatriot of the Alexandrian philosopher. It was not until the sixteenth century that full attention was given to Philo. He was rescued from oblivion by Azariah de Rossi, an Italian Jewish scholar, himself a remarkable character and almost a romantic figure. Although incapacitated by a fatal illness, de Rossi mastered the whole of Jewish literature and recovered many forgotten treasures of the Jewish literary genius, both original works and translations. His scholarly and literary distinction rests on his *Moor Enayim* (Light of the Eyes), a work unique for its vast research in Jewish history and literature and which brings together men and topics widely diverse but inwardly related. Thus, after centuries of neglect, Philo reappeared in de Rossi's pages, as do Josephus and even the Church Fathers. Azariah is the first Jewish scholar to enter upon a full discussion of Philo, his time, philosophy, and relation to the Bible and the Septuagint. He is also the first Jewish writer to take the Alexandrian sage sufficiently seriously to devote a whole chapter to him, with a review and critique of his work.

Philo, whose given Hebrew name was Yedidiyah (Beloved of God), was born into a family which for generations had enjoyed the prestige that went with wealth and with social and political distinction, in the year 10 B.C.E. He was therefore contemporary with Hillel and Jesus, although neither of them was conscious of his existence. Little is known of his antecedents or the source from which his ancestors had derived their wealth and political distinction, although the latter must have been in the family long before Philo was born. Philo himself seems to have been well provided for, sufficiently, at any rate, to allow him to give free rein to his preference for the meditative life without concern for the material things of existence, and his brother Alexander was governor of the Jewish community and ruler of the whole of the delta region of Egypt. Indeed, so secure was he in the favor and confidence of the Roman ruling class that Mark Antony appointed him guardian of his daughter Antonia, who was later to be the mother of the Roman Emperor Claudius. Philo writes that besides his brother's high political connections, he possessed one of the greatest fortunes in the ancient world. And Josephus states that Alexander provided the silver and gold plates that covered the nine gates of Herod's

Temple at Jerusalem, a gift which must have been of inestimable value.

Alexandria, the city in which Philo was born, as were probably his forebears for generations before him, stood at the crossroads of two civilizations—Hellenic and Judaic. In the arts and sciences, in philosophy and culture, Alexandria, the most Hellenized city in the Roman Empire, was heir to all the wisdom and glory that was Athens. Its Jewish community ranked next to Jerusalem in population and importance, and had schools and communal organizations of its own, even a Sanhedrin for the guidance of the religious and secular affairs of the community.

The Jews were not strangers or recent arrivals in Alexandria; they were among the most ancient inhabitants of the city. Indeed, the Jews may be said to have been present at the very founding of the city, when Alexander, in establishing the town which he called by his name, had settled there many of the Jews who were in his army. The kind and friendly treatment of Palestine Jewry by the Macedonian conqueror created among the Jews a kind of romantic sentiment for the city, so that through frequent and numerous immigrations Alexandria absorbed more than one-third of the million Jews living in Egypt. The relations between the Jews and their Gentile compatriots were friendly and considerate. The early successors of Alexander were kind and benign rulers; they did not retreat from his mild and tolerant policy toward the Jews, who were permitted to follow their religion and organize their community life. The Jews were assigned the Delta District for their settlement—not, however, as a ghetto, but in order that they could more safely practice the requirements of their religion and preserve their historic national identity. Both Philo and Josephus maintain that the Jews were scattered throughout the city with their synagogues, schools, and organizations. They enjoyed a degree of self-government, with an Alabarch who exercised almost complete control over their economic and political affairs. They engaged in the crafts, commerce, and industry. The freedom the Jews enjoyed in the Hellenized Roman city in their economic, religious, and

cultural life was such that an outstanding Palestine authority regarded Alexandria as a "sister" of Jerusalem.

The Jews, on their side, won the confidence and friendship of
the Alexandrians by their rapid Hellenization. The impact of the
new cultural environment affected powerfully the sons and daughters of the old Jewish settlers in Alexandria. While the old generation continued in their love of Hebrew and cherished nostalgically
their old memories, their children adopted Greek as their language
not only in their social and economic relations but also in their
religious and cultural life. The Sabbath was strictly observed by
the Alexandrian Jews, but when they gathered in their houses of
worship, which they called by the Greek name "synagogues," for
holy repose, the Torah and portions from the Prophets were read
to them not in the Aramaic idiom, as was instituted by Ezra the
Scribe, but in the Greek language. It was under the pressure of
these circumstances that the need arose for a translation of the
Bible into Greek for the Hellenized Jews of the Roman empire,
which was accomplished by the Septuagint, the "Translation of the
Seventy," in the year 270 B.C.E.

It was in such an environment, half Greek and half Jewish, that
Philo was born and lived his life. His schooling in all likelihood
was not different from that of most children of affluent aristocratic
parents. Hailing from a family socially and politically well connected, the aim of his parents must have been to provide him with
an education that one day would qualify him for holding public
office. His education, therefore, was thoroughly in harmony with
the requirements of his age and his family's social position. It
included a thorough grounding in the Greek classical philosophies,
and a wide acquaintance with Greek literature, including poetry
and the drama; and, since athletics was the mark of a Greek gentle-
man, it is not surprising that he had a very considerable knowledge
of boxing and chariot races, both of which he witnessed and may
have participated in during his youth. It is not surprising, either,
that, born in a slave-holding society, Philo should consider life
without slaves unthinkable. Thus, by training and family tradition,

Philo was prepared for the life of the leisure class to which he belonged.

Philo's parents must have been greatly disappointed when, on maturing, he rejected the plans they had made for his future. He despised the mercantile career despite the wealth and prosperity it had brought his family; he would not go into government service, notwithstanding his brother Alexander's success; nor did he respect the leisure class of society, with their indolent and inactive lives. Instead, he chose for himself the studious, meditative life of the philosopher. He studied hard; he worked incessantly. He absorbed himself completely in the products of Greek culture and civilization. Antagonistic forces though they were, Greek philosophy had always sharpened and fertilized the Jewish consciousness. He loved and admired Greek culture and the Greek mentality so greatly that they thoroughly possessed him. He familiarized himself with the thoughts of Zeno, Pythagoras, and the Stoics, and he all but worshipped Plato. No other Jew of day was as well-read in the culture and philosophy of the Greeks. He knew all that was to be known of Hellenic culture and civilization in the Alexandria of his time. His style assumed a classical form. He wrote so completely like Plato that people humorously wondered who was imitating whom.

His character and disposition were no less striking than his accomplishments. He was honest and liberal, loving his countrymen and loving all human beings. The man who chose to live the life of the mystic and enjoyed the contemplation of the scholar apart from the din and noise of the world at the same time held himself ready to assume the responsible place in society that was expected of one of his wealth and position. When he was driven from the ethereal heights into the practical affairs of life which deluged him he did not run away, but unhesitatingly answered the call even at the peril of his life. He knew nothing of the evils of envy, ambition, and self-seeking which darkened the life of another highly gifted man of his age—Josephus. He thanked God, rather, that he escaped the temptations of mortal life and that God had opened his eyes and "flooded them with the light of wisdom, so that I am not abandoned for the whole of my life to darkness."

His priestly descent weighed heavily with Philo, and it deepened his Jewish consciousness. It was to him a kind of *noblesse oblige.* Philo felt his Judaism keenly. The Hellenic culture which he imbibed and which he loved and admired did not weaken or shake his Jewish consciousness. The sublimity of the Hebraic moral and ethical genius was passionately alive in him. It is still a question among scholars as to how much Hebrew he knew, although from references in his writings it is quite certain that he knew some Hebrew and was acquainted with the Jewish tradition which was being shaped in Palestine. But whether he read the Bible in the language in which it was written or in available translations, certainly no other man of his time outside Palestine knew it so well and wrote of it so enthusiastically as he did. Indeed, if there was a conscious mission that gave meaning and purpose to his life it was to spread the Jewish thought revealed in the Scriptures among the nations and to make it loved and respected and to serve as the basis of a universal religion.

Philo fraternized intellectually with the Greek philosophers, who were his constant companions, but spiritually he remained a true son of Israel. He loved Plato of all philosophers and called him "holy," but Moses was to him not only the most perfect man and the greatest legislator but the greatest philosopher. He had a high respect for Greek culture and civilization, but he derived his highest moral and ethical ideal from the ancient Hebraic writings. The Torah was for him the true standard to which all outside knowledge was to be subordinated. And by the Torah—the Five Books of Moses—Philo meant not only its religious and ethical conceptions but also its customs and ceremonies. With Pharisaic insistence Philo demanded literal obedience to the precepts of the Torah, even if their meaning and purpose are not easily grasped. He found the greatest fulfillment of the Law in the characters of the men—Abraham, Isaac, and Jacob—who lived pious lives pleasing to God before a single statement of the Law was made at Mt. Sinai. He wrote biographies of the early pre-Sinaitic spiritual heroes of Israel, but the only one that survived is his *Life of Moses.*

In his later life Philo abandoned one ideal he cherished in his youthful days. As a young man he thought that the path to virtue and happiness lay in the ascetic solitary life. In a life-weary world, sated with the pleasures and enjoyments of the senses which brought no inner peace and satisfaction, Philo surrendered himself to the ascetic life of the Essenes, a semimonastic group of men on the edge of the Dead Sea, described by him in *The Meditative Life*. But, fortunately, the noble pessimism of Philo's early days, as Bentwich aptly phrased it, was replaced by a nobler optimism of his maturity when he felt himself called upon to play his part in the world of action. Following the passage in which he pays glowing tribute to the contemplative life, he writes: "God has dispersed the cloud that beset my soul and taught me that favorable and unfavorable conditions are not brought about by differences of place, but by God who moves and leads the car of the soul to whatever He pleases." Indeed, he sternly rebukes those who "live by themselves as though they were in a desert or were disembodied souls, men who recognize neither city nor village nor household nor any organization of men whatever, and despise in their quest for naked and abstract truth the things prized by the populace." Professor Goodenough calls attention to a passage on the Decalogue in which Philo points out that the Jewish Law is divided in the Decalogue into two tables—one concerned with piety and holiness to God, the other of justice to men and brotherly love. The one is the task of the soul, the other of the body; so the true life combines both the theoretical and the practical. In observing both alike, man is following the highest Law.

The life of action Philo recommended he himself experienced comparatively late in life, when he had not many more years to live. It came in the wake of an anti-Semitic agitation set up by the Jew-hating demagogue, Apion, which resulted in an outburst of mob violence against the Jews of Alexandria. A number of Jews were killed, their homes and businesses sacked and pillaged, and thirty members of the Council of Elders were dragged to the market place and flogged. Unwittingly Agrippa, a grandson of

Herod and Mariamne whom Caligula, the Roman emperor, appointed as king of Upper Galilee, supplied the spark which started the anti-Jewish conflagration. The Jews naturally rejoiced in the appointment, and since on his grandmother's side he was a descendant of the Hasmonean family they regarded his kingship as restoration of Jewish independence. When, therefore, on his way to take possession of his throne and kingdom he passed through Alexandria the Jews made his coming an occasion for celebration and paid him royal honors. This embittered the Egyptians, who, having no king of their own, construed the kingly honors accorded to Agrippa as a slight to the emperor.

It did not take much to infuriate the emperor against the Jews, notwithstanding his friendship and intimacy with Agrippa. His megalomaniac vanity was piqued by them when they refused to join in the airs of divinity he gave himself and to set up his statue in their synagogues to be worshipped as a god. The Egyptians who worshiped frogs and animals in their temples had no difficulty in executing the mad emperor's order, but the Jews naturally and understandably refused. Petronius, the Roman governor of Syria, tactfully countermanded the emperor's order to have his statue installed in the Temple at Jerusalem, knowing the trouble and bloodshed it would cause, but Flaccus, the emperor's henchman in Alexandria, at one with Apion, construed the refusal of the Jews as disobedience to the king's command.

In his overweening conceit, and beclouded mind, Caligula, in the second year of his reign (36 A.D.), became obsessed with the idea of his divine rank with a terrible earnestness. With him the worship of the emperor was not a mere form of homage which the Roman emperors had taken over as a heritage from the Greek kings, but he actually believed in his divinity and regarded the refusal to worship him as proof of hostility to his person. The Jews, therefore, who for religious reasons could not join in the divine honors paid to the king, were marked men for the Jew-baiting Alexandrians, who by persecuting them hoped to curry favor with the emperor.

There was consternation among the Jews in Alexandria and their co-religionists throughout the Roman empire. Caligula was no longer a normal human being; he was mentally and morally decayed by his self-destroying debauchery and would not listen to the appeals made to him. To punish his Jewish subjects for their refusal to carry out his insane demand for divine worship, he revoked the legal enactments for their protection passed by previous emperors. In vain did his boon gambling companion, King Agrippa, appeal to him, subtly reminding him of the impressive numbers of Jews, their wide dispersion, and the danger that would accrue to the empire by provoking their hostility. Caligula would not listen; Flaccus was deposed, probably at the instance of Agrippa, and sent into exile, where he was later executed. But the hostility fanned by him and Apion remained unchanged and the worship of the emperor continued a burning question involving the Jews in danger.

Although skeptical of the results, there was nothing left for the Jews to do but to try to argue the insane emperor out of his dangerous resolve. They decided upon an embassy to Rome and, of course, there was but one man in all Alexandria who by prestige and standing, by culture and eloquence, was fit to head the delegation; and that man was Philo. He was known and respected by all classes of men and his reputation extended to the capital city of the empire. Philo was not quite sixty years old at the time of his mission to Rome, but he described himself as an old man, without, however, flinching from the task that was assigned to him. It is the only phase of his life which the philosopher-sage of Alexandria reported in detail without glossing over the exasperating indignities and humiliations he was made to suffer.

It was a vain and futile mission from which nothing was to be expected, for what chance had the man who spoke and wrote in Homeric accents against the purple-dressed maniac who had an ear only for the flattering sychophants who surrounded him? The emperor had neither the time nor the patience for the brilliant oration Philo had prepared. He was busy giving orders to the gardeners and architects of the royal estate. When he paused to listen or to put in a word, it was with the raving madness of one

who but half understood what was being said. The crowding
flunkies cheered the emperor's every word, while jeering the hapless
Jews, who were more frightened than disappointed by the outcome
of their impossible mission. Philo himself was neither frightened
nor disappointed, but took the whole matter in the philosophic
calm befitting his profession. Indeed, when his fellow delegates
stood before Caligula quaking and trembling, not knowing what
the crazy monarch's next deceitful word might be, Philo braced
them with the memorable saying, "To die in such cause is a kind
of life."

The situation changed with the death of Caligula at the hand of
an assassin. Claudius, the new emperor who succeeded him, saner
than his predecessor, annuled Caligula's discriminatory laws
against the Jews, affirmed their previous privileges, warned the
Alexandrian populace against further bloodshed and restored peace
and order in his empire.

Philo's political activity ended with his participation in the
Jewish embassy to Rome, and he died shortly afterward at the
age of sixty. To students of Philo's life his public activity, for which
he had neither the natural taste nor liking, is of less interest than his
intellectual and spiritual achievements, which, indeed, made him
one of the most fascinating characters of his age. He thanked God
that he was not hurled down into the vast sea of political care, that
he did not have to grovel for glory, wealth, and bodily comforts, but
lived in constant communion with sacred utterances and teachings
and achieved the enjoyment of what is truly beautful, desirable,
and blessed.

He was an intensely religious man with a mystical contemplation
of God. The God-consciousness had sunk deep into his soul and it
dominated his life and thought. He not only loved and revered the
Bible but he identified himself with its prophetic spirit. In his
mystical state he sometimes believed that he had attained a union
with the divine spirit and worked directly under its influence. He
refers to seizures when he was in the hands of a power greater than
he knew. He writes of one such occasion: "My soul is wont to be

affected by a divine trance and to prophecy about things of which he had no knowledge. . . . Many a time have I come with the intention of writing, and knowing exactly what I ought to set down, but I have found my mind barren and fruitless and I have gone away with nothing done. But at times I have come empty, and suddenly have been full, for ideas were invisibly rained down upon me from above, so that I was seized by a divine frenzy and was lost to everything, place, people, self, speech and thought. I have gotten a stream of interpretation [of the Bible], a gift of light, a clear survey of things, the clearest the eye can give." What a choice example this would have made for the late Professor James! But we must remember that it was written by a healthy-minded Jew in Alexandria precisely nineteen hundred years before *The Varieties of Religious Experience.*

Philo was the greatest apostle of Judaism in the pagan world. He believed implicitly in the prophetic destiny of Israel to be a light unto the nations. He lived in an age of social and moral decay. The best Greek and Roman moralists were looking forward to a religion that would harmonize their intellectual life with the deeper demands of the spirit. Judaism had neglected its opportunity; the Rabbis, for good political and historic reasons, were undecided and contradictory on the subject of proselytism, although not only was Ruth the Moabite a convert to Judaism but Shemaiah and Abtalion, Akiba and Meir, were either themselves or descendants of proselytes. Yet, notwithstanding the little encouragement Jews held out to converts, it was a missionary age in which Philo lived and he was its noblest representative. Greek and Roman writers speak with chagrin of the spread of the Jewish religion among all classes of the population. Horace tells of his friend in Rome who was "one of the many who observed the customs of the Jews," and the historian Josephus writes: "There is not any city of the Greeks, nor of the barbarians, nor of any nation whatsoever, to which our custom of resting on the seventh day has not been introduced. . . . As God himself pervadeth all the universe, so hath our law passed through the world."

Philo was the first active missionary to the world. At a time Paul was preaching a perverted self-destroying Judaism, one torn from its roots and disloyal to its historic development, the Alexandrian philosopher was teaching a pure and undiluted Judaism harmoniously in keeping with the national character and tradition of the Jewish people. He was saturated with a prophetic love for his people. Indeed had he lived in the time of the Prophets he might have been counted as one of them, for there was something prophetic in his spiritual fervor and exalted moral and ethical utterances. What more beautiful observations can be found in religious literature than his sayings, "They who offer themselves offer the highest sacrifice," and "God delights in altars on which no fire is burning but around which virtues dance"? And what more elevated optimism in the essential goodness of man than, "Assuredly, there is in the soul of every man, however undistinguished he may be, a detestation of evil."

It was to the Bible that Philo devoted his deepest thoughts and love. In all likelihood the Holy Writ was all he knew of Judaism. Scholars are undecided on how much he knew of the Palestine schools although, according to Lauterbach, the Palestinian halakah was known in Alexandria before the time of Philo and that, conversely, many of his ideas are found scattered in the Talmud and the Midrashim. But, at any rate, the Mishnah did not come into existence until one hundred and fifty years after his death, and the Gemara at a still later time.

Philosopher and superb stylist that he was, Philo loved the Bible for its lofty style and unmatched narratives, not unworthy of being compared to those of the Homeric poems. But to him the Bible stood for something infinitely greater than the Homeric poems—greater, indeed, than everything he knew of the Greek philosophers. It was a book of divine revelation containing the sum of knowledge and the highest moral and spiritual goals that man can aspire to. He read into the Bible all the deep learning and profound wisdom of the Greek and Roman schools and set before himself the task of presenting the Mosaic Legislation as the one code to bring about a perfect order of life and happiness. The great body of Philo's writings is devoted to this purpose—to demonstrate to the world the unique greatness and value of the Torah for attaining the noble and virtuous life.

But how could the simple stories and incidents of the Jewish Bible be made to square with the sophisticated Greeks, who created a philosophy, a cosmogony—indeed, a whole scientific view of the world—that was diametrically opposed to that of the scriptures? It was plain to Philo that to make the Holy Writ acceptable to the Hellenized world it had to be interpreted, and his own scientific conscience dictated such a procedure. And so he adopted the allegorical method of interpreting the scriptures which would make it palatable by contemporary cultural standards. Philo had an untroubled conscience about arraying the most unlikely stories, precepts, and events of the Bible in the raiments of his own philosophical notions. He saw that the Septuagint was far from a literal translation of the Pentateuch and, as for the Greeks, they often explained their theories and doctrines on the basis that they were allegorically contained in Homer's poems. "Essential as allegorism was to the Palestinian Jews," writes L. Ginzberg, "it was not less to the Alexandrian Hebrews, who were made to feel the derision of the Hellenes at the naïve presentation of the Bible. The Jews replied by adopting the Hellenes' own weapons; if the latter made Homer speak the language of Pythagoras, Plato, Anaxagoras and Zeno, the Jews transformed the Bible into a manual of philosophy, which also was made to contain the teachings of these philosophers."

Philo contended, as indeed Maimonides did, later, that there were two ways of reading the Bible—the literal way, which is the manner in which the ordinary people read the sacred volume, and in a deeper allegorical sense embodying the spiritual purpose of the Bible. On this principle, our philosopher uncovers the profound wisdom of the most trivial incidents in the Torah, teaching that there is nothing so common and ordinary in the divine legislation but is filled with sublime thought and meaning. Every precept of the Torah, every law and commandment, is suffused with light and wisdom; there is nothing that is superfluous or unnecessary in the divine legislation, anticipating Rabbi Akiba by about a hundred years. The spirit of humanity breathes through the Judean law from beginning to end. Against the boasted Greco-Roman morality Philo advances a long array of Mosaic benevolent duties toward animals, servants, widows, orphans, and strangers. He finds the love of one's enemy contained in the law of Moses—"Thou shalt not abhor an Egyptian" (Deut.23:8), and he comments: "In spite of all the wrongs the Egyptians did to us, love of man must triumph in us over hate of the enemy. Love of man extends itself to all mankind, even to foreigners and enemies."

So far so good, and one may almost agree with Graetz who, considering the three moralists of the century—Hillel, Jesus, and Philo—grants the palm to the Alexandrian philosopher for his beauty of style, eloquence, and depth of thought. He glorifies Judaism far more fervently than did any other man. But in allegorizing the Torah, in dwelling upon the symbolic purpose of the *mitzvot,* he exposed Judaism to the danger of emasculating the Bible of the strength and vigor that go with the practical fulfillment of the commandments. If the spirit is the thing, why, then, bother about the literal observance of the law? This was, of course, a distortion of Philo's meaning and intention, and he severely lashed his co-religionists who made his allegorical interpretation an excuse for neglecting the observance of the ceremonial law. He taunted and ridiculed them for spiritualizing the Sabbath without observing it, esteeming the Abrahamic covenant without circumcising their children, and thinking highly of the dietary laws but not carrying them into practical effect. In his own life Philo was a pious Jew who lived up to every demand of the Mosaic Law. While he treated the stories of the scriptures allegorically and found profound universal values in every figure and every episode, he was perhaps the strictest Torah-observing Jew in Alexandria and he found spiritual blessedness in the literal fulfillment of the Law.

Philo's philosophy is basically Jewish and his dominant interest was Judaism, although his thinking was influenced by Plato and the Stoics. What he received from the Greek philosophers he modified and fashioned to suit the Jewish pattern of thinking. According to Professor Wolfson, Philo's philosophy is not only Jewish and original but he is the father of a religious philosophy that prevailed from his day down to the time of Spinoza. He gave fresh and original expression to what he assimilated from foreign sources. In the more than one thousand years that elapsed between the time of the Alexandrian sage and the Jewish Arabic period there was little new added to his body of thinking.

Philo's dominating aim was to make philosophy square with the ethical and philosophical ideas of the Bible. His pronouncements are the pronouncements of the Bible; his conception of God and of man and his spiritual destiny is Jewish. If he deviated from the strict line of the Bible and held with Plato that God did not create the world-stuff but found it ready at hand, it was because, while believing in the divine inspiration of the Bible, he did not believe in the literal truth of its words. He set out to prove that between sound philosophy and revealed religion there is complete accord— they are but two ways of expressing the divine truth.

He stood firmly on Jewish ground in his theological conceptions of Judaism. God as He is conceived in the Mosaic legislation and by the seers and prophets of Israel is the bedrock of Philo's religious convictions. He is not always literally the God of the Bible, any more than was the God of Maimonides. He has no human attributes, qualities, and emotions. For that reason He cannot be perceived by human eyes. He is always the same; He cannot change; He can never perish. He exists, but He has no relation with existing things. Philo characterizes the anthropomorphisms of the Bible as a "monstrous impiety." All good things our theologian says, proceed from God, but not the evil ones. God stands in a special relation to man, through his soul, for the soul is a reflex of God, a part of the divine reason.

The ethics of Philo are Jewish, tinged with Stoic influence. Man, he says, is a moral being, his soul's inclination is toward the good, for it bears a reflex of the divine image. It is only the body, with its lusts and passions, that makes for evil. When it is in control all the higher aspirations toward God and virtue are stifled. The end is complete moral and spiritual turpitude, the annihilation of all sense of duty; not a particle of the soul remains whole. The worst consequence of this moral death, says Philo, is absolute ignorance and the loss of the power of judgment. Sensual things are placed above spiritual, and wealth is regarded as the highest good. The life of man is a continuous, never-ending battle between the higher impulses of his soul and the restless desires of the flesh. The characteristic difference between the Philonic and the Stoic attitude is that, whereas the latter believes in man's ability to fight off the evil and conquer in the name of the good, Philo holds that man himself is helpless in the titanic struggle and needs God to assist him.

Nevertheless, while Philo regards the physical part of man as defective and an impediment to his moral growth and advancement, it is not to be despised. It is indispensable in view of the nature of his being. It is even an advantage to the spirit, since the spirit arrives at its knowledge of the world by means of the five senses. Knowledge can no more thrive without the senses than the soul can operate without the body. It is characteristic of Philo—and this, indeed, distinguishes him from the Stoic ethicists of his day—that he looks to religion as the basis of man's ethical life. It is God who implanted the ethical sensitivity in man, and it is by our ecstatic contemplation of Him that we may hope to keep it alive within us.

The dual personality of Philo—the intellectual and the mystic—makes him speak, as it were, with two voices: at times with excessive regard for knowledge and wisdom, and at others deriding the pride and arrogance of the philosophers who think that with their intellect they can comprehend God and the world. Philo parted company with the Greek sophists when he insisted upon the insufficiency of reason—when, with Job (11:7), he cried out: "Canst thou find God by searching?" Only a mind equal to God can know God. It is sentiments like these which make Philo unique in Jewish literature—which, indeed, couple his name with those of the Bible prophets and with Ibn Gabirol, Judah Halevi, and Maimonides.

Philo reflects the high standard of Jewish morality in the importance and value he sets on man and human life. He makes man the barometer of all morality. It is by our relation to our fellow men that our conduct and actions are judged. For man is the creation of God, a fragment of His own Being; indeed, he is part of God; he is endowed with an immortal soul. He must not be shamed or humiliated. He must not shame and degrade himself. Philo abhorred human slavery and approved of the biblical provision (Exod. 21: 5–7) for boring a slave's ear when of his free choice he persists in slavery and will not be set free by his master. He is likewise stern toward the taking of human life, since he reckoned nothing so precious and sacred.

Philo affirms his belief in immortality. When the body dies, he says, the soul does not depart with it; for, indeed, how could the soul perish since it is a part of God's own essence? When man dies the soul returns to her pretemporal state. The souls of the righteous are taken up by God and live forever, while those of the wicked are reincarnated within the human species. In the matter of the Messiah, Philo reflects the intensity and prevalence of the messianic hope of the philosophic Hellenists who lived in comparative freedom in Egypt. Philo, the greatest exponent of Alexandrian Judaism, gives two versions of his conception of the Messiah and the messianic era, one universal and one national. At times his Messiah is presented as a man of war who will usher in an era of prosperity and universal peace and turn men to God; at others, he is pictured as one who will bring "unexpected liberty to those who but a short time before were scattered about in Hellas and in the countries of the barbarians, in the islands over the continents." In other words, Philo endows his Messiah with all the color and richness of the Palestinian writers. Like the Messiah of the Jewish tradition, he does not set aside the Jewish teachings but accepts and affirms them in their minutest detail.

Philo was the greatest writer and thinker Alexandria produced. He was a much greater man than Josephus, who was not a philosopher and whose loyalties to the Jews and their convictions were not quite above doubt. Philo lived in the most interesting Jewish period in the Greco-Roman world. His life was divided between two loves—his love for Judaism and his devotion to Hellenic culture and civilization, both of which he served with almost equal loyalty and affection. But being a Jew, his greatest enthusiasm was for his inherited religion, for which, by his personal life and through his writings, he tried to enlist the heathen world's honor and esteem.

Philo lived in what was for the Jews a disturbed and troubled time. The relations between the Jews and Rome were correct and calm on the surface, but were seething underneath with unrest and the danger of eventual hostilities. Intellectually and spiritually the time was marked by numerous sects and heresies. The philosophers were attacking the Bible and the religious position of the Jews; and the followers of Christianity, still in its infancy, were promulgating a doctrine destructive of the teachings of Judaism. Philo was the unrivaled teacher of his age and the superb defender of his faith. While on the one hand he taught a Torah-supported Judaism without the heresies that tended to weaken and undermine it, on the other hand he sought a formula that would adjust Judaism to the culture and civilization of his age and make each acceptable to the other. This adjustment or compromise—the allegorical interpretation of the Bible, worked out to his own satisfaction—would make Shem and Japheth dwell together in harmony; and, however disapproved of by contemporary and later Jewish authorities, it was of tremendous influence in saving the Jews of Alexandria from religious disintegration. Indeed, one wonders what might have happened to the largest Jewish community in the Greco-Roman world had it not been for him.

The question naturally arises as to why, then, does Philo enjoy so little standing in Jewish history that it was not until the sixteenth century, at the hands of Azariah de Rossi, that a full account was given of him in the roster of great Jews? The assertion that Philo was more Greek than Jewish is contradicted by the fact that in his personal life and writings he was thoroughly Jewish, that he took pride in the name of "Israel," which he interpreted as *Yasar-el* (one who beholds God), and that, as pointed out by students of Philo, there is striking resemblance in much of his writing to that found in the Talmud and Midrash. In essence and quality, his Jewish background outweighed his Greek training. His Jewishness was stronger and more fundamental than was the cultural influence that came to him from the outside world. There are poetry and rapture in Philo's words when he speaks of Judaism, its beliefs and practices, its ethics and morality. He extols Abraham as the progenitor of a whole nation, "dearest of all to God, which has received the gift of priesthood and prophecy on behalf of all mankind," thus fusing the national and the universal elements of the Hebraic ideal.

Of no greater validity is the rejection of Philo on the classical score that around the word "Logos," a Greek philosophical term of uncertain connotation, he spun a theological doctrine which the Christian church manipulated and distorted until it became an unfailing testimony to the Nazarene. Unprejudiced Christian scholars—Professor Erwin R. Goodenough the most gallant and courageous of them—have long since repudiated the fraud and branded it as such. In an outstanding essay, "Philo of Alexandria," in *Great Jewish Personalities,* he writes: "I am confident that Philo would indignantly have repudiated Christianity had he ever heard of it." And again: "Everything I have read in Philo assures me that such a perversion of Jewish tradition would have seemed to him utterly blasphemous. However much of his ideas may later have been what he would have considered misused by Christianity, he himself remained loyal to the Jewish people and the Book."

Philo can no longer be ignored by Jews; he cannot be lightly dismissed from the Jewish record. The weight of evidence of his love for the Jews and the Torah is on his side. He stands high in the honorable list of those who championed the Jewish cause without thought of self. His name cannot any more be erased from the pages of Jewish history because of distortions of his writings than the Book of Isaiah can be torn from the Bible because of the monstrous distortion by Christianity of one of its most poetic chapters. Philo was a philosopher and a teacher who spread the knowledge of the Torah in an age that was teetering on the brink of religious disintegration. His influence on Jews in the Greco-Roman empire was no less striking and decisive than was that of the Judaic teachers of the Babylonian captivity. The future will reclaim him for a place in the Jewish household beside those other children of the Jewish spirit whose life was a source of strength to their faith and people.

Saadia Gaon

THROUGHOUT HISTORY the Jewish genius has never ceased creating and expanding. From the time of the Bible to the present there has been neither pause nor let-up in Jewish cultural activity. The peculiar quality of Jewish creativity is its many-sidedness. There was an aura of talent about many men of past generations which enabled them to achieve mastery in almost all things. Their gifts were not confined to one single interest but, like a mighty stream, flowed in many directions. They possessed encyclopedic minds. While religion was their principal concern, they worked and achieved greatness in most cultural and scientific fields. They were philologists and jurists, theologians and philosophers, astronomers and mathematicians, physicians and poets.

Saadia ben Joseph (better known to posterity as Rav Saadia Gaon, belongs to that versatile, highly gifted group of men who embodied in themselves a whole university of knowledge. A mere enumeration of what he did, the books he wrote, his travels, struggles, and controversies with the greatest Jewish powers of his day, all in the brief span of sixty years, leaves one bewildered. Of all his contemporaries and near contemporaries, his career was the most tumultuous and exciting. He knew poverty and persecution, excommunication, exile, and loneliness in foreign lands. But be the times fair or foul, not for a moment was his spirit ever completely crushed. And it was while he was in the abyss of despair in a strange country that he produced his masterpiece, *Kitab al-'Amanat,* translated into Hebrew as *Sefer Emunot v'Deot* (The Book of Beliefs and Opinions), which preserved his name for more than a thousand years.

Saadia ben Joseph was born under the mild Mohammedan rule

of Egypt in the small village of Dilaz in the Upper Egypt district of Fayyum in the year 882. Something like a veil of mist hangs over the youth and antecedents of the second greatest Jew the land of the Pharaohs ever produced. Saadia glamorized his descent by tracing it back to Shela, the son of Judah, fourth of the sons of Jacob, and by counting among his ancestors Haninah ben Dosa, a saintly rabbi of the second century, about whom, so legend has it, a divine voice from Mount Horeb was heard calling daily. "The entire world is being sustained on account of my son Haninah." Saadia's enemies, however, were less complimentary about his ancestry. They spread malicious stories about Saadia's father, maintaining that he had not only engaged in degrading occupations but was not even of Jewish stock, having descended from Egyptians who were converted to Judaism.

Not much more is known of Saadia's early education or of his teachers, whom he never mentions by name. It may, however, be taken for granted that he was not self-taught but had both Jewish and Arabic teachers. As paradoxical as it may seem, according to some scholars one of his early instructors and the first to awaken his interest in the subject of Hebrew philology was a Karaite. Be that as it may, it can in no sense be maintained that Saadia grew up as a lonely palm in a desert land. Living within easy reach of the Palestine and Babylonian academies, the interest of his Jewish neighbors in Torah-learning could not have been neglected. While Saadia's early education was derived from Egyptian-Jewish sources, it was considerably enhanced and amplified by the learning and scholarship which came to the Nile country from the Palestine and Babylonian talmudic academies.

Saadia matured early, as men of his type usually do. He was not long out of his teens when he was already recognized as a scholar. Some of his literary plans and ideas took shape in his mind before he reached the age of twenty. He was about that age when he pioneered in the field of Hebrew philology by the publication of *Agron,* the first Hebrew dictionary and the one that set the pace for the Hebrew renaissance in Spain a generation or two later. He followed it up with *The Book of Language,* in twelve parts, a surviving fragment of which proves to have been the first Hebrew grammar on record. He pioneered in comparative philology in a short treatise in which he discusses rarely occurring words in the Bible and their relation to kindred words in the Mishnah and the Talmud.

He was a great Jewish personality in an age in which few Jewish scholars attained fame and distinction. He invested Judaism and Jews with life and power in a time when life and power seemed to have gone out of them. He was one of the few Jewish scholars who stood in active relation to his time and to its spiritual and intellectual challenges. He was intimately acquainted with the movements and perplexities of his generation, and he dealt with them wisely and constructively. He was among the first to recognize the danger of the Karaite heresy, which threatened to undermine Judaism, and he energetically exposed and demolished its fallacies. When he realized the religious ignorance of the Arabic-speaking Jews, many of them were no longer able to read the sacred volume in the language in which it was written, he translated it into Arabic and wrote an appropriate introduction and commentaries. Finding the synagogue ritual in a deplorably disordered and chaotic condition, he compiled the first scientifically organized prayer book. And at the climax of his literary career, sensing the mental climate of his age and its religious doubts and confusion, he met the situation with his *The Book of Beliefs and Opinions.*

Saadia was a keen student of the Bible. He mastered it more perfectly than any other man of his time. He loved the Bible for its literary grace and beauty, for its high moral and ethical quality, for its humanizing and civilizing value, and as an instrument through which to reveal to the world the character and genius of the people that created it. He differed from the rabbis in his knowledge and appreciation of the scriptures. The rabbis barely knew the Bible; their knowledge of it was desultory and haphazard; they had not entered into its spirit as a great literary and cultural document. Saadia found in the Bible treasures of thought and beauty but dimly realized by his contemporaries. With the sole exception of Rashi, Saadia was the most perceptive student of the Bible, its greatest lover and interpreter. The Bible figures more prominently in his writings than in the works of most other Jewish authors. While his references to the Talmud and the Midrashim are comparatively few, his allusions to the Bible are legion.

Saadia was born and spent his youth in a Karaite environment. The Jews of Upper Egypt were predominantly Karaites. While they rebelled against Tradition and did not recognize the Talmud, they were accomplished students of the Bible and could give a better account of themselves than some of the more learned scholars of the Talmud. They were fine Hebrew grammarians and stylists, and because of their expert knowledge of the Bible they held themselves out as the only legitimate representatives of Judaism. The rabbis deplored the heretical Karaites (or "Ananites" as they were called, after Anan ben David, who founded the sect about 767), but they could not stand up to them in argument because of their opponents' linguistic superiority. To take the Bible out of the hands of the Karaites and bring it into the lives of the Jews, both as a source of knowledge and of inspiration, Saadia set himself to the task of translating it into the Arabic language, the vernacular spoken by the Jews from the extreme West to India. To make his translation available both to Jewish and non-Jewish readers, unlike the practice of Jewish scholars at the time, he composed his work in Arabic characters. Scholars disagree as to whether he translated all or only part of the Bible; but from the part of his translation that has been preserved, the magnitude of the task, his vast learning and tremendous energy appear almost incredible. He accomplished his purpose. He took the Bible out of the hands of the Karaites and made it accessible to the people who had almost forgotten it.

Saadia's translation was the first rendition of the Hebrew scriptures into the language of the Koran by a talmudic Jew, and it was epoch-making. Had Saadia done nothing else, this monumental achievement alone would have entitled him to the gratitude and reverence in which posterity holds him. His translation accomplished for his fellow Jews in Moslem lands as much as the Greek and Aramaic translations of the Holy Writ had done for the Jews of Alexandria and Palestine centuries before—even more, indeed; for neither the Jews of Alexandria nor those of Palestine were confronted with the religious problems which faced the Jews in the Mohammedan countries at the time of Saadia's translation of the scriptures. Seven years of extraordinary labor and energy Saadia is said to have spent on his Arabic version of the Torah; but he had the satisfaction of seeing it supersede Karaite renditions of isolated books of the Hebrew religious classic. In Yemen Saadia's translation was held in great reverence and was hallowed by the traditional name *Targum,* the name also given to the Aramaic translation of the Bible, which forms part of the Jewish traditional literature.

Scholarship, skill, literary artistry, and an exceeding love for Judaism lie back of Saadia's translation. Guided by his own love of the Bible, he strove to kindle in the hearts of his fellow Jews the same enthusiasm for it. For the Bible was to Saadia more than merely a collection of religious precepts and homilies, more than a grand text for scholars to exercise their ingenious legal interpretations upon. It was an exquisite literary masterpiece, to be loved and cherished for its sheer beauty and delight.

It was Saadia's conviction that nothing in the Book was in opposition to reason and that apparent contradictions were only on the surface. He followed the Onkelos or *Targum* method by using metaphorical translations of words offensive to reason. To make the Bible better understood and appreciated, as well as to counteract the influence of the Karaite expositors of the scriptures, Saadia accompanied his translation with an elaborate, although, as Ibn Ezra charges, often labored explanation and commentaries. The century in which Saadia wrote was not a critical age, especially in its attitude to the Bible. The Bible was regarded as a holy book, every word of which was held to be divinely inspired. It is, therefore, not surprising that, rationalist in many respects though Saadia was, he did not rise much above his time in his belief in the literal truth of the incidents and miracles reported in the Bible. He thus believed the miracle of the manna and the quails as "the most amazing of all miracles, because a phenomenon of an enduring nature excites greater wonderment than one of a passing character." He believed that all the prophetic books of the Bible were written by the Prophets after whom they were named, that all the Psalms had been composed by David and all the Proverbs by Solomon, notwithstanding the fact that the Bible itself gives other headings for their compositions.

By his translation and commentaries, Saadia aimed to make the Bible an encyclopedic source of knowledge for the enlightenment and instruction of the Jews. "Saadia," wrote M. Simon in a chapter in *Aspects of the Hebrew Genius,* "created in his contemporaries the sense of historic continuity with Israel of the past, and this sense was like the infusion of new blood into the veins of the Jewish people. . . . The Student of the Talmud, to whom the Bible was little more than a jumble of verses, each one of which could apparently be made to mean anything, was taught by Saadia to read the Bible consecutively with an open mind, and to derive from it a national consciousness based on his own affinity to the great thinkers of Israel." As though anticipating the later Bible surgeons, who divided the Holy Book into minute segments, assigning to them different times and places, Saadia taught that the scripture sequences had a meaning and logic of their own.

Saadia was an intensely spiritual person—religion was the one yearning of his heart. He waxed eloquent in his demand for the wholehearted inwardness of prayer. He regarded the lack of *kawannah,* or concentration, in prayer as the one thing that stands between God and man. He anticipated the founder of Hasidism in insisting on Rabbi Simon's injunction, "When thou prayest, make not thy prayer into a fixed mechanical form." Saadia's religious sensitivity was jarred when he noticed on his travels the lack of uniformity of the synagogue service and the want of poetic elegance of the Hebrew prayers. The *Siddur,* the Hebrew Order of Prayers, was in a fluid and chaotic state. Every community improvised its own form of divine worship and it was not always in the best taste and style. The *payyatanim,* the medieval liturgical poets of the synagogue, twisted the Hebrew language out of all form, until their compositions bore no more resemblance to the language of the Bible than the Hebrew characters in which they were written. The halakists, on the other hand, were more interested in the talmudic regulations of the prayers than in their emotional quality. Between the two, the religious feelings of the people remained unexpressed, their emotions starved, and their souls, full of love and yearning for God, unarticulated.

Saadia was a pioneer in the field of Jewish liturgy, as he was in everything to which he put his hand. He was exceptionally gifted for this most delicate of religious tasks. He was ardently and passionately religious; he was an enthusiastic devotee of the synagogue and he wanted to see its influence deepened by stirring hymns and songs of praise. He had complete mastery of the Hebrew language, which responded to his every demand, and he possessed a poetic sense which was evident in his prose writings. He composed his prayers neither in the obscure idiom of the payyatanim nor in the style of the halakists, but in the language of the Bible. A man of deep religious consciousness, he felt the need of placing into the hands of the Jews a systematically ordered prayer book, at once clear and comprehensive, and expressive of their profound religious yearnings while written in an elevated and dignified style.

Saadia's *Siddur* bears the stamp of the author's genius. In conception, style, and arrangement, the *Siddur* may be considered as another of Saadia's major contributions to Judaism and to the Jewish people. It is neither a compilation nor a new edition of the old prayers, but an original creation by a man who combined a profound religious sense with a fine literary talent. The *Siddur,* like his translation of the Bible, was part of Saadia's educational program intended for the enlightenment and religious edification of the Jews. As he did with his translation of the Bible, Saadia adorned his *Siddur* with an introduction in which he considers the significance of the prayers, their history and composition. In addition to the prayers stemming from old sources, Saadia composed a number of prayers *(Bakashot)* of his own, of which Henry Malter said, "In grace and purity of style, and in fervency of religious emotion they rank among the best the synagogue has ever produced."

Saadia's *Siddur,* the expression of his personal religious urge, superseded the other texts of Hebrew prayers, especially the one of Amram Gaon, which was more of a liturgical legal code than an expression of prayer and petition, and it received the praise and commendation of later authorities. Abraham Ibn Ezra acclaimed Saadia's *Siddur,* and Moses Maimonides was sufficiently influenced by it to use as model for his own Order of Prayers. Apart from its value as a text of Hebrew prayers of wide influence in Jewish congregations in the Islamic world, Ismar Elbogen recognizes in the *Siddur* "an invaluable historical document mirroring the spiritual life of the Jews more than one thousand years ago, and the manner in which they expressed their religious thoughts and sentiments." The manuscript of the Saadia *Siddur,* which was identified by Steinschneider, was published almost one hundred years later in Jerusalem through the initiative of the late Israel Davidson.

In the ninth and tenth centuries it was not only the Bible but also the Talmud—indeed, especially the Talmud—that had to be recovered from the neglect into which it had fallen. To be sure, during the *Kallah* months of Adar and Elul the academies were crowded with multitudes of scholars who came from far and wide for instruction and enlightenment. It was perhaps at that very time that Saadia realized the need of extending to the Talmud the educational program which he had so successfully carried out for the Bible. As Gaon of Sura, letters came to him from Jewish communities in the Islamic world, inquiring about passages in the Talmud they found difficult to understand and about obscure words, unfamiliar terms, phrases, and expressions the meaning of which baffled them.

Abraham Ibn Ezra characterized Saadia as "the principal speaker in every place." But not only was Saadia the chief speaker in every place but the first and foremost worker and authority in every field. He was practically the first of the Geonim to write commentaries on the Mishnah and the Talmud and to quote

Alexander Marx, "the first to write an 'introduction' on the methodology of the Talmud . . . and compose a number of halakic compendia, in which he, for the first time, discusses the laws systematically without regard to their sequence in the talmudic sources. . . . It goes without saying that, like all the Geonim, he answered questions directed to him from various countries even as far as distant Spain."

It was, however, Saadia's polemic against the Karaites, a heretical Jewish sect in opposition to rabbinic Judaism founded by Anan ben David in Babylon about the middle of the eighth century, which revealed to the world his forceful character, vigorous personality, and stupendous energy. Saadia was all of twenty-three years old when he fired his first salvo into the Karaite camp, but so stunning was its effect that it spread havoc and consternation among the Bible literalists. For the first time the followers of Anan realized that they had a real opponent to contend with. Taken by surprise, they answered the young man's challenge with nothing more than invective and diatribes. But Saadia would be neither silenced nor frightened. He was a brilliant pamphleteer and a fighter with a relish for battle. His first attack was followed by still other offensives, which made the enemy furious.

Saadia was an implacable foe of Karaism and everything it implied. He was the first great rabbi of his time to recognize its danger to Judaism and to the unity of the Jewish people. He regarded his struggle against the Karaite perversion as a holy crusade for the preservation of the purity of the Jewish faith and its high moral and ethical teachings. The heads of the academies and their learned colleagues had not been fully awake to the situation. They were too steeped in their study of the Talmud to realize that right under their very eyes a menace had arisen which threatened to destroy both them and the Talmud. For Karaism was not a religious sect within the framework of Judaism but a cunningly devised perversion to destroy Judaism by destroying its legitimate custodians, the Rabbis of the Talmud. Had Anan, the founder of the movement, succeeded and had Karaism become the practice of the Jews, Judaism, both of the Bible and the Talmud, would have disappeared or would have degenerated into one of those sectarian cults that infested the Islamic world.

Although Saadia emerged on the battlefield comparatively late, when the "Bible Loyalists," the name by which the Karaites called themselves, were already well organized and had a following spread over almost all the Islamic world, the enthusiasm and moral earnestness he devoted to the campaign and the high level of scholarship with which he conducted it did much to weaken its influence of Karaism and stem its further spread. For Saadia was an adversary even the best informed Karaites dared not take lightly. He was a superbly gifted man, a Rabbinist with a profound knowledge of the Bible and a Talmudist able to expose the shallowness of the anti-talmudic creed.

Saadia's polemical writings make up the largest, if not the most important, part of his literary activity. From the first to the last of his controversial writings, he was tireless in his defense of Judaism against its traducers. He followed up his original refutation of Anan with several tracts, and returned to the subject in works not ostensibly directed against the Karaites, such as *Sefer ha-Galui* and his principal philosophical treatise, *The Book of Beliefs and Opinions*. The traditional-minded Jews regarded Saadia as their religious guide and defender, the savior of rabbinic Judaism, and as the man who met the challenge of a crisis and carried victory before him. Indeed, the contemporary Jews beheld in him a new kind of rabbi —a man who combined general culture with profound Jewish learning, an erudite Talmudist and an accomplished student of the Bible, a traditionalist and at the same time a philosopher who attained mastery of the sciences—such a combination of gifts and talents as the extraordinary times in which they lived demanded.

While the Karaites were the most numerous and vociferous assailants of traditional Judaism, there were other influences, some sly and subtle, some loud and raucous, which threatened to undermine the religious faith and convictions of the Jews. The ninth and tenth centuries, in which Saadia lived, were critical for the maintenance of the Jewish religion. The collision between Judaism and

Greek philosophy in Arab garb had done considerable damage in shaking faith in the Bible and the divine origin of the universe, and Jewish philosophers spent much time and ingenious effort to fuse the two opposite forces into one. Nor was this all. At the time of Saadia, the Orient was a veritable battlefield rampant with all sorts of religious vagaries, heretical views, and outright rabid attacks on Judaism. It did not take long for the intellectual confusion to penetrate into the Jewish camp, which all but destroyed the ramparts of the ancient Jewish faith.

There is no better indication of the debased and demoralized condition of Jewish life of the time than a book which questioned the unity and omnipotence of God, denied the divine revelation of the Torah, refuted the miracles of the Bible, especially those of the Pentateuch, and dwelt on the conflicting and contradictory statements in the scriptures. This book had not only obtained a wide circulation among the Jews but, until challenged and banned by Saadia, was used as a textbook in Jewish religious schools. The author of this audacious volume, inimical to both the Talmud and the Bible (to the latter perhaps even more than to the former), and seeking the destruction of both, was the strange individual, Hivi Al-Balkhi, a Persian-born Jew of possible Zoroastrian or Christian tendencies, or both. He demonstrated his implacable hostility to Judaism, with special accent on the Bible, in a list of two hundred questions, offering interpretations of Biblical stories and narratives in most instances more bizarre and fantastic than the text itself. For example, he explains the story of the passage through the Red Sea by claiming that Moses knew of a spot in the Red Sea which ran dry once in a thousand years. Thus the Hebrew lawgiver led the Israelites through in perfect safety, while the less well-informed Egyptians drowned in the resurgent waters. The manna, Al-Balkhi said, was but a fairly common variety of desert plant, and made other similar objections to miraculous Bible incidents. He attacked circumcision and sacrifices, the belief in reward and punishment, and argued against God's omniscience by citing His failure to ward off personal calamities and world catastrophies. Briefly, Hivi dared dispute the very fundamentals of the Jewish faith. "To be sure," writes Salo W. Baron in his *Social and Religious History of the Jews,* "Hivi is an exceptional phenomenon. . . . . He seems to have been one of those 'smart-alecky' eclectics who took his arguments wherever he could find them, without necessarily committing himself to any particular set of beliefs." But whatever his personal religious convictions, it is, to say the least, surprising that the new "Torah" he concocted, probably made up of revised portions of the Pentateuch, enjoyed a wide circulation and was used by teachers for the religious instruction of the young.

In 915, when Saadia was thirty-three years old, he suddenly and without warning quit Egypt for foreign lands leaving his father, children, and disciples behind. It has never been determined what motivated Saadia to leave his country at a time when his reputation was great and his fame was spreading. Was it an involuntary departure caused by his enemies in influential political quarters, or was it ambition for a position which he failed to realize in his native land. Both were likely, for Saadia, as a militant defender of traditional Judaism, cannot have had many friends in Fayyum, where the majority of the Jewish population were Karaites who made his stay in the country uncomfortable. But, on the other hand, his personal ambition cannot be excluded as a contributory cause of his leaving the country. At the age of thirty-three, Saadia was certainly one of the most celebrated Jews of his time. He had rendered yeoman service to both Judaism and the Jewish people by his learning, scholarship, and the defense of the ancient faith— all of which, however, he accomplished, so to say, as a free-lance and not as an officially recognized authority.

Saadia's itinerary covered several countries—Palestine, Syria, and Babylonia. First he went to Palestine, where he intended to settle, and privately he harbored the ambition of an appointment in one of her great talmudic academies. He was generally received with due respect, and honors were paid him by Aaron ben Meir, head and Patriarch of the Palestine Jewish community; but the appointment on which Saadia had set his heart eluded him, for then, as now, academic honors did not always go to men of recognized talent and ability but often to scions of important aristocratic families. Saadia bore his disappointment the best he could and, after tarrying in Palestine for a few years, left for Babylonia, where, in her unrivaled center of Jewish learning and culture, he hoped for an active sphere of activity.

It was not fated that the man born to controversy should escape involvements even on his travels. Saadia was in Aleppo when he became the center of a dispute about the fixing of the Jewish calendar between the Palestine and the Babylonian authorities. Ostensibly the controversy was between Ben Meir, head and Nasi of Palestine Jewry, and David ben Zakkai, the Babylonian Exilarch, but it was not likely that Saadia, in view of his fame and reputation, could fail to be drawn into so grave and vital a matter as fixing the days and dates of the Jewish holidays. The details of the problem which threatened to divide the two largest Jewries of the world are involved and intricate, and the controversy came about when the learned official head of the Jews of Palestine insisted on carrying out the ancient prerogative of the Holy Land to regulate the Jewish religious calendar. In the days of the Temple, when the people were not trained in the art of chronometric tables, the calendrical calculations were in the hands of the Sanhedrin. Later, they were passed on to the Patriarchs of Palestine, descendants of the House of Hillel, who through messengers announced the days and dates of the holidays to the Jews of the Diaspora.

But matters changed in the course of time. Numerically and culturally Palestine ceased to be the most important center of Jewish life and her hegemony over the Jews of the world was disputed. Babylonia, with her great schools of learning, came upon the scene, and the question arose as to whether in all religious matters Jews must follow the dictates of the Palestine authorities. When, therefore, Ben Meir issued his calendar, ordering the Jews to celebrate the Passover Festival two days earlier than the calculations made by the Babylonian authorities, the latter refused to follow his mandate but acted according to their own light and advised inquirers to disregard the Palestine calendar. Ben Meir did not take the slight to his prestige lightly and a battle royal between the two contending parties raged for some time.

When the news of the conflict came to the Happy Warrior, he lost no time in ranging himself on the side of the Babylonian academies, declaring the Palestine calendar to be inexact and misleading, and calculated to divide the unity of the Jewish people in the observance of their holidays. He threw himself into the fight with all his proverbial energy and initiative. He wrote letters, made a personal appeal to his friends and disciples in Egypt, and wrote a book, *Sefer ha-Moadim,* (The Book of Holidays). Ultimately the struggle ended, in 922, with victory for the Babylonian scholars.

Recognition of Saadia's part in the struggle was swift and ample. He had stood in the thick of the fight, and he carried off its richest prize. It was but natural that David ben Zakkai, the Babylonian Exilarch, should feel impelled to reward his principal aide in the contest, which he did in 928 by appointing Saadia as Gaon, or head, of the academy of Sura, the more celebrated of the two Babylonian schools of learning. It was indeed an honor well merited by the man so extraordinarily gifted. At the same time it was a rare distinction for one so young as Saadia (he was only thirty-six years old at the time of his appointment, and a foreigner besides!) to be called upon to fill a position created by Rav, one of the two founders of Jewish learning in Babylonia seven hundred years before Saadia was born.

It is easy to surmise what must have been in Saadia's mind when he became master of the halls of learning once presided over by the Amoraim. It was an honor indeed to be principal of the academy where the Babylonian Talmud was founded. But it was also a crushing responsibility. For, to his chagrin, Saadia soon realized that, with all her fame and glory, not the faintest echo of Sura's old-time greatness remained. Only the name and reputation of the old school survived—all else was gone with the passing of time. The geonic dignity of Sura had been held in hereditary possession of a few families, and they were not always of the highest order.

It was to no easy task that Saadia was assigned but one which called for his greatest powers of organization. For two years he worked with almost superhuman energy. He had to build every-

thing from the bottom, filling in gaps, removing intellectual cob-
webs, and raising the school's status in order to give it a semblance
of its former glory and distinction. Expert teachers took the place
of political appointees and students with a genuine desire for study
were attracted, and the halls of learning, silent for so long, rang
out once more with the words of Torah. Saadia triumphed. To his
reputation, epoch-making in so many branches of activity, was
now added the revival of the Sura academy.

Unfortunately, however, his triumph was short-lived, and the peace
and quiet he needed after his stupendous labors were denied him
by the bitterest conflict of all his embattled life—paradoxically
enough, with the very man who raised him to his position of
eminence. There were rarely two men more unlike each other in
character and disposition than the Gaon of Sura and the head of the
Babylonian Jewish community. One was a scholar, the other a politician; one derived his authority from the Torah, the other from the
good will of the flunkies who surrounded the Caliph's throne. While
the Exilarch ruled over the temporal affairs of the Jews, the Gaon
had charge of their religious and cultural life. When, therefore, the
two men by reason of their respective offices were thrown together,
nothing short of a collision could be expected.

History records that the immediate cause of the feud between
them was an overcharge by the Exilarch for his part in an inheritance lawsuit involving 70,000 gold pieces, which Saadia, claiming special knowledge of the laws of inheritance, considered excessive. But while this may have been the direct reason for the
conflict between them, its real cause was far more fundamental. It
lay in the nature of the divided functions of their respective offices.
Briefly, it was a contest between temporal and spiritual powers over
the Jewish community. While both the Exilarchs and Geonim were
elected officials confirmed by the government, with their respective
duties and responsibilities clearly defined and marked, the Exilarchs, banking on their mythical Davidic descent, lorded over the
heads of the schools. They looked down upon them as their subordinates, dismissing disobedient scholars and appointing in their

stead men of mediocre learning. Saadia's predecessor, for instance, was a weaver with no other qualification for his position than his submission to his master's wishes.

Saadia was not a man wholly after ben Zakkai's heart, and he was warned against his appointment. He was learned and extraordinarily gifted, it was maintained, but he was stubborn and unyielding when provoked, and was not entirely above playing politics. But the Exilarch appointed Saadia over the protests of his friend. He saw in the young scholar the only person fitted to carry out his cherished ambition—the revival of the old academy of Sura, which was in such a state of decline. But to guard himself against the boundless ambition of which Saadia was accused, the Exilarch, according to Baron, imposed upon him an oath that Saadia "would not transgress my words, nor conspire against me, nor recognize anyone else as prince of captivity, nor side with any of my opponents." But Saadia had other plans in mind. He aimed to have the Gaonate restored to its former position of prestige and to make the tradition of Jewish learning independent of the Exilarch.

To keep up the fiction of their Davidic descent, the Exilarchs conducted themselves in semiregal style, lived luxuriously, entertained lavishly, arrayed themselves in princely clothes, and supported a large retinue of aides and escorts—the cost of all of which came from the earnings of the heavily taxed people. When this income did not cover their expensive living plus the cost of the gifts they were obliged to present annually to the court, certain Exilarchs proved not to be above corruption. In his "letter," Sherira, a contemporary of the geonic period, complained of the arbitrary, even tyrannical rule of the Exilarchs, their oppression of the people, and their interference with the heads of the academies in the performance of their duties. Nevertheless, despite occasional dissatisfaction, the Jews were proud of the Exilarchs and gladly gave them their loyalty and support. They gloried in their power and position at the court and in the fact, that without a fatherland of their own and living as captives in exile, the Exilarchs were a symbol of hope and the promise that "The scepter shall not depart from Judah nor a lawgiver from between his feet." (Gen. 49:10.)

The office of the Exilarch, in contradistinction to that of the Gaon, which was ostensibly purely religious, was to represent the Jews at the court of the Caliph, collect taxes, appoint judges, supervise the courts, and select scholars as heads of the academies. But although the Exilarch had complete jurisdiction over the courts, certain civil decisions required the endorsement of the heads of the two academies, Sura and Pumpadita, to make them valid. In the matter of the inheritance settlement referred to, if there had been no other issues at stake the 16,000 dirhams David ben Zakkai claimed for himself and his court would have been too paltry a sum to justify all the sound and fury. Saadia, Salo Baron argues, was after all a stranger in the country and was not familiar with the much larger tax Moslem courts imposed upon litigants. And so, suspecting the legality of the titled leader's decision, Saadia refused to sign, although the verdict had been endorsed by his Pumpadita colleague.

It was a public rebuke of the Exilarch, as well as an affront to his honor and dignity which, understandably, he could not take in good grace. When pressed for his signature, Saadi equivocated by saying that one endorsement was sufficient, knowing well that it was not. Messengers were sent to him, but Saadia remained implacably unyielding. Ben Zakkai's son, Judah, came to argue with him, and, failing to persuade the Gaon, he raised his hand to strike him, but Saadia warded off the blow and had him unceremoniously turned out of the house. "Ye shall not respect persons in judgment," was the Gaon's defense of his stubborness. What had begun as a trivial matter, a kind of tempest in a teapot, turned into a first-class sensation much to the glee of the gentiles and the humiliation of the Jews. Opposing parties were formed, street fighting took place, defamations, and invectives flew back and forth with unrestrained vehemence. Excommunications and counter-excommunications, deposition and counter-depositions were indulged in. The Exilarch excommunicated and deposed the Gaon, and the latter in turn excommunicated and deposed the Exilarch. Influential authorities, the Jewish court bankers who furnished the financial support to both of the heads of the academies and the Exilarchs were called in to settle the controversy and, what was worse, Moslem officials were resorted to in an effort to arbitrate what was a purely Jewish controversy.

For three years the battle of words raged. The fortunes of the controversy alternated with the changing Mohammedan administrations. Scandalous pamphlets were aimed at each other by the contending parties. Saadia assailed the Exilarch in a very un-geonic *Sefer ha-Galui* (Open Book), which was answered in kind by his opponent. When, after prolonged duelling, the tide turned against Saadia, more likely because of bribed officials than the merits of the case, the Gaon was deprived of his position and was compelled to leave the country.

There was no place in all Babylonia better calculated to heal Saadia's wounded pride than Bagdad, the marvel city of the eastern world, that home of caliphs, viziers, beggars, thinkers, and poets, so vividly described by Haroun al-Rashid in *Arabian Nights*. Situated on the Tigris and in close proximity to Sura and Pumpadita, Bagdad was a center of Jewish learning and culture and a sort of intellectual retreat for scholars and men of letters from foreign lands.

Saadia lived in retirement, but not for long in discouragement. Despite his tribulations, he was above total defeat. His troubles, it was later shown, had sharpened rather than dulled his mental and spiritual faculties. His mind had not permanently lost its freshness and originality. At first, though, he had his moments of dark brooding; and his health had been undermined. At fifty he felt himself an old man with not many more years to live. He was a stranger in a city of a teeming population, with few friends. But, like most great men, after defeat, he quickly roused himself, and his old dash and energy again manifested themselves.

The years Saadia spent in retirement proved to be the most active and energetic of his life. High-souled thinker that he was, he looked ahead to the still unexplored tasks in the field of Jewish learning and scholarship instead of grieving over his past disappointments. As energetic as he had been before, his accomplishments were still more prodigious now that he left his controversies behind him. The literary and scholarly tasks he planned during this period were destined to make him famous for centuries to come.

The Jewish philosophical literature of the Middle Ages was the product of an age of intense intellectual and spiritual struggle and conflict. Those were times of fierce doubt and unbelief. Men were puzzled and mystified by the contradictory demands of reason and religion, faith and knowledge, that were being made on them. The humanistic spirit had not yet been born, but its stirrings in the womb of time were unmistakable. As a result of the recovery of the Greek heritage there was a new appreciation of life and nature. For the second time in history Jewish culture collided with Hellenic thinking—this time in the garb of Arabic literature. Men were no longer inclined to believe blindly, credulously, fanatically. They asked questions and demanded answers. The foundations of revealed religion were shaken. Plato and Aristotle reappeared upon the scene and usurped the power and authority that formerly belonged to religion.

Saadia, whose heart ached at what he saw, felt, and experienced, gives us a vivid picture of the general spiritual havoc of his time in his book, *Kitab al-'Amanat,* translated into Hebrew by Judah Ibn Tibbon two hundred and fifty years later under the title, *Emunot v'Deot* (The Book of Beliefs and Opinions). "My heart grieved for mankind," he writes, "and my soul was moved on account of our people Israel as I saw in our times many of those who adhere to our faith entertain impure beliefs and unclean ideas; while those who deny the faith boast of their own unbelief and triumphantly deride the men of truth, albeit they themselves are in error. I saw men sunk, as it were, in the sea of doubt and overwhelmed by the waves of confusion, and there was no diver to bring them up from the depths, and no swimmer to rescue them. But as God has granted me some knowledge by which I can be useful to them, and endowed me with some ability which I might employ for their benefit, I felt that to help was my duty, and guiding them arright a moral obligation upon me."

Saadia Gaon was the first Jewish philosopher to explore the

whole range of Jewish lore in an effort to bring it in harmony with the prevailing thought of his age. He was a pioneer; he blazed a path in which many succeeding Jewish thinkers, including the great Maimonides, followed. If he did not attain to the heights of medieval Jewish thinking he still must be given the credit for having legitimatized philosophy within the framework of Judaism. "Any Jew," writes M. Simon, "who wishes to indulge in philosophic speculation, can claim a charter of right in *Emunot v'Deot;* and, broadly speaking, it may be said, that all Jews who have been persecuted for philosophizing, have brought their trouble on themselves through not sticking to the *Emunot v'Deot*. 'Orthodox' Jews may find matter of charge against Maimonides; but be they never so obscurantist, they can hardly banish the work of the man who sat in the chair of the Amoraim and Geonim."

Averring that there is nothing in Judaism which sets it against independent thinking in matters of religion, Saadia strikes his religious-philosophical credo clearly in his own words: "The warning of the sages against philosophic thought was intended to keep us only from that one-sided speculation which does not take into account the truth of Scripture. Limitless speculation can give rise only to error, and should it even eventually lead to truth, it has no firm foundation because it rejects Revelation and puts doubt into its place. But when philosophy works hand in hand with faith, it cannot mislead us. It confirms Revelation, and is in a position to refute the objections that are made by unbelievers. . . . Should, however, some object that if speculation arrives at the same conviction as Revelation, the latter is superfluous, since human reason can arrive at the truth without divine interposition, I should reply that Revelation is necessary, inasmuch as without it, men would have to go a long way round to reach clearness through their own thought."

From the above, it will be seen that Saadia is a rationalist only so far as the interests of reason and religion do not conflict. When, however, they are found to differ, he stands staunchly by the latter without yielding an inch. There is, therefore, nothing in *Emunot v'Deot* to provoke the heated controversy and opposition which the

Moreh Nebukim encountered. His postulates are not the postulates of the philosophers but those of the Torah, which is to him the only reliable source of truth. His Judaism is the Judaism of the Bible, the Talmud, Revelation, and Tradition. A keen student of the Bible and intimately acquainted with its every word and thought, he makes it the warrant for and foundation of his every statement and argument. And it is indeed remarkable with what dexterity he marshals biblical texts to support his every contention, however farfetched. It is his conviction that the faulty reasoning of the philosophers and the erroneous claims of both Christianity and Mohammedanism are due chiefly to their fallacious interpretation of the scriptures.

Unlike Maimonides centuries later, who attempted to mystify the *Guide,* preferring to address himself to one intelligent man rather than take notice of the unenlightened multitude, Saadia wrote: "My intention is to place the subject throughout the book within the grasp of the reader and not beyond him; to speak a language which is easy and not difficult; to adduce only the principal proofs and arguments, not their ramifications, so that the reader may find his way about without too great difficulty; that his study may be made straightforward, and through it he may attain his object." Nevertheless, *The Book of Beliefs and Opinions* is a severely difficult volume, comparing poorly with Maimonides' philosophical *magnum opus,* addressed to a select circle of students rather than to the general reading public. While the book is at times solemnly eloquent, even rising to the heights of inspiration, its style is as often harsh and diffuse, making its reading far from an entertaining exercise.

Wide and varied as were Saadia's fields of activity, he was primarily—one might almost say instinctively—a philosopher. His philosophical attitude is plainly manifest in almost everything he thought and wrote, even on subjects not in themselves philosophical. He is linguist, mathematician, and metaphysician in his commentary on *Sefer Yezira* (Book of Creation), a mystical work of unknown origin; he is exegete, historian, and philosopher in the introduction to his Arabic rendition of the scriptures; he is a philosopher of Judaism and defender of its historic faith against the Karaite heresy. But it is in his *Emunot v'Deot* that the philosophic genius of the author rises to its greatest heights, making it one of the most significant contributions to the religious thought and literature of the Jews in many a century.

The book was written in the Arabic language with Hebrew characters, and is arranged in nine chapters, with a concluding chapter or essay dealing with the principles of the practical and ethical conduct of life as part of the Jewish religious system. It is by far Saadia's greatest work aside from his translation of the Bible, and is the only one, by the way, that has been preserved in its entirety to our time. Unlike the *Kuzari* and *The Guide for the Perplexed*, which appeared in translation almost immediately upon their completion, *Emunot v'Deot* had to wait nearly seven hundred years before being rendered into Hebrew by Judah Ibn Tibbon, and almost as long again before it was made accessible in European languages.

Rav Saadia stands firmly on Jewish ground; he is traditional throughout and one of the most conservative of Jewish philosophers. *Emunot v'Deot* is a defense of the principles and teachings of Judaism as revealed in the Bible and the Talmud. His sources are the traditional sources of Judaism, and when he refers to Greek philosophy or to the writings of the Arabic thinkers it is to refute them rather than to build a bridge between them and the Jewish religious outlook.

Saadia grapples with the eternal problems of God, Creation, Revelation, and man, and comes to conclusions not always convincing but always in the spirit of the Jewish faith and tradition. To Saadia, God is not an object of reasoning, speculation, or argumentation. He is an Absolute. He is the source of Knowledge, the fountain of Truth, the Lord and Master of all Creation. He revealed Himself to His people and gave them the eternal Law. Saadia assigns to Him the attributes of Unity, Incorporeality, Life, Wisdom, and Power. He discusses lengthily the subject of Creation, and defends the biblical doctrine of *creatio ex nihilo*. Revelation is the process by which God made Himself known to man. Without revealed religion, Saadia says, man would stray and stumble in his search after truth, and without its precepts he would be floundering without a safe guide or support. Man, Saadia maintains, is the ultimate aim and purpose of the cosmic process. It was for his happiness that God had the world come into being and He endowed man with the power to carry out His divine plan.

He regards the Bible as the only available source of Truth and maintains, against the claims of both Christianity and Mohammedanism, that God had never intended the Bible to be abrogated by any other religious system. He denies the miracles of Jesus as proof of his prophetic authority, for the true prophet, he avers, is recognized not by the miracles he performs but by the ethical value and content of his message. Judaism is not so much a philosophy as a divine legislation, he declares, anticipating Moses Mendelssohn by eight hundred years. "Our nation," he asserts, "is a nation by reason of our Torah."

He discusses with a display of warmth and a wealth of Biblical citations the nature and destiny of the soul, man's short life upon the earth, the disparity between virtue and happiness, his longing for higher bliss than can be achieved on this earth, resurrection of the dead, the Messiah, and a Hereafter in which the recompense for good and evil will be properly adjusted. The soul, Saadia says, is a substance created by God as the instrument of the body, but it has its own separate existence when the partnership is dissolved by death. This world, the philosopher maintains, with all its restlessness and disappointments, with all its misery and wretchedness, can never have been planned by God to be man's only and final existence. Both the Bible and the rabbinic writings are replete with references pointing to the existence of another world in which the good and the evil will receive their share of reward and punishment. We need but cultivate a wiser attitude and more patience in the face of every loss and buffet of fate, knowing that there will be a righting of every wrong, a compensation for every sorrow, an unalloyed bliss and happiness for every grieving and bereaved heart.

It is entirely in keeping with Saadia, the traditionalist, that he should hue close to the orthodox line in not only maintaining the resurrection of the dead but in holding that the resurrection will be physical. In a statement in which he almost literally anticipated Maimonides' declaration in his *Ma'amar Tehiyat ha-Metim,* Saadia naively says: "We know of no Jew who opposes this doctrine, or finds it difficult to believe from the point of view of reason that God should revive the dead, since it has already become clear that God created the world *ex nihilo*. He can, therefore, find no difficulty in believing that God should by a second act create something from something disintegrated and digested." Saadia terms Resurrection synonymous with Redemption, and pronounces this miracle no less plausible than *creatio ex nihilo*. Resurrection, Saadia says, will be for all Jews, except those who have no faith or disbelieve in it.

There is a special flavor to Saadia's treatment of the suffering and redemption of the Jews not to be found in the writings of the later Jewish philosophers. For Saadia was a warm-hearted thinker, a man of feeling and emotion; and the pain and anguish of his people tore at his heart. In one of the concluding chapters of his book he reviews the position of the Jews in the world, the taunts by their revilers, and the persecution by their enemies, and with prophetic compassion he bitterly cries out his protest to God. With exceeding tenderness, supported by a long array of prophetic promises, he soothes and comforts them: "Our Lord," he says, "has informed us through His prophets that He will deliver us, the congregation of the children of Israel, from the state in which we find ourselves; that He will gather our dispersed from the East and West, and bring us unto His holy place, and settle us there permanently. . . . For this reason we patiently endure our sufferings, and wait for Him without casting any doubt on His promises. We do not despair nor does our courage falter, but we grow in strength and firmness, as it says, 'Be strong and let your hearts take courage, all ye that wait for the Lord'."

Although Saadia was not the first Jewish philosopher—he was preceded by Philo and Isaac Israeli—he was the first to complete a system of Jewish religious philosophy and the first to recognize the difference between the Greek and Hebraic type of thinking. There were philosophic vagaries among the Jews at all times. The Prophets waged war against the deniers of the existence of God; the Psalms scornfully denounced the unworthy who saith in his heart "there is no God"; the Books of Job and Ecclesiastes are replete with skeptical ideas; the first chapters of Genesis and Ezekiel were built up as physical and metaphysical philosophies. Likewise the Tannaim and Amoraim are represented by highly speculative ideas. The Talmud speaks of only four who penetrated into the *pardes,* the garden of philosophy, but the venturesome ancient spirits must have exceeded that number. Hillel, Akiba, Hanina bar Homa, and Rav delivered themselves of observations that bear a distinct philosophical stamp.

Nevertheless Saadia may justly be spoken of as a pioneer in many fields, and, especially, as the first to endeavor to work out a system of doctrines in harmony with the traditions of Judaism. He explains writing his book on the ground of the confusion of his contemporaries who were afflicted either by blind faith or arrogant disbelief—equally injurious to a rational understanding of Judaism. It is characteristic of Saadia's fight against the "purblind" in Israel that, in order to defend his view that the principles of Judaism are based on philosophic insight, he injected into his interpretation of the Bible thoughts and opinions which the Biblical writers had not reached.

Saadia considers the question of ethics, or the practical conduct of life, in the tenth and final chapter of the book, in which he selects for examination and criticism thirteen principles by which men should guide and conduct their life. The list contains such items as asceticism, hedonism, materialism, too great devotion to study, pursuit of love, lust for power, and lust for money. He cautions against excesses and sees the attainment of the highest good in a balanced and co-ordinated distribution of one's physical and spiritual forces and faculties. He closes his work with the warning, "Nothing in this book will be of benefit save to him who has purified his heart and is intent on his moral elevation."

Although upon completion of his major philosophical work Saadia was barely fifty-five years of age, he considered himself an old man. He had reached his goal and fulfilled his life's task, not without sacrifice to himself. He was easily the greatest man of his time and did more for his faith and people than any of his contemporaries. In the long line of Geonim there was none to equal him in learning and in service to Judaism. He fought unbelief and was the first to stand up against the Karaite heresy which threatened the destruction of Jewish tradition. He was vigorous in his campaign against corruption and waged unrelenting war on what he considered the despotic rule of the Exilarchs. By his translation of and commentary on the Bible, he became the religious mentor of a large part of the Jewish people living in Mohammedan lands, and by his *Siddur* he made it possible for Jews to express their spiritual yearnings in an elevated style. By his *Emunot v'Deot* he revealed himself not only as the first Jewish thinker to furnish the world with a comprehensive system of the fundamental principles of Jewish belief and thought but cleared a path which many fellow Jewish thinkers followed. In Henry Malter's estimate, "Saadia did not merely influence the Judaism of the Middle Ages, but to a very large extent, he created it."

When, however, in his depression and loneliness Saadia reviewed his life, dark thoughts, after all his years of optimism, assailed him. The man who was to become immortal felt unhappy with his lot. He saw nothing but failure in his career on earth. An unkind fate had shadowed his steps almost from his birth. He was an alien all his life; the wanderer's staff had not rested long in his hand. He wandered from country to country, but found happiness nowhere. He left few friends in Egypt, little good feeling for him in Palestine, he was alone and forgotten in Bagdad. He had quarreled with Ben Meir of the Holy Land and with David Ben Zakkai in Babylonia. He hoped to unify the Jews but, instead, he lived to see them riven apart as never before. The academy he had raised from decay was in the throes of decline again and he, under the ban of excommunication, could do nothing to help salvage it. Was he, now that he had nothing more to look forward to, to die and be buried in a foreign land?

This was not to be. The greatest man the Jews had produced since the Babylonian Talmud authorities was not to remain homeless and alone in the closing years of his life. Saadia's star, like a guttering candle, flamed up for another moment with unwonted brilliance. The Jews of Babylonia, wearied of the long struggle which had brought them nothing but shame and humiliation and had lowered the prestige of the school of learning of which they were proud, demanded of the Exilarch that means be found for a reconciliation with the man whose genius they held in high esteem. Ben Zakkai, who had suffered from the rift no less than his opponent, was more than willing to see past differences forgotten and to meet the man whom he secretly held in high regard.

The reconciliation was fully as dramatic as their feud had been. The contestants were tired of the long-drawn-out strife and in their hearts they welcomed the opportunity to end it. But proud and stubborn men that they were, neither one would take the first step. It, therefore, fell to the lot of Kasser Ben Aaron, a representative member of the Jewish community of Bagdad, to act as peacemaker. He discharged his task with such tact and delicacy that it caused little embarrassment to either of the parties to the controversy.

When he secured an agreement between Saadia and the Exilarch, he formed the outstanding Jewish personages of the city into two groups, to act as guards of honor—one to conduct the Exilarch and the other, Saadia. Each group was to proceed toward the other till they met. The whole community joined in the rejoicing and many an eye dimmed by tears of happiness when the two men, who for three years had fought each other with every available weapon, now embraced and kissed in perfect harmony and friendship. It was a memorable day for the Jews of Babylonia and a memorable day for the Sura academy when Saadia was restored to his former position. The cloud that had spread over the school under the

the incompetent management of the two unknown men who had succeeded Saadia quickly vanished under his energetic leadership after his restoration.

Fate, however, willed that the renewed cooperation between the Exilarch and Saadia should be of short duration and they both soon died within a period of two years. Their deaths almost coincided with the waning influence of Babylonian Jewry, no little aggravated by the constant friction and quarrels between the Geonim and the Exilarchs. For another half-century the flicker of glory and prestige hovered over the Jews of Babylonia, due to their famous academies. About the year 1000 the cultural leadership of the Jews was transferred to Spain. As Saadia was the last brilliant representative of the Sura Gaonate, Sherira and his son Hai marked the closing chapter of the Pumpadita school. The three terminated a period in Jewish history that was rich in cultural activity and leadership. The Exilarchate feebly struggled against extinction for some time and attempted to wield influence under the old, honored name. But their authority, such as it was, was limited to their own country, without respect and recognition by the Jews of the world.

No greater loss ever befell the Jews of the Islamic empire than the premature passing of Saadia Gaon. He died at the age of sixty on the 26th day of the month of Iyar (May 16th), 942. In the course of history it sometimes happens that the spirit of an age becomes personified in a single human being, and it is no exaggeration to say that the spirit of the age he lived in was reflected in the life of no other man as clearly and profoundly as it was in the life of Saadia. He was the voice and symbol of his time, and its greatest religious teacher. He not only absorbed all the wisdom and learning of his generation but he put them to practical use. He was an educator in an age in which there were few inspired teachers, and a philosopher who held up a torch to those of his fellow Jews who were drifting and stumbling in their tracks. He worked in many fields and his range of knowledge was extensive, but he had but one theme: it was Judaism; and to making it clearly understood he devoted all the energies of his heart and mind.

But even more striking than his mental and spiritual powers was his character, as strong as flint. He was not a man of compromises; he made no adjustments but persevered in what seemed to him just and right. He was a personality not to be bribed or influenced by those of superior power and standing. Naturally such men do not walk in a path of roses; and Saadia, who made Truth his goal, was not spared the hardships it imposed. Nevertheless his was a great victory; for while he chafed at times under the sting of defeat and exile, the glory of having been one of the greatest of Babylonian Jewish teachers belongs to him, and more than a thousand years after his death his name is still held in deepest reverence.

Rashi

UNTIL COMPARATIVELY recent times Jews have shown but little concern about biographies of their great men. While the characters of the Bible are studied with great fidelity and their every act and thought noted, no such attention, with few exceptions, fell to the lot of the heroes of our rabbinic literature—as if their spiritual achievements and influences alone counted and not their private, individual lives. How one should like to get a glimpse of Rashi's early life, his childhood, his youth, his parents, his education! Was there nothing in his youth besides work and study? Early as he must have matured, the child in him cannot have been completely killed and forgotten. On the contrary, upon reading his commentaries, especially on the Bible, one gets the feeling that Rashi was one of those men who always retain something of the child nature. Indeed, there is a youthful feeling and emotion in his lines that overshadow his usual learning and make him the friend and intimate of his students. Practically nothing is known about his parents. Strangely Rashi, who occasionally refers to his teachers, never mentions his father. We do not even know whether he was a scholar nor what his interests and occupation were.

According to the best available information, Rashi was born in the year Rabbenu Gershom died, which was 1040, at Troyes, a town in Champagne, Northern France, where he spent most of his life. His parents were unquestionably pious and God-fearing people, as were most Jews of their time. Rashi was married quite early, as was the custom—possibly at the age of fifteen. His wife presented him with three daughters, but no sons. Two of them became the mothers of sons celebrated for their learning. Like their grandfather, they wrote commentaries on the Bible and the Talmud. Although Rashi was in every respect the spiritual leader of his community, his position was purely honorific in character, like that of most Jewish scholars of his time who disdained to profit by their knowledge of Torah, and he supported himself and his family by cultivating a vineyard.

This, and no more, is what the historians have to tell us about the personal life and affairs of the man who influenced more lives and counted more disciples than any other man in Jewish history. But, as if to fill the void, there has evolved a body of anecdotes and legends which surround Rashi and his family with a nimbus of rare glory. Thus, his father, described as a pious and scholarly man, is supposed to have cast a costly gem into the sea rather than part with it for a fabulous amount of money which, he feared, would be used for idolatrous adornment. Thereupon he heard a voice announcing that a son would be born to him more precious than the jewel he had lost. With complete disregard of chronology, a genealogy was invented for Rashi's mother, which traced back her ancestry to Johananha-Sandler, a talmudic sage of the second century and a disciple of Rabbi Akiba. When she was imperiled by a runaway horse during her pregnancy, a wall miraculously opened to receive her, so that no harm might come to her and the child she was carrying under her heart.

Rashi, himself, as well as his parents, was made the hero of a number of fanciful stories and legends. The famous Worms chapel was built several centuries after the renowned commentator's decease; but until comparatively recent years it was pointed out to visitors as the Rashi Chapel. Likewise, as late as the middle of the nineteenth century tourists in Troyes were shown a butcher shop which allegedly was never bothered by flies, because it was supposed to have been built on a spot formerly occupied by Rashi. The man whose interest in foreign countries had led him no farther away from home than Mayence and Worms, whither during his *Wanderjahre* he went to study, is represented to have traveled extensively through Europe, Asia, and Africa; and the scholar who, besides French and a smattering of German, knew no language except Hebrew, in which he wrote his great commentaries, is fictitiously reputed to have been a linguist with a command of the Latin, Greek, Persian, and Arabic tongues.

Discarding the mythical and legendary accounts of his life, what was Rashi's early education? It could not have differed much from the elementary training of most Jewish children of his time and place, which was primarily religious and ethical, with inculcation of the love of Torah and the practice of its precepts. The educational ideals of the Jews in those faraway days were few, but they were sufficient. Basically they were a training in the art of Jewish living. The education of a Jewish child began at home. No sooner had he learned to lisp than a talmudic precept made it his father's duty to teach him words of Torah. The women, whom the Law originally exempted from active participation in most religious duties, likewise played their part in the training of their little ones by amusing them with songs and lullabies based on verses from the Bible. Thus before they were ready for school they were already equipped with the essentials necessary for the life of a Jew.

Although theoretically a child's formal education did not begin until he was six years old, anxious Jewish parents did not wait that long but brought their offspring to *heder* ceremoniously dressed in his best holiday clothes and wrapped in a *talit* sometime before that age. A quaint and impressive ceremony followed, which had for its purpose to win the heart of the youthful scholar for the study of Torah. The parents of the child and their invited guests participated in the initiation, which usually was conducted with a dignity and distinction that remained a treasured memory in the lives of young and old alike.

While there was no universal compulsory education among the Jews there was not a Jewish community, however small and poor, that did not gladly provide for the competent instruction of the young. Indeed, a curse of destruction was laid by the rabbinic sages upon a community that proved derelict in the religious instruction of its children. "A town which fails to send children to school," says Maimonides, "shall be excommunicated until it appoints school teachers. If it persists in its failure, it shall be outlawed, because the entire universe is maintained only by the breath of schoolchildren."

The *heder* or the Hebrew primary school, spoken of by Louis Ginsberg as "one of the greatest institutions of post-biblical Judaism," has been unjustly maligned and ridiculed. It suffered decay and corruption in the Russian-Polish form due to the depressed social and economic life of the people who maintained it, but one needs not accept Solomon Maimen's shocking, distorted, and biased picture of the *heder* without considerable skepticism. The records prove that at the time of Rashi, Jewish communities in France vied with each other in expenditures for schoolhouses that far exceeded in size and value the private ghetto buildings. Indeed, so lavish were they with their money for school buildings that the warning by the author of the *Book of Saints,* a century after Rashi, that "a living wage for scholars is more conducive to good education than an elaborate structure which would more directly flatter the vanity of the donor" could well apply to them.

While nearly all educational establishments followed, with slight variations, the same pattern, the same cannot be said for the elementary and secondary schools, that flourished among Jews in Moslem countries. Both the Franco-German Jews and their brethren across the Pyrenees had their philosophy of the function of Jewish education; but while to one it was to serve God, cultivate piety, and make possible their union with God, to the other it was to serve as systematic consolidation of the Jewish spiritual treasures of the past with the culture and enlightenment of their own age. The educational goal of the schools of one part of Jewry was the study of Mishnah, Gemara, and the ethical-religious classics, while the curriculum of the Sephardic school included, besides the Bible, Hebrew grammar and philology, rhetoric, mathematics, philosophy, the natural sciences, and the Arabic language.

It was fortunate for Rashi—and the Jews—that he did not share the educational program of his sophisticated Sephardic brethren or he might not have had the marvelous combination of learning and humility, extraordinary expository genius and undivided subordination in Torah which distinguished the Master of Troyes. He was the product of the same education that fell to the lot of thousands of Jewish children of his generation. One may venture to suppose that, being precocious, he learned and absorbed more than most of his young colleagues in school. And while there was no admixture of foreign elements in his school curriculum, one may likewise surmise that he was not completely ignorant of the secular sciences or many tractates of the Talmud that required some study, at least on an elementary level, would have remained totally incomprehensible to him.

While Jewish learning was cultivated on both sides of the Rhine, it was the French school, or the one founded by Rashi and continued for two centuries by the *Tosaphists,* his successors, that attained the highest results. The economic and political conditions of the country in which they had lived since the dawn of Christianity favored their preoccupation with the finer things of the spirit. For a considerably longer time than in any other country in Europe the Jews lived in France in comparative tolerance and they had the right of citizenship. They were not allowed a part in the political life of the nation and there were frequent controversies between the ecclesiastics of the two religions and, occasionally, more serious disturbances that involved extortions and tragically large numbers of forced baptisms. On the whole, however, their travail was not nearly as severe as that of their German brothers. For the most part, Jews and Christians lived on fairly friendly terms with one another and their respective scholars, when not adversely inspired by the Church, often met and conversed together.

For the first time in the European annals of the Jews, with the sole exception of their history in Spain, which, culturally, was almost thoroughly Arabized, the Jews of northern France presented a picture of nearly complete integration with the customs and manners of the country in which they lived. They managed their own affairs, had their own tribunals, were not subject to either civil or ecclesiastical jurisdiction. They engaged in commerce and industry, possessed tanneries and vineyards, attended the great fairs, accumulated considerable wealth, and even Latinized their Hebrew names. Except for their common religion and pursuit of knowledge in which all Jews shared alike, there was little resemblance between the proud, urbane French Jews, conscious of their superior social and economic position and the shabby ghost-like figures of their German-Jewish brethren with the somber shadows of persecution ceaselessly haunting their steps.

The German Jews enjoyed neither freedom nor security, neither social standing nor material wealth, but their high intellectual and spiritual level made them at least the equals of their French co-religionists. Living in close proximity they formed a cultural unit, the Franco-German school, which lasted nearly half a millennium. Scholars who were not content to study under but one master wandered from school to school, especially when one became famous because of a celebrated teacher. When, therefore, the word had spread that the Law went forth from the Rhine country it was but natural that the scholarly vinegrower of Troyes, emulating the example of Rabbi Akiba, should leave home and hearth and travel to the schools of Worms and Mayence over which hovered the spirit of the great Rabbenu Gershom through his disciples, who carried on their Master's tradition and his methods of teaching.

It was Gersham ben Judah of Mayence (960–1040), styled "Light of the Exile," who was first in the procession of German-Jewish scholars to make possible the dissemination of talmudic scholarship. He not only collected manuscripts of the Talmud and corrected them but, so that future copyists might have an authorized text, he transcribed with his own hand the whole Mishnah and the Talmud. It was a colossal task and was possible only to one himself intimately acquainted with the entire rabbinic literature and possessed of tremendous energy, unheard-of patience, and extraordinary love for and devotion to Torah.

Rabbenu Gershom made the totality of Jewish learning his province. He worked in Bible, in Talmud, and in midrashic and geonic literature. He wrote commentaries and responsa; he established a school for Jewish learning with disciples from a number of near-by provinces. He became the greatest legal force and authority in the Franco-German Jewish world. He transferred to the Western hemisphere something of the fame and glory which formerly belonged to the Babylonian geonate. His generation indulged in no superfluous oriental hyperbole when it called him *Meor ha-Golah,* the "Light of the Exile," nor did Rashi exaggerate when, speaking of him, he said, "Rabbenu Gershom has enlightened the eyes of Captivity." By his wisdom and learning, by his character and personality, and, best of all, by the moral and spiritual influence he exerted, he was indeed a torch and guide unto his people in the dark and dismal days in which they lived.

Rabbenu Gershom gave a fresh impulse to Jewish learning and made the Rhine province resound with the words of Torah. His exacting labors covered many fields, not the least of which was his extensive correspondence with individual scholars and whole communities, who turned to him for enlightenment on ritual and civil questions, on marriage and business contracts, and on diverse other matters pertaining to private and communal affairs. But to the wide masses of Jews he was more than that. He was their legislator and reformer, an authoritative voice that was listened to respectfully in the far-flung reaches of the Diaspora. In a time of confusion and disunity, when there was neither authority nor discipline in Jewish community life, he became the first in the annals of Jewish history to convoke a synod, which enacted important legislation for the amelioration of the social and economic conditions of large numbers of Jews. To make the Talmud a living force and influence down the ages, however, more than merely a correct text was necessary. What was needed was a man of genius and of no smaller stature than the creators of the Talmud itself, who, by his skill and learning, by his love for Torah and his imagination, should explain and interpret the vast accumulation of knowledge of more than half a millennium for the waiting students. Such a man was Rashi, whose full name was Rabbi Sh'lomo Yitzhaki (Solomon, son of Isaac). After completing his commentary on almost all the books of the Bible, he undertook and completed his still more stupendous commentary on the Babylonian Talmud, second only to that of the masters of the Talmud themselves.

He was the typical Jewish scholar. The love of Torah permeated his whole being; he knew no other love or life outside it. He not only loved Torah but disseminated its knowledge among others. What sustained Jewish scholarship through the ages and made possible the perpetuation of Judaism was the fact that every scholar in Israel felt himself called upon to gather disciples about him and instruct them in the words of Torah, in accordance with the precept of the Mishnah: "Raise up many disciples." Rashi was twenty-five years old when, on the death of his teachers, Rabbenu Gershom's disciples, he founded a school at Troyes which, in light of its intrinsic results and the number and quality of the students it attracted, soon became the greatest center of Jewish learning in the Franco-German community. It was both a school and a laboratory, for, while the Bible and the Talmud were taught there with an ingenuity and insight not known since the days of the Babylonian academies, it was at the same time the workshop from which emerged those great commentaries that secured the correct interpretation and understanding of the Bible and the Talmud for nearly a thousand years.

Although it was Rashi who made Troyes famous in the Jewish world, the city contained an imposing Jewish community for at least a hundred years before Rashi was born. It was an active community, both commercially and religiously. The Jews drew their living from vineyards in which they must have been prosperous, for they supported a Hebrew school of more than local fame. As already observed, Rashi also earned a living for himself and his father from the cultivation of grapes. It is interesting to note that one of the greatest scholars in history, at whose feet sat generations of students and lovers of Torah, was anything but a bookish recluse. In order to keep his vineyards going and provide for the material needs of his family, he occasionally had to visit the fairs and keep himself informed on prices, and until his daughters were old enough to help he had to wait on his customers.

He was indeed *Parshandata,* the Great Illuminator, for without his commentary the Babylonian Talmud might have suffered the same neglect as did the Palestinian Talmud. He was a master commentator, both by reason of his stupendous learning and his method of interpretation. He was concise, precise, and clear. He never used two words when one word would suffice. He was never at a loss for the exact word or a fitting expression for the thought or explanation he had in mind. His almost incredible economy of words called forth the comment, "In Rashi's time, a drop of ink was worth a piece of gold." It is only in exceptional cases, when a talmudic passage is particularly involved and difficult, that he abandons brevity and is more detailed and lengthy in his explanation. When Rashi was ill, and Samuel ben Meir, his grandson, himself a great scholar and a Bible and Talmud commentator, undertook to complete his grandfather's unfinished commentary, Rashi, upon recovering, weighed Samuel's written pages in his hand and remarked: "If thou hadst commented the whole Talmud in this fashion, thy commentary would have been as heavy as a chariot."

Rashi wanted to be a commentator and he was a superb one. He kept off every digression and avoided every discussion not strictly connected with the subject. He knew the whole of rabbinic literature and was at perfect ease on his home ground. His purpose was to make Jews love the Talmud and find joy in its study. The dialectic method of Talmud study was still centuries in the future, but Rashi sensed its danger and warned sharply against it. He criticised "one who is over sharp and clever" and, in another instance, condemned "wrong interpretation that comes from one who is a clever dialectician." When stumped by a difficult word or passage, Rashi, rather than attempt a farfetched explanation, was modest enough to admit, "I do not know this word;" "I do not understand its meaning;" "I have no satisfactory tradition regarding this."

With all his modesty, however, he did not hesitate to take issue with older authorities when he disagreed with them with such expressions as "I do not see it that way;" "It seems to me that it is not so;" "they are in error;" and even stronger ones.

Rashi's influence on Jewish learning is enormous. He stimulated rabbinic studies more generally than any other scholar of his time and of centuries afterward. He became both a model and an indispensable guide to his people—the former because of his incomparable style and manner of interpretation and the latter because he provided a commentary that is the only tool needed for the study of the Talmud. Any man with a fair knowledge of the language of the rabbis and their style of reasoning can, with the help of Rashi's commentary, read the Talmud without too much effort. While Moses Maimonides, who died almost exactly one hundred years after Rashi, feared for the neglect of the Talmud and composed his monumental *Mishneh Torah* to serve as a substitute, Rashi through his commentary provided a key to the Talmud which secured its preservation and study for all time.

Rashi's commentary had no sooner appeared than it became the classic textbook of rabbis, students, and laymen alike. It was hailed in countries which boasted Talmud commentators of their own. He became the supreme interpreter, teacher, guide, and illuminator. Thousands came to know the Talmud through his commentary. To this day there is not an edition of the Babylonia Talmud without Rashi's commentary framing its pages. Alexander Marx calls attention to the interesting fact that half a century ago, when an enterprising publisher decided to print a one-volume edition of the Talmud in small type, he left out all other glossaries and commentaries, but did not dare to omit Rashi's. The most meticulous scholars are likely to pay attention to the older commentaries but none will overlook Rashi.

He is more fortunate than his predecessors; he is more fortunate than his successors. He became a blessed godfather to all who would know and understand the rabbinic lore. He was more fortunate than Maimonides, writes a biographer of Rashi, for while he founded a school and raised many disciples, the philosopher-codifier labored in unplowed ground and it was only after the lapse of time that, little by little, he made his way. Rashi's influence has been enduring, his fame widespread; generations brought up on Rashi find it quite difficult to conceive what talmudic scholarship would have been like without him. He not only inducted students into the colossal mazes of rabbinic literature but guided their every step and made the hours they spent there an unutterable spiritual delight.

If by his commentary upon the Talmud Rashi won for himself the gratitude and admiration of students and scholars, his commentary upon the Bible, especially the Pentateuch, secured for him the lasting love and affection of all classes of Jews. While as commentator he is the teacher of one's maturing years, as expounder of the Bible he is the friend and companion of one's childhood. Men grown old in years and experience still remember with a springlike warmth in their hearts the time when Rashi first shone in their lives. To thousands of children Rashi was more than a commentator; he was a kindly and genial instructor and guide who stirred their hearts and roused their imagination.

There was no Grimm nor Andersen, no Arabian Nights, no story books of special interest to children. But when they read their Rashi, replete with the tales and legends culled from the Talmud and the Midrashim with which he embroidered the words of Torah, they were stimulated and enthusiastic. To learn Humish (the Five Books of Moses) with Rashi was an achievement; it signified an introduction into the inner sanctum of Jewish learning. His every word was followed breathlessly by thousands of young and eager children. He himself drank in the beauty and poetry of the Bible and knew how to make it a living book. Rashi was a master educator who subtly, almost magically, understood how to capture the hearts of his students and win their lifelong love and devotion. He was an accomplished pedagogue and invested everything with soul and endowed his every word with his great, warm personality. Unnumbered little ones gamboled their way into Judaism through him. He filled their souls with holy longing for the Jewish past and abiding faith in the Jewish future. Through him the words and incidents of the Bible throbbed with life. He made the patriarchs, heroes, and prophets of the scriptures, stand out lifelike in his pages.

Few authors had such a public as it was Rashi's good fortune to have. Both young and old found him not only instructive but stimulating and inspiring. He not only helped to bring the ancient Jewish heritage to the wise and the learned but the masses, the untutored, and heavy-burdened, who had not trained their minds for the fine and exquisite subtleties of the scholars, loved their Rashi for reasons of their own. Other commentators of the Bible wrote for the elite and learned Jews, while Rashi had uppermost in mind the plain and simple people. He knew their great hunger for Torah and sought to feed their starved and yearning hearts. Their education may have been neglected; they probably could read only their prayers, and, at best make out a simple passage in the *Aggadah,* or the ethical portion of the Talmud. But knowing Rashi—and what Jew of old had not at least a smattering of knowledge about Rashi? —they could no longer be counted among the *amei-ha'aretzim* (ignorant) and could hold their own among the moderately learned.

Rashi in his eagerness to be clear and concise so that every Jew, be he ever so humble, would understand, made a special effort to find the words best fitted to reach his readers. He was often forced to borrow foreign words for which there were no equivalents in Hebrew. This frequently led him to use the French vernacular. He was the first medieval Jewish Western scholar to employ a foreign language in interpreting the Scriptures. He adopted words of the French tongue spoken during the eleventh and twelfth centuries, calling it *Laoz.* His commentaries contain about thirty-five hundred of such old French words. This earned him lasting gratitude for preserving this old French dialect.

Rashi's commentary on the Bible penetrated the religious life of all classes of Jews as did no other work besides the text of the Bible itself. It met with the universal encomium of scholars as the greatest achievement by a single individual. His grandson, Jacob ben Meir, known as Rabbenu Tam, a famous talmudic scholar who did not always agree with his grandfather on matters of interpretation, remarked, "So far as my grandfather's commentary on the Talmud is concerned, I might do as well, but it would not be in my power to undertake his commentary on the Pentateuch."

Reviewing the weekly lesson of the Torah with Rashi's commentary became as much a religious duty expected of a Jew as the study of Torah itself. Indeed, Joseph Karo (1448–1535), author of the *Shulkhan Arukh,* and Isaac Luria (1534–1572), the famous Safed kabbalist, recommended this procedure as a religious precept not to be deviated from, the latter even going so far as to prefer Rashi's commentary over the Aramaic translation of the Pentateuch which the law required to be read on the Sabbath, since Rashi's commentary is more easily understood and renders the text more intelligible. Gradually Rashi became the favorite commentator on the Torah, and until recently there was not a Jew to be found who could not quote at least a word or phrase from Rashi. So popular did Rashi's commentaries become that, according to Alexander Marx, there appeared numerous supercommentaries, with at least ninety of them in the library of the Jewish Theological Seminary alone.

The unique qualities of Rashi, which make his commentaries so indispensable and himself so popular, moved the historian Graetz to state, "Rashi, as commentator, may be called an artist"; and similar words of praise and admiration came from other admirers. Of how many scholars can the same be said—especially commentators, of whom little originality or creative genius is expected? But when applied to Rashi, who will question the correctness of the historian's estimate? For in sober truth he was an artist, indeed. He was an artist in his style and diction and in his qualities of perception and imagination—an artist with such a range that he could speak at times with the tongue of the learned and at other times with the simplicity of a child and who richly deserved a former teacher's tribute: "We owe it to you that this age is not orphaned, and may many like you arise in Israel."

Rashi was a man of feeling and emotion. He approached the Bible with a childlike mind and with a childlike faith. He thought of everything in terms of symbols and figures of speech. He was not scared by the anthropomorphisms of the Bible, as were some of his sophisticated Spanish brethren. He animated everything and everything was animated for him. One can imagine him a successful writer of children's stories, an occupation in which one cannot picture a metaphysician like Moses Maimonides or a Bible critic like Abraham Ibn Ezra, who ran the gamut of all the sciences of his time. He searched the Bible with the imagination of a poet rather than with the mind of a critic. "In his works there is not one rational explanation out of a thousand," Abraham Ibn Ezra complains of the French commentator. Others deplore that he does not always give the literal meaning of a text but wanders far afield and introduces stories and parables from the Talmud and the Midrash. But these are exactly the characteristics that made Rashi so unique a commentator and his work so loved and admired by young and old.

The uniqueness and art of Rashi's commentary is not to be sought so much in its interpretation of this or that word or verse of the Torah as in its total result in disseminating Jewish learning and culture. For instance, what better preparation for the study of the Holy Scriptures than Rashi's commentary; what more adequate introduction to the Talmud and the Midrash than his interpretation of the Bible, which is in itself a marvelous anthology of all that is best and finest in rabbinic literature? "The commentary of Rashi," says Louis Ginsberg, "had peculiar qualities that made it an eminently fit introduction to the study of the Holy Scriptures. A simple, natural system of exegesis which, through the simple use of the Midrash, was presented with warm, deep feeling, made the Bible a living book to the child-student. It enabled him to penetrate to its very recesses. At the same time, the study of the Scripture with Rashi was the best possible introduction to rabbinic literature —the Midrash and the Talmud—from which Rashi gives frequent quotations in his Bible commentary, making them intelligible in his unsurpassed way."

The exhausting, almost superhuman, energy the writing of his commentaries required did not prevent Rashi from participating in the active, daily life of his people. He dared not—indeed, his position did not allow him—to become one-sided and absorbed only in his books and studies. The authority exercised by a great teacher does not radiate exclusively from his learning but from the totality of his life and personality. "The learned caste among the Jews of antiquity and the Middle Ages is a unique phenomenon in history," writes Louis Ginsberg. While, of course, it was his learning that gave him his status, he discharged many other functions besides teaching the knowledge of Torah. He was the counselor, judge, arbitrator, and tribune of his own and other communities. He answered questions, he decided differences, he interpreted the law, he attended personally to an enormous correspondence without the help of secretaries or assistants. He was also the comforter and spiritual healer of his people when dark days of suffering and persecution fell upon them.

Rashi's love for Jews was unbounded and he bore their burdens with saintlike tenderness and patience. Indeed, nowhere is his kindly, gentle spirit so richly manifested as in the letters he wrote to widely scattered communities. Meek and modest, he was like Moses, who did not know that his face shone. When he was appealed to in a controversy in a community outside his jurisdiction, his reply was, "What am I that I should consider myself an authority in other places? . . . I am a man of little importance, and my hands are feeble like those of an orphan." His profound, overflowing humanity is particularly exemplified in his correspondence, known in rabbinic literature as Responsa, about the tragic consequences of the First Crusade, proclaimed by Pope Urban II for the purpose of rescuing the Holy Land and the tomb of Jesus from the hands of the "vile race," the Moslems. Thousands of Jews perished in the mass slaughter that resulted, among them a number of Rashi's friends and disciples. Scores of Jews who lacked the courage for the supreme sacrifice submitted to baptism, but when the terror was over they longed to return to their old faith.

Much to the chagrin of the ecclesiastical authorities, Emperor Henry IV, never a favorite of Rome, permitted the forcibly baptized to return to Judaism. But some Jews found it difficult to show any leniency to or to consort with those of their former brethren who had deserted their faith, not considering the circumstances under which they had acted. When the matter was brought before Rashi his decision was prompt and unequivocal. He was not only for forgiving the sinners—sinners under such extraordinarily cruel circumstances—but pleaded with the Jews not to offend or spurn those who wished to return. "Take heed," he wrote, "in your conduct toward those whose defection was under the menace of the sword and who escaped as soon as the danger was over." He not only welcomed their return but even permitted the use of the wines of the renegade Jews for sacramental purposes and the exercise of their priestly rights, if they happened to be of Aaronite descent.

Rashi's fame went far beyond the Jewish community and extended to almost the whole world, particularly among Christian students of the Bible. Indeed, Rashi's share in the chapter of Christian-Jewish cultural relations is by no means an insignificant one. The field of Jewish learning during the Middle Ages had widened, and it included a number of Christian scholars. In the century—the thirteenth—we are considering, there were contacts between Jews and Christians other than the contact of persecution. "Christian and Jewish scholars lived in an atmosphere of deepening polemics," says Herman Hailperin, and, while the purpose of the disputations was to convert the Jews, there developed a need on both sides to search the Scriptures for the light they might cast on the subject under discussion. The Jews, of course, had their Bible and commentaries, but it was not until Nicolas de Lyra (1270–1349), a Franciscan monk regarded as the most famous Christian scholar of his age, that the Christian world for the first time was given the opportunity to regard the Jewish Bible as the Jew saw it. For de Lyra was a man remarkable both for his profound knowledge of the sources of Judaism and his fairness. He not only knew his Rashi and held him in high esteem but followed him so closely in his own exegetical work that he was dubbed *Simius Solomonis* (Rashi's Ape).

The ideal artist, be he poet, writer, painter, or musician, never regards his work as complete. There is always a word, line, stroke, or note he should like to change. "Rashi," writes Jacob Z. Lauterbach, "throughout his entire life, worked continuously at his commentaries, revising, correcting, retracting some of his opinions, and modifying some of his interpretations, thus preparing what we may call new and revised editions of his commentaries." He began his work while still a young man, when he was studying in Worms, and kept at it until the very last. He himself is known to have prepared at least three revised editions of his commentary to several tractates of the Talmud, and, as far as his Bible commentary is concerned, he is reported to have admitted to his grandson Rashbam that if he had the time he should like to rewrite it in agreement with more recent findings.

There is no finer and more eloquent tribute to Rashi than the one penned by the late Jacob Z. Lauterbach. "There is a legendary report to the effect," he writes, "that Rashi was engaged in the work of revising his commentary to the Talmud up to the very end of his life, and that when in the revision of his commentary to the tractate *Makket,* he reached the explanation of a passage (19b) containing the word *Taher* 'pure', his pure soul expired." That, of course, is merely a legend, but like so many legends it contains a kernel of truth. With naïve embellishment this legend tells us, and we have no reason to doubt it, that all his life, even to his dying hour, Rashi busied himself with his favorite task of interpreting the Talmud, and that he breathed his last in the spiritually and intellectually pure atmosphere of his studies. He died in 1105, with the knowledge that he had made a contribution that would greatly stimulate the study of the Talmud and would help to make it understood and appreciated by a large circle of students and scholars.

Judah Halevi

JUDAH BEN SAMUEL HALEVI, Abul Hasan Ibn Alawi, as he was called in Arabic, the sweetest singer in Israel since biblical days, belonged to that unique period in Jewish history characterized by historians as the Golden Age. In his songs as in his life Judah Halevi was the Jewish spirit incarnate—indeed, he was himself a perfect poem fashioned in flesh and blood. He was the greatest Hebrew poet of his time and one of the great Jewish poets of all time. No other man captured the heart and imagination of the Jewish people as did this Castilian-born Hebrew singer. The historian Graetz did not exaggerate the love and affection the Jews bear their Poet Laureate of nearly a thousand years when, in a burst of enthusiasm, he wrote: "To describe him fully, one would have to borrow from poetry her richest colors and her sweetest song."

Judah Halevi was the most creative and versatile of Jewish poets. There were many strings to his lyre, and he played upon them with equal grace and beauty a great variety of themes. He was a prodigious synagogue minstrel, and his liturgical pieces are chanted to this day in Jewish congregations all over the world. He sang of love, wine, and friendship, and the passing years have not faded the charm and freshness of his verses. He loved nature with the heart and imagination of a poet, and his lyrics are unequaled for their sparkling beauty. But great Jew and loyal lover of his people that he was, their fate and future were the predominant motifs of his songs. He sang the ballad of his people, the ballad of their pains and sorrows, their silent grief and suffering.

Yet Halevi is not a gloomy poet nor a prophet of doom. He declaims the wretched fate of his people and veils his head in mourning because of their suffering, but his muse is also merry with bright and gay tunes that shine and glisten like the morning dew. For Halevi loved life with the faith and confidence of a trusting heart. He looked at the world with clear and steady eyes and saw nothing but love and beauty. His poetry is a harmony of tears and smiles, of despair and exaltation, of defeat and triumph. He lamented the fate of his people, and their suffering almost broke his heart, but in his mind's eye he beheld their future radiant with ancient prophetic splendor.

It is of such glorious stuff that the Jewish nation's poet was made. He was the spokesman of his people—a truer representative than any of his distinguished contemporary bards. He came with a new light, and in that light we are still walking today. No poet before or since has been so loved and esteemed by his people, unless it be Hayyim Nahman Bialik, who followed him by about eight hundred years. Many poets, writes Halevi's English translator, "tried to rival Halevi's poetic genius, but they appear to us like stars after the moon has risen." Judah Albarizi, himself a poet, who followed Halevi by a single generation, was no more extravagant in his praise than were others of the Castilian poet's admirers when he wrote of Halevi: "He entered the treasure-house of song and took all its choice vessels, and going out, he closed its gates behind him."

The biography of this "pure and faithful, ever spotless son of his people," is so shrouded in uncertainty that it is only of his inner life, as revealed in his poetic and prose work, that we can speak with certainty, everything else being mere conjecture. Not even the year of his birth has been definitely established, Kaufmann, Graetz, Geiger, and Harkavi each suggesting a different date. It is, however, generally accepted that Judah Halevi was born in 1085 in Toledo, capital of the Christian state of Castile. His youth, of which but little is known, seems not to have been unusual. He was a precocious child, but precocity is not a rare quality among Jewish children in any generation. Good fortune favored him in that he was born and brought up in an atmosphere of affluence and was spared the agonies of poverty and loneliness which soured the lives of a number of his contemporaries who rose to fame and distinction.

The future sage and poet, destined heir to King David's lyre, matured early. When after his elementary education the city of his birth had little more to give him, his father sent him to Lucena to perfect himself in his talmudic studies under the auspices of Isaac Alfasi, a brilliant rabbinic luminary, famous for his talmudic compendium. Endowed with extraordinary talent, the youthful student absorbed everything he was taught with little effort or difficulty. He mastered the Hebrew language, and his style became as precise, lucid, and supple as the language of the Bible; he explored the depth and intricacies of the Talmud, and he so thoroughly familiarized himself with the niceties of the Arabic language that he could vie with the best Moslem scholars in the grace and beauty of the language of the Koran.

His craving was for knowledge, his ambition to enlarge the empire of his mind. As if his other studies were not enough, he devoted himself to the physical sciences, delved into the subtleties of metaphysics, and paid his tribute to the Greco-Arabic philosophy, which was the intellectual fashion of the day and which he later did much to oppose and refute. Poet and visionary though he was, with heart and mind fixed on the intangible things of the spirit, he nevertheless remembered the practical demands of life and, looking forward to an independent existence of his own, he took up the "vanity of the medical science," as he called it, for a profession. At the home of his schoolmaster he met kindred spirits, who, like himself, were lovers of the Torah and masters of the learning and culture of the time, and with whom he formed abiding and intimate friendships.

Halevi progressed; he matured; his years of apprenticeship served him well. He returned to the city of his birth laden with learning, honors, and experience. His poetic genius had not yet fully matured but its growth was clearly in evidence. The silken magic of his speech had not yet revealed itself but there was a warm mellowness in his lines which heralded the coming master. He tuned up his lyre with verses on joyous occasions in his own life and in those of his friends; he gladdened with his music the hearts of newlyweds and muted his harp in mourning over the loss of a friend or a scholar. When his friend and teacher, Isaac Alfasi, died, his elegy was so sad and stirring, that he was hailed by the considerably older and more practiced poet, Moses Ibn Ezra:

> How can a boy so young in years,
> Bear such a weight of wisdom sage,
> Nor amongst the greybeards find his peers
> While still in very bloom of age?

A brilliant company of friends and admirers, who valued his talent and paid tribute to his accomplishments, gathered around the young poet while he was still in his teens. His name echoed all the way from Toledo to Granada, Seville, and Cordova. It required all his moral force and character not to succumb to the incense that was burned before him. Together with his slightly younger contemporary, Abraham Ibn Ezra, a roving poet and master of many fields of knowledge, he established himself in the Castilian capital, which was beginning to recover something of her lost position as the center of Jewish learning and culture.

Not long after his return, Judah Halevi married, and, sentimental young man that he was, it may be taken for granted that it was a love match. Unhappily, however, all that we know of the poet's wife are the adoring poems he addressed to her while she was alive and the moving lament he raised when she died. Otherwise, Halevi left us in complete ignorance of his wife's name, family, background, and looks. She presented her husband with an only child, a daughter, who, in turn, bore a son, whom she called by his grandfather's name, Judah. While there is little allusion in Halevi's poems to his home and family life, in his ode written on the eve of his departure for the Holy Land he left a ringing farewell to his daughter and grandson, his wife having already died.

Halevi had no faith in his medicines and incessantly prayed to God for deliverance from the profession for which he had little liking. In a short poem he writes:

> To meet the fountain of life of truth I run,
> For I weary of a life of vanity and emptiness,
> To see the face of my King is mine only aim;
> I will fear

My medicines are of Thee, What be good
Or evil, whether strong or weak.
It is Thou who shalt choose, not I:
Of Thy knowledge is the evil and the fair.
Not upon my power of healing I rely;
Only for Thine healing do I watch.

The poet with the irresistible song of Zion in his heart regrets the time he is compelled to waste on things in which he finds no satisfaction. Medicine is to him not so much a science as it is a vanity and a delusion. He is nevertheless obliged to practice his profession because of the importunities of the sick and the dying before him. In a letter written at an advanced age to a friend, he bares his feelings and prays for deliverance: "I occupy myself in the hours which belong neither to the day nor to the night, with vanity of the medical science, although I am unable to heal. The city in which I dwell is large, the inhabitants are giants, but they are cruel rulers. Wherewith could I conciliate them better than by spending my days in curing their illness? I physic Babel, but it continues infirm. I cry to God that he may quickly send deliverance unto me, and give me freedom to enjoy rest that I may repair to some place of living knowledge, to the fountain of wisdom."

But with his desire for independence, and possibly with the tragic examples of Solomon Ibn Gabirol and Abraham Ibn Ezra before him, he resorted for a living to the calling for which he had prepared himself and, according to his own statement, not without success. Although, either humorously or in earnest, he poked fun at the medical profession, his thorough training in the physical sciences, his skill, and, above all, his great sympathy for the sick and suffering made him a good doctor with many more patients than he could care for.

But he was not happy and the wanderlust possessed him. He was bored by his wearisome, humdrum existence and it made him restless. He who had it in his power to create the most refined and delicate poetry chafed under the fetters of the prosaic needs and demands of his daily life. History does not record the mental turmoil that made Halevi leave his home and family and become a wanderer, nor the details of his journey, but his steps have been traced to Granada, Seville, Málaga, and Cádiz. Everywhere the Castilian singer was received with pleasure by young and old, for he was an amiable and jovial young man who did not despise the wine houses and who was fond of jokes and riddles.

From town to town the poet wandered, everywhere bestowing little gifts from his rapt heart. He sang of the joys of life, of the beauties of nature, of the blossoms of spring, of the blushing maiden's cherry lips. On and on, in place after place, the pilgrim-poet's lyre poured forth merry little songs at the nimble touch of his hand. We do not know how many other towns the wandering minstrel visited, but it is fairly certain that he brought his odyssey to an end at the gates of Cordova, where the greater and most creative part of his life was spent.

It was in Cordova, the capital of Andalusia—the Bride of Andalusia the Arabs fondly called her—that our poet's wings achieved their highest flights. Cordova encouraged the arts and prized poetry highly. The Andalusian capital was to Spain what Florence was to Italy during the Renaissance, some five hundred years later—a city of commerce and learning, of scholars, thinkers, and poets, of magnificent parks and palaces, and vineyards bathed in marvelous sunshine. Roman buildings spoke of the early foreign occupation of the city and Moslem mosques displayed the exquisite art of Moorish architecture. Colleges and learned fraternities made the city a center of learning and culture for students from far-away Christian and Mohammedan lands.

Jews have their happy memories of the capital of the western Arab empire—memories of a flourishing Jewish community, of an intensive literary and spiritual activity, of talented scholars, poets, and philosophers, under the influence of whose luminous accomplishments we are still living today. It was in Cordova that the foundation of the post-biblical Hebrew revival was laid, where the Jewish spirit was fostered and preserved, where, indeed, the national Jewish consciousness was kept alive with extraordinary love and devotion. Under Hasdai Ibn Shaprut, prince and Maecenas of Jewish learning, talmudic scholars thrived and prospered until the academy he founded rivaled the Babylonian schools.

Judah Halevi liked the environment in which he found himself and responded to its spirit enthusiastically. There was a frankness and freedom of spirit in the Andalusian capital that suited his poetic temperament admirably. With all the rashness and impetuosity of youth, he sang lustily of love and friendship, of the juice of the grape, of the eyes of his beloved and her raven locks. Whether the dozens of love poems he composed were meant for his wife or for the enchanting female creatures he met is now questioned, but many of them are as audacious as any phrased in the language of the Bible. Thus, the Castilian bard sings:

> Through the veil are seen two serpent-eyes,
> A snake coils o'er your cheek—your hair;
> It stings the hearts of many from afar, my fair.
>
> Awake, O my love, from your sleep,
> Your face as it wakes let me view;
> If you dream someone kissing your lips,
> I'll interpret your dreaming for you.

One can picture Halevi as the darling of the Cordova salons, the toast of every gay party. There was something grand and magnificent about the young Castilian singer who with happy and effortless ease charmed from his lute such beautiful strains of love and joy. But lovely though they were, they were out of step with the mood of the Jewish people of the time, and one can understand the resentment of the older and more serious-minded of Halevi's friends. They knew the greater potentialities of Halevi's genius and when they remonstrated with him for frittering away his time and talent on trivialities, the poet retorted:

> Shall one whose years scarce number twenty-four
> Turn foe to pleasure and drink wine no more?

Halevi returned to Toledo, and for a while his lyre lay idle. The political atmosphere of the country of his birth had suddenly changed and the events that transpired spread a blight over the poet's life. Alfonso VI, the Christian ruler of Castile, was a wise and judicious monarch, and it served his interests to be on good and friendly terms with the Jewish element of his country's mixed population. But Pope Gregory VII was disgruntled. It hurt his Christian conscience to see such un-Christian conduct on the part of a Christian king, and he remonstrated with Alfonso angrily on the subject. Riots and plunder of Jewish homes and shops followed. In one such attack Solomon Ibn Farissol, scholar and leader of the Jews of Castile, was brutally murdered.

It was a shattering blow and it shocked the poet out of his youthful complacency. When he resumed his poetry he was no longer Abul Hasan, the warbler of the dainty love ditties, but Judah Halevi, the inimitable singer of Israel, the mighty voice of his people, at once their hope and their conscience, their seer and patriot-philosopher. In an exquisite transitional poem, the now-matured bard acknowledges the change that came over him:

> Asleep in the bosom of youth how long wilt thou lie?
> Know that boyhood is like shaken tow,
> Shake thyself from the lure of time—like birds
> Shake themselves from the dewdrops of the night.

The man who with his lilting songs and ballads had paid his tribute to the passing mood and temper of his time, sang now of *erah hayyim l'ma'alah,* the upward way of life. Had Halevi persisted in his simple songs and written nothing else, he might have been remembered as a gifted poet who infused fire and passion into his music, but he certainly would not have lived in the hearts of his people for nearly a thousand years. But having made God and Israel the passion of his song, he vies with the Psalmist for immortality, and his poetry has become part of the holy lore of the synagogue.

"If one may speak of religious geniuses," writes Max Schlessinger, "Judah Halevi must certainly be regarded among the greatest products of medieval Judaism." No other man drew as near to God as he and none clung to Him as closely or felt so safe in His shadow. He sought God always, in his waking and sleeping:

> Longing I sought Thy presence;
>   Lord, with my whole heart did I call and pray,
> And going out toward Thee,
>   I found Thee coming to me on the way.

His love of God knew no bounds—without Him his soul would shrink and wither away:

> When I remove from Thee, O God
> I die whilst I live, but when
> Clinging to Thee I live in death.

He enriched the synagogue liturgy with many sacred melodies. He put music into his songs which the Levite chorus of the Temple might have envied. What can match Halevi's "Ode to Zion," about which Lady Magnus correctly observed that fifty translations have not spoiled its fervid lines. Solomon Ibn Gabirol may rank first and foremost as synagogue minstrel. He adorned his Maker with a "Royal Crown" which nearly a thousand years have not tarnished. But while Gabirol sang the song of the Lord with the voice of the philosopher and the theologian, Judah Halevi sang with such bell-like clarity that everyone can hear and understand.

He adorned the religious homelife of his people with his song. He was particularly touched by the joy and peace with which the Sabbath transforms every Jewish home, and he sang:

> On Friday doth my cup o'erflow,
> What blissful rest the night shall know,
> When in thine arms, my toil and woe
> Are all forgot, Sabbath, my love!
>
> 'Tis dusk, with sudden light distilled
> From one sweet face the world is filled;
> The tumult of my heart is stilled—
> For thou art come, Sabbath, my love.
>
> Bring fruit and wine and gladsome lay,
> Cry, 'Come in peace, O restful day!'

It was, however, from his patriotic songs—the laments that burst from his heart over Zion's fallen glory and the dreams of her future greatness—that Judah Halevi gained his greatest reputation. In him all that the Jews have loved and lost, their severest defeats and greatest hoped-for triumphs, are distilled in songs and prayers which have rung through the centuries. He is the typical lover of Zion, the typical mourner over her faded grandeur, the typical poet and prophet of her restored splendor. He combines the qualities of

Jeremiah, Isaiah, and Ezekiel. Like Jeremiah, he weeps and mourns over his nation's misfortunes, and like Isaiah and Ezekiel, he sings exultingly of his visions of its miraculous rebirth.

Michael Sachs, a German-Jewish scholar, preacher, and historian, assessed Halevi's genius correctly when he said that, in his utter love for and devotion to his people, he was the most national and patriotic of Jews. To the Jews Judah Halevi is more than a great poet, a great thinker, a towering figure in the Jewish cultural renaissance. He is their heart, their conscience, the man in whom all that is best and noblest in their lives finds glorious expression. He is the spokesman of the Jewish folk, their voice and symbol. The ancient prophets loved their people, yet they often rebuked and chastised them; while Halevi saw no inequity in Jacob and no perverseness in Israel. He looked deep into the hearts of his people, and knew their wretched lives and acute suffering, and he forgave their small sins and transgressions.

The memory of Zion and Jerusalem was like a sacred fire in his heart and mind. It gave him no rest; it fired his thoughts and gave shape and form to his every song. None of his contemporaries so fully represented his people's love of home and freedom as he did, and none could with equal boldness, and justice, proclaim, *"Ani Kiner l'shiraik"* (I am a harp for thy song). He remembered the loveliness of Zion's youth and the glory and splendor of her prime, when the great ones of the earth sought and wooed her. Jerusalem is to him the city of the world, the life of souls where the *Shekhinah* dwells; sweet would it be to him to walk naked and barefoot upon the desolate places where the holiest dwellings were:

> O, city of the world, most chastely fair,
> In the far West, behold, I sigh for thee,
> O, had I eagle wings, I'd fly to thee,
> And with my falling tears make moist thine earth.

Next to his religious hymns, Halevi's patriotic songs are the noblest outpourings of his heart. Never is his speech so tender and his words so soft and mellow as when his thoughts are attuned to the memory of Zion and Jerusalem.

My heart is in the East, and I am in the uttermost West—
How can I find savor in food? How shall it be sweet to me?
How shall I render my vow and my bonds, while yet
Zion lies beneath the fetters of Edom, and I in Arab chains?
A light thing it would seem to me to leave all the good
    things of Spain
Seeing how precious in mine eyes it is to behold the dust of
    the desolate sanctuary.

When in their despondency he saw his people despair of redemption, he soothed their failing spirits:

Bide thou thy time—within thy soul be peace,
Nor ask complainingly when thy pain shall cease;
Speak, rhyme and sing, for victory is thine,
Nigh thee my tent is pitched, and thou art mine.

Halevi was not only the most loyal and patriotic of Jews but also the most farseeing. Had the Jews listened to the message of his songs, how different their history might have been! He beheld the fate and future of his people more clearly and realistically than any of his contemporaries. He disdained the imaginary peace and prosperity of his Spanish brethren. While they were drowsing happily in their sumptuous homes and easy circumstances, he heard the rolling thunder, the tramping feet of the Christian Crusader, the sound and fury of the Mohammedan destroyer who would soon turn to ruin and ashes the glory of their seductive life; and bitterly the poet cried out:

Have we either in the East or in the West
A place of hope where we may rest?

Zion became the mistress of his heart, the devotion of his life, the crown and climax of his choicest songs. The whole power of his creative genius he lavished upon her. To see her, embrace her, to kneel in her dust he would surrender everything that was dear and precious to him. Nor was it a poetic dream or rhetorical fancy. He had resolved upon his pilgrimage to the Holy Land and nothing would deter him—neither the remonstrances of his friends nor the pleading of his daughter, his only child, and his grandson—his wife was dead.

I have no care for worldly goods,
Not for treasures nor for aught that may perish—
Even so far that I can forget her that went forth from
    my loins,
And I can forget her son, though it pierce my heart,
And I have nothing left but his memory for a symbol.

Had he reached his goal or was he lost in the mist that shrouded his steps? The final episode in his story will help answer that question. Meanwhile, the long centuries have retained his memory as bright and radiant as when he walked the streets of Cordova with the divine music of his lyre.

It took another great Jewish poet, the tortured and tormented Heinrich Heine, to portray in winged words the genius of Israel's Prince of Singers:

Yes, a great and famous poet,
Star and beacon of his age,
Light and lantern to his people,
A superb and a resplendent

Flame of song, a fiery pillar,
Burning in the van of Israel's
Endless caravan of sorrow
In the desert waste of exile.

For his song was like his spirit;
Pure and perfect without blemish—
When Halevi's soul was fashioned
The Creator kissed it, glowing

With his happy inspiration;
And distinguished by God's favor
All the poet's fervent measures
Echo with that kiss forever.

When a poet turns philosopher there is danger that one phase of his genius will overshadow the other. No such fear, however, need be entertained in the case of Judah Halevi; for no matter to what form of work he turned he was the incomparable master always. When, therefore, some time before he embarked upon his great pilgrimage, he produced his celebrated work, *Kitab al'Khazari*, which became known in Judah Ibn Tibbon's translation as *Sefer ha-Kuzari*, he created a masterpiece that in form and content is as great as any of his poems.

The *Kuzari* is a brilliant and fascinating work, a dramatic poem in five parts, in which the author's genius is poured out in a steady stream of thought and feeling, of learning and eloquence, making it one of the most striking contributions to Jewish philosophical literature. Written more than eight hundred years ago, it is as fresh and challenging today as it was when it emerged from the writer's hand. It is timeless—a book for the ages and more enduring than some other philosophical works that created greater stir and controversy. "Its popularity," says Hartwig Hirschfeld, the English translator of *Kuzari* from the original Arabic, "is evidenced by the fact that edition after edition followed from the earliest days of the printing press down to our own time. Indeed, the most elaborate edition was undertaken by an un-Jewish scholar."

Halevi's genius was stupendous and diversified. He was not satisfied with poetry alone, but distinguished himself also in other forms of writing. He was perhaps the least medieval and the most modern of the Jewish poet-philosophers. He was the minstrel of Zion, the guide and conscience of his people. The fate and destiny of his nation are nowhere else as clearly mirrored as they are in his writings. Zionist philosophy has made little headway since Judah Halevi. We still think and speak in terms of the *Kuzari*, although many may never have seen or read the book. Some of its leading ideas have passed into the vocabularies of Jewish people who are unaware of their source. He was foremost Zionist of his age and the first to formulate a philosophy of Jewish nationalism; to advocate the return of the Jews to their ancient homeland; to regard Palestine as an essential factor in the destiny of the Jewish people; and to look upon the Jewish restoration as a practical ideal instead of a shining fantasy.

Halevi's love of Israel flames and blazes in each of his hymns and poems, but it thunders and reverberates with a mighty force in the pages of the *Kuzari*. The writings of no other medieval Jewish philosopher reveal such love and tenderness for the people and land of Israel as does Halevi's great philosophical work, which is in reality a glowing panegyric of the Jews, their history and traditions, their land and language. Their sins and failings disappear in the love he bears them, in his sympathy and understanding of their fate and suffering.

The *Kuzari* is Jewish throughout. There is not the slightest trace of alien influence in its pages. Although composed in the Arabic language, the spoken and written idiom of the Jews in Spain, the book is as uniquely and characteristically Hebraic as if it were the inspired product of the land and language of the prophets. For Judah Halevi was all Jew, superbly and harmoniously Jewish in all his thoughts and feelings. He was not influenced by his environment nor affected by his keeping pure and unadulterated the holy flame ignited at his birth. Traditional Judaism—the Judaism of the Bible and the Talmud—was to him the whole and only truth, and to him it mattered little if that truth clashed with the so-called truths of the philosophers. When he was confronted with the conflicting ideas of the Hellenic thinkers, his pithy reply was:

> Be not enticed by the wisdom of the Greeks,
> Which only bears fair flowers, but no fruit.

The *Kuzari* took its name from one of the most romantic stories in the otherwise drab and prosaic life of the Jews in the medieval world. For decades this dramatic episode lived and throbbed in the poet-philosopher's mind, until finally it took shape in his great work. In his youth Halevi must have heard the story of the conversion of the Khazar kingdom to Judaism in 750, and the correspondence between the last of its princes and Hasdai Ibn Shaprut (915–990), the scholar-diplomat at the court of the Caliph Al-Rhaman and the head of the Jewish community in Spain. He may even have known personally some of the Khazar descendants who took refuge in Spain after the destruction of their kingdom in 1016 by the Russians.

With the story of the Khazar conversion lingering in his mind, it was but natural that Halevi, poet and lover of his people that he was, should be set off on a train of thought that led him to write his book. Always alert for the defense of Judaism he could have found no more fitting theme than the decision of King Bulan, when considering a change of faiths, to reject the triumphant religions of Christianity or Mohammedanism in favor of that of the despised and persecuted Jews.

Halevi dramatizes the story of King Bulan's conversion by telling of his persistent admonition from heaven that, while his intention was good and acceptable to God, his deeds were not. At the very opening of the story Halevi makes the point for Judaism that God cannot be served by good intentions only but by all the actions of one's life. To set his mind at ease, the Khazar monarch invited a philosopher and representative of Christianity and of Moham- medanism, the two major religions of his realm, to discuss the merits of their respective faiths. He had not, however, called for a Jew, because of the generally despised status of the Jewish race. It was not until after the two theologians referred reverently to the Holy Scriptures of Israel that he also summoned a rabbi.

The philosopher is easily and quickly disposed of. He teaches that motive and purity of heart are all that count and that, possess- ing these, one can make his own religion. He speaks in abstractions of reason and speculation as the only way to pure religion. The king, however, is dissatisfied, since he knows how pure and just his ways have been, and yet God has not approved of him. The king is equally dissatisfied with the Christian and Moslem theo- logians. They speak dogmatically of love, faith, and humanity, but they are fighting and killing each other in the name of serving God —an oblique reference by Halevi to the First Crusade.

When the Jew's turn came, he did not speak of theology or philosophy or the nature of God, but only of God's activity in the history of Israel. It is this history in which he professes his faith. He speaks as if the Jews had no faith apart from their history; but their history is the history of the deeds and actions of God; it is history viewed as something that takes place between heaven and earth. To follow Martin Buber: "He [the Jew] does not believe that it is possible to reach the point the king wants to reach on the paths of theological dogma . . . as to become like the Creator in wisdom and justice . . . but from the living witness of His rule in human history." In other words, the Jew, Halevi's spokesman, takes his stand on history. The fundamental difference between Judaism, Christianity and Mohammedanism, and philosophy, he maintains, is not a difference of creed and doctrine, marked though that difference be, nor is it a difference in explanations of the existence of God. For Judaism, he protests, is neither a philosophy nor a theology, but a factual religion, a historic manifestation of God which a multitude of six hundred thousand Israelites saw, felt, and personally experienced. The Jews were not persuaded into the existence of God by creed or doctrine or philosophic argumentation, but they experienced His Being by direct, personal contact with Him, as it were. God spoke to Moses; He redeemed them from Egypt; He revealed Himself on Sinai; he gave them the Ten Commandments; He led them through the wilderness for forty years; He sent them the manna; He fought their battles; He brought them to the land of Canaan; He raised them to a great nation and a kingdom of priests.

It was Halevi's contention that the Jews had a more direct and accurate knowledge of God than the philosophers, who, having no verified tradition to support them, are like blind men feeling their way in the dark. Unlike Saadia, he does not hold that the belief in creation out of nothing is fundamental to the whole concept of God. "The question of Eternity and Creation," he says, "is obscure, while the arguments are evenly balanced. The theory of Creation derives greater weight from the prophetic tradition of Adam, Noah and Moses, which is more deserving of credence than mere speculation. If, after all, a believer in the Law finds himself compelled to admit an eternal matter and the existence of many worlds prior to this one, this would not impair his belief that this world was created at a certain epoch, and that Adam and Noah were the first human beings."

He enters into a lengthy discussion on the anthropomorphisms of the Bible, which he regarded as necessary means of dispelling the corporeal sensuousness of the Deity. God, says Halevi, cannot be known by means of rational proof; He may be apprehended but not comprehended by the human mind. Metaphors and figures of speech are a convenient method by which to interpret the gross materiality of the Deity one often finds in the Bible. He defends free will against the Epicureans and Fatalists, both of whom teach a doctrine opposed to the spirit of Judaism. It is given to man to fashion his own life, be it good or bad, and there is a reckoning in the Hereafter. "It does not agree with common sense," Halevi says, "that when a man perishes, body and soul should disappear with him." He taught that immortality is the prerogative of all men who live a pure and righteous life and is not the reward only of those who acquire wisdom, as taught by Aristotle. Although other religions make much greater ado about reward and punishment and lay greater stress on immortality than does the Bible, there are ample allusions in the Prophets to the immortality of the soul and to reward and punishment after death to justify a Jewish belief in them.

Through his *alter ego*, the rabbi, our poet-philosopher pours out his soul before the king in a series of conversations which make his book a memorable milestone in Jewish philosophical literature. He instructs his royal master in the special place Israel occupies in the scheme of Divine Providence. Again and again he reminds him of the vital connection between God and the Jewish people. They are the elect of God, the heart of nations, His peculiar possession. The Divine Influence is with them; other nations may acquire learning and wisdom but to Israel alone was prophecy given. The good deeds of all men will be rewarded, but priority belongs to Israel, for they stand near God and for His sake they bore shame and reproach and exile. If there were no Israelites there would be no Torah. They did not derive their high position from Moses, but Moses received his for their sake. We are not called the people of Moses but the people of God. When the king is irked by the rabbi's high appraisal of Israel and refers to their worship of the golden calf, Halevi's quick retort is that some excuse may be found for them since, of six hundred thousand souls, the number of those who worshiped the idol was less than three thousand.

But the sufferings of the Jews, their poverty and degradation—how can these be explained in view of their piety and virtue and God's special care of them, the king urges. But the best of other religions, retorts the rabbi, boasts of these things. Does it not glorify him who said, Who smites thee on the right cheek, turn to him the left also, and he who takes away thy coat let him have thy shirt also? The nations of the earth glory in the poverty and humiliation of the teachers of their faith and not in their strength and power. Besides, Israel's suffering is voluntarily endured, for if they wanted to be friends and equals of their oppressors they could do so by speaking but one word. The travail of Israel in exile, the rabbi insists, and all the vicissitudes which come their way have the effect of purifying the spirit of Torah within them, purging them of all dross, and refining the pure metal, so that the Divine Influence may be made manifest unto the world.

In glowing poetic terms from the lips of his spokesman, the rabbi, Judah Halevi describes the high standing of the Holy Land as the abode of the *Shekhinah,* the font of prophecy, the source of all the spiritual good and blessings that come to the world. Step by step, in an effort to win the king's love for Zion, he dramatizes all the high moments of her history, her epic grandeur in the days when other nations, although believing in laws not recognized by the Torah, sent pilgrimages to her and honored her and fought to possess her. All roads lead to Palestine, but none from her. Whosoever prophesied did so either in the Holy Land or concerning her. She is the center of the world, a decisive factor in space and time. Even today all nations love and revere the land, although the *Shekhinah* no longer dwells there.

The king, who listens patiently to what he is told of the blessing and holiness of the land, is quite prepared to admit that, in Israel, God had selected suitable material from the human race with which to achieve His purpose; but he finds it difficult to understand why any part of the earth itself is to be chosen as the land of God above any other. In answer, the rabbi replies that the Divinity selects the most suitable terrain in which to accomplish his purpose. You will have no difficulty in understanding, he says, that one country may have higher qualifications than others; that there are places in which particular plants, metals, or animals are found which are not found in other places. The noble vines need the special soil that is more favorable to their growth than any other, although they still must be planted and cared for properly in order to produce the golden wine. The vines are the Chosen People, the terrain is the land of Israel, the cultivation is the work which must be performed in the land of Israel and cannot be performed anywhere else. No other place could share the Divine Influence, just as no other place might be fitted to produce good wine. There is a primeval relationship between the Chosen People and the Chosen Land so that the Jew can most perfectly serve God by spending the whole of his active life in Palestine. What is done in the lands of exile is necessarily imperfect, since perfect action is only possible in the perfect land, which is Palestine.

The poet, as though he were listening to his own accusing conscience, feels ashamed and humiliated when the king of the Khazars replies to the rabbi's enthusiasm about Palestine by asking why he does not personally go there and make it his abode, in life and death. He reminds the rabbi of his God-serving ancestors, who made their ascent to Zion and did not leave it in dearth and famine, and, when they were exiled, directed that their bones be buried there. Halevi hears echoed in his heart the words he has his rabbi say to the king. The rabbi admits that all his protestations of love for Zion—"Have mercy on Zion, for it is the house of our life"—when not accompanied by action are of no more value than the chatter of starlings. Bitterly he admits that the Jews are remiss and that they prefer the life of craven slaves in the galut to the freedom and independence of their own land. Halevi no doubt had in mind the Jews of his own day, but he pointed to the Jews of Babylon, when the call came for their return to the homeland, only the poor and the God-fearing heeded, while the rich and prosperous remained in captivity, with their successful businesses. "No," cries out the poet-patriot, "Jerusalem can only be rebuilt when Israel yearns for it to such an extent that they embrace her stones and dust."

After the discussion of the greatness of the Holy Land is closed, the author finds it necessary to introduce the king, in a series of dissertations by the rabbi, to the faith and practices of the Jewish religion, which are strange to him. Halevi rather skilfully alludes to the fact that, unlike Christianity and Mohammedanism, in which faith is discharged by the mumbling of certain words, Judaism requires the active exercise of the whole life and regulates one's conduct to the smallest detail. He contrasts somewhat caustically the heavenward gaze and outward piety of the followers of other religions to the attitude of the Jewish believer—his submission to God, his patience under suffering, his devotion to Torah, which sanctifies every act and consecrates every thought.

Halevi is unsparing in his attack on the Karaites, opponents of traditional Judaism, who, in his day, the middle of the eleventh century, were very active in most Islamic countries. He criticizes what he calls the perverse doctrine of those who reject the rabbinic interpretation of the Bible, without which, he contends, its meaning is virtually incomprehensible. The view of the rabbis, he says is based on the tradition of the Prophets, while the opinion of the others is based on speculation. There is harmony and unanimity among the Sages, while there is perpetual strife and discord among the Karaites. The rabbinic tradition is a source of comfort and peace, while the Karaites are always in doubt and confusion. The writer has strong feelings on the subject, and if, in discussing it he is more controversial than poetic, he must be excused on the score that his book is a polemical work which, in the style of the Middle Ages, gives no quarter to the opposing viewpoint. The author concludes his argument with an enthusiastic survey of the rabbinic authorities of the Talmud, exclaiming, "Only he is hostile to it who does not know it, and never endeavors to study it."

There is no perceptible difference between the socio-ethical philosophy of Halevi and the ethical outlook of most other medieval Jewish thinkers. It is based on the teachings of the Bible supplemented by the wisdom of the rabbis and their interpretation of the Talmud. Man, he says, is not a lone solitary creature, but is part of a whole. He is not intended to live for and by himself, but as a segment of a society. Spiritual or moral perfection is attainable only when one merges his life with the life of the community. United with those around him, one enjoys safety at small expense. Political duties, he teaches, are intimated in the Biblical regulations on tithes and imposts. It is the duty of the individual to live for the community, bear hardships, and even risk death for it.

Prayer, says our poet-philosopher, is no less a social than a religious function. While it is well to pray in the privacy of one's home and heart, one prays best with the community. A person who prays for himself is like one who retires alone into his house, refusing to assist his fellow citizens in the repair of their walls. It has been ordained, therefore, that the individual recite the prayers with the community, and, if possible, in a community of not less than ten persons. He is critical of asceticism, which in his day was considerably in vogue among the Christians and the Mohammedans. The Divine Law, he says, does not approve of voluntary abasement and suppression of one's physical desires and pleasures. It rather calls for moderation—that we give every physical and mental faculty its due without overburdening one at the expense of another. According to the Jewish view, a pious servant of the Lord is not one who detaches himself from the world or flees from it, but one who loves the world, with all its gifts and opportunities, because they afford him the means of deserving the world to come. Judah Halevi regards suicide as an anti-social act because, he says, no rational being seeks death voluntarily. If Saul killed himself, it was not to seek death but to escape torture and derision.

In the fifth, and concluding part of the book, Halevi discourses lengthily, through the rabbi, on a number of subjects to which he has referred briefly before. He reverts to the subject of Creation and warns the king not to be confused by the sophistications of the philosophers. The difference, he says, between the philosophers and the believers is that, according to the former, the world came about by chance, while the latter ascribe the creation of the world to the Divine Will. He calls the soul a spiritual substance which cannot be encompassed by space; it endures forever and is not subject to decay. It is distinct from and independent of the body. Old age attacks the body but not the soul; the activity of the body is limited, but not that of the soul.

Judah Halevi may be said to have been a philosopher by intuition. If he did not use the actual word in describing his philosophy, its use is implied in his critique of reason and the senses. The senses, he says, cannot perceive the essence of things. They can only perceive the external and accidental peculiarities of things. Our intellect, grounded in matter, cannot penetrate to the true knowledge of things. God therefore planted in man a special sight, an inner eye—imagination Halevi calls it—which enables him to see beyond the concrete. The Prophets possessed this faculty to the fullest extent—they saw the divine world with the inner eye. They saw the attributes of God with their feeling, imagination, and poetic insight. The corporeal qualities they ascribed to Him harmonized completely with the inner sense with which they regarded the Deity. Halevi, through the character of the rabbi, censures the philosophers and scientists, especially those who attempt to attribute ideas to the Bible. He reveals striking familiarity with the Greek and Mohammedan philosophies, and displays considerable courage in his critique of the Koran, "which strongly inclines toward limiting man's own freedom of will almost to a vanishing point."

Later the rabbi reverts again to his overwhelming love for the Holy Land and his desire to go to Jerusalem. The king, loath to see him go, points out the dangers of the voyage and argues that with a pure heart and mind, one can serve God anywhere. To the king's arguments our poet-philosopher replies that heart and soul are perfectly pure and immaculate in the place believed to be specially selected by God. The king is favorably impressed with his mentor's resolve to betake himself to the Holy Land and, without interposing further objections permits the rabbi to fulfill his heart's desire.

Judah Halevi's actual romantic voyage to Palestine, discussed at such length through his character of the rabbi, introduced a new phase into his already rich and abundant life. The troubadour of God and love added a new facet to his poetic genius. Judah Halevi may be said to have been the only great medieval Hebrew poet in whom we hear the song of nature. The medieval Jew knew little of nature. He lived an urban life among merchants, books, and scholars. It was not so in Bible times, when the Jews' love for nature radiated from the Scriptures in a hundred lovely guises. Alexandder Humboldt, a great German naturalist, proclaimed the 104th Psalm one of the most magnificent nature poems in all literature. But what Jew in the Middle Ages, with his life in constant danger, had a chance to cultivate a love and feeling for nature?

When Judah Halevi had left Spain and was at sea on his way to the Holy Land, his poetic muse caught the song of the waves, which he transmuted in his own inimitable way. In "A Storm at Sea," he gives us a superb word picture of the vessel, which he humorously calls a "coffin," swaying and staggering in an unruly sea like a bird caught in a tempest. It is one of the most beautiful poems portraying the might and terror of the sea. Although the poem is too long to quote, the first stanza will give an idea of the writer's mood and feeling:

> The waves roar
> As the wheels roll o'er;
> They fall and roar
> On the face of the sea.
> The heavens grow black,
> For each wave as a stack
> Rises up, then rears back
> Till the depth you can see;
> The cauldron boils o'er,
> With a hiss and a roar,
> And none can restore
> Its tranquility.
> And mighty waves hide,
> And waters divide,
> And a mountain with pride
> Rises near a valley.
> And my heart stands still,
> But bows down to His will
> Who to Moses gave skill
> To divide the Red Sea.

Hardly anything is known of the poet's last great adventure—not even whether he ever reached the goal of his passionate journey. But we do know that wonderful poems full of love and longing for Zion blossomed in his mind on his way to the Holy Land. He visited Alexandria, Damietta, Cairo, Tyre, and Damascus. Everywhere he was received with great honor, and attempts were made to detain him. He was feted and toasts were drunk to him from golden goblets in a vain effort to persuade him to change his mind. The poet immortalized his new friends and benefactors in unstinting lines. But their entreaties that he abandon his journey fell on deaf ears. His love for Zion obsessed him and he would not be swerved from his goal. A holy compulsion drove him on to his "highest moment."

Did he realize his "highest moment?" After Damascus, the poet's steps are lost in an unsolved mystery. On the basis of disputed evidence, Israel Zinberg, the Yiddish literary historian, maintains that after a fruitless journey Judah Halevi returned to Spain, where he died shortly afterward. But even if he did reach his goal, what he found in the Holy City must have been far different from the glory and splendor he had pictured in his imagination. The City of David was in the possession of Christians and was not too friendly to Jewish pilgrims. It is altogether possible that his passionate lament, quoted below, whose effect Nina Salaman says that fifty translations have not spoiled; was written in chagrin and disappointment as Halevi approached Zion's holy mount:

> Zion! wilt thou not ask if peace be with thy captives
> That seek thy peace—that are the remnant of thy flocks?
>
> From west and east, from north and south—the greeting
> "Peace" from far and near, take thou from every side;
>
> And greetings from the captive of desire giving his tears
>   like dew
> Of Hermon, and longing to let them fall upon thine hills.
>
> To wail for thy affliction I am like the jackals; and when
>   I dream
> Of the return of thy captivity, I am a harp for thy songs.

Whether or not the great poet reached the Holy Land and composed his deathless lament upon approaching the sacred mountain, legend says that he did, and that line after line of heart-breaking beauty filled the silence of the night. But little, the legend goes on, did the singer know that he was overheard and that behind him a Saracen stood, with jealousy and hatred in his heart. Himself a poet, he envied the fire and passion of the stranger's song. Spurring forward his horse, he struck down the old man with a savage blow of his lance. The poet fell back, mortally wounded, with his immortal song unfinished.

Moses Maimonides

IN MOSES MAIMONIDES, familiar to the great mass of Jews as the Rambam, Judaism produced one of its greatest personalities of all time. His genius and achievements were not limited to his own age and people, but are world-wide in scope and influence. To millions of Jews he is an exalted scholar and teacher. They study his writings, ponder his thoughts, and conclude their morning devotions with his Thirteen Articles of Faith. Indeed, so great is the Jews' love and reverence for their twelfth-century sage and teacher that they liken him to Moses, "the man of God," and when he died, they inscribed upon his tombstone, "From Moses [the son of Amram] to Moses [the son of Maimon], there was none like unto Moses."

His literary activity was stupendous. He was the most prolific of Jewish writers—a unique, many-sided genius who absorbed all knowledge and labored in many fields. As jurist, philosopher, and scientist, he wrote learnedly on the Bible and the Talmud and on logic, mathematics, and astronomy. Storms of bigoted opposition raged about him, and once not long after his death Jewish obscurantists united with Christian fanatics in making a public bonfire of one of his philosophical works. But while the parchments were burned, the spirit and reputation of the writer remained unblemished, and to this day when one of his volumes accidentally falls to the ground it is picked up and reverently kissed, as if it were the Bible or a tome of the Talmud.

Moses Maimonides and the time and place of his birth were perfectly matched. Had he lived a hundred years or so later he might have been a statesman or a financier under one or another of the Spanish Christian monarchs, and *The Guide for the*

Perplexed would never have been written. Had he been born and lived in medieval France or Germany, with a single-hearted devotion to the Talmud, he would still have composed codes and commentaries but not in the form and spirit of his *Mishneh Torah*. A kind Providence decreed that he see the light of day in Mohammedan Spain, at the time of his birth one of the most tolerant and enlightened countries in Europe, where men were free and unrestrained in their mental and spiritual aspirations.

Moses Maimonides was born in Cordova, the beautiful capital of Andalusia on the Guadalguivir, on March 30, 1135 *(Nisan* 14, 4895). He hailed from a long line of distinguished rabbis and scholars, his father, Maimon, having been a *dayyan* (judge) at the rabbinical court of the city. Maimon, a highly cultured man who knew his Bible and the Talmud, was also proficient in the secular sciences and the literature of the Mohammedans. It was a proud and illustrious family that Moses was born into, one that traced its descent through Judah the Patriarch, compiler of the Mishnah, to the royal house of King David.

Cordova, Moses Maimonides' birthplace, was an ideal city for students in pursuit of knowledge. Under the Umayyad dynasty, which ruled Spain for almost three hundred years, the Andalusian capital in learning, wealth, and cultured refinement, was the jewel of the vast Arab empire—indeed, the "jewel of the world," a German Benedictine nun called her. She rivaled Bagdad in the East in the splendor of her life, in the magnificence of her buildings, and in population, which at the high noon of her prosperity numbered several hundred thousands. But what gave the city her greatest fame and distinction were her liberal atmosphere, broad tolerance, and the fraternal spirit in which Arab, Jew, and Christian met and lived together. The Moravides were the political masters of Andalusia, and they loved learning and cultivated the arts and sciences. They were strong in their faith but not to the point of fanaticism; they prized learning above conquest, and the scholar above the man of war.

It was in such free and cultured atmosphere that Moses the son of Maimon was born and spent his early childhood. His father was his first teacher and instructed him in the sacred and secular sciences, without, however, denying him the tutelage of other scholars, possibly Arabic, who led him through the course of studies usual at that time. Extraordinary diligence and native genius combined in the young student in perfect harmony, so that at an early age he was already an acknowledged scholar, able to steer his own course without the help of teachers.

Fate, however, willed that Cordova, which witnessed the blossoming of young Maimonides' genius, should not see its full maturity and development, for a change of political dynasties drove the Maimon family from their home and sent them into exile. The blow came from the north, in the wake of the bigoted Berber Almohades, who, although at one with the Jews in their belief in the absolute unity and incorporeity of God, were yet fanatically hostile to both Jews and Christians and sought their conversion or destruction. In rapid, successful campaigns, they swept through North Africa and Moslem Spain, compelling the closing of all synagogues and churches, and making the acceptance of Islam a condition for residence in the land.

The Jews suffered irretrievable losses at the hands of the North African hordes. Their magnificent synagogues were destroyed, their renowned academies of learning were closed, and an end was put to the labors of Samuel ha-Nagid and Hasdai Ibn Shaprut, of an earlier generation; and the Jews, without being physically molested, were offered the choice of the Koran or banishment. Some Jews reconciled themselves to the conversion demanded, giving mere lip service to the religion that was forced upon them while in their hearts and homes remaining loyal to the faith of their fathers and carrying out all its precepts. Only the most conscientious among them disdained the religious deception and submitted to the alternative of exile. Maimon and his family belonged to the latter group of the Jews of Cordova, and, sacrificing their home and fortune, they left the country. Young Maimonides was not quite thirteen years old when he was compelled to leave the Andalusia he loved, for the hard life of an exile.

History does not record the itinerary of the Maimon family, but no matter what frontiers they crossed the youthful student's passion for knowledge did not cool for a moment. How ruefully he must have looked back to the great library that lined the walls of his father's study! But nature had endowed him with such an unfailing memory that he never forgot anything he ever read or studied. He made his debut as a writer on philosophical and mathematical subjects, probably at the age of sixteen, with *An Introduction to Logic* and *A Treatise on the Calendar,* of no great importance or significance in themselves but marking the trend of the future scholar's mind.

After years of wandering, the roving Maimons made their home in Fez, the Moroccan capital, at one time a center of talmudic learning presided over by the celebrated Isaac Alfasi. The years (1159–1165) Moses Maimonides spent in his new abode were years of comparative peace and security. The fanatical Almohades were more tolerant toward religious nonconformists in their own country than they were in the territories they conquered, where they stamped out "heresy" with an unrestrained hand. Maimonides found in the city an alert, active Jewish community, with schools and scholars, like himself, devoted to the pursuit of Jewish and secular learning. He resumed, or rather continued, his literary work, writing in the fashion of the day commentaries upon the Talmud, not many of which, unfortunately, were preserved. In the tradition of his forebears, he added a medical course to his several other studies.

In Morocco, at the age of twenty-three, Maimonides began his work on his *Mishnah Commentary,* one of the great literary masterpieces, which took him ten years to complete and which is universally regarded as one of the most brilliant achievements of rabbinic learning. A collection of laws compiled and edited by Rabbi Judah the Patriarch (135–220 C.E.), the Mishnah had to wait almost a thousand years for a commentator. In the meantime, a resurgence of intolerance in Morocco, with many acts of violence against the Jews, resulting in the brutal murder of his colleague and teacher, Rabbi Judah Ibn Shoshan, forced Maimonides to interrupt his work and come to the assistance of his hard-pressed brothers. At a time when the Jews were crushed by a burden of sin for having outwardly to profess a religion which inwardly they scorned and rejected, Moses Maimonides, only twenty-five years of age, but already an acknowledged authority, wrote his famous, *Ma'amar Kiddush Hashem* (Essay on the Sanctification of God), known also as *Iggeret Hashemad* (Letter Concerning Apostasy). Contrary to a contemporary rabbi who condemned any tampering with the Jewish religious law, even in appearance and to save one's life, Maimonides, without denying that there was something to reproach in a policy of pretended submission, quotes an impressive array of authorities who had not disdained to save their lives by feigning heathenism in times of persecution. He differentiates between the conversionary demands upon the Jews in times involving idolatry and those made under the Moslem formula. He, therefore, concludes: "Any Jew who, after uttering the Moslem formula, wishes to observe the whole 613 precepts in the secrecy of his home, may do so without hindrance. . . . If a man asks me shall I be slain or utter the formula of Islam? I answer, Utter the formula and live."

Maimonides, however, also counseled that "we should go forth from these lands and go to a place where we could fulfill the Law without compulsion and without fear"—advice that he himself was before long to follow. The *Letter*, which was written in Arabic and which he ordered to be kept in strict secrecy, could not long escape the attention of the Moslem authorities, with results that Maimonides knew only too well. His position was extremely hazardous; he remembered the tragedy of Ibn Shoshan and was anxious to escape a similar fate. But what could have moved him to sail with his family for the Holy Land, which was then in the Latin Kingdom of Jerusalem and was no safer for Jews than Morocco? He found Palestine a waste land, without schools or scholars to refresh and stimulate his mind. What Jews there were in the country were poor and scattered, most of them petty traders and workmen. Therefore, after remaining in the country about a year and visiting its holy places, he settled in Egypt, where he hoped for a better opportunity for his expanding scholarly ambitions and energies.

At the time of Moses Maimonides, Egypt was for the Jews the only oasis in an almost universal wilderness of intolerance. In a time of religious persecution in Spain, fanatical pressure in Morocco, and unremitting oppression in European countries, the Jews lived in comparative peace and security under the Fatimid rule in the land of their ancient persecutors. They enjoyed a well-organized community life of their own, resembling that of their Babylonian brethren under Persian domination. They had their schools, scholars, and lay leaders, who bore high-sounding titles. The Nagid, counterpart of the Babylonian Exilarch, was in charge of the political affairs of the Egyptian Jews and enjoyed considerable standing and influence at the court of the caliphs.

When Moses Maimonides made Egypt his home after his years of wandering, he chose Fostat, with her sparse Jewish population as a place of residence, rather than Cairo or Alexandria, with their many more Jews. He hoped to find in the smaller community the peace and quiet he needed for the completion of his *Mishnah Commentary,* which he had begun years before in Morocco. However, the peace he had longed for was not granted him, for no sooner was he settled in his new home than a series of misfortunes befell him—first, the death of his father; and then, before he had recovered from this blow, his brother David, a businessman and the supporter of the family, was lost in a shipwreck in the Indian Ocean.

The death of his brother plunged Maimonides into deep and lasting grief. In a letter to a friend years later, he wrote: "It is the heaviest evil that has befallen me. . . . For a full year I lay on my couch stricken with fever and despair. Eight years have passed, and still I mourn. He grew up on my knees; he was my brother, my pupil. He was engaged in business and made money that I might stay home and study. He was learned in the Bible and the Torah, and was an accomplished grammarian. My joy was to see him; now my joy was turned to darkness. . . . I should have died in my affliction but for the Law, which is my delight, and for philosophy, which makes me forget to moan."

Upon the death of his brother, Maimonides inherited the responsibility of providing for his own family and that of his brother. He gave lectures in philosophy to a select group of students and served as rabbi, judge, and teacher of the Jews of Fostat. But adhering to the rabbinic injunction, he would not accept compensation for instruction, and lived on the edge of poverty. Fortunately, however, he had studied medicine in his youth, and he now put this training to practical use. Before long he became a widely sought-after physician. In 1168, while engaged in his exacting professional and communal duties, he completed his first great work, the *Mishnah Commentary*, written in the Arabic vernacular with Hebrew characters.

The *Mishnah Commentary* is the first product of Maimonides' mature genius, and it established his reputation as a great figure in Jewish learning and scholarship, although he was only thirty-three years of age. While ostensibly a commentary upon the Mishnah, it is in reality a philosophy of Judaism in its widest ramifications. While he elucidated obscure words and passages in the Mishnah, his greatest concern was with its religious and ethical content. He prefaced every one of its six tractates with comprehensive forewords and provided the Mishnah as a whole with an illuminating introduction, in which he explained the history, character, and structure of the first biblical code. He prefaced his commentary on the Sayings of the Fathers, the most widely known tractate of the Mishnah with his famous Eight Chapters, which is an adaptation of Aristotelian psychology and moral philosophy in Hebraic garb. He seized upon the opening words of the tenth chapter in Sanhedrin— "All Israel have a share in the world to come"—and formulated his celebrated Thirteen Articles of Faith.

Maimonides' reputation extended to the far-flung reaches of the Arabian empire, so that Jews not only in Egypt but in distant parts of the Moslem world turned to the Fostat sage in all matters pertaining to their religious and communal life. The religious persecution of Jews which had driven Maimonides from Spain and

Morocco had spread to other countries under the Crescent, especially to the southwestern part of Arabia, where thousands of Jews lived in a region whose legendary history went back to King Solomon. Like their North African brethren, the Jews of Yemen were confronted with the choice of apostasy or martyrdom. Internal dissension aggravated the plight of the troubled Jews. Unscrupulous renegades attempted to present Mohammedanism as a religion divinely ordained to supersede Judaism. A young visionary proclaimed himself a precursor of the Messiah, urging the Jews to prepare for his imminent coming. Fortunately there were clearheaded Jews who were not deluded. Jacob al-Fayyumi, the most learned and respected member of the Jewish community of Yemen, appealed to Maimonides for advice in the crisis.

Iggeret Teman, the letter of counsel and consolation Maimonides addressed to the Jews of Yemen, in its sympathy and tenderness is one of the most striking of the philosopher's minor writings. He sought to raise the downcast spirits of his suffering brethren by reminding them that the Jews are a unique and indestructible people and that, while persecution will never cease, neither can Israel ever be destroyed. With unbounded love and depth of feeling he appealed to his harassed people: "Our brethren of the House of Israel scattered to the remote regions of the globe, it is your duty to strengthen one another . . . and let not persecution frighten you, because it is only a test from God to see how strong your faith in Him is." He ridiculed the claim of the apostates that Judaism had been superseded by Mohammedanism. Not the least interesting part of the letter is Maimonides' list, recorded for the first time, of the bogus Messiahs in Persia, Morocco, and Andalusia, who had brought considerable suffering upon the Jews and who in the end turned out to be nothing more than irresponsible madmen. The letter accomplished its purpose—the spirits of the sorely tried Jews were raised and the persecution soon ended— and Moses Maimonides was the hero of their deliverance. Indeed, so great was their gratitude that they included his name, while he was still alive, in the Kaddish, an honor formerly accorded to the Babylonian Exilarch.

In 1180, twelve years after the completion of the *Mishnah Commentary,* Maimonides climaxed his career in rabbinic scholarship with his *Mishneh Torah* (the Second Torah), a complete compendium of the biblical and rabbinic law, religion, and ethics. It is also known as *Yad ha-Hazakah,* an allusion to the last verse in Deuteronomy. According to Maimonides' own statement, he devoted ten long years to the task, working day and night. But, as Graetz observes, "Really, time stands in no relation to the magnitude of the performance," for it represents the greatest attempt ever made by any one man to bring order, clarity, and coherence into such a titanic maze of confusion as the Talmud. The artist and the scientist are fused in the *Mishneh Torah;* the philosopher and the theologian join hands in its pages. For the work is more than a prodigious compendium of rabbinic jurisprudence; it is a survey of the theology, philosophy, and ethics in their relation to the faith and practice of the Jewish people. It was a novel and daring attempt to make the philosophical concepts of religion as much an integral part of Judaism as the detailed regulations of its ceremonies and rituals. Thus, the first part, *Sefer Hamadda* (the Book of Cognition), belongs more properly to the domain of philosophy since it deals with metaphysical concepts of God, providence, free will, prophecy, and such subjects. It is not surprising that so unique a procedure should have stirred up criticism and controversy. The rabbis were critical of Maimonides' rationalistic tendencies, his failure to supply sources, and his disregard of talmudic references to omens, amulets, and astrology; some of them even charged him with trying to supersede the Talmud.

His critics claimed ample justification for their charge was to be found in his own words in the Introduction to *Mishneh Torah.* In explaining his motives for writing the *Mishneh Torah* he asserts that both the Babylonian and Palestinian Talmuds were unintelligible to all but the scholars and that it requires special knowledge to divine "the things permitted and forbidden, and concerning all the other commandments of the Law. Therefore, I, Moses, the son of Maimon, the Spaniard, have studied all these works and made up my mind to collect the results derived from them in precise language and concise manner, so that the entire Oral Law may be made accessible to everyone without any arguments . . . in clear and unmistakable terms in entire accord with the decisions . . . existing since the time of Rabbi Judah the Patriarch, compiler of the Mishnah until the present day. In short, my intention is that no man shall have any need to resort to any other book on any point of Jewish law. . . . For this reason I have called the name of this book *Mishneh Torah,* for all that a man has to do, is to read first the Written Law and follow it up by this work, and he will know the entire Oral Law without the need of reading any other book."

But far from setting himself above the Talmud or trying to supplant it, Maimonides had by his Code clarified and simplified the Oral Law and greatly contributed to its deeper study, so that to this day the two, the Talmud and the Code, are studied as one. What Maimonides had in mind was to help the ordinary Jew, untrained in the talmudic dialectics, who, in his efforts to know and observe the law, found himself confused by the countless claims and counterclaims of the rabbis. Maimonides would have been embarrassed—even angry—had he known that his Code, even as the Talmud itself, was to become the subject of numerous commentaries. The late Alexander Marx cites a bibliography of commentaries on the Code, compiled by Adolf Jellinek in 1893, listing no less than 220 titles. Due to the popularity and intensive study of the Code, the number of commentaries has by now considerably increased.

Sefer ha-Mitzvot (the Book of Commandments), is an introductory volume to Maimonides' stupendous Code. Before approaching his main work, his orderly and methodical mind impelled him to arrange in systematic manner the traditionally agreed upon 613 commandments of the Pentateuch, 248 positive and 365 negative. Various attempts at tabulating the precepts of the Torah had been made through the ages; but, dissatisfied with the result, the Rambam decided upon his own enumeration. He did not, however, follow the order of the commandments as they apppear in the Bible, but devised his own arrangement, giving priority to the idealogical teachings of the Torah and to its ritual laws. Maimonides wrote *Sefer ha-Mitzvot* in the Arabic language, in contrast to *Mishneh Torah,* which he composed in Mishnaic Hebrew.

After paying his debt to traditional Judaism with his *Mishnah Commentary,* the *Book of Commandments,* and *Mishneh Torah,* Maimonides turned to helping those Jews who, though well versed in the Torah and loyal to their faith, were baffled by the seemingly irrational teachings of their religion and especially by the literal interpretation of the Bible. They were puzzled and confused by the inconsistency they were led to believe existed between the life of reason and the precepts of the Torah. Such men, Maimonides felt, must not be allowed to drift away and become ultimately lost to Judaism, but should be shown the fallacy of the idea that the only alternative to religion without reason was reason without religion. It was for such perplexed Jews that Moses Maimonides wrote his *Dalalat al-Hairin* (The Guide for the Perplexed). The book was written in the Arabic language, but, having regard for the religious sensitivities of the extreme Mohammedan traditionalists, Maimonides used Hebrew characters.

While his *Mishnah Commentary* and the *Mishneh Torah,* established Maimonides' reputation as a great talmudic authority, *The Guide for the Perplexed* made him world-famous as a philosopher. It is the climax of his literary-philosophic career—the first Jewish work since the Bible to become a part of world literature. Until the opening of the eighteenth century, the *Guide* was the only channel through which post-biblical Judaism flowed to the non-Jewish world. The Jewish philosophical literature which preceded the *Guide* is rich and stimulating but, because it was written primarily for Jews and with a strong national flavor, it failed to arrest the attention of the non-Jewish public. It is the unusual wealth of thought and ideas and the novelty of its approach to a philosophy of religion that made the *Guide* timeless in its appeal and influence. In European countries there was scarcely a Christian scholar of any importance who did not take a position for or against the work of the "Egyptian Moses." "Maimonides was the teacher of the whole Middle Ages," Abraham Geiger concludes his study of the medieval Jewish philosopher, "and every enlightened mind that arose later drew eagerly from him, found stimulation in him, and gladly acknowledged himself his pupil."

The Guide for the Perplexed is one of the world's classics of which it may be said that it became more popular in translation than in the language in which is was originally written. Had not a redeemer appeared in the person of Samuel Ibn Tibbon, of Lunel, who translated it in the author's lifetime and under his supervision, *The Guide for the Perplexed* might have suffered the fate of many another neglected Jewish classic which had to wait for centuries before being discovered. Shortly after the time of Maimonides, Arabic influence ceased to be a determining factor in Jewish creative activity and its place was filled by the influence of Jewish communities in Christian countries; and it was in these communities, notably those in southern France, that the *Guide* enlisted its greatest following. Indeed, so great was their enthusiasm that ten years after Ibn Tibbon's translation a new Hebrew version of the book was made by Judah ben Solomon al-Harizi. The style of the second translation is more polished than that of the first, but Samuel Ibn Tibbon's version is regarded as the more authoritative and is more generally used, since it carries the author's *imprimatur*.

The *Guide* owes its origin to the author's chance acquaintance with a young man, Joseph Ibn Aknin, a physician and a talented writer, who wrote Arabic poetry in the style of the Koran and Hebrew verse in the language of the Bible. A devoted student of the sciences, while at the same time a good Jew, he found it difficult to reconcile the precepts of the Torah with his scientific inquiries. When he met the Sage of Fostat a strong bond of friendship developed between them, and Aknin spent several years under Maimonides' tutelage. After Aknin had left his teacher Maimonides continued his instruction in a series of essays. "When, by the will of God, we parted, and you went your way, our discussions aroused in me a resolution which had been long latent. Your absence has prompted me to compose this treatise [*The Guide for the Perplexed*] for you and those who are like you, however few they may be. I have divided it into chapters, each of which shall be sent to you as it is composed."

The Guide for the Perplexed is not easily summarized. It is an encyclopedia of Jewish theology, philosophy, and biblical criticism, of which even a table of contents would require considerable space and be of little use without lengthy explanations. Briefly stated, it discusses the Bible, God, His attributes, His names, the world, its origin, changes, and destiny, man, free will, the origin and mystery of evil and the resurrection, the essence and meaning of prophecy, Moses and the significance of the Law, man's supreme duty and happiness, his knowledge, and his passion for God.

Maimonides does not attempt to prove the existence of God, for in the time in which he lived neither Jew, Christian, nor Mohammedan doubted or questioned His existence. Instead, he devotes almost half of the first part of the book to divesting the Deity of the material qualities with which the Bible had endowed Him. He was one of the first of Jewish philosophers to make use of the term *homonyms* to imply that words which have one meaning when applied to man have another meaning when applied to God. Thus, such words as unity, existence, life, kindness, mercy, knowledge, seeeing, hearing, and standing have a different meaning when used with regard to God and to man. God's attributes, therefore, are not positive but negative, for God cannot be defined, He cannot be comprehended by human senses. Time and space have no relation to Him; we can only know what He is not, never what He is. If He can be known at all, it is by his acts and not in his essence.

Maimonides trusted reason; he is the philosopher of reason and his philosophy of Judaism is an expression of his implicit faith in the reasonableness of religion. There is no better definition of the Maimonidean philosophy than Ahad Ha'am's description of it as the "Sovereignty of Reason." Maimonides admired Aristotle as the philosopher of reason and followed him faithfully, even to the point of proclaiming him to be but a little lower than the Prophets. Yet he did not trust him blindly or slavishly; and when he found the Greek philosopher's theory of an everlasting world contradicting the Bible's statement of its creation, Maimonides declared: "The traditional opinion regarding *creatio ex nihilo* is a high rampart erected around the Law of our teacher Moses. . . . If we were to accept the eternity of the Universe as taught by Aristotle, that everything in the Universe is the result of fixed laws, that nature does not change, and that there is nothing supernatural, we should necessarily be in opposition to the foundation of our religion." Indeed, Maimonides' disagreements with his Greek mentor were greater and more numerous than were their agreements. Aristotle ruled out miracles from the order of the universe; Maimonides taught that the same God who created the laws of nature could also alter them; one denied free will, the other affirmed it. Aristotle limited providence to the *genus,* the species; Maimonides extended it to every individual of the human race. The former did not recognize uniqueness among the peoples of the world; the latter affirmed the biblical teaching of the "chosen people" as the sole recipient of the divine law. He was willing to agree with Aristotle concerning the sublunar but not the superlunar world. What the Greek called natural law was, to the Jew, design—all the regularities of nature contingent upon the existence of a rational, designing God. In other words, as remarked by the late George Sarton in summing up the differences of the two men, "he [Maimonides] bowed to Aristotle the scientist, and even to the philosopher, but rejected the theologian; he could not do otherwise."

There is a touch of religious fervor in his discourse when Maimonides makes the purpose of life and man's place in the universe the subject of his discussion. The philosopher turns poet and the rational becomes almost a mystic. There can be no question of purpose in Aristotle's uncreated world. Everything runs with clock-like regularity, unchanged and unchanging. There is no favoritism or partiality in the philosopher's order of the world. Man, beast, and plants all emerge from the same hand of nature and are fated for the same destiny. There is no higher purpose of man than his lower kin of the field and forest. They exist for no other or higher goal than that, by their existence, they preserve and perpetuate the shape and form of their species.

Maimonides is both philosopher and poet. He raises man above the stars and makes even the spheres revolve for his sake. Man is lord and master of all things, the final aim and purpose of creation. All things exist for man; he is a free moral agent; he has freedom of will and choice. He is unique for his knowldge of God, the formation and acquisition of ideas, and for his mastery over his desires and passions. Virtue and honor lie open to him, and there is no limit set to his moral and spiritual potentialities. Unless a man fully realizes his heaven-granted gifts of mind and soul in the service and contemplation of God his life is barren, his existence wasted, and he is not even certain of a share in the world to come.

There is a refreshing, healthy-minded breeziness about Maimonides that pervades even the more heavy and solemn pages of the *Guide;* for with all his insistence upon metaphysical knowledge and correct ideas about God, our philosopher knew life and encouraged the enjoyment of it, with all its color and loveliness, with all its delights and pleasures. He disdained the practice of asceticism by certain religious groups who fled from the world and human society on account of the latter's sinfulness. Human life, he said in paraphrase, cannot be lived in a vacuum; man is a social being and he needs the association of his fellow men for the full flowering of his intellectual and spiritual qualities. Between the excesses of the thoughtless and the total abstinence of the ascetic, Maimonides proposed Aristotle's *golden mean*—that is, midway of the two extremes.

Maimonides attempts to account for the evil and suffering in the world, but with no conclusive results. The problem is an old but ever recurrent one, and arises even today. Job cried out to God for justice, and Moses was so oppressed by the evils he saw practiced in the world that the rabbis quote his plea to God, "Master of the Universe, let me know Thy ways. Why is it that the righteous suffer and the wicked prosper?" Maimonides' answer to this problem is a denial of the existence of evil; what seems to be evil, he asserts, is the absence of good, as darkness is the absence of light, sickness the absence of health, and death the nonexistence of life. The numerous evils to which persons are exposed are not made by God but are due to our own defects. We suffer from the evils that, by our own free will, we inflict upon ourselves, and then we attribute them to God. Our judgment is faulty, our standards inadequate; but, if we look at life objectively, we find that what our reason pronounces bad is not bad in accordance with the order of the universe.

The discussion of prophecy called for Maimonides' greatest care and delicacy of treatment, for it is a subject on which the followers of the great religions—Judaism, Christianity, and Mohammedanism—stand sharply divided. With the Moslems the prophecy of Mohammed is their greatest article of faith and the slightest disparagement of it would have involved our philosopher in serious difficulties, if not the loss of his life. Instead, therefore, of rejecting the prophetic office to any other people but the Jews, as did Judah Halevi, Maimonides proceeds with great ingenuity and psychological insight to discuss the nature and meaning of prophecy and the necessary conditions for the discharge of its function. Maimonides does not deny the divine or supernatural element inherent in prophecy; on the contrary, the divine election is not only implied in the prophetic calling but is basic to its vocation and message. The illumination comes from God; it is He who endows man with the power, spirit, and will to prophesy. But man must be physically, mentally, and morally ready and prepared to receive it. The divine influence, says Maimonides, will only come to one who is perfectly co-ordinated in all his faculties—the imaginative no less that the intellectual and spiritual.

Maimonides sets the office of the prophet above that of the philosopher. The philosopher arrives at truth by his intellectual faculty, by proof and investigation—the prophet, by intuition and divine illumination. The philosopher's truth is only for his time and it may be disproved by later findings; that of the prophet is eternal, timeless. The position of the prophet is higher than that of the philosopher in that he is not only a thinker but a revealer, teacher, and religious legislator. Not all prophets occupy the same high level of prophecy, and Maimonides enumerates eleven degrees of prophets, ranking Moses at the top. Moses, he asserted, received the divine communication directly—not in sleep or visions, as did some of the other prophets. "He was chosen by God from the whole human kind. He comprehended more of God than any man in the past or future. There was no veil he did not pierce. No material hindrance stood in his way, and no defect, whether small or great, mingled itself with him." It has been well suggested by A. Cohen that Maimonides attached importance to the uniqueness of Moses to the point of formulating it into a principle of faith, because of the rival claims of Judaism's daughter religions that they produced prophets greater than he.

If it had not been for the chapters in the third part of the book, in which Maimonides attempted to rationalize and assign reasons for the commandments of the Torah, *The Guide for the Perplexed* would not have been any more violently attacked than similar unconventional statements by preceding Jewish philosophers had been. But to Maimonides the laws of the Torah are reasonable laws and their binding force moral and ethical, instead of arbitrary. He says, therefore, that when we encounter in the Bible laws and precepts whose meaning is obscure and which, on the surface, have no influence upon our moral and spiritual life, they must be explained, so that their intent and purpose is revealed. Israel, he says, must obey with knowledge, for they are called "a wise and understanding nation." He strongly resents the statement of the rabbis that there are in the Torah *hukim* (ordinances) with no obvious purpose, and which must not be probed into.

With characteristic boldness, Maimonides explains the motives and reason for these laws, some on the ground of hygiene and self-discipline and some on the score of foreign influence. In their early history the ancient Israelites lived among pagan nations and adopted some of their idolatrous rites and superstitions. Among the heathen practices absorbed by the Israelites, Maimonides does not hesitate to include the sacrifices, despite the importance assigned to them in the Pentateuch. Maimonides the psychologist maintains that the reason for the retention of the sacrifices in the Bible is God's understanding of human weakness. The Israelites had practiced the pagan form of worship too long for them suddenly to eradicate it. For this reason, says Maimonides, God allowed this kind of service to continue, transferring to Himself that which formerly served as worship of idols.

Maimonides' reputation as a physician matched his fame as philosopher and theologian. He turned to medicine as a means of earning a livelihood for his own family and that of his brother David. But he soon came to love the medical science, both for its own sake and for the opportunities it offered to help suffering human beings. His medical education was begun in Morocco, where he either practiced independently or as an apprentice to famous physicians. The medical science was highly developed among the Arabs, who had available an abundant literature of translations from Greek sources which a man as inquisitive as Maimonides probably lost no time in exploring and making his own. One cannot read Maimonides' *Mishneh Torah,* which was certainly the product of his Morocco sojourn, without being impressed with its numerous references to the medical science and its medical allusions and illustrations. The fourth chapter of *Hilkot Deot* in the Code with its many sanitary rules and regulations, could not have been written by anyone other than a man with professional training and experience in scientific hygiene.

But it was not until after Maimonides' arrival in Cairo in the spring of 1165 that his interest in medicine, either as a science or as a profession, awakened in earnest. As a novice and a Jew, his practice of medicine could hardly have been expected to thrive immediately. But, in time, his energy, his skill and learning, his deep understanding of human nature, combined with his great personal charm, made him one of the most sought-after physicians in the capital. It was the patronage of the powerful Vizier and Judge al-Fadil Abd al-Rahim al-Baisani that led to his appointment as physician at Saladin's court and ultimately to the summit of his medical career. In 1190, when at the height of his medical reputation, he wrote to Joseph Aknin, in Aleppo, that he had acquired great eminence in medicine and counted among his patrons members of the nobility—observing obliquely that the income from that source was not great.

His medical standards were high. Medicine, he said, should be practiced only by conscientious scientists with knowledge, the gift of observation, and open minds. To Maimonides, medicine was not merely a profession for earning a livelihood but a sacred calling, a religious occupation no less important and spiritually rewarding than the precepts of the Torah. He derived this attitude from the religion which made the preservation of life a divine commandment. Maimonides fought quackery in medicine as he did bigotry and superstition in religion. "Do not allow yourself," he wrote, "to be misled by writers of amulets; their writing, like their speech, is full of deception."

Maimonides occupied so commanding a position in the medical world of his time that, notwithstanding his being a Jew, he was invited by the English king, Richard the Lion Hearted, to serve as his personal physician. Maimonides wisely rejected the offer, feeling that he was safer in Egypt than he would be in England. Non-Jewish scholars paid tribute to Maimonides as philosopher and medical scientist. Ibn Usaibia, the renowned physician and Arabic historian of medicine, closes his biographical sketch of Maimonides with a verse by a Mohammedan judge, which, notwithstanding its oriental exuberance, testifies to the universal regard in which the philosopher-physician was held:

> Galen's art heals only the body,
> But Abu Imran's [Maimonides' Arabic name] the body and
>   the soul.
> His knowledge made him the physician of the century.
> He could cure with his wisdom the disease of ignorance.

Maimonides was as prolific a writer on medicine as he was on philosophy and jurisprudence. A number of his ten books on the theory and practice of medicine, all written in Arabic, were promptly translated into Latin and Hebrew. Dr. Hermann Kroner (1870–1930), a German rabbi, edited and translated some of Maimonides' medical works into German, and a new Hebrew translation of his ten volumes is now in process of preparation in Israel. Not all these books are original—some are collections and quotations from Greek and Arabic medical authorities; nevertheless, Maimonides' energy and industry are surprising when it is remembered that medicine was not his only interest and that he was also a philosopher and theologian, and a rabbi to whom the Jews of almost half the world turned for instruction and guidance. Maimonides lived in an age of tradition and authority, when it was not safe for any man to proceed independently without inviting the reproach and censure of his colleagues. Yet he did not hesitate to deviate from established authorities when his observations contradicted their teachings. The *Aphorisms,* better known in its Hebrew title *Pirke Moshe* (Chapters of Moses), his largest and most popular medical work, though derived from Galen and other Greek masters, is more than a mere compilation of their writings. It was extensively revised and amplified by Maimonides.

Maimonides' medical success was no doubt a well-merited reward for the years of study and labor he devoted to his profession, for his conscientiousness, accuracy of judgment, and amiability. But it was due no less to his extraordinary skill and ability as a writer. A gifted literary craftsman whose pen responded with equal grace and readiness, no matter what subject he would have it serve, he wrote with clarity and distinction; and, as observed by Dr. Israel Wechsler, being articulate in writing was then even more than now the broad highway to fame. Maimonides was a perfect synthesis of the physician and the psychologist. He was a healer both of physical and of mental ailments. He was among the first physicians of his time to draw attention to the relation between physical and mental illness. He held that mental depression was caused as often as not by physical disorders. He regarded the study and practice of medicine, as we have noted, as a religious calling, and he treated it as such. Every day, before leaving on his rounds, he recited a prayer imploring God for guidance and for freedom from pride and vanity.

This prayer by the Fostat-Cairo physician became famous in medical literature and was described by Sir Willliam Osler, the noted Canadian physician, as "one of the the most precious documents of our profession, worthy to be placed beside the Hippocrates Oath." When a controversy developed over the authenticity of the prayer, Sir William Osler wrote to Dr. Joseph H. Hertz, the late

Chief Rabbi of Great Britain, for an opinion. After due investigation, Dr. Hertz expressed the opinion that the prayer was the
product of Dr. Markus Herz, a friend and pupil of Immanuel
Kant and Moses Mendelssohn, originally written in German and
published in a Hebrew translation in *ha-Measef*. The English version, reported to have been taken from the Hebrew translation, first
appeared in the London paper, *Voice of Jacob,* Dr. Hermann
Kroner and other authorities on the medical works of Moses
Maimonides, who made the prayer the subject of special study have
concluded, however, on the basis of internal evidence, that
Maimonides was the author of the prayer, since in form and spirit
it is in complete harmony with the Fostat philosopher-physician's
other writings.

Moses Maimonides was a sadly overworked man. He was mentally and physically exhausted. His appointment to the medical
staff of King Saladin's court was no mere honorific position. Fostat
was two miles from the Cairo court and Maimonides made the
trip each day on a mule, leaving home early in the morning and
returning late in the evening. His duties called for his attendance
on the Sultan and the latter's numerous wives, courtiers, and high
officials. After Saladin died, Maimonides continued in the service
of his eldest son and successor al-Malik al-Afdal Nur al-din, a man
of unsteady character and habits, whose frequent attacks of depression kept his doctor in a state of constant concern and anxiety.

At the beginning of a new century, in 1200, Maimonides had
but four years more to live. But he did not spend them in idleness,
resting on his laurels, but in incessant work. There was still a
surging energy in his tired frame. He never stopped correcting his
Mishneh Torah, revising and adding to his medical books, and
taking personal care of his heavy correspondence from many parts
of the Jewish world. The supervision of the Hebrew translation by
Samuel Ibn Tibbon of *The Guide for the Perplexed*, which by
mutual agreement they named *Moreh Nebukim,* gave him the
greatest satisfaction. When the translator expressed the desire to
meet the master in order to discuss some difficult passages with

him personally, Maimonides discouraged his coming, because of his onerous duties at the court and the many patients who waited for him at his home. "In consequence of this," writes Maimonides, "no Israelite can have any private interview with me, except on the Sabbath. Then they all come to me after the morning service when I instruct them as to their proceedings during the whole week. We study together a little until noon, when they depart. Some of them return, and read with me after the afternoon service until evening prayers. In this manner I spend the day."

Maimonides was no longer alive when the last chapter of the *Moreh Nebukim* reached his home. Toiling to the end, he died on December 13, 1204 *(Tevet* 20, 4965), while dictating to his nephew, who acted as his secretary, the last chapter of the revised edition of his *Aphorisms*. He had not quite completed his seventieth year. Public mourning at his death was declared in all Egypt. Jews and Moslems, admirers and former opponents—all united in lamenting his loss. In Jerusalem a general fast day was proclaimed, and on the Sabbath a portion of the first book of Samuel containing the verse, "The glory is departed from Israel, for the Ark of God is taken" was read in the synagogues. According to his wish, he was taken to Palestine for burial, and was laid to rest in Tiberias, where his tomb attracts pious pilgrims from all countries, who come to pray and to meditate upon the life and teachings of the man who marks a lofty peak in his nation's intellectual and spiritual life.

Joseph Albo

JOSEPH ALBO was the last of the philosophical and theological writers of the Spanish School, the last of a cultural tradition that had lasted for nearly half a millennium, the last of his co-religionists to search for a synthesis that would make philosophy more Jewish and Judaism more philosophical. He was perhaps not the most original thinker of the Spanish School. The Jewish philosophic genius manifested itself in profounder and more independent minds than his. Indeed, with the death of Hasdai Crescas, whose classroom discussions Albo is said by Dr. Harry Wolfson to have repeated, there was a hiatus in Jewish philosophy which lasted for more than two hundred and fifty years. Philosophy was ill-adapted to times that called for steadfastness and loyalty rather than for abstract thinking. Oppression and depression had done their work and, instead of aspiring to new heights of the spirit, Israel retired behind the citadel of tradition. In contrast to the former liberality of the Jewish spirit, Jewish teachings became more fixed and formalized, and greater store was set on observance and obedience than on free and untrammeled speculation. Joseph Albo must be given credit for having been among the foremost of his race to have blended philosophy with religion—indeed, to have made them identical. In the words of his biographer and exponent, S. Black, "He not only invested Judaism with a philosophic foundation, but endowed philosophy with a pre-eminently religious content."

Joseph Albo's *Sefer ha-Ikkarim,* the book which made him famous, was not so much a bold flight into the philosophical heights as a restatement of the views and opinions of his predecessors, and was not so much an independent and novel contribution as a presentation in crisp summary form of the principal teachings of the Jewish religion. Indeed, as shown by Dr. Isaac Husik, philosophy

196

was not Albo's forte, nor was it his chief concern. Many of the doubts and perplexities which arose in the minds of Jews had been, if not completely solved, at least discussed by Jewish philosophers from the time of Saadia down to Hasdai Crescas, Albo's teacher. They had been abundantly argued, debated, and written about by greater and stronger minds than Albo's. It was the latter's goal to give his people the quintessence of Judaism, its leading teachings and tenets, brief and unadorned—which in their struggle for spiritual existence they sorely needed.

The formulation of the teachings of Judaism in sharp and fixed terms, it must be remembered, was born of the Jewish struggle to maintain their Jewish identity. When the Jews were an independent people and their religion followed its own free and unhampered existence, there was no need to reduce their teachings to fixed forms and principles. Indeed, Jewish teachers from the days of the prophets down to the destruction of the Jewish state looked askance at any such attempt, regarding it as an offense against the sovereignty of the human mind. Thus, there is no suggestion of creeds in the Bible and in the Talmud only the faintest trace of their presence may be discerned. And, indeed, what room could there be for vital concepts of a religion in which every letter and word of the Torah was regarded as equally important and binding on the believer?

In Judaism, therefore, articles of faith had never acquired that authority and importance they exercised in other religions—as in Christianity and Islam, for instance. They never became conditions of salvation which one rejected only at the cost of losing everything. While the Rabbis enumerated the 613 religious precepts of Judaism, "Thou shalt believe" is not one of them. The ethos of Israel is realistic; it seeks to curb the evil instinct rather than enforce belief. Broadly speaking, therefore, if one is searching Judaism for its fundamental tenets he is likely to find them in pious conduct rather than in abstract belief.

Also, religious dogmas obtained no such sovereignty in Jewish life as they did in other religions, because the synagogue lacked the power and instrumentality to enforce them. Of what avail would it be to legislate inviolable principles when there was no ecclesiastical or state authority to enforce their obedience? There were no popes, no bishops, no community councils to carry them into effect. Even when, from time to time, such authoritative bodies did arise, as, for instance, the Men of the Great Assembly and later the Sanhedrin, they were not vested with power in matters of faith. They could penalize those who denied but could not declare or legislate what to believe.

It was only when Judaism came into contact with alien influence, and religion became a matter of knowledge instead of a matter of faith, that the Jewish struggle for existence began and the need was felt for the establishment of rigid and uncompromising articles of faith. When Rabbinism was challenged by Karaism and when first Islam and then Christianity engaged Jews in religious disputations and called upon them to vindicate their faith, the need arose for a precise and conceptual determination of the basic creed of the synagogue. It was then, and not until then, that, in the confusion of the times and the dismal conditions of their lives, the necessity not infrequently arose for short, concise statements in which the principal doctrines of Judaism would be summed up and which might be more conveniently handed down. "My heart sickens to see the belief of my co-religionists impure and their theological views confused," wrote Rab Saadia Gaon; and he proceeded to clarify the confusion by constructing a number of articles of Jewish faith—an attempt that was followed by other Jewish thinkers from Moses Maimonides down to Joseph Albo.

In less than one hundred years from the time of their formulation the Thirteen Articles of Moses Maimonides became the accepted creed of the synagogue and embodied in its ritual, and, although frowned upon by critics, were almost universally acknowledged. Poets made them the subject of lyrics for songs and numerous homilies and commentaries were written on them. But soon conditions arose that made them burdensome, even dangerous, to the people who received them with enthusiasm. The Jewish center of gravity was shifted from Mohammedan to Christian lands. To further conversion, church dignitaries forced Jews to accept the challenge of religious disputations. It was a pious fraud that invariably succeeded; for, no matter who won the debate, the Jew always paid both with his life and his faith. It was thus that the church was enriched, although in most cases the Jews submitted to nothing more than mock conversion. Joseph Albo figured as a participant in one such debate—the famous Disputation of Tortosa, the greatest and longest of them all, which, with interruptions lasted eighteen months.

But fruitless as the religious discussions between Jews and Christians were, the Tortosa Disputation drew upon it the attention of the Christian world, not so much for its religious issue as for its political implications. The Disputation was sponsored by the former Pope Benedict XIII, who, disowned and discredited by almost all Christendom and banished from his throne, but retaining a following on the Pyrenean Peninsula, hoped to repair his damaged reputation by the wholesale conversion of the Jews. The plan was cunningly designed and, if all went well, what greater victory could there be for any man than this greatest of all triumphs of the Church Militant? Would it not silence the former pope's enemies, restore him to his throne, and enter his name in history as the greatest of pontiffs?

While Benedict's propaganda among the Jews was purely political, conceived and carried out for his personal advancement, the theological arguments on the Christian side were supplied by one Geronimo de Santa Fe, formerly Joshua Lorqui, an ex-Jew, a renegade from the synagogue, and a traitor to his faith and people, whose acquaintance with Jewish literature gave him an advantage in his attack on his former co-religionists. The Jewish turncoats were no less a burden to themselves than they were a plague to the people to whom they once belonged. As apostates, they were a pathetically unhappy lot of men. Scorned and despised by their former brethren, they were not much more popular with their new friends. They simulated devotion to the church, but they inspired a feeling of suspicion among their new associates which caused the best Christians to shun their company. As quoted by Marvin Lowenthal, Conrad of Magdeburg bluntly summed up the Christian attitude toward the Jewish converts. "The faith of a converted Jew," he said, "is like the droppings of a sparrow; hot when it falls, but cold as it hits the ground."

Tortosa—indeed, all Christendom—was breathless over the outcome of the Disputation. Grandees and burghers, as well as the titled hierarchy of the Church from the lower ranks to mitered bishops turned out in their holiday attire for the theological tournament. The Jews, had they been permitted, would gladly have stayed away, for they had no illusions about the outcome. They knew in advance that, win or lose, they would be destroyed. They were not afraid to meet the opponent in verbal combat, for they knew their Bible and Talmud and were masters of debate. But they also knew by experience that, in spite of Benedict's hollow promises that no harm would come to them for speaking their mind freely, they were summoned not for the purpose of convincing or being convinced but for the purpose of being converted.

Twenty-two of the most learned rabbis and scholars of Aragon were summoned for the Disputation, among them Don Vidal Ibn Labi of Saragossa, a physician and distinguished man of culture, and Joseph Albo of Monreal, a philosopher and disciple of the great Hasdai Crescas. The apostate Geronimo raged and fulminated and predicted dire consequences for his adversaries. Benedict found it necessary to intervene and apologize for Geronimo's bad temper on the ground of what he called his "native Jewish rudeness." In a speech of garbled sophistries and specious arguments, the venomous renegade proceeded against the Jews and Judaism by trying to prove their hostile attitude to Christians and the Christian religion. The principal point at issue touched upon a vital doctrine of Christianity and an important creed of the synagogue. Had the Messiah come; and if he had, was he realized in the person of Jesus? The Jewish representatives might have pointed to the twelfth creed of Maimonides' Articles of Faith and settled the matter. But would it have been politic? Would it not have offended the church, which had her own definite views on the subject?

The spirited debate went on, fiery speeches, threats, and denunciations, on the one side, and courageous rebuttals on the other.

When, after eighteen months, from February 1413, to November, 1414, there was no sign of victory for either side, the Disputation was abruptly called off. Benedict was disappointed and bitter. He finally realized how hard it was to convert the Jews, and he gave up the attempt. Not one of the Jews wavered; not one of them was frightened into submission. But Benedict wreaked vengeance on them in others ways. The Jews of Aragon were forbidden to study the Talmud, to have social or commercial intercourse with Christians, or to disinherit their children who were baptized as Christians.

Under the conditions the Jews were called upon to face, the Thirteen Articles of Maimonides were a hindrance, if not a positive danger, instead of a help. Without them, they could evade or parry the Christian attack, but how could they avoid giving offense to the prevailing faith when Maimonides made the immutability of the Law and the coming of the Messiah fundamental doctrines of the synagogue while Christianity considered the opposite view the cornerstone of the church? In their hands the dogmas obscured rather than clarified the cardinal teachings of Judaism. Highly contested individual opinions were set down as creeds, so that they confused rather than clarified the expression of Judaism.

Seeing the confusion that existed among the philosophers on the principles of the Jewish religion, Joseph Albo found that there were three essentials from which no revealed religion can deviate —the Existence of God, Providence, and Reward and Punishment after death. These *ikkarim* (principles) do not, however, exhaust the credal content of Judaism. For from these issue, like branches from the stem of a tree, *shorashim* (derivatives) which are incumbent upon every religionist, and particularly upon every Jew, to believe, if he is not to be guilty of heresy. Albo enumerates eight such *shorashim* which he considers vital to a Jew if he is to share in the world to come.

However, the novelty of Albo's doctrine consists of still another division into which he classifies the beliefs and teachings of Judaism. For Joseph Albo was a surprisingly liberal thinker—in many respects, centuries ahead of his time. He was far ahead of the legalists of his time and of those who regarded with awe, and demanded inflexible obedience to, every letter and precept of the Torah. On the contrary, Joseph Albo took an almost startlingly modern view of the Torah—a view which not only in his day but even today might seem to some Jews curious, if not heretical. Thus, in his broad survey of the religious content of Judaism, he found that it was heavily embroidered with precepts and ordinances not necessarily vital to the genius and teachings of the Jewish religion—observances and practices which may confer happiness upon the pious but the neglect of which does not place one outside the Jewish community or impede his progress toward religious perfection. Indeed, his interpretation of the religious requirements of Judaism was so broad that under his doctrine it would be difficult to impugn the orthodoxy of even the most liberal of Jews. The minor customs and traditions, which abound in every religion, he called *anafim* (twigs), which, although they embellish the tree and make it look beautiful, do not affect it basically. They may wither and die or may be hewed off without doing serious harm to the trunk of the tree itself. "Likewise," Albo says, "a person who violates a commandment of the Torah is called a transgressor, and is liable to the penalty prescribed in the Torah for that commandment, but he is not excluded from those who profess the Torah, and is not regarded as a denier of the Torah who has no share in the world to come."

It has become customary among some critics to belittle Joseph Albo's standing as a philosopher. But credit for having been a great and, in many respects, an original thinker, cannot be denied him. He was a man with a great diversity of gifts and talents. The breadth and variety of the genius of Spanish Jewry is exhibited in him as in few other men. He was daring and courageous, and one must marvel at the freedom with which he criticized the views and opinions of his predecessors, especially those of Moses Maimonides. He distilled the wisdom of his ill-fated age and presented it with fluency and eloquence. He was the first Jewish philosopher to classify law as natural, conventional, and divine, and to invent a philosophical terminology all his own. If he leaned heavily upon his predecessors, he rejected their views as often as he accepted them.

His book *Sefer ha-Ikkarim* proves that he was a matured and well-informed man who read widely and wisely and was thoroughly at home with his subject, and, although sometimes diffuse, he was never obscure or unintelligible. Few other men show such intimacy with the philosophical currents of his time and those of previous generations. He was familiar with the works of the classical Greek and Arabic thinkers and, as for the Jewish philosophers, hardly anything they taught escaped him. Although Plato, Aristotle, Euclid, and Hippocrates figure largely in his pages, as do Ibn Sina, Ibn Roshd, and Algazali, among the Arab philosophers, there is no better and more complete appraisal of the philosophical speculations of Jewish thinkers than in Albo's *Sefer ha-Ikkarim*. One finds the most hallowed names in his procession, from Rab Saadia down to Hasdai Crescas. He shows considerable acquaintance with the *Kabbalah*, which in his day excited almost sensational interest, and quotes the *Zohar* on several occasions, although, as one might expect of a philosopher, warning against the indiscriminate acceptance of its doctrine.

But what is particularly surprising is his expert knowledge of Christianity, his familiarity with the New Testament, and his more than superficial acquaintance with Christian church theology—a field in which he may be said to have excelled many another Jewish philosophical writer. From a man who joined in the Judeo-Christian controversies of his time and who represented his community at the Tortosa Disputation one might expect some acquaintance with the theological teachings of his opponents. But his knowledge of the religious teachings of the predominant faith was more thorough and complete than that. He displays a familiarity and depth of insight astounding in a man who was a rabbi and a Talmudist and whose whole life was steeped in the sacred lore of his own people. Besides casual references to the New Testament, found all through the four parts of his book, he devotes more than twenty-five pages to a refutation of Christian doctrine in the third part of his work alone. One must indeed marvel at his erudition;

more than that, one must admire his courage in criticizing the fundamental teachings of the dominant faith when to do so was to invite the displeasure of the all-powerful church.

To explain Albo's philosophy a whole treatise would be necessary. A few brief notes on the characteristic features of his teaching as they affect or perhaps helped evolve, current Jewish thinking reveal that, with the exception of Maimonides and Halevi, he was probably the best informed Jewish philosopher. Is it not likely that the tenor of Jewish thinking was in some measure determined by this sage of Soria?

Writers do not classify Joseph Albo as a rationalist. Indeed, the rationalist school of medieval Jewish thinkers is said to have come to a brilliant climax in the work of Moses Maimonides. But there are flashes in *Sefer ha-Ikkarim* which remind one of the noblest representatives of that school—flashes which, considering the time and environment in which he lived, seem surprisingly modern. Indeed, one is led to feel that although Albo was affected by his time, he looked far beyond it.

The open-mindedness of Albo was indeed remarkable and is one of the outstanding qualities of his work. While he believed in Revelation and was devoted to the Torah, he was at the same time one of the stoutest defenders of the sovereignty of human reason. There is in his work no enslavement of the human mind, no shackling of the intellect, no blind adherence to the traditional concepts of Judaism. Thus, in one of the surprisingly illuminating passages in his work, he makes himself responsible for the daring statement, "For the Torah does not oblige us to believe in absurdities, nor put our faith in anything reason cannot conceive. . . . Absurd ideas, therefore, which cannot be conceived by the mind need not be believed even if it is plainly expressed in the Torah." One is not surprised that he met with opposition during his life and was the subject of much bitter criticism long after his death. For much milder utterances men were charged with heresy and were roundly abused and persecuted by their contemporaries.

Albo was on the side of free discussion of religion, even to the point of questioning the validity of one's faith and how it squared with the doctrines of other creeds. In support of his viewpoint he quotes Maimonides, who in *The Guide for the Perplexed* says that it behooves every man to investigate the religion he professes. Albo, of course, is so sure that in such investigation Judaism would come out triumphant that he entertains no fears on that score; but the very fact that more than five hundred years ago he encouraged the critical study of religion is significant.

He even went further than that and declared himself in favor of a free interpretation of the tenets and doctrines of Judaism in accordance with the changing conditions of the times. For an illustration—and there is nothing in Albo that is not made crystal clear by a wealth of illustrations—he draws on his medical profession. The physician, he says, has to adopt his medicaments to the various stages through which his patient passes. That he changes his prescription does not, however, imply that his medical knowledge is imperfect or that his earlier remedies were unwisely chosen. The varying conditions of the invalid is the cause of the varying treatment. A daring doctrine—indeed, daring in some quarters five hundred years after it had been uttered!

Joseph Albo was a man of warmth and feeling. He saw his generation struggling under a load that was crushing to many of them. Thousands despaired because, upon examining their religious conduct, they found they were remiss in one or another of the divine commandments. Would they be saved? Would they attain to that state of spiritual perfection, or *hashlamat hanefesh,* which, acording to Albo, is the aim and purpose of religion? "If every one professing the Law of Moses must fulfill all the many commandments mentioned therein before he can attain any degree of future life, then the Law of Moses would hinder man from the acquisition of perfection rather than help him. . . . Human perfection may be attained by fulfilling even a single one of the commandments of the Law of Moses. And when a man's heart is that poor and humble that he can find nothing wherewith to merit heaven, it is enough if he merely abstains from doing what is evil." What a comforting doctrine; almost *Hasidic* in spirit, it must have seemed to the men and women of his time who, to escape persecution, had to suffer many of the precepts of the Torah to go unobserved.

In a supreme crisis in civilization, when forces of evil have arisen to crush the worth and dignity of human personality, what better lesson than that of the kind and gentle teacher of Soria who in words of solemn beauty had taught: "Man has a personality which is in the likeness of God. And therefore he must be careful not to disgrace it either in himself or in his neighbor, and he should see to it that it should survive death and unite with the celestial beings in that place from which it originally came. This is what Scripture metaphorically implies, 'In the day that God created man, in the likeness of God He made him'."

What greater tribute could be paid to this preacher of good will and human cooperation of five hundred years ago than to say that even as he was beholding with his own eyes men being burned for clinging to their religion, he still taught the equality of all men and the validity of all faiths that led to the moral and spiritual better-ment of the believers? For this is what Albo actually says at the conclusion of the first part of his book: "This shows that there may be two or more divine laws existing at the same time among differ-ent nations, and that each one leads those who live by them to attain human happiness."

Albo's religion is a joyous and ecstatic faith, a rapturous absorp-tion in God reached by means higher than human reason. But it is not the religion of the mystic who shuns and despises life. Indeed, he castigates severely those religious sects which would seek God along the parched roads of the denial of life. Living in an age when life was degraded and held cheap, Albo preached and affirmed life. No words occur more frequently in his pages than *haslama enushit* (human happiness). He refers to Kabbalah, but it is doubtful that he was ever one of its devotees.

Unfortunately, little is known of the personal life of Joseph Albo, if he had a life outside the one that was merged with the community which he served as a kind friend, wise teacher, and noble guide. For Jewish scholars and thinkers had rarely enjoyed a private or individual life of their own. Their teachings radiated from personalities keenly aware of the needs of the people in whose midst they lived and whose lot, for the most part sad and tragic, they shared. Indeed, herein lies the secret of their greatness and the wondrous influence they exerted on their environment. They towered above other men of their generation not so much by what they wrote and taught as by what they were and did.

Not even the dates of Albo's birth and death are established with any degree of certainty. Scholars are still in disagreement about both. It is only by computations and deductions that we are led to surmise that he was born about 1380 and died about 1444, fourteen years after the completion of his book. From what little is known, he was born in Monreal, Aragon, and lived in Soria, Spain, where he exercised the functions of preacher and physician to his community. Judging by his book, which is simple, direct, and fluent in style and contains a wealth of illustrations and allegorical interpretations of biblical and talmudic texts, he must have been an exceedingly effective preacher indeed. One can almost visualize the people, inspired and uplifted by his gentle tone, his eloquence, and the magic and warmth of his personality. For Joseph Albo was not a harsh teacher. One cannot conceive of him as a fanatic—he who had seen so much sorrow and suffering, and who knew so well the tremendous burdens the humblest Jew had borne for his religion. Indeed, he asked for little; for what more could he ask of people who had already given so much? He was satisfied with a minimum of conformity, if only they kept what he considered the essentials of their religion.

His career came to a brilliant climax when, as a young man, he was summoned by his people to represent them at the celebrated Disputation of Tortosa. It was an honor, and a challenge, too; indeed, it was one of the gravest responsibilities that could come to a man so young—he was less than forty years old; for upon the issue of that debate depended everything the Jews of Spain held dear—their freedom, their religion, their way of life. No record was kept of the famous Disputation, or if any was kept, it has long since been lost. We, therefore, do not know how Albo figured in the renowned verbal contest, what part he played, or how successfully he parried the attack of the adversary. But his part could not have been an undistinguished one, for he possessed many of the qualities necessary for just such an exchange of wits. He was an excellent theologian, acquainted with the teachings of both the church and the synagogue, and courageous to the point of recklessness. We have referred to his intimate knowledge of the New Testament. But his acquaintance with Christian teachings went far beyond it—indeed, to the writings of the church fathers, since in at least one place in his book, he ventures to correct a mistranslation of a biblical verse by Jerome.

Little more is known about the composition of *Sefer ha-Ikkarin* than about the personal life of its author except that it was completed in the year 1428, or fourteen years after the Disputation of Tortosa. It was written at a time when the Jewish world was in confusion, chaos, and dissolution, when Spanish Jewry was living through the deepest martyrdom and events were aligning themselves for its final tragedy. What survived the persecutions of Ferrand Martinez was overwhelmed by the terrors of Vincent Ferrer. Their inner life was all but extinguished, their external life all but destroyed; nothing was left of the fame and glory that once was Spanish Jewry. A people, a great people, of poets, thinkers, and scientists was again making ready for the fate that had overtaken it throughout the centuries of its tragic history.

Albo's book senses the coming doom, but he never once directly refers to it. He who had seen so much, felt so much, and experienced so much, the kind and gentle shepherd of his flock, neither laments nor mourns but, instead, soothes, comforts, and consoles. Indeed, he never even mentions the clouds and storms through which he has passed. His faith is too strong and his confidence in Israel's destiny too great to be shaken by passing events, no matter how grave and serious. It is with *ikharim* (principles) that he is concerned—not with the din and noise of a wicked world.

It seems that the lay people, who took so kindly to Albo, had a higher opinion of him than had some of the professional philosophers, who patronized him, treated him almost with disdain, and regarded him as having departed from the high intellectual level of his predecessors. No sooner was *Sefer ha-Ikkarim* made available to the general reading public than it became unusually popular. And this perhaps not so much because of its subject matter as because of the brilliance of its style and its frequent use of stories and illustrations. Reading it, one feels the exhilaration experienced in reading Rashi's commentary on the Bible or choice portions of the Midrash rather than the emotions usually aroused by reading the speculations of a philosopher. Preacher that he was, and therefore unaccustomed to brevity, Albo often takes up long chapters with what he might have condensed into a paragraph or two. But, even so, he is seldom tiresome. If there are no new horizons in his book, one may always expect to be surprised by a new phrase, a subtle expression, a fresh use of a word, or an ingenious explanation of a biblical or talmudic passage. The qualities gave Albo's book a popularity not enjoyed by the work of any other Jewish philosopher.

Sefer ha-Ikkarim might very well have ended with the first part without any serious loss of its essential ideas. But, as the writer himself states, he was prevailed upon by friends to further clarify his views, which he did by adding three more parts to the original argument. The first edition of *Sefer ha-Ikkarim* appeared in Soncino in 1485, and was published with a commentary, *Ohel Ya'akob*, by Jacob ben Samuel Koppelman ben Bunem, of Brzesc.

Joseph Albo was the last bearer of the torch carried for more than a thousand years in Moslem and Christian lands; for with him the philosophical genius of the Jews—a genius fed from Jewish and not alien sources—may be said to have exhausted itself. Now and again it still flickered dimly, in men such as Isaac Arama, author of the homiletical *Akedat Yizhak*, in Don Isaac Abravanel, and, less clearly, in the latter's son, Judah Leo Abravanel. It flickered and sputtered, but its original strength was spent. The expulsion from Spain, which came less than half a century after Albo died, put an end to a tradition that had been maintained for centuries and that gave the Jews many of their most eminent men. One must, however, be grateful that before the flame had died down it made a last effort to burn bright again in the person of

Joseph Albo, who lived a life that produced for us a book for which thousands have blessed him.

Don Isaac Abravanel

DON ISAAC ABRAVANEL belonged to the third generation of a family which, because of their wealth and their social and political position, ranked high among the Jews of the Iberian Peninsula. There are no rabbis or outstanding scholars recorded in the Abravanel lineage. Don Isaac's ancestors belonged to the lay aristocracy and were prominent figures in politics and philanthropy. Don Isaac was the first of his line to carve for himself a brilliant career in Jewish and general scholarship. It flattered his vanity to claim for his family descent from King David and their settlement in Spain in pre-Roman days. Neither of these claims had either been proven or denied, but so strong was the family tradition in him that it gave him a feeling of *noblesse oblige*.

Seville, in the Kingdom of Castile, was the original home of the Abravanels. There they lived for centuries, and, because of their financial acumen, ability to manage state finances, and diplomatic discernment, they rose to a high position in government affairs. Not many of Don Isaac's ancestors are known. But his grandfather, Don Samuel Abravanel, was renowned among his contemporaries for his piety and intelligence and for his generosity to the poor and to impecunious scholars. He was a leading member of the Jewish community in Spain and their representative and protector at the court of King Henry II, whose finance minister he was. He served as envoy to Pope Martin V, to plead for his people when Rome showed signs of hostility to the Jews. He established a tradition for generosity and Jewish leadership from which his family had never departed.

It was not given, however, to Don Samuel Abravanel to reap the full measure of reward for his generous and distinguished life. In

211

1391 a wave of "holy hate" broke over the Jews of Spain, with pillage, murder, and forced conversion in its wake. In Seville, a prosperous community of seven thousand Jews, four thousand were killed outright and the survivors sought safety in conversion to Christianity. Rather than fire or blood, they chose the water of baptism. The aged Don Samuel Abravanel, a confidant of the king and loved and esteemed by all, lacked the strength to resist pressure, and so became a Christian; but he secretly remained loyal to the religion in which he was born. For six years he remained in the king's service under his baptismal name of Juan Sanchez de Seville, while waiting for the opportunity to cast off the mask and return to his inherited faith. The opportunity came in 1397. Leaving behind his palatial home, his fortune, and a brilliant career as statesman, he crossed the border with his son Judah and fled to Portugal. The blot of conversion on the family escutcheon made such a painful impression on Don Isaac that he never mentioned his grandfather's name in any of his copious writings.

Although Portugal bordered upon Spain, there was an atmosphere of freedom and tolerance there and sympathy for the fugitives from religious persecution. The Jewish community in Portugal was quite large and prosperous. Whole towns and villages were inhabited by Jews, but they were particularly numerous in Lisbon. Without fanaticism to harass them, their life was comparatively safe and secure. They could move about the country freely and were not molested in the practice of their religion. The Jews of Portugal did not reach the high level of intellectual and spiritual development that their Spanish brethren attained, but they nevertheless had a well-organized community, with synagogues and educational establishments.

Don Isaac Abravanel was born in Lisbon in 1437. At the time of his birth the Abravanels had already lived in Portugal a comparatively long time, and had acquired wealth and social and political status. Don Judah and Don Samuel, father and grandfather of Isaac, were friends of the royal house of Portugal and served their state in distinguished capacities. The family was religious yet modern; intensely Jewish but at home in the secular environment. They created for young Isaac an atmosphere conducive to the development of the future scholar and leader.

Don Isaac's education was the usual training of children of the Jewish upper class. He was exposed to all that was best in both Jewish and secular culture. While religion was the foundation of that education, it was broadened and amplified by a liberal training in the arts and sciences of the day. Thus, young Isaac's schedule of studies included the Hebrew, Latin, Portuguese, and Spanish languages, arithmetic, physics, astronomy, and logic, not counting a passing acquaintance with the Talmud—and all this without regard to the student's ultimate goal. "Merchants and financiers, doctors and rabbis went through the same course of literary, scientific and philosophic instruction," writes A. Wolf.

It was in such a school that Don Isaac's mind was deepened, his intellect sharpened, and his faculties developed. As if the knowledge he acquired was not enough, he later supplemented what he had learned with his own researches, which were vast and thorough. He interested himself in the works of the Greek and Roman classicists; he quotes Seneca in his commentary on *The Ethics of the Fathers* and devoted a whole dissertation to a refutation of Aristotle. He acquainted himself with the literature of the Christian and Moslem scholars; he mentions Albertus Magnus and shows high regard for Thomas Aquinas. He is the first Jewish exegetical writer to take notice of Christian Bible commentators, such as Jerome, Nicholas de Lyre, and even the baptized Paul of Burgos, extracting from them what he found to be good and valuable. He hailed Moses Maimonides as the greatest and deepest mind the Jews had produced, and devoted himself enthusiastically to his *Guide for the Perplexed,* which he all but memorized, without, however, following blindly all its teachings and theories.

Don Isaac's philosophic thinking matured early. He was not long out of his teens when he surprised his friends with a philosophical essay, *Zurot ha-Yesodot* (The original Form of the Elements)—fire, water, air, and earth—from which, according to Aristotle, the sublunary world developed. Closely following it, and of greater interest to Jews, was *Ateret Zekenim* (The Crown of the Elders), of which B. Netanyahu writes: "When he wrote this book, he had already developed the fundamentals of his world outlook. All the major themes of his writings are to be found in this brief dissertation on the concept of God and the meaning of prophecy . . . his admiration for the cabalists, 'the bearers of truth,' and his criticism of the philosophers who walk in darkness. The only exception was Maimonides from whose influence Don Isaac could not free himself."

Abravanel was determined on a new commentary to the Bible because of his dissatisfaction with the older commentators. In his opinion, Ibn Ezra was too cryptic, Rashi too brief, Gersonides too bent upon extracting moral and ethical maxims from the biblical stories, and Kimhi more of a grammarian than an expositor. He was pleased with Nahmanides, but he resented his mystical involvements. His own method, not very popular today, was to preface each chapter of every book of the Bible with a lengthy introduction, often the length of a dissertation, in which questions and uncertainties of a philosophical, theological, and historic nature were raised and resolved. The style and chronological sequence of the books, no matter what their traditional arrangement, are considered, and, what is perhaps the most important, he casts upon the Bible episodes light drawn from his own experience, which could not have been done by the other commentators. He hails Moses Maimonides as the greatest and deepest mind the Jews ever produced, both as philosopher and expositor, with serious reservations on the questions of creation, miracles, and bodily resurrection of the dead.

Abravanel had another goal for his commentary. He was anxious to reveal to his readers the creative and ennobling spirit of the Bible, its inner beauty and spiritual grandeur. These qualities had often been obscured rather than clarified by many of the commentators. Their work was pedantic rather than illuminating, occupying itself with the words and letters of the Torah rather than with the spirit that vitalizes its pages. Abravanel correctly felt that the approach to the finest things in the Bible lies not in its outward form but in its inner content.

There was another consideration that made the work attractive to him. His commentary to the Bible was inspired by the practical exigencies of the time in which he lived. In the hands of zealous priests and apostate Jews, the Bible was made to serve as a weapon against the Jews. With utter disregard of their meaning, texts and verses of the Bible were twisted for the purpose of Christian propaganda. The great public disputations, in which both the Bible and the Talmud suffered at the hands of their detractors, had been over for a century when Abravanel was born, but their baneful effects continued. It was an ambitious program on which he embarked, but few men were better qualified for the task than he. His knowledge of the Talmud, although not outstanding, was sufficient. His Hebrew style was fluent, elegant, and graceful. He was at ease in the Latin language and, as already remarked, he was acquainted with the works of the non-Jewish writers on the Bible. He had been a student of history, and his knowledge of statecraft afforded him an insight into the ways and habits of courts, kings, and princes. His keen historical and analytical faculty helped him sense the nuances inherent in the time, authorship, composition, and chronolgy of the Holy Writ.

Don Isaac's commentary on the Bible, which lay clearly outlined in his mind, had to be temporarily suspended in favor of more immediate duties to which he felt himself committed. A student and scholar by inclination, he was a man of large business affairs by family tradition. His father and grandfather, and possibly generations of his ancestors before them, had been great personages. They knew the dazzle and glamor of court life, and when in his early manhood Don Isaac sampled its delights he found them congenial to his tastes. His father, a powerful courtier but already in the sixties, instructed his son in the duties and responsibilities of the high office which he knew would fall to his lot before very long. He instructed him in the intricate business of statecraft, in the national budget and taxation, in foreign and domestic commerce, and, above everything, he conveyed to him what he knew of the temperament and disposition of the king and the high officials surrounding the throne.

When the student and scholar turned courtier and business man, he flung himself into his new life with the energy and passion he had formerly given to his books. The family reputation was not only undiminished in Don Isaac's hands but was greatly increased and augmented by him. He won the confidence of King Alfonso and the trust and friendship of the political and financial magnates of the kingdom. His warm personality, winning manner, and practical wisdom gained for him the recognition and admiration of a large circle of friends. He became associated both personally and professionally with the powerful House of Braganza, the most influential nobility in the country, and especially with Duke Ferdinand, its head, who was lord of fifty towns, castles, and fortresses, almost rivaling the reigning monarch in prestige, wealth, and magnificence.

Don Isaac Abravanel took advantage of his opportunity to act as a shield and protector of his Jewish brothers. By virtue of his own never-wavering love of his people and by the example of his forebears, he recognized the responsibility of his great position for the life and safety of his fellow Jews. Unfortunately, there was ample need for such protection, both within and without the Portuguese kingdom. Hostile voices for the restriction of the rights of Jews were not absent in Portugal, even under the mild and tolerant rule of King Alfonso. A particular instance of Don Isaac Abravanel's devotion to his people and his readiness to stand by their side was furnished in 1471 when Alfonso, after a successful attack on the African port city of Arzila, brought back with him a large number of captives, among whom were two hundred and fifty Jews. To save the Jewish victims from being sold as slaves Don Isaac organized a committee, collected a fund of ten thousand gold doubloons, about eighty thousand dollars, ransomed the captives, and housed and fed them until they could shift for themselves. On another occasion, when the king of Portugal sent a delegation to Rome to congratulate Pope Sixtus IV on his accession to the throne of St. Peter and appointed as a member

John Sezire, a learned friend of Abravanel and well disposed to the Jews, Don Isaac wrote to Yehiel of Pisa, a pious and learned Jew and a banker and financial magnate of Tuscany, to extend him every courtesy.

It was a happy and tranquil life that Don Isaac Abravanel for some time spent in Portugal, seemingly secure in his position and firm in the regard of his friends. "I lived," he writes in the introduction to his commentary to the Book of Joshua, "in peace in my inherited house in the renowned city of Lisbon, the capital of Portugal, where God had given me blessings, riches and honor. I built me great houses with many rooms. My home was a meeting place of the wise and the noble. I was beloved in the palace of Alfonso, a just and mighty king, under whom the Jews enjoyed liberty and prosperity. I stood near him and he leaned upon my hand; and so long as he lived, I went in and out of the palace." He was happy, too, in his married and domestic life. While not much is known of his wife, it is established that she presented her husband with three sons—Judah, Joseph, and Samuel, and one daughter. Very little is known of the daughter—not even her name. But it is quite certain that Don Isaac did have a daughter, that her husband's name was Joseph, and that he was a business and political associate of his father-in-law, with whom he later fled from Portugal. The natural happiness Don Isaac derived from his offspring was augmented by their extraordinary ability; two of them attained lasting fame.

But the "blessings, riches and honor" on which Don Isaac Abravanel had prided himself in Portugal, were short-lived; they vanished with the death of his patron, King Alfonso V, on August 18, 1482. Abravanel's trials commenced with the ascent to the Portuguese throne of Jaoa, a ruler in every respect unlike his father. Henceforth, in Don Isaac Abravanel we behold no longer an important personage and a great statesman, but a man stricken and impoverished, fleeing through many lands, lingering for brief respites here and there, but nowhere finding rest—the very symbol of his race and people.

When King Jaoa assumed the reins of government, Portugal was seething with discontent and rebellion. The old monarch had been a mild and tolerant ruler but not always a wise and sagacious one. His expansionist policy brought ruin and disaster to the country. As against his successful campaign in North Africa, his operations against Sicily ended in national disgrace and catastrophe. A disheartened and starving population was made to pay heavily in taxes for the wars they did not want but could not prevent. Then there was the baronial system, which Alphonso encouraged and endowed with great power and large gifts of land. Under this system the Duke Ferdinand of Braganzas, for instance, to mention but one, grew so powerful that, in addition to the many estates over which he lorded, he could at any time put into the field an army of thirteen thousand men—not many less than the national army of Portugal commanded by the king.

The failure of his father's mild and temperate policy made King Jaoa resolve upon a sterner course. Although only twenty-nine years old upon his accession to the throne, King Joao was an astute and firm ruler with a fully developed personality and definite views of government, which he lost no time putting into operation. He was jealous of his royal prerogatives and brooked no interference from feudal lords of the realm. The capital was tense with excitement and apprehensive of the future. The conflict between the king and the nobility spread an atmosphere of suspense. The king, set and determined, struck at the head of the Braganzas first by confronting him with a charge of treason against the throne in conspiratorial correspondence with the king of Aragon. The prince, unable to clear himself to the king's satisfaction, was summarily sent to the block. The unfortunate man's brothers escaped a similar fate by fleeing to Spain.

It was not likely that Abravanel would escape the king's purge of the Braganzas and other members of the nobility. Although not a member of their caste, he was an intimate friend and associate of the executed prince and was closely identified with him in personal and business relationships. It was unlikely, according to the reasoning of the king and his henchmen, that the man who shared the prince's confidence did not know of his treasonable conspiracy. Had Abravanel been more cautious and less trusting he would have realized the implications of the Braganza tragedy and, being an intimate at the court, he would have had advance knowledge of what was happening. As it was, Don Isaac Abravanel not only did not know but was not even in the capital at the time of the dramatic events, having spent the summer with his family in a villa close to Lisbon.

It was at the villa that Don Isaac Abravanel was appraised of the shocking news. He had hardly recovered when a messenger came to summon him to appear before the king. It was a grand opportunity to face the king, protest his loyalty, and recount his own and his family's services to the crown. But he knew his monarch's dark mind and his ruthlessness once he was determined upon a course of action. The Duke of Braganza was arrested while he was conversing with Jaoa at a royal cabinet meeting. Nevertheless, Don Isaac was ready to obey the king's summons and started out for Lisbon. While on his way, he was accosted by an unknown friend who urged him not to return to the capital but to flee for his life. Don Isaac was confronted with a difficult decision. He faced the alternative of returning and attempting to clear his name, with almost certain death as the price, or fleeing like a criminal, which would only confirm the suspicion of his guilt and endanger the life of his family, to say nothing of the confiscation of his property. After considering the problem from every angle and consulting with his family, he came to the conclusion that flight was his only course. After a ride of a day and two nights, he therefore crossed the Portuguese border into Castile on the night of May 31, 1483.

Scholars are in disagreement on Don Isaac Abravanel's first residence in Spain on his flight from Portugal. Graetz says it was in Toledo, where he met and struck up friendship with Isaac Aboab, the last representative of Jewish scholarship in Castile, and Abraham Senior, collector of the king's tithes. Recent authorities, however, point to Segura, a small town but one with a sizeable Jewish community, hard on the Portuguese border. Abravanel may have chosen Segura because of its proximity to Portugal, in order to keep an eye on affairs in his native country, where he had left many friends with whom he kept up an active correspondence. To keep himself beyond the reach of King Joao's agents, Abravanel later moved frequently, spending some time at Alcalá, Plascencia, and Segura.

In Segura, his new home the statesman-philosopher-commentator at the age of forty-six started his life over again. He managed to rescue some capital from his confiscated fortune and in an unexpected show of generosity the Portuguese monarch permitted Abravanel's wife and children to join him in his exile. The Jews of Segura, proud of the great visitor in their midst, showed him every mark of honor and respect. Discouraged by his experience but undaunted in spirit, Don Isaac Abravanel resumed his literary work which he had long neglected. His reflections were sometimes sad and bitter. Was not his misfortune a rightful punishment for deserting the Torah for the empty tinsel of worldly honors, for the gratification of his pride and vanity? With renewed enthusiasm he threw himself into his work—the work for which he felt himself divinely chosen and on which alone his reputation would rest. The creative urge stirred him; he worked uninterruptedly day and night: ideas for his commentary on the Bible surged through his mind faster than he could put them down on paper. As though fearing that he might be interrupted, he worked at a furious pace, turning out book after book—commentaries on Joshua, the Judges, the two books of Samuel—in the almost unbelievable time of two and a half months. When one remembers that this output was the product of wide critical reading, vast research, and personal observation, the magnitude of the task he accomplished will be understood. Abravanel's commentary upon the Bible is no less significant for its social and political comments on the time in which he lived and played his part than for its religious and philosophical views. "It was the first and perhaps the only time," remarked Netanyahu, "that the main political part of the Bible was interpreted by a statesman."

Had Don Isaac Abravanel been allowed to continue his work undisturbed he might have realized his dream of completing a commentary on the whole Bible. This goal, however, was denied him. It was inevitable that his reputation for achievements in finance and statecraft in Portugal should reach the ears of the Spanish rulers and once more open up a path to his door. Was it Abraham Senior, collector of King Ferdinand's revenues, or the surviving members of the Braganza family, now fugutives in Spain, who spread the fame of the distinguished Jewish newcomer? In any event, it was only about a year after Abravanel's arrival in Castile that he received a summons from their majesties, King Ferdinand and Queen Isabella in March, 1484, to appear at the Spanish court.

The appointment to a high office in service to the Spanish sovereigns could not have been displeasing to the man who still smarted under humiliation by an ungrateful king. What better vindication of his character and ability than, as a fugitive, to be called to the service of the greatest court in Europe, and this in spite of the laws against Jews holding public office and the protest of Pope Sixtus IV! Abravanel welcomed the appointment for still another personal reason. Don Isaac was essentially a man of action, accustomed from his youth to the din and clamor of big affairs and the handling of intricate state matters. He loved the atmosphere of books and learning, but it did not completely satisfy his energetic nature. He longed for wider fields, for greater activity and a fuller life.

At no more critical time in the fiscal affairs of Spain could Don Isaac Abravanel have been summoned. The unremitting wars with Portugal and the protracted campaign in Granada had drained the last ounce of gold from the Spanish treasury. The war on the Moors, though popular, was appallingly expensive. No new revenue could be raised from a people already heavily burdened. The difficulty was further complicated by a renewed show of strength on the part of the Moors. It became clear that what had promised to be a short and victorious expedition actually demanded a tremendous cost of blood and treasure. In their desperation, the royal pair looked around for the man who could perform the miracle of pulling the country out of the mire in which it found itself, and they discovered him in Don Isaac Abravanel, who, in somewhat similar situations in Portugal, had mobilized his country's resources and supplied the armies in the field.

Don Isaac Abravanel advanced quickly at the court of Ferdinand and Isabella. He was tactful and cautious, prudent and circumspect in his conduct at the most strongly Catholic court in all Christendom. He served his masters well. He built up the country's resources and enlarged his own fortune. Abravanel himself relates how he grew rich in the royal service and purchased for himself lands and estates, and how from the court and the highest grandees he received great consideration and honor. He was impressed with the gracious attitude of his rulers, and to encourage their friendship toward him and his fellow Jews, he personally advanced a considerable sum toward the rehabilitation of the country's treasury.

But could Don Isaac Abravanel have been unconscious of the policy of total extermination of his people being planned by the Spanish monarchs? Was he not aware of the expulsion of the Jews from Andalusia only three years before he received his royal commission, and their subsequent expulsion from Aragon in 1487, while he presumably was basking in the regal favor and patronage of Ferdinand and Isabella? What illusions about his own and his people's future could Abravanel have had in a country terrorized by so savage and brutal an instrument as the Inquisition? In one of his works he speaks of "the thousands and thousands of renegade Jews who were consigned to the flames by an impious and fanatical clergy, motivated not by religion, but by greed, ambition and self-seeking."

Why, then, did not Abravanel try to prevent the wholesale destruction of the Jews by counseling them to emigrate to some other country? For what miracle could he have been waiting? Under the sinister domination of Torquemada, the evil genius of the Inquisition, Abravanel might have known that there was no future for the unbaptized Jews in Spain and that, after having finished with the Marranos, he would turn his bloody hand against all Jews in the kingdom, baptized and unbaptized. Abravanel sensed it in the priest's growing insolence and in his complete control over the minds of his sovereigns, who would deny him nothing, no matter how extravagant his demands. Ferdinand could not for the moment agree to his confessor's frenzied demand for the total expulsion of the Jews, for Granada had not yet capitulated and he was badly in need of the ability and experience of his Jewish subjects in the fields of finance and taxation. But their doom was irrevocably sealed and decided upon.

Still, like their brethren in Germany nearly four and a half centuries later, they did not believe that the blow would fall with such crushing, annihilating force. They had faith in their leaders and in their influential friends at court. They had contributed mightily to the greatness and prosperity of their fatherland, and the very marriage of Ferdinand and Isabella, which joined the kingdoms of Castile and Aragon under one common rule and made possible a united Spain, was largely the work of patriotic Jewish Spaniards, especially Abraham Senior, a rich and influential Jewish financier and statesman. Paradoxical as it may seem, this Ferdinand, who wrapped himself in the mantle of Christian piety and was titled by the Pope as "Ferdinand the Catholic," could not himself have withstood the scrutiny of the Inquisition because of the Jewish blood passed on to him by his mother, who was the granddaughter of a Jewess of Toledo.

Don Isaac Abravanel doubted that the king, notwithstanding Torquemada's untiring urging, would carry out the total expulsion of the Jews. He was confident that the "pious" zeal of the churchman would burn itself out, that the people themselves would rise in revolt against him, as the Pope had denounced his methods, and that the sovereigns, realizing how slight were the gains from the Inquisition as compared with its power for destruction, would soon disown it and its principal sponsor. Moreover, as Don Isaac Abravanel saw it, the situation of the Jews everywhere in the world was quite hopeless. If they were not treated in other countries with the extreme violence they experienced in Spain they nevertheless were regarded as unwelcome strangers almost everywhere. But, above all, Abravanel did not have the power he was credited with. His functions were strictly financial and administrative and he had no influence on the political affairs of state. When, therefore, the blow fell, he and all the other Jewish representatives at the court were helpless.

It was written in the stars that the two men, Don Isaac Abravanel and Christopher Columbus, who, according to Salvador de Madariaga, Spanish diplomat and historian, was really named Colón and came from Marrano stock, should meet in a critical moment in their lives at the court of Ferdinand and Isabella, as they may have met before at the court of Alfonso of Portugal. Both came to Spain at almost the same time—Abravanel in 1483, Columbus a year later. One came as a fugitive in need of rest and peace, the other as an adventurer seeking fame and fortune. Abravanel had brought with him his unfinished commentaries, Columbus his vision of the splendor and opulence of the East.

While full documentation of Columbus' Jewish, or Marrano, ancestry is lacking, there is the circumstantial evidence of his many Marrano-Jewish connections. He knew Abraham Zacutto, a celebrated scientist and cartographer, whose astronomical charts he used on his voyage; he left in his will a small legacy to a Jew; he was fond of quoting from the prophets and entertained messianic illusions, considering himself a messenger of Jehovah. Jews were the first to befriend and assist him in his poverty and pave the way for his success. When the wars with Granada exhausted the royal treasury and it was unable to promote his expedition, Don Isaac Abravanel and his two Marrano friends, Luis de Santangel and Gabriel Sanchez advanced almost 3,000,000 *maravedis* to equip Columbus' fleet and make it ready for the voyage.

The man who signed the order to expel the Jews on the very same day put his signature to one of the most important papers in history, bidding Colón-Columbus to go to "certain parts of the Ocean Sea on some errands required by our service." Little wonder that later Colón-Columbus was to connect in one sentence subjects of the expulsion of the Jews and of the discovery of the Indies. With the royal order in his wallet, he left for Palos, a small seaport in Andalusia, from which he sailed on his expedition when the country was already astir with the economic and social effects of the uprooting of his old race from the soil in which it had thrived for so long.

The Semitic group at court had not remained passive. Both the *conversos* and the professing Jews had not abandoned the fight. As the day drew near on which the edict of expulsion was to be proclaimed, they redoubled their efforts. Don Isaac Abravanel was among those who were most active. Besides exerting all his personal influence with the king and queen, he implored his many friends at court to assist him. His activities in behalf of his people at this time were truly herculean. He missed no opportunity in his attempt at least to mitigate the horrors of the impending catastrophe. In his struggle he did have the assistance of many influential persons at court who resented the vain masqueradings of the arrogant monk Torquemada. They saw through his sham piety and mock holiness, and did what they could to defeat his barbarous designs.

The royal court became a battleground of plots and counterplots among those who were loyal in their support of Don Isaac Abravanel and those who were fanatical in their zeal for Torquemada. It was a struggle of reason against fanaticism; of merciful justice against inhuman cruelty; of the lives of three hundred thousand people against the frenzied hate of one demoniacal being. What chance did Abravanel have against such odds?

History has preserved a record of the historic meeting between Don Isaac Abravanel and his sovereigns. Don Isaac argued the cause of his condemned people with moving eloquence. "I pleaded with the king," he writes, "many times. I supplicated him thus: 'Save, O king. Why do you thus to thy servants? Lay on us every tribute and ransom, gold and silver, and everything that the children of Israel possess, they shall willingly give to their fatherland.' I sought out my friends, those who stand near the king and enjoy his confidence, and begged them to beseech and petition him to revoke the evil decree concerning our destruction and annihilation, but all in vain. Like an adder which stoppeth its ears, he remained deaf to our appeals. The queen, also was standing by his side, but she would not listen to our plea. On the contrary, she argued in favor of carrying out the plan. I neither rested nor spared myself, yet the calamity was not averted."

Still, Abravanel did not cease his efforts. He pledged his own fortune of thirty thousand gold ducats and the entire wealth of the Jews—a sum being sufficient to cover the entire cost of the war with Granada. Here was a treasure to whet the appetite of any monarch, even one less greedy than King Ferdinand, and, at last, at the sight of so much gold, he wavered. Although the queen remained adamant, Ferdinand was ready to accept the ransom and rescind the edict of expulsion. But Torquemada was suspicious and never for a moment relaxed his vigilance. When he learned what was happening, he burst into the audience chambers with a crucifix held aloft in his hand, screaming with frenzied, fanatical boldness:

"Behold the crucified whom the accursed Judas Iscariot sold for thirty pieces of silver. Your majesties are about to sell him for 30,000 ducats. Here he is, take him and sell him. I resign my post. No one shall impute this guilt to me. You, however, shall have to answer to your God." He threw the crucifix into the faces of the monarchs and then rushed out of the hall. The king and queen were stunned by the attack, and Torquemada prevailed, as fanatics invariably do over minds so much weaker than their own.

It was Abravanel's last meeting with the sovereigns of Spain. A friendship lasting eight years now ended abruptly. Once again, as in Portugal, ingratitude was to be his only reward for years of faithful service.

It was on the 31st day of March, 1492, during the very same year that had witnessed their triumphal entry into Granada, that Ferdinand and Isabella issued the proclamation ordering all Jews to depart from the Spanish dominions of Castile, Aragon, Sicily, and Sardinia. They were given but four months in which to leave their homes and were allowed to take with them their movable property except gold, silver, and coins of any description, and those goods whose export was forbidden. In other words, they were allowed to take practically nothing.

The first reaction to this edict was utter panic and desolation. Abravanel writes: "When the Jews learned of the evil that had befallen them, they wept and mourned. Wherever the news of the king's decree was received, there was great wailing and lamentation, for no such sorrow had befallen the Jews since they had been driven out of their own land and sent into exile to live among strangers." Although they had long expected the blow, its coming found them unprepared. They had been unable to believe that the measure would be so cruel, so savage.

The four months which they were allowed in which to prepare themselves were altogether too short. They could not collect debts owed them, which they would soon forfeit because of their absence. The market became so glutted with commodities that no sales were possible. Few were willing to buy what the proprietors would soon have to leave behind them. The sacrifice of property was so great that a chronicler of the times stated that he saw a house exchanged for an ass and a vineyard for a suit of clothes.

But as soon as they had weathered the first shock a strange, almost mystic calm settled over the outcasts. They accepted their fate with patience and resignation, putting their faith in God and in the ultimate destiny of their people. "Every man," writes Don Isaac, "said to his brother, 'Be strong and of good courage for the sake of our faith and the Law of God. If he lets us live, we shall live. If, however, we are to die, we shall not be faithless to our covenant. Nor will we falter, but march onward in the name of our God.'"

When the hour of exile struck there were some defections in the ranks of the departing Israelites. A contemporary writer, Joseph Ya'abez, notes that it was the poorer people who were most ready to accept exile and suffer rather than abandon their religion, while many of the wealthy were willing to accept baptism. Among the latter was Abraham Senior, financial advisor to the crown.

Although an influential leader of the Spanish Jews, he could not bring himself to leave his country, and, at eighty he was induced to accept Christianity. He was more typical of the wealthy Jews than Abravanel, who willingly surrendered his fortune and position out of loyalty to the faith of his fathers. Yet who can censure those other men and women, who had already experienced the worst forms of savage brutality and were terrorized by what the future might hold for them?

A foul attempt was made to prevent the departures of Don Isaac Abravanel and his son, Judah, who was a talented surgeon and the personal physician to the king and queen. Ferdinand was anxious to retain their services and secretly arranged to seize Judah's year-old son, hoping thereby to force both the Abravanels to remain in Spain. His plot, however, miscarried. Judah Abravanel learned of the scheme and quickly sent the child to Portugal with its nurse, intending to join them later. It was the beginning of a tragedy that was to spread a blight over the lives of both father and son, who were never to meet again.

On the second day of August, 1492, after a respite of two days, which Don Isaac had obtained for them, three hundred thousand Jews sorrowfully departed from their native Spain. By a strange coincidence, the day happened to be the Ninth of Ab, on which, fourteen hundred and twenty-two years before, their forefathers had lost their national independence through the fall of Jerusalem. But it was also the very same day on which Christopher Columbus set out on his historic voyage which was to result in the discovery of the new continent, America. In his diaries, Columbus himself noted the peculiar coincidence of the two events. "In the same month," he wrote, "in which their majesties issued the edict that all Jews should be driven out of their kingdoms and territories, in the same month, they gave me the order to undertake, with sufficient men, my expedition to the Indies."

It was a miserable and wretched army of fugitives that left the country in which their sires had lived for centuries. Life seemed pitiless and every hand was raised against them. To help them was irreligious; to rob, pillage, and murder them was considered an act of piety. To quote Don Isaac Abravanel: "The expulsion was accompanied by pillage on land and on sea. . . ."

Many of the sufferers, driven mad by hunger, sought nourishment from the scanty grass covering the rocks and sands of the deserts, and attempted to quench their thirst with the water of muddy pools. Disease and famine exacted a frightful toll. According to Abravanel, of the three hundred thousand Jews who left Spain, scarcely more than ten thousand survived after their wanderings were over. And their wealth, which at the time of their departure from Spain amounted to the considerable sum of thirty million ducats, was now entirely gone.

Thus Spain ceased to be a center of Jewish life and culture. The sunny land of Andalusia was to know the Jew no more. She had proven an ungrateful and faithless mother to the children who had loved her. Henceforth, other lands were to be enriched by the hearts and minds and hands that Spain had spurned. In their flight, the Jews left everything behind—their fields and their gardens, their beautiful homes, their stately buildings and magnificent synagogues. All these possessions were immediately seized by the state and the church and converted into either state property or churches and monasteries. But the spoils failed to enrich the despoilers. The glory of Spain began to diminish. With the fleeing exiles, all that had made her great vanished. The country was to pay for centuries for the sufferings she had inflicted upon an unfortunate people.

Don Isaac Abravanel did not flinch from sharing the fate of his people. To him it was unthinkable that he should preserve his fortune by disloyalty to his suffering brethren. He not only shared their hardships but was among the first to go into exile. Whatever little he managed to save from his wrecked fortune he distributed among the poor and distressed. Almost all his writings contain some reference to the frightful plight of his fellow Jews, with never a word about his own misfortunes.

Abravanel asked no immunity for himself or his family. The same Joseph Ya'abez, to whom reference has already been made while censuring the rich and aristocratic Jews, has nothing but the highest praise and admiration for the courage, heroism, and endurance of Don Isaac. When Abravanel arrived in Naples after many months of weary travel, he came, like the rest of his stricken brethren, a poor and penniless exile, bringing with him nothing but his unshakable faith in the future glory of the Jews.

At fifty-five Abravanel felt himself an old man, broken in spirit and courage. Although the Jewish community in Naples welcomed him warmly and showed him every mark of honor and respect, Abravanel felt himself a stranger in a country whose habits, customs, and language he did not understand. Gloomy and despondent, this man who had so often cheered others was himself now in need of encouragement.

Abravanel might have turned again to his books and his studies, but the atmosphere of Naples was not congenial to scholarship. The Jews there were traders rather than thinkers; business was their chief occupation. Before the arrival of Abravanel Naples was devoid of the barest essentials that mark a true Jewish community. It had neither rabbis nor teachers, schools nor scholars. To a man like Abravanel, however, the cultural poverty of his new home constituted a serious challenge. With every ounce of his remaining energy he set about to raise the spiritual level of his environment. He installed a rabbi, trained teachers, and created facilities for the religious education of the young.

Attracted by his presence, other Jewish scholars came to Naples and settled there. The Jewish community of the city was no longer in the desolate state in which Abravanel had found it. Though seared by his past experiences, he wanted to resume his work. In the stress and hurry of his active life, many things had remained undone. There were manuscripts to be completed, more commentaries to be written, and, above all, there was the despairing, anguished spirit of his stricken people to be strengthened and comforted. As a result of their suffering the faith of many Jews was crumbling. Their exile and martyrdom had engendered religious doubts and uncertainties, and missionary priests were taking advantage of their lack of faith. It was a situation that Abravanel could not ignore. In this connection, he began a program of writing that would require many years to complete.

But as had happened before in Portugal and in Spain, he was again "betrayed" by his fame and reputation. His renown as a statesman had followed him into exile, and he was again to be denied leisure for his scholarly work.

King Ferdinand of Naples, in striking contrast to his royal name-sake in Spain, was an enlightened and humane ruler. Although historians have recorded a different impression of Ferdinand and his son, Alfonso, attributing to them all kinds of vices and cruelties, Abravanel called them "princes of mercy and righteousness." It was probably not disinterested kindness alone that prompted the king's generosity. The king of Naples knew of Abravanel's services to the Spanish sovereigns and of his reputation as financier and statesman, and he attempted to attract the refugee statesman to his court by extending every kindness and courtesy to the Jews.

Thus, for the third time Abravanel joined the court of a reigning monarch and lived in the familiar splendor of kings and princes. Though he arrived in Naples a stranger and all but a beggar, one among thousands of stranded refugees, he was sought out and entrusted with the duties of a high office in less than a year. Abravanel served his royal patron well, and when Ferdinand died and was succeeded by his son, Alfonso II, he continued at court. During this period Abravanel managed to complete his commentary on the two books of Kings, in which, besides carefully elucidating the text in its historic setting, he commented upon the Spanish exile, the suffering of the Jews in the Diaspora, and the disastrous effect upon their faith.

But fate pursued Abravanel relentlessly, robbing him of lasting peace. The dangerous war with France, which Naples was now unable to avert, resulted in its capture by the armies of King Charles VIII. The French ruthlessly destroyed everything in their path, including Don Isaac's priceless library. His account of what then befell him is brief: "I amongst the exiles came to Naples, where, however, likewise I had no rest, for King Charles VIII of France ruined us. His soldiers plundered all my possessions. The French were masters of the city, the very inhabitants having abandoned the government."

After the death of Alfonso, Abravanel fled to Corfu for refuge. The fatigue and hardships involved in his frequent changes of residence would have proved almost unbearable were it not for the fact that in Corfu he discovered the manuscript of his commentary on Deuteronomy, which had been lost during his travels. In Abravanel's own words, "I embarked on board a ship, and by God's mercy, came to the Island of Corfu, and whilst there, got hold of what I had before written on this book, and joyfully resolved to enlarge it."

While in Corfu Abravanel also wrote the major portion of his commentary on Isaiah, whom he considered as the greatest of prophets, although it was not to be completed until three years later. It is a curious work, with its lengthy introductions entirely devoted to the belief in resurrection, a subject much discussed in those days. Since life offered the Jews so little their thoughts frequently turned to the contemplation of death and life after death.

Abravanel then set out for Monopoli, a small seaport near Naples, where he was to spend the next seven years, from 1496 to 1503—the period of his greatest literary activity. His family had scattered. "My wife and my sons," he wrote, "are away from me and in another country, and I am left by myself alone, an alien in a strange land." One must marvel at his sheer power of endurance.

Freed from the political activities which had hitherto absorbed him, he surrendered himself to the literary labors with a zeal and an enthusiasm far too great for a man of his years. But in his work he found the solace and comfort he sought and felt compensated for all the sorrow and suffering he had endured. Books on a variety of subjects issued in rapid succession from his busy pen.

Driven by a mighty desire to bring a measure of hope and comfort to the exiles, Abravanel turned with particular love and tenderness to the messianic prophecies of the Bible. With incomparable love and imagination he set out to restore their waning faith in their redemption. Under the horrors of their wretched existence, a mood of defeatism seized upon the fugitives. Many, even the most loyal and faithful, despaired of the future and were receptive material for the proselytizing church. Young and old, their spirit broken, uttered words of blasphemy against God and his Anointed. Abravanel was critical of the Jewish philosophers who treated the Messiah allegorically; he deplored and rejected their tendency to rationalize the Messiah out of existence and create a kind of nebulous, mythical figure without relation to the physical and spiritual needs of the Jews. The times, he insisted, demanded a real and living Messiah, able to redeem and save, instead of the veiled, glorified vision of the imagination the Jewish rationalists created. Much as he admired Maimonides in other respects, he could not accept his statement that there will be no difference between the present and the messianic era save in Israel's later freedom from subjection to the nations of the earth, and he interprets Samuel's declaration in the Talmud on this point as not denying the transcendental prophecies of the Bible concerning the messianic era.

Abravanel presented his own conception of the Messiah and the messianic era in three books which demolished the rationalist views and the Christian messiahship of Jesus in a clear and ingenious manner and which to this day survive as unsurpassed classics of messianic literature. In the order of their composition, they are *Mayene Yesua* (Wells of Salvation)—1496; *Yesuat Meshiho* (The Salvation of his Annointed)—1497; *Mashmia Yesua* (Announcement of Salvation)—1498. *Mashmia Yesua* is a valuable collection of all the passages in the Bible relating to the Messiah. Abravanel also wrote, at the request of his son Samuel, a student in Salonika, a commentary on *Abot* under the title *Nahlat Abot* (Inheritance of the Fathers)—1505, and *Zebah Pesah* (The Passover Sacrifice), based on the tales relating to Israel's first redemption. Abravanel's messianic treatises were widely read by Jews everywhere and still are read to this day, as testified by their frequent publication.

Distressed by the wretchedness and hopelessness of his people after their expulsion from Spain, Abravanel not only tried to relieve their despondent mood by preaching belief in the Messiah but actually predicted the very time of his advent. Regarding himself as a descendant of the Davidic Dynasty, he entertained the idea that the promised redeemer would come from his house and that his own eyes would behold his appearance. Supported by vague allusions in the Book of Daniel and passages in the Talmud, he set the year 1503 as the time for the coming of the Messiah. His computation of the "end" proved an illusion, and he must have smarted under the pain of disappointment. But the intensity of his belief in the immediacy of redemption spread a feeling of hope and comfort among the despairing exiles.

But pure and holy as were Abravanel's intentions, it was but natural that his magnificent faith in the speedy end of his people's suffering through the coming of the Messiah should fire the imagination of deluded dreamers and visionaries, many of whom presented themselves as the hoped-for-Redeemer. In the East and in the West they appeared, in Christian and Moslem countries, bearing the glad tidings of the Messiah, influenced by, if not actually repeating Abravanel's fervid words. Messianic pretenders like Asher Laemmelein, Diego Piros (or, as he later called himself, Solomon Molko), David Reubeni, and the notorious Sabbatai Zevi, were either acquainted with Abravanel's messianic writings themselves or knew of them by reputation.

Venice provided the last glow to light up the career of the aging statesman-philosopher. Although sixty-six years of age, the unwearied wanderer took up his staff once again so that he could spend the remaining years of his life in the classical city of democracy, popularly known as the Pearl of the Adriatic. Although in that age of almost universal intolerance Jews had their occasional difficulties in the Venetian Republic, also, they nevertheless established in its capital city an active community life of their own, with rabbis, scholars, and schools of learning. Jews all along the Dalmatian coast made Venice their trading center, and with them came merchants of another kind, with knapsacks filled with spiritual goods, which they dispensed freely for the religious and cultural enlightenment of their Venetian co-religionists.

Don Isaac Abravanel was happy in his new home, where for the first time in his life he could maintain cultural relations with Jews of other lands. But, above all, he was overjoyed to be reunited with his two sons, Judah and Joseph (Samuel was still studying in Salonika), both of whom possessed qualities almost equaling those of their father. He derived a large part of his happiness from the fact that he was free from the burden of state business and would be able to complete the work he had left unfinished in Monopoli.

If, however, Don Isaac planned to pass his days in Venice unknown and with no other responsibility than his work, he cherished a false hope. For 1508 was a critical year for the Venetian Republic, which was on the brink of war with Portugal on account of their conflicting maritime trade interests. It is not known whether Don Isaac offered his services or was commissioned by the Venetian Senate to negotiate a trade treaty with Portugal, which only twenty years before, in 1485, had passed a death sentence upon him. The treaty for which Don Isaac worked did not materialize, but he himself was long remembered for his ability, tact, and personality in his negotiations.

The last act of his diplomatic career was now over and he could devote himself, undisturbed, to his literary work. He worked hard and without pause. Notwithstanding his increasing years, his style was fine, his ideas were presented with clarity and precision, and his material invariably well organized. He completed his commentary on the entire Bible, except the Hagiographa, and his commentary to the *Guide*, and wrote two new books in addition. His fame was universal. He was known in the East as well as in the West, in Middle Europe as well as in South Europe. Letters came to him from every country where Jews resided, asking for his counsel and guidance in all sorts of matters.

Some of these inquiries were of a scholarly nature. For example, Saul Ashkenazi, a learned rabbi of Candia, wrote to him about certain obscure passages in Maimonides' *Guide for the Perplexed*.

Abravanel's reply is particularly valuable for the information it contains about his life and writings. "These books," writes Abravanel, "were written after I left my country. Before then, all the time I spent at the courts and palaces of kings was given to royal service. I had no leisure for study, and knew no books, but spent my days in vanity and my years in trouble, achieving only riches and honor. And now these very riches have perished and the glory is departed from Israel. It is only after I had been a fugitive and a wanderer on earth from one kingdom to another, and without money, that I sought out the Book of the Lord, according to the words of him who says in the Talmud, 'He is sadly in want, and therefore he studies'." He regretted the hours spent on what he called "unsatisfying knowledge," and wrote to Ashkenazi: "I confess my guilt that in the vanity of my youth I spent much time on the natural sciences and on philosophy. Now, however, that I have become an old man and seen much affliction, I say to myself, 'Why devote so much attention to Greek literature and other such matters foreign to me?' Therefore, I have limited myself to the contemplation of *The Guide for the Perplexed* and to exposition of the books of the Bible. These are the sources of all knowledge, and in their wisdom all doubts and perplexities are disolved."

The letter, written when Don Isaac was seventy, is depressing and unlike his usually uncomplaining nature. Advanced age had done much to weaken and enfeeble his physical powers but his mental faculties remained unimpaired and, had he not already covered almost everything in his field, he might still have attempted new tasks. What embittered Don Isaac Abravanel and made his closing days dismal and dejected was the fact that, instead of witnessing the redemption of his people as he had hoped and predicted, he saw fate cruelly harden against them. There were clouds on the horizon of his storm-tossed brethren in Italy, and he feared that the violence and ferocity with which Ferdinand stamped out the Jews and Judaism in Spain would now be repeated in the Italian provinces under Spanish rule. Fortunately, Abravanel did not live to see the full culmination of these events. He died either on

November 25, 1508 or January 13, 1509, according to respective authorities, at the age of seventy-two years.

Great honors were shown him by the leaders of his own people, as well as by the non-Jews of the Republic; but since under the law the burial of Jews was not permitted in Venice, his body was taken for interment to Padua. Fate, however, willed it that the man who enjoyed little rest during his life should find no greater repose in death. For not long after Don Isaac was laid to rest the Venetian Republic, to which Padua at the time belonged, was involved in a war with Maximilian, emperor of Germany, and in the fighting Venice was sacked and destroyed as was also the old Jewish cemetery of Padua. The slabs and tombstones were demolished and every mark of identification obliterated. It was not until four hundred and sixty-seven years after his death, in 1904, that the Jews of Padua made amends for the ravages of time and war and erected a monument in the center of the cemetery to the memory of Don Isaac Abravanel, with appropriate inscriptions in Hebrew and the Italian language. But more striking than the epitaph itself is the poem composed by his famous son, Judah:

> A tower of strength to his people was he,
>   A buckler and shield in their need:
> Repairer of breaches, restorer of paths,
>   Consoler in words and in deed.
>
> In counsel profound, in station supreme,
>   The Captain, his hand at the helm!
> The princes came daily to seek his advice;
>   The nobles and chiefs of the realm.
>
> Great master of knowledge, of science and wit,
>   Counsellor wonderful, prince of peace;
> The Law of the Lord was his constant delight;
>   His thoughts therein *sans* surcease!

Rabbi Meir of Rothenburg

THE JEWS OCCUPIED an anomalous position in thirteenth-century Germany. They had duties but no rights, the responsibilities but not the privileges of citizens. Indeed, they were not regarded as persons but as chattels, not as human beings but as property. They were the livestock of kings, dukes, and bishops, who sold, pawned, and ceded them without their own will or consent. They were vested interest *servi camerae,* chamber serfs, of those in power, lay or ecclesiastical, in the territory in which it was their misfortune to live. Classed as property, the Jews had not the right to change or choose their place of residence. Disputes often arose over the ownership of Jews, and bishops and boroughs not infrequently fought acrimoniously to establish their claim to them.

The end of the crusades did not end the misery of the Jews in medieval Germany, for the kings and princes realized that living Jews were worth more to them than dead ones. Rudolph of Habsburg, the pauper prince who managed to seize power and establish himself as emperor of Germany, justified his plunder and confiscation of the property of his Jewish subjects by shamelessly declaring that "all Jews, without exception, are our crown servants." He was one of a number of German princes to conduct a lively trade in Jews by selling or hiring them out and pledging them to creditors. Rudolph must have been in dire need of money, indeed, when he once pawned five Jews for three hundred marks and another time pledged the Jews of Lemburg for a like paltry sum.

The Jews of thirteenth-century Germany were a depressed and dejected lot. Although they had lived and trafficked in the Rhineland for centuries, perhaps since Emperor Constantine in the fourth century, when the native barbarian Germans were still clad in buck skin and roamed the primeval forest, the only privilege they had was to suffer and die without resistance. Changes in the world around them were of comparative indifference to them, for invariably the result was the same and only the method of persecution changed. They were naïve in the sciences, disinterested in the arts, and, unlike their contemporary co-religionists in Moslem Spain, they had not distinguished themselves as poets, philosophers, and men of letters.

To compensate for their deficiency in the things in which their brethren to the southwest ranked so high, the Jews of the Rhineland developed what Solomon Schechter in his admirable essay, "Jewish Saints in Mediaeval Germany," calls a "religious delicacy," a depth of feeling, and a spiritual inwardness that were rarely equaled by their brethren in any other country. They cared more for Torah than for the arts and sciences, more for piety than for philosophy, more for prayer than for the rationalizing sophistications of the wise and the learned. It was from these "naïve" and simple Torah-minded Jews that sprang that group of rare and remarkable men who became famous as *Hasidei Ashkenaz,* the Pious Men of Germany. These men stamped their religious and ethical genius on future generation; indeed, so great was their faith and so deep their devotion to Judaism that they left behind them an unparalleled record of martyrdom. While thousands of Jews in Spain and Portugal betrayed their faith because of their unwillingness or inability to make the extreme sacrifice, their brethren in benighted Germany not only submitted to their fate without a murmur but even introduced into their ritual a regular benediction, thanking God for the opportunity and privilege of dying for the sanctification of His Name. The benediction runs: "Blessed be Thou, O Lord, our God, King of the Universe who has sanctified us by Thy commandments and bade us love Thy glorious and awful Name, Who was and is and will be, with all our hearts and all our souls, and to sanctify Thy name in public. Blessed be Thou, O Lord, who sanctifies Thy name among the many."

That the Jews of Germany were not broken by their experiences but later even produced great and holy men and scholars in whose hands the lamp of learning was unextinguished was due to a large extent to the faith and genius of Rabbi Meir of Rothenburg, the greatest talmudic authority in Germany in the second half of the thirteenth century. He was a wise and courageous leader, a clear thinker, and an exemplary spiritual personality who served and helped save his people in the hard and trying times with which they were confronted. He belonged to that extraordinary company of the *Hasidei Ashkenaz,* which, among others, produced in the twelfth century the mystic-saint Rabbi Judah ha-Hasid, of Regensburg, author of the well-known *Sefer Hasidim* (Book of the Saints), and his famous pupil, Eliezer ben Judah of Worms, popular for his ethico-mystical work, *Rokeah.*

But while their concentrated mass suffering produced among the Jews of Germany a tendency to mysticism and idle speculations, and while fantastic dreams of a golden future sometimes led to deplorable consequences, Rabbi Meir was one of the more tough-minded of the German Jews. His love was for the Torah, his devotion to talmudic learning. He towered over the preceding and following generations, Rabbenu Gershom and Rashi alone having measured up to his scholarly stature. He knew the whole rabbinic literature, the Babylonian and the Jerusalem Talmud, as well as the geonic Responsa. Reliable texts of the Talmud were scarce in those days and to meet the needs of his students he often had to follow the example of Rabbenu Gershom, who copied the whole Mishnah and Talmud with his own hand, at the same time revising many faulty sections.

Rabbi Meir was, in addition, a prolific liturgical poet. His compositions are included in the liturgy of the Day of Atonement and of the Ninth of Ab. "Although he was a German," writes Louis Ginzberg, "he modeled his poems on the style of Judah Halevi, although not equaling him. Still, his *piyutim* show great command of language and, to a certain extent, true poetic inspiration." In Rabbi Meir's time, the synagogue ritual was not completely organized but was in a rather fluid and chaotic state, so that it required of a *hazan,* or cantor, more than a pleasant voice to render the prayers in their proper order. Reb Meir, therefore, discharged the function of a *hazan* for his congregation, in which capacity he was instrumental in stabilizing and consolidating the Ashkenazi liturgy.

"Of Rothenburg" is added to Rabbi Meir's name, although he was not born there and did not die there. During the course of his many wanderings he stayed longer in that city than anywhere else and established there his school of talmudic studies, with its many pupils. He was born in the year 1215 at Worms, Germany, in the city made famous by the legendary Rashi chapel and her schools of learning. He hailed from a family of rabbis, scholars, and judges, some of whom he mentions in his legal decisions with great respect and deference. His father, Baruk, from whom Meir received his early education, was a man who added to his reputation for scholarship and piety a brilliant gift of oratory. His son frequently refers to him in his Responsa with a natural filial love and reverence.

Rabbi Meir—he was titled "Rabbi" at a young age—followed the custom of many other students of the Law who left their native towns and migrated to schools of learning famed for their learned teachers. After whiling briefly in his own country in one town after another, he was rewarded for his intellectual odyssey in Paris, where he studied under the celebrated Rabbi Yehiel. He was in France during the famous controversy over the Talmud at La Rochelle in 1240, instigated by the notorious apostate Nicolas Donin and conducted in the presence of Pope Gregory IX. The attempted conversion of the Jews by controversy, or public disputations, after every other attempt had failed, followed the familiar pattern. Learned Jews and Christians were ordered to argue the merits of their respective religions. But to make sure that the Christians, aiming for the souls of the Jews might not lose their own souls, apostates learned in Jewish lore were pressed into service.

In this case, it was Nicolas Donin, a Talmudist excommunicated by the French rabbis for his heterodox views who, burning for revenge against his former co-religionists, incited the temporal and spiritual powers against them and the Talmud. He framed fraudulent and disgraceful charges against the Jews and the Talmud, charging that it was the latter which hardened the Jews against accepting Christianity and that once the Talmud was destroyed, their conversion would be easy. Rabbi Yehiel was one of the four

Jewish representatives at the debate. But if the renegade's ambition for the conversion of his former brethren was not realized, he was more successful in his attack on the Talmud. On March 3, 1240, while the Jews were in their synagogue, all Jewish books were seized; in June, 1242, twenty-four carloads of the Talmud and other Hebrew books were committed to the flames in Paris. Rabbi Meir was a witness of the infamous destruction of the Jewish holy books, and commemorated the sad event by his elegy, *sha'ali serufah baesh,* recited on the ninth day of the month of Ab.

For no accountable reason, unless it was for her proximity to Worms, the city of his birth, on his return to Germany Rabbi Meir settled in Rothenburg and founded there his school of talmudic learning. In any event, like Rabbi Yohanan ben Zakkai in a similar situation hundreds of years before, Rabbi Meir felt the need of overcoming the despair and hopelessness of the Jews of the Rhineland after the century of bloodletting by the crusaders. Reb Meir was only thirty-seven years old at the time, but his fame had spread, and his school assumed something of the dignity and importance that once marked the Babylonian academies of learning, not only in the eyes of Germans but of people in the adjacent countries as well.

Reb Meir lived in a large house of twenty-one rooms, with special apartments for his students, whom he wanted always to have near him. Did he receive any other emoluments besides the house which was probably given to him by the community? If not, it may have been because it was not until comparatively late in the Middle Ages that rabbis consented to be remunerated for the services they rendered to their congregations. In the case of Reb Meir, he had independent means from private investments. Reb Meir not only supported himself and his family from his private income but provided for the needs of his impecunious students who had no other means of supporting themselves. He was, therefore, an ideal rabbi—one who did not derive his power and authority from the *Parnassim,* the lay authorities of the community, but lived, spoke, and acted independently of them.

Rabbi Meir reflected the times and spiritual condition of

the Jews in thirteenth-century Germany. He was their greatest scholar and the most generally recognized religious teacher of his generation. But his scholarship was more erudite than brilliant, more learned than acute. He followed the traditional line without deviating an inch. It was a trait of the man and of his scholarship that likewise characterized the spiritual life of the German Jews of his time, who were more strict and punctilious in their observance of the law than the Jews of most other countries. They represented a type of spiritual backwardness which, seared by the world, finds refuge in extravagant beliefs and practices. Thus, Rabbi Meir encouraged German Jews in their custom of observing Yom Kippur for two days—the tenth and eleventh days of Tishri. He was somewhat eccentric in his piety; he locked the stove of his apartment for the Sabbath and hid the key to prevent his gentile servant from warming the house, even on the plea that the servant was doing it for the master's own benefit. On the Sabbath he would tie his hat to his body by a string, lest he desecrate the day of rest by stooping to pick it up if it fell from his head.

"The thirteenth century," writes Irving A. Agus in his scholarly work, *Rabbi Meir of Rothenburg,* "was the beginning of isolation for the Jews of Germany. . . . Their minds as well as their experiences were considerably narrowed. . . . The strengthening of religion in general, and the growing veneration for saintliness in particular among the Christians over all Europe, was a great factor in focusing the attention of the Jews on the details of their own behavior." They were concerned that every act of theirs, every utterance and every ritual performance should be in strict conformity with what they thought to be the religious law. They questioned Rabbi Meir on such trivial details of ritual observance as how to cut the loaves of bread on the Sabbath, whether one was permitted to open a window on the day of rest, and whether one might drink water on the afternoon of the fourteenth day of Nisan. In his younger and more liberal days, Reb Meir dismissed such questions as *shtut* (nonsense); but as he grew older he became more conservative and stringent in his religious views, and was emphatically in favor of every local religious custom.

He was certainly the greatest legal authority of his age and country, and his leadership was acknowledged by Jewish communities beyond the borders of Germany. His correspondents, some of them outstanding scholars themselves, lavished extravagant praise on him, crowning him with such titular honors as "Gaon," "The Light of Exile," "The Father of Rabbis," "The Father of all Israel." His pupils who lived with him paid him the homage and veneration due a saint or a holy man. They observed and described carefully and in great detail his every habit, custom, and behavior by which the German Jews shaped their lives. The books, writes Irving Agus, "compiled by his students formed a mine of information on his views and practices. These books were studied and consulted by the scholars of the succeeding generations, by authors of codes and Responsa, and especially by R. Moses Isserles, who incorporated many of these views in the *Shulhan Aruk*."

The question has been raised as to how and by whom Reb Meir was appointed or elected to his position as Chief Rabbi of the Jewish communities in Germany. Reb Meir himself never refers to any such official appointment or election. It is not likely that he owed his appointment to Emperor Rudolph of Habsburg, for when governments claimed a voice in the election of rabbis in the Middle Ages the Jews strongly resented the assumption of any such right on the ground of interference in their internal affairs. Least of all would Reb Meir have countenanced any such interference at the hands of the man with whom he was in lifelong conflict. Dr. Louis Ginzberg clinched the matter when he said in his article, "Meir of Rothenburg" in the *Jewish Encyclopedia,* that "merely on account of his great scholarship he was everywhere recognized as the spiritual leader, whose decrees and institutions were considered as authoritative."

Rabbi Meir had an active literary career. Besides his onerous duties as spiritual leader of his community, he was a prolific writer. Not all his writings have survived, but from references and quotations from his works it is evident that his literary operations covered a large and varied field. He wrote commentaries and glosses on a number of tractates of the Talmud. But his Responsa, which became standardized rules of Jewish religious behavior, although addressed to individuals as well as to communities, attracted the widest attention in his own and later generations, gained for him a world-wide reputation, and were entered into the Law books of Jewish religious codifiers.

The Responsa—in Hebrew *She'elot u-Teshubot* (Questions and Answers)—is an ancient but still existing method of learning the authoritative interpretation of the religious law by writing to eminent scholars or heads of academies. Since no provision could be made in the legal codes for specific or contingent cases, the Responsa form an invaluable supplement to the codified law. The Responsa, however, serve a purpose apart from the one for which they were intended. "The Responsa contain invaluable material for general history," writes J. Z. Lauterbach in his article on *She'elot u-Teshubot* in the Jewish Encyclopedia, "as many events are cursorily mentioned in them which are either noted obscurely or totally ignored by contemporary historians, yet which illustrate and explain the conditions of the times. The Responsa thus contribute much to a knowledge of the cultural circumstances of the Jews and of the people among whom they have lived. From these questions based on the problems of daily life, falls much light on the moral and social relations of the times, on occupations and undertakings, on the household, on customs and on usages, on expressions of joy and of sorrow, on recreations and on games."

Rabbi Meir's Responsa, of which there are eight hundred, follow the old pattern developed in the East in the geonic period of the ninth and tenth centuries. Letters of inquiry came to him from various adjacent communities, and also from rabbis and laymen in France, and they covered a large range of questions pertaining to civil and ritual law. His opinion and decision, as judge and supreme legal authority, were solicited on such matters as business transactions, real estate, inheritance, marriage contracts, partnerships, sureties, employees, informers, community government, and taxation. The questions addressed to Reb Meir covered practically the entire gamut of religious and mundane life and illustrate the confidence the people had in his judgment.

He answered the questions addressed to him in a clear and concise style, sometimes in a word or two. He also showed great patience and forbearance, even when irritated by what he regarded as foolish questions. To rabbis who addressed him in exaggerated terms and looked to him as the final authority in all matters of rabbinic law, he protested that they overestimated his learning and importance. He was gentle and considerate toward his colleagues, and when he was compelled to refute or override their decisions, it was with great deference and respect for their position. He was noted for the independence of his mind and judgment, and never hesitated to maintain his position even against authorities whom he held in the utmost reverence and veneration. Thus, while he would not upset decisions of Rashi and Rabbenu Tam, he sometimes cited usages he had observed which agreed with his own position.

Reb Meir would not be involved in intercommunity disputes, and recommended to his correspondents that they abide by the rules of their localities. Indeed, his true greatness is reflected in his relations to the Jewish communities in Germany and their peaceful existence with one another. But the kind and gentle teacher was often provoked and replied angrily when correspondents tried to use his authority in matters outside his jurisdiction. In the Middle Ages local custom *(minhag)* was in chaos among the Jews of Germany, each community following usages handed down from earlier generations which were not always in strict obedience to the law. Indeed, the Talmud accepted the authority of "custom" and gave it the validity of law; but later scholars were dissatisfied and insisted that the letter of the law prevail. In the case of a community in which it was the custom to give presents to gentile servants on Purim—a custom to which a rabbi objected on biblical grounds (Hos. 2:10), Reb Meir wrote: "In places where the custom has already been well rested, it should not be discontinued lest it disturb peaceful relations with the Gentile neighbors."

Gambling was one of the vices to which Jews were addicted in the Middle Ages. Lacking outdoor sports, to which, due to their repressed condition, Jews had no access, they found in games of chance an outlet for the relief of their physical and mental strain. Was gambling among Jews resorted to for profit or merely as a pastime? It evidently was the former or the moralists would not have thundered so vehemently against it. Indeed, the Mishnah declared gambling (dicing) infamous and excluded players of the game from the right to give evidence in a court of justice; and Maimonides in the twelfth century forbade that any game be played for money. While there may have been other kinds of gambling among Jews in the Middle Ages (the Talmud mentions betting on pigeon races), it was wagering on games played with dice against which the Jewish authorities raised their voices in protest. For, despite assertions to the contrary, there is no reference to cards in Jewish sources before the fifteenth century, writes Israel Abrahams, when the game became the rage all over Europe. In Rabbi Meir's time the gambling habit seems to have been widespread among his co-religionists and it is frequently mentioned in his Responsa. Indeed, so addicted had they become to it that many found it hard to abstain. When vows to shun gambling were broken, Reb Meir imposed severe penalties upon the transgressors.

Rabbi Meir was a kind, warmhearted man. The poor and unhappy, the divorced woman, the deserted wife, the workingman, the hired laborer cheated by his master, the teacher denied his fee—all such occupied a special niche in his heart. His decisions in such cases were quite unique for the period—full of warmth, sympathy, and understanding. He was generous and chivalrous toward women, and there are few more touching parts of his Responsa than those which deal with the conduct of husbands toward their wives, which should be tender, respectful, and affectionate. In a rough and violent age, in which women occupied a position of semislavery, Reb Meir not only advocated for them just and correct treatment at the hands of their husbands but a gentle and tender relationship.

The biblical and post-biblical attitude to wives is reflected in Reb Meir's saying: "Husbands must honor their wives even more than they honor themselves." Indeed, "Jewish mystics in the Middle Ages," writes Israel Abrahams, "compared a man's love to God with a man's love for his wife." But not only is a woman to be honored by her husband but she is entitled to his companionship. When in his struggle to seek a livelihood for his family a man is compelled to leave his home for long periods of time the law obliges him to make ample provision for his wife's maintenance during his absence, and Reb Meir ruled that one should not be away from his wife and home for more than eighteen months at a time. By such regulations the tender-hearted teacher of Rothenburg tried to make woman's lot easier in a crude medieval society not always sensitive to her special needs and nature.

Divorces were deplorably common among Jews in the Middle Ages, and sometimes were granted on the flimsiest trumped-up charges of conjugal infidelity. Marriages were contracted at so young an age that divorce often occurred before marriage was fully consummated. Marriage by proxy, common in the whole of medieval Europe, also contributed no little to the frequency of divorces among the Jews. But whatever the cause, the evil was widespread, brought untold distress and hardship to the women involved, and cried out for remedial measures to improve their lot. While the benign and saintly teacher of Rothenburg, with his great respect for authority, could not change or tamper with the long-established divorce laws, he did his utmost to mitigate the evil by curbing the advantage unprincipled husbands took of it. Divorced women were not easily remarried, for divorce carried with it a certain stigma. Rabbi Meir, therefore, insisted that when a divorce was granted, it must be for good and sufficient reason. Marriage and divorce laws occupy a considerable portion of Reb Meir's eight hundred Responsa, in almost all of which the tenor of his decisions is mild and lenient toward the woman. He invalidated the betrothal of a woman entered into in the presence of but one witness (the law calls for two), declaring, "We do not require that she receive a divorce for the mere sake of strictness, since such an act would bar her from marrying a man of priestly lineage." He pronounced legal a betrothal with a copper ring in which the man said,

"I betroth thee with this ring," instead of "with this ring of gold." He declared mock marriages null and void when there was no previous courtship or serious intention to marry whenever a contrary decision would involve the woman in grave legal complications. He refused a husband's request for a divorce from his wife on the ground of her suspected illicit relation with another man. His rabbinical colleagues and the community leaders not infrequently took exception to his lenient interpretation of the law; but the humane and considerate scholar would not be moved from his position of pity and compassion for his distressed and troubled people.

In a religion of such high domestic morality as Judaism, in which, indeed, the Scriptures had used the relation of husband to wife as a type of God's relation to His world, there could be no question of legislating against wife beating. There is no reference in either the Bible or in the Talmud to such monstrous crime. Nevertheless it must be regretfully admitted that the wife beater was not altogether an unknown figure among the Jews in the Middle Ages. Jewish authorities spoke out against wife beating as a debased and depraved practice and public opinion treated the culprits with utmost contempt. It may be cited as proof of the rare occurrence of physical ill usage of Jewish wives by their husbands that in the eight hundred Responsa of Rabbi Meir there are comparatively few which deal with wife beating. His claim was that "Unlike other people, we are not accustomed to beat our wives." When, however, rare incidents of such domestic violence were brought before the scholar-saint of Rothenburg, he was stern to the full extent of his legal authority. On one occasion he accompanied his decision with the remarks: "A Jew must honor his wife more than he honors himself. If one strikes his wife, one should be punished with greater severity than for striking another person. For one is enjoined to honor his wife but is not enjoined to honor the other person. . . . If he persists in striking her, he should be excommunicated, lashed, and suffer the severest punishment, even to the extent of amputating his arm." On another occasion, he authorized a woman to demand a divorce, with full dowry rights, from a husband so destitute of humanity as to physically abuse her. At a considerably earlier period, Rabbi Tam, a grandson of Rashi, forced a wife beater to provide his wife with separate maintenance.

Rabbi Meir was a social philosopher, and the Jewish community organization was his greatest concern. The autonomous government of their community was one of the rights the Jews of France and Germany had succeeded in wresting from their oppressors. In the course of time the authority of the self-governing community became so independent of outside interference that it almost resembled a state within a state, and was often attacked as such. The Jewish community controlled its own courts, regulated taxes, managed its religious and educational institutions, conducted marriage and divorce proceedings, imprisoned offenders, imposed fines, flogged and banished criminals, and, in extreme cases, passed and carried out the death sentence. In other words, the Jewish community was a self-governing body with practically unlimited power over its members. "It was a system of government," writes Irving Agus, "based on high ideals of justice and human rights. . . . This government evolved under no military pressure of any kind, but out of the great need of a group of people for mutual help and co-operation, and was genuinely democratic while, at the same time, it protected the individual against the tyranny of the majority. . . . Such a system of government, essentially democratic, is dependent for the enforcement of its authority entirely upon public opinion, the subtle forces of social approval, the deep religious feeling of the group and its unusual reverence for a study of what constitutes humanity and justice."

Reb Meir was the philosopher and theoretician of the community organization. He pondered deeply on its functions and responsibilities, and on its rights and limitations, and his Responsa are replete with reflections upon various problems surrounding it. His conception of the community is that of a completely sovereign, august, and solemn body, with authority not only over an individual's religious, moral, and ethical conduct but also over his social and economic life. Thus, based on talmudic authority—and the

Talmud was the final and ultimate authority in the community organization—the community arrogated to itself the right to fix weights and measures, prices and wages, and set penalties for the infringement of its rules and regulations. A sense of justice, if not the strict talmudic precept, dictated that the individual who is helped and protected by the community, should submit to its authority.

But while its power in religious matters, such as that to build synagogues, erect houses of study, appoint rabbis, was generally recognized, the question arose among scholars as to its right to interfere in the secular affairs of its members. For be it said, that the Jewish attitude is exceedingly democratic. "Thou shalt choose" is a frequently occurring phrase in the Mosaic legislation, and the Talmud emphasizes over and over the inalienable rights of the individual against the encroachment of the majority; and later authorities shaped their legal enactments and regulations in accordance with the talmudic principle that the sovereign rights of the individual shall not be invaded or coerced by any outside power. Irving Agus marshals a whole array of universally recognized authorities, including Rabbenu Gershom, styled the "Light of the Exile," Rashi, and Rabbenu Tam, among others, who stood for the absolute rights and freedom of the individual in the secular affairs of his life. Does this weaken or undermine the power and control of the community over its members? Not necessarily, writes the author of *Rabbi Meir of Rothenburg*. For one may of his own free will and consent surrender his individual right to the community in which he chooses to live.

Reb Meir was not only in accord with his predecessors on the question of one's personal rights and privileges but, as we shall see, he went far beyond them. Reb Meir was consistent in his theory of freedom in all cases, not even excluding those involving religion. He had strong ideas on this point. He preached the dignity and sanctity of the human personality, which on no account may be abused or violated. His thoughts on this matter are predicated on the assumption that every human being is sovereign unto himself and is free to follow his own choice and will. The *herem* (ban or excommunication—one might call it religious boycott) is an age-old Jewish institution to preserve the authority of the synagogue and the community from offenders against their rules and regulations. In olden times it was a disciplinary measure for maintaining the social and spiritual cohesion of the Jewish group. There were various forms of the ban, depending upon the nature and gravity of the offense. In no case, however, was the penalty so severe that the recalcitrant, by mending his ways, could not be restored to his former position in society. But Reb Meir, with his unbounding love for and devotion to freedom, all but destroyed this protective measure of the community by ruling that the *herem* is effective only when the individual thus penalized submits to it of his own free will and consent. Briefly, the legal basis of the community government is not arbitrary, capricious, or despotic, but is moral and ethical, grounded upon the voluntary consent and agreement of the governed. It is on this principle that Reb Meir explains or justifies the binding authority of the Torah upon Israel—not because it was forced upon them but because it was voluntarily accepted by them. Thus, in his view, it was not under the strained circumstances of Mount Sinai that the *berit,* the binding compact between God and Israel, was consumated, for it was there not voluntary and therefore not obligatory, but it was rather in the time of Mordecai and Esther, when it is said explicitly *kimu v'kiblu,* the Jews had freely and voluntarily "taken upon themselves and their seed," that the fulfillment of the laws and commandments of the Torah became mandatory upon them.

The most dramatic episode in the career of Rabbi Meir as teacher and spiritual leader of his generation did not take place until almost the end of his life. It reveals the man not merely as a great scholar and author of books and Responsa but as a great historic figure in the spiritual heritage of his people, a brave and gallant fighter in his nation's struggle for a free and dignified existence. It was his lot to live in one of the most tragic and calamitous periods in medieval Jewish history. The crusades had come and gone; the Knights of the Cross had relieved their conscience, troubled by their unpaid debts to the Jews, by plundering and murdering them. The liberation of Jerusalem from the Moslems had failed, and their next of kin, the Jews, were made to pay for the disappointment with the death of tens of thousands. All the Jews had to set against the carnival of pillage and massacre was their loyalty to God.

After more than a century of bloodletting the Jews of Germany were physically weakened, exhausted both in body and mind. How could any people go through such unparalleled ordeals without paying heavily with their physical and mental powers. A generation, says a Jewish historian, grew up dazed and timorous, always peering suspiciously into the future and waiting for the next blow to fall. Unhappily they had not to wait too long, for the agony had not ended with the Crusades. Ever-new weapons were devised for the demoralization and degradation of the Jews. For no sooner had the severest storm passed, than there were fabrications of poisoned wells, ritual murder, and heavy tolls of pillage and slaughter. That the Jews survived at all was due to their two traditional endowments—the capacity to endure suffering and the capacity to recuperate quickly from suffering. These two qualities the Jews of Germany exhibited to an amazing degree in the great disasters that befell them. For no sooner did a storm subside than they picked up the scattered pieces, so to speak, reorganized their lives, and started anew toward their religious and cultural destiny. They developed schools and scholars, heroic and saintly men, who glorified the pages of their nation's history. More than that, there was a revival of their old-time moral vigor and stamina, their pride and courage to stand up to their oppressors, which served them in good stead in the days ahead.

In medieval Christian Europe the Jews largely financed the activities of their temporal and ecclesiastical rulers. They were the mainstay of the support of their overlords' extravagant manner of living. A monarch's wealth was often determined not so much by his country's trade and commerce as by the number of his Jews. It was not the economic wealth and prosperity of the Jews nor the high rate of interest they charged that inspired the antagonism and hostility of their Christian overlords. For these they were not only forgiven but their acquisitive talent was actually encouraged for the rulers knew that one day all the Jews' accumulated wealth would revert to their own coffers. The charges of usury against the Jews was never sincere; it was merely a hypocritical gesture toward the church, which officially forbade usury but privately practiced it. In truth, the charge of usury against the Jews was a cynically concocted sham to legalize their policy of spoliation and extortion and to reduce the Jews to a position of serfdom.

The term *servi camerae,* thralls or vassals of the king, was not invented by Emperor Rudolph of Germany. It had been coined and used for the repression and oppression of the Jews no one knows for how long a time, perhaps for centuries. But as applied by the Habsburg emperor it became a means not only for the physical and economic subjection of the Jews but for their personal and moral degradation. For, as the king's personal serf or vassal, the Jew, as remarked above, ceased to be a free human being with a will and dignity of his own and became an animate property subject to the whim and caprice of his master; in other words, a living chattel which could be sold, mortgaged, and in any other way disposed of as the owner's property.

Emperor Rudolph arrived at the doctrine of *servi camerae* not so much because of his peculair distaste for Jews as because of the rather extraordinary circumstances of his life. He succeeded to the moderate territory of his father Albert IV, which, in the spirit of his time, he tried to augment and expand by military enterprise. When, in the year 1273, he was elected and crowned as emperor of Germany, he found that he had nothing on which to draw to conduct his sumptuous court and pay off his creditors for his military campaigns with the exception of the Jews he had inherited with his kingdom. But their taxes were already committed to their ecclesiastical overlords and to the burghers of the towns in which they lived. He would have levied a special king's tax on the Jews, but they refused to pay the impost. It was in this dilemma that the impoverished emperor formulated the doctrine that "they [the Jews] and all they owned were the king's property."

The Jews would have submitted to the crushing burden of still another tax and satisfied the king's greed; but they could not accept the phrasing of the decree—*servi camerae*—which would make them crown slaves of the German ruler. Their inborn human dignity and their pride as Jews revolted against it. What was most surprising was the fact that their good and patient rabbi, Reb Meir, who usually met every stroke of ill fortune with a resigned, "God wills it," was not only sympathetic with the popular resentment against the king's humiliating order but, with an outraged sense of justice, became a leader of the opposition.

There was no more effective weapon the Jews could employ against their rapacious sovereign than mass emigration, which would result in the loss by the emperor and by the bishops and the burghers of the towns of their lucrative incomes. Reb Meir led the exodus and hundreds of Jews, according to some estimates, followed him. Among them were many wealthy Jews from the districts of the Rhine and the Maine. It was the first time in history that Jews took matters in their own hands to escape oppression and avenge themselves on their oppressors. The goal of Reb Meir and his followers was the Holy Land. Unfortunately, however, they did not progress very far, for in Lombardy, Rabbi Meir was recognized by a baptized Jew and handed over to the local authorities. The emperor had the rabbi arrested and placed in confinement in the tower of Ensisheim, in Alsace. This was in June, 1286, the same year in which the monarch had issued his brutal edict.

Authorities are uncertain what punishment was meted out to the followers of Rabbi Meir; but it seems likely that under the strict application of the serfdom law, the property, real and personal, of those who left the country without the king's permission was confiscated. With his chief prisoner, the Rabbi of Rothenburg, the emperor dealt leniently. Outside his incarceration he suffered no personal hurt or indignity. The king well knew the esteem in which the Rabbi was held by his people and Reb Meir suffered no further consequences. Indeed, he was treated with every mark of respect by his jailers; he was permitted to receive visitors, to teach and carry on the duties of his position as rabbi and leader of his flock. He did not, however, have his library with him in prison, and when he quoted authorities it must have been from memory. Rabbi Meir deplored his lack of books, and appended a note to a decision: "I do not possess the *Tesafot* to tractate *Gittin,* nor the code books from the south (Alfasi and Maimonides). I composed the above with the help of heavenly guide; if you find that the *Tesafot* and the codes hold another opinion, my opinion is nullified by theirs; for what does a poor man know, one who dwells in darkness and gloom for three and one-half years."

The Jews of Germany were in "darkness and gloom" no less than their beloved rabbi. They entered into negotiations with his jailer, the emperor, and offered a large sum of money—twenty thousand silver marks—for Reb Meir's release. The emperor, perpetually in need of money, first agreed, but afterwards rescinded his decision, hoping that by waiting he could strike a still better bargain for so valuable a hostage. By that time, Reb Meir had already spent seven years in jail. When he learned the high price being offered for his freedom, he protested and would not consent to be released. He not only was aware of his emperor's greed but feared that others might follow his example and use similar means of extortion from their Jewish population.

However, the Jews were prepared to pay enormous sums of money for the ransom of their beloved teacher, but, covetous of the wealth of the prosperous Jewish communities, the emperor raised his demands. The Jews would still have bargained, even though they knew how unknightly Rudolph was in his dealings. But Rabbi Meir was determined to die a martyr rather than allow the Jews to encourage such outrageous conduct on the part of the crown. When Rabbi Meir died in 1293, after outliving his emperor by one year, his "martyrdom" did not end, for besides his kingdom Rudolph bequeathed to his son and heir the corpse of his distinguished prisoner. For fourteen years Rudolph's successors kept the sainted martyr's body in prison, haggling, bargaining, and negotiating with the Jews for its release and the privilege of giving it a Jewish burial. At last a childless Jew, Susskind Alexander Wimpfen, from Frankfurt, sacrificed his entire fortune for the release of the corpse of the great and pious rabbi. The only reward

Wimpfen asked was that he be buried beside the bones of the beloved rabbi.

Israel Baal Shem Tov

Israel Baal Shem Tov, the founder of Hasidism, is one of the most fascinating and compelling figures in Jewish history and, indeed, in the history of the religious movements of the world. He was a unique character, a novel personality, a man of feeling and emotion. He was a dramatic figure in spiritually undramatic times, a rebel, innovator, and liberator in an age in which such qualities invited opposition and hostility.

His childhood was spent in loneliness and his early manhood in poverty and destitution. He came into the world without the credentials which mark men for honor and distinction. He had neither great scholarship nor a distinguished ancestry. His knowledge of the Torah was in all likelihood not much above that of the average layman. He was not a teacher in the ordinary sense of the word, yet he drew to himself scholars, thinkers, and kabbalists by the sheer force of his dynamic personality.

The great rabbis of his day were barely aware of his existence, for he was not a product of the learning of the schools. He was an undisguised Jewish peasant, simple and unaffected and with an unsophisticated faith in God in his heart. He associated with the common people, whom he considered his friends and brothers. The gentle slopes of the Carpathian mountains of his native village were very nearly the only school he knew, and the hours of meditation he spent there the only preparation for the life he chose to live. Yet he enunciated a doctrine and created a movement that gave new direction to the thinking of thousands of Jews.

Who was Israel Baal Shem Tov, or "Besht" as he is commonly referred to—a name formed from the initial letters of Baal Shem Tov, Master of the Good Name—and what was the secret of his

258

extraordinary power and influence? Scores of books have been inspired by his remarkable life and the movement he brought into existence, but they fail to reveal the real image of the man. Legend portrayed him in many a light and posterity has enlarged and gilded his image, as it does that of most men who rise to fame and distinction. But his authentic likeness remains a mystery. His disciples repeated his words and indirectly quoted his sayings, but they disclosed little of his personality, as though they were reluctant to lift the veil that concealed the Master. His literary legacy is scant. The Besht not only spurned writing himself but he discouraged it in his disciples. When he discovered one day that one of them was taking notes on his discourses, he quickly repudiated what had been written. A few of his letters have come down to us, but the material is too insignificant for an authentic picture of the Besht as a living personality.

Shibhe ha-Besht (In Praise of the Besht), the nearest approach to what might be regarded as a biography of the founder of Hasidism, is a curious collection of stories, anecdotes, and legends, which, because of their fantastic exaggerations, belong more properly to the realm of fiction than to that of history. But Israel Baal Shem Tov is not a legendary figure. He is a historical personality who existed in time and space. He is a concrete personality, by the authentic documents of his age, by the reliable tradition of his followers, and by the power and influence of his life. The very myths and legends that were circulated about him, incredible as they are, prove the presence of a great and highly individualized personality behind the mists.

At the turn of the eighteenth century Jewish life was surrounded by darkness which seemed as though it would never end. While the entire world was on the eve of a mighty outburst of activity in all spheres of human endeavor the Jews were nursing the wounds inflicted upon them in one of the severe catastrophes of their history in the wake of the Terrible Decade (1648–1658), the name given to the Bogdan Chmielnicki massacre in which more than half of the Jews of Poland met their death. The survivors bewailed the disaster and called it "the third hurban"—the third destruction of the Temple. And a destruction of the Temple in a spiritual sense it indeed was. For Poland was a great center of Jewish culture and learning.

The Jews accepted their affliction, as they always had. They searched their hearts, rehearsed and confessed their sins, and justified the ways of providence. But, try as they might, they could not reconcile themselves to what had happened. Blindly they groped for the meaning and purpose of their latest martyrdom. For, surely, unless God had utterly forsaken them and had cast them off, they could not have been made to suffer in vain. Out of their misfortune the old mystic faith in *heble moshiah,* the pains heralding the advent of the Messiah, was revived. Redemption must be near, they argued; the Messiah was on his way. Their tortured souls could conceive of no other solution to the tormenting question that haunted their minds.

For a time it seemed as if, indeed, their prayers were heard and their suffering was at an end. For out of the chaos and confusion of the time emerged a man who cast a glow of hope and promise over the wretched lives of the Jews and caused them to hail him as the promised Messiah. Conscious fraud or self-deluded fanatic, Sabbatai Zevi, the son of a Jewish small trader in Smyrna, Turkey, represented the collective longing of the Jews for redemption. The great masses of the people accepted him as, indeed, in their misery, they were ready to accept anybody who held out to them the faintest promise of relief and succor in their unfortunate existence. When, however, in the appointed year of destiny, 1666, the mask was off and the "King Messiah," to save his life, adopted the Moslem faith and a substantial financial grant, the Jews of the world were overwhelmed with shame and humiliation. It seemed as if everything had failed them and that all they had waited and hoped for had turned to ashes.

In their stinging humiliation a wave of despondency spread over great masses of Jews. Desperately and passionately they cried out for leadership. They needed firm hands to guide them and strong shoulders to support them. They needed to be told and instructed how to live and what to believe. They needed to fill the vacuum of their shattered hopes and expectations—an elixir that should both revive and stimulate them with new pride, faith, and courage.

The Terrible Decade, and the Sabbatai Zevi messianic fiasco that followed, might not in themselves have brought the emotional world of Hasidism into being any more than had similar experiences in the past; but one wonders whether without them the Hasidic movement would have arisen and taken such a forceful and influential place in Jewish life as it did. As a result of the terrible blood-letting the Jews were spiritually spent and weakened to the point of exhaustion, and in consequence of their bitter messianic disillusionment their moral and mental faculties became numb and barren. They longed for a new beginning, for a new type of leadership. Rabbinism and Kabbalism had both failed them; one could not support their ebbing strength in their severest travail and suffering, and the other had brought them to the verge of utter destruction.

The spiritual tragedy of the Jews at the time we are describing lay in their geographic distribution. While in northern Poland, including Lithuania and White Russia, the Jews lived fairly prosperously, Jewish learning was cultivated, and talmudic scholarship stood in high esteem, matters were different in Podolia, Galicia, Volhynia—indeed, in the whole southwestern region. Great masses of Jews lived in small rural communities in a highly deplorable condition, politically and economically. They had no social status, no rights of citizenship, no dignity or standing as human beings. They were the serfs and sharecroppers of their Polish landlords, whose estates they farmed and whose taxes they collected but by whom they were despised and looked down upon.

Their life was without joy, their days without comfort, their suffering without compensation. Although they were honest and pious folks, even to the point of fanaticism, they were spurned and derided by their more fortunate educated brethren. Living far from the great centers of Jewish life and culture, their education was neglected, so that many of them could not even read their prayer books. In an age in which only scholarship counted, when neither wealth nor piety nor any other qualification entitled a man to social or public recognition, the illiterate, the *am-ha-aretz,* the man not trained in solving intricate talmudic problems, could expect but little at the hands of his more scholarly brethren.

With no attempt made to enlighten and instruct them in their helplessness they passed from one absurdity to another. Their suffering had narrowed their religious outlook and they became victims of superstitious fears and terrors. The slightest infraction of the law appeared to them as a mortal sin for which they were fated to suffer grievous punishment.

The late Simon Dubnow the historian quotes a writer of the beginning of the eighteenth century as saying, "There is no country in the world where the Jews are so much given to mystical fancies, devil hunting, talismans, and exorcism of evil spirits as they are in Poland."

Deep down in the hearts and minds of the great masses of Jews there were revolt and indignation and an irresponsible cry for a changed order of things. The learned rabbis had utterly disappointed them; indeed, they but rarely came in contact with them. The rabbis were rigid and pedantic, and they failed to satisfy the religious cravings of the common man. The simple and illiterate folk longed for the good and godly life, the God they could serve truly and well, and they were offered only dry and uninspired hairsplitting talmudic casuistry.

It was into this kind of atmosphere that Israel Baal Shem Tov made his appearance and touched off the revolution which was destined to become such a decisive factor in the religious life and history of the Jews. The word "revolution" must be used guardedly in the case of the founder of the Hasidic movement, for there was nothing rebellious or mutinous about the man and his teaching. Indeed, he was one of the mildest and most modest of men, happy in his piety, and never guilty of departing from the slightest requirement of the rabbinic law. All he aimed at, what he lived and strove for, was to bring a little cheer and happiness into lives that were dismal and joyless, to scatter the fears that oppressed them, to lift the burdens that weighed them down and to make them feel that, although they were neither wise nor learned, there was a place in God's kingdom for them.

Israel was born in the remote village of Ukop, on the borderline between Podolia and Wallachia, in the year 1700, to humble but pious and upright parents. One would only waste his time should he try to locate on the map the village made famous by the great and holy man who happened to be born there. Legend has woven many a story into the circumstances of Israel's birth and the name he was given. For example, it is told that when his parents, Eliezer and Sarah, had reached a childless old age and had given up all hope of offspring, the Prophet Elijah appeared to them, and said: "Because of your piety and steadfastness, a son will be born to you who will lighten the eyes of all Israel, and Israel shall be his name, in fulfillment, 'Thou art my servant, O Israel, in whom I will be glorified'." They were nearly one hundred years old when their son was born and they passed away shortly afterward, according to this old legend.

The young orphan became a community responsibility. Themselves struggling for their daily crust of bread, his custodians bestowed upon their helpless charge what love and care their hearts were capable of. But Israel was a difficult child—a problem child he probably would be called now. For the boy was certainly odd and unlike most other children of his time. In an age when it was the ambition of most Jewish children to become well versed in knowledge of the Torah, Israel hated nothing so much as the confining and stifling atmosphere of the *heder,* a one-room school. As often as he could manage to evade the vigilant eyes of his teacher he would desert the little school and run away to the woods, where, it is said, he learned about trees and birds, animals and flowers.

Israel persisted in his strange conduct, much to the chagrin of the elders of the synagogue, who frowned upon his apparent idleness. But they let him have his way, for was he not an orphan, the child of the God-fearing Eliezer? Although he seemed to have no worldly ambition other than that of performing odd jobs requiring the least physical and mental exertion, Israel, now past the *Bar Mitzvah* age, perhaps to the surprise of everyone about him, found suitable employment for himself as *behelfer,* or assistant school master. Although his task was an ordinary one, he discharged it in an extraordinary manner. Every morning the youthful school assistant made his rounds of the Jewish homes, gathered his little flock of children, and conducted them to school; and in the evening, when their lessons were over, he led them home again. But on the way he taught them to sing the synagogue melodies with such ferver as to break through the clouds of gloom and soar straight up to heaven.

But his nights he spent in the little synagogue, where he made his bed on a hard bench. Late in the night, however, when the evening devotions were over and the worshipers had gone and the *shamash* had put out the last candle, Israel arose from his feigned sleep and pulled out of his bosom a much-worn kabbalistic manuscript by a mysterious rabbi, Adam, and pored over its pages by the light of the moon. Legend says that an illumination descended from heaven which filled the prayer house with a radiant beam of light. Passers-by were startled, for they believed that the light came from the spirits of the dead, who were believed to take possession of the synagogue in the night.

Israel was growin up and his mind was maturing. But what prospect did the future hold for him in Ukop? Vague intimations of his calling came to him; but how was he to realize them? Inwardly he rebelled against his lot. He wanted to be free—as free as the birds and the flowers he had loved in his childhood haunts. He dreamed of a new life which would be bound by no authority save the commanding Voice. But the difficulties were staggering in the way of his playing a part in his dream's fulfillment since he had at that time no means of support.

He spent several years in visiting one community after another, serving alternately as *shohet,* teacher, cantor, and as arbitrator in disputes. He settled finally at Tlust, near Brody. There was a holy seriousness about the man and his words which made people love and trust him. They brought to him their business and domestic differences to be straightened out. It was on such an occasion that he met the rich and learned Ephraim, of Kuty, who was so impressed with him as arbitrator that he offered Israel his daughter Hannah in marriage, without, however, informing her of the arrangements.

When Ephraim died, and Israel, dressed in the shabby and uncouth garb of a peasant, presented himself before Rabbi Abraham Gershom to claim his bride, the learned rabbi was shocked, and insisted on annulment of the betrothal. But Hannah would not listen to her brother and was for carrying out her father's wishes. After many vain attempts to instruct his brother-in-law, whom he considered an *am-ha-aretz,* ignorant of the Torah, Rabbi Gershom urged Israel to leave Brody. The future Besht wanted nothing better. He found urban life stifling and felt nature luring him with her myriad voices. After trying to make a home in a number of places and engaging in a variety of occupations, Israel settled down with his loyal wife in one of the loveliest spots in the Carpathian Mountains, where nature was serene and friendly. He built a little hut high up in the hills and spent his days and nights in song and meditation. He eked out their existence, such as it was, by digging clay, which his wife carted to the city for sale.

Israel found in the mountains a world entirely to his liking. His soul was exalted by everything he saw, felt, and experienced. With abounding joy, he roamed days on end in the balmy air of the virgin hills, dreaming, singing, and praying, and the mountains re-echoed his songs and prayers as if they sensed their meaning and understood what was in his heart. He found joy and holiness in everything—in the murmur of the brook, in the calm of the day, and the solemn stillness of the night. He saw God in everything and everything in God; indeed, he saw the whole universe, the God-created Universe, alive with God and holiness. There was nothing real in life and the world which did not emanate from God and flow back to Him.

He learned to see God with a new mind and a new heart. He learned to see God in the heights and the depths, in good and what might seem evil to others, in the saint and the sinner. He saw and found God in all the normal acts and concerns of life, in man's strength and folly, in his passions and virtues. He saw nothing that is profane and common, nothing not endowed with holiness. Every act of living is holy, or may be made holy.

Israel's love of nature persisted, and he spent much time in roaming through the fields and forest, where he learned the medicinal properties of plants, herbs, and grasses. With abounding tenderness he tried to apply what healing art he acquired to the sick and the ailing he found all about him. Legends soon spread and fantastic stories were circulated about the healing powers of the "man from the hills." There were no hospitals or asylums for the sick, and the rumor of a healer in their midst brought scores of patients to his door. He was under constant pressure from the sick and their friends. He brought relief to the physically and mentally afflicted. It is not at all surprising that the mere presence of such a spiritual personality as Israel, the touch of his hand, the gentleness of his eyes, should help the unfortunate more than drugs and herbs.

Had Israel pursued his healing profession he might have fared no better than the other Baal Shem who traversed the countryside with their medicinal cures and conjurations. But Israel was not of their tribe. There was something about the man—his gentleness of tone and attitude, his sympathetic participation in the lowly people's toils and tasks—raised him high above the ordinary Baale Shem, and they called him Baal Shem *Tov,* Man of the *Good* Name, probably in allusion to Eccles. 7:1.

But Israel, fired with a spiritual mission, deprecated and sought to avoid the reputation of being merely a healer of the body. What he wanted, what he believed his mission to be, was to bring a measure of cheer and happiness to the starved hearts and sick spirits of his people. He assumed but temporarily the role forced upon him by his sympathy for their bodily suffering and distress. When he was rebuked by a man who later became one of his admiring disciples for writing amulets with the secret name of God, Israel opened one such amulet and showed his accuser that it contained nothing more magical than his own and his mother's names, "Israel, son of Sarah."

He mingled with the people and was adored by the masses. He made friends with all sorts of men, including the rejected and the downcast. Simple and warm-hearted, he knew how to win their love and confidence. Teamsters, cobblers, and even men of unsavory reputation in the community were among his companions. He rejected no one, for all men, he said, were equal in the sight of God. He knew their pains, their fears, and suffering, and his heart was filled with compassion and pity. He sought out the good in every human being, even in the sinner who strayed from the path.

On the Sabbath many came to the synagogue or to his home to hear him expound the words of the Torah. He spoke to them of God and love, of faith and piety, of goodness and holiness, and he illustrated his discourses with stories and parables from the Bible, the Talmud, and the Kabbalah. His discourses were not in the language and manner of the rabbis—involved and learned and hard to understand—but were simple and unaffected talks. The plain and simple folks were inspired and instructed by him. They heard him and carried his message to their friends and neighbors. His fame grew, his reputation spread, and disciples gathered about him and called him Master.

Contrary to the teaching of the so-called Practical Kabbalah, he insisted that excessive fasting and other ascetic practices were not only useless but were even harmful and injurious to the true service of God. They are Satan's invention to alienate man from God, he said. He preached the joyous acceptance of God. "Serve the Lord in gladness; come before Him with song," he quoted from a psalm of David. He encouraged active participation in all human experiences. The surging passions and desires of the heart, he said, are not to be shunned or stifled, for there is not a seemingly profane act or thought but can be bound to God. "Nothing is unholy in itself; nothing is evil in itself," he taught. "What we call evil are the undirected energies waiting to be set right."

He held up prayer as the simple man's approach to God and his union with Him. It is the most important medium by which man can establish a correlation with the Deity. But such prayer must be ecstatic and rapturous and not a mere perfunctory repetition of words, which is worse than no prayer at all. On every occasion, in his private talks with his disciples and his public discourses on the Sabbath, the Besht condemned and ridiculed the mechanical, lifeless prayers which are recited without inner feeling and warmth. He called them dead and wooden prayers, unable to lift themselves to God.

He laid great stress on the ethical precepts of religion, on those ideas and ideals of Judaism that stimulate righteous conduct toward one's fellowmen. He preached the unification of the ethical and religious domains. The pious man, he said, should serve God not only by observing the religious customs and ceremonies but also in his daily affairs. The Besht paid high tribute to learning and regarded it, next to prayer, as the most effective method of realizing one's communion with God. He regarded the kind of knowledge that does not lead to the practice of good deeds as worse than useless. He urged his disciples to devote themselves to such study as inspires piety and reverence.

There was little new or original in anything that Israel Baal Shem Tov said or taught. He did not introduce any new ideas into Judaism. His personality attracted his followers perhaps more than his teachings. Students will find it easy to point to parallels of most of his sayings in the Talmud, the Midrashim, and the Jewish ethical literature of a thousand years. He did not create, he did not originate; he only revived and repeated what had been said numberless times before. But when spoken by him, as evolved and developed in his own peculiar way, it assumed a novelty that sprang like a stream of cool, refreshing water in the desert of his people's hearts. For the Besht was a poet and a mystic, and he endowed his words with a marvellous power and imagination.

A new world, as it were, opened up to the multitudes that crowded to hear him speak. They learned to worship God with an enthusiasm and devotion they had not felt before. He infused a sense of dignity and self-respect into masses of men who regarded themselves as neglected. He restored the joy of life to men burdened with gloomy superstition. He came as a holy optimist, throbbing with joyous enthusiasm and an unlimited faith in God and man. His sympathy, his tenderness and understanding, wove a romance of happiness over lives that were sad and bitter. He made them conscious of their power and their unlimited potentialities. They could raise their heads; they were no longer timid and abashed: the delights of heaven were also theirs.

No wonder he became the idol of the masses. The lovely simplicity of his words and his marvelous stories were talked of wherever Jews met. With almost miraculous power he laid his spell over the souls of men. They believed in him and they loved him, although many had never seen him. Legends began to circulate about him—strange and fantastic tales spun from pure imagination. He was said to have cured the blind, revived the dead, and covered great distances in a single night, and that he had but to spread his mantle to pass safely over lakes and rivers.

But the learned rabbis of his time bitterly opposed and attacked him, for they only believed what was written in books and quoted in the name of great authorities, while the Besht paid little attention to books and took but scant notice of authorities. They accused him of undermining religion and charged him with mocking tradition, belittling talmudic learning, and encouraging ignorance. They felt their position and influence threatened by him. They saw their authority over the people slipping away from them. But their opposition failed to dampen the enthusiasm with which the Besht was received by the masses. With incredible rapidity his teachings spread to almost all classes of Jews.

There was one powerful ambition on which the Besht had set his heart but which in the heat and turmoil of his busy life remained unsatisfied—to go to Eretz Yisroel. The Holy Land stood high in the mystic longings of the Hasidim, and a pilgrimage to her holy places, especially Safed, where studied the saints and seers of the Kabbalah with whom Hasidism is so closely linked, was their pious dream. After seeing his creed firmly established the Besht thought the time was ripe to realize his long-cherished hope. He prepared for the journey and got as far as Stamboul and was well on his way to the Land of Israel when, mysteriously, a halt was called to the pilgrimage, and he turned back. Was it that the Besht realized that the time had not yet come, that his work was still not finished, and that the Hasidic brotherhoods springing up everywhere needed his personal attention? On this the record is not clear. Whatever the immediate reason, he deeply felt the disappointment and regarded it as a sign from heaven that he was not deemed worthy of the Holy Land.

After his abortive pilgrimage Israel Baal Shem Tov took up residence at Medziboz. Admirers came from far and near attracted not alone by his reputed miraculous deeds but to be instructed and blessed by him. At first the plain and ordinary country people came—the peasant Jews and farmers of small estates. But before long scholars, also impressed by his fame, joined his circle. Only rarely has a religious ideal sprung from the heart of a single man spread so rapidly and attracted so many followers. As the Besht's followers grew in strength and numbers they became known as Hasidim, from the Hebrew word *hasid,* signifying men of piety, religious devotion, and fervor.

The Besht was fortunate in his disciples. While the gentleness of his spirit reached out to the lowly and the meek, he soon felt the need of more intelligent and influential adherents to gain for his doctrine universal acceptance. It was, therefore, a great and decisive moment in the life of the Besht when he succeeded in winning to his creed such able and gifted converts as Dob Baer, a Volhynian preacher and kabbalist, Jacob Joseph of Polonye, a scholar and prolific writer, and Gershon Kutover, a former rabbi of Brody, his brother-in-law, who first despised Israel as an ignoramus and later admired him as a saint and a holy man. One and all they were men of high character, great talmudic learning, and undisputed piety, besides being talented organizers.

It was to these ardent and devoted disciples of the Besht that the success and expansion of Hasidism was largely due. During the lifetime of the founder, they traveled widely, preaching the new doctrine and spreading the knowledge of the new Hasidic creed among the educated and the unschooled alike. While the preacher of Meseritz, the greatest of the Besht disciples, undertook the proselytizing mission of the Master among his learned associates, and Jacob Joseph of Polonye advocated his teachings in sermons and books, laying the foundation for a Hasidic literature which grew with amazing rapidity in volume and content. Gershon Kutover settled in the Holy Land and founded branches of the Hasidic creed there.

The Besht was an excellent teacher. He not only knew how to win the love and devotion of his disciples but he trained them in the propaganda of his faith. He poured into them all his strength and the powers of his heart and mind. He surrounded them with the aura of his influence and subtly made them instruments of his will and spirit. He taught them to live and associate with the ordinary Jews, whom he had not for a moment forgotten. That they might always live in his presence he had them lodge in his house. In this way a unified life developed between the Besht and his disciples, which greatly contributed to the close and intimate attachment to each other.

Jews do not deify their religious leaders. Instead, they weave about them stories and legends which reveal the love and admiration they bear them more truly than any form of deification. At the same time, the Besht's enthusiastic followers saw in him something more than a man, and he was made the hero of Hasidic folklore. According to legend, he had access to heaven and glimpses of paradise; he met and conversed with the Messiah, who told him the exact time of salvation. The Besht revealed to his disciples the secrets he had overheard in heaven and the forgiveness he obtained for the sinners. It was said that he crossed turbulent streams on his belt, that brigands were afraid to harm him, and that once, when lost in meditation, he found himself slipping down a dangerous precipice a cliff opposite where he had been sitting saved him by closing up the gap. Fantastic as the stories are, their accuracy was not questioned. But as Solomon Schechter correctly observed, "It is not as a worker of miracles, but as a religious teacher and reformer that Baal Shem is interesting."

The Hasidim revered him and revere him to this day, more than two hundred years after his death. Perhaps the best illustration of the love and admiration in which the Besht was held by his disciples is the story told by Martin Buber. "Rabbi Leib, son of Sarah, the hidden Zaddik, said to persons who were talking about the Besht,

'You ask me about the Baal Shem Tov? I tell you: if he had lived in the age of the Prophets, he would have been a prophet; and if he had lived in the age of the Patriarchs, he would have been one of them so that just as one says, "God of Abraham, Isaac, and Jacob," one would say: "God of Israel." ' "

What was the source of Israel Baal Shem Tov's power and influence? What, in essence, was his message that was received so enthusiastically by his admirers and that created so much opposition on the part of his critics?

The ruling principle of the Besht, as gathered from the writings of his most trustworthy disciples, is that God is an imminent universal Being, manifest everywhere in all things, in matter as in mind, in the mundane affairs of life as in the sacred things. He is not the God of the pantheist, because He may be spoken to and He answers; neither is He the God of the ascetic, because He is not outside this world but in this world.

From this follows Besht's polemic against asceticism, the product of the Lurian Kabbalah, which became almost a religious dogma among a certain class of Jews. For since God is in matter as He is in spirit, there is nothing that is common or profane, and the care of the body is as much a religious duty as the care of the soul. If the whole universe is a manifestation of the Divine Being and all things are forms in which God reveals Himself, one may serve Him with all his senses and faculties, with his worldly desires and appetites, as well as with his holy thoughts and acts, as expressed by the words, "In all thy days thou shalt know Him." (Prov. 3:7).

The Besht exemplified his uncompromising opposition to every form of asceticism in his famous letter to Dob Baer of Meseritz, known as the "Great Maggid." When word came to the Besht that his disciple had imposed upon himself heavy penances which, in his frail condition, would injure his health, he chided him: "My soul is outraged at your determination. By the Counsel of God, I abjure you to abandon such dangerous practices, which are the outcome of a disordered brain. Is it not written, 'Thou shalt not hide thyself from thine own flesh?' Fast no more than is prescribed. Follow my counsel and God shall be with you."

Related to his attitude toward asceticism are his unconventional views of sin and evil—unconventional in the opinion of the ordinary rabbi of his time. He took a singularly optimistic view of human frailties. He knew that sin existed and that evil and wickedness existed; but he regarded them as transitory and not absolute or inherent qualities. All temptations are from God, a disciple said, reflecting the thought of the Master; our lusts and our passions are from Him; our good and our evil are from Him. The true believer, recognizing the likeness of God in everyone, should try to restore that likeness when he finds it obscured by sin.

He gladdened the hearts of the wayward by assuring them that they were not lost, for no man is sunk so low that he cannot be raised to God again. "I let sinners come to me," said the Besht; "for if they know that they are sinners and therefore consider themselves base, God is with them." None knows the heart of man and none should judge his neighbor. When it came to Israel's ears that one of his disciples was preaching admonishing sermons, he reprimanded him: "What do you know about admonishing? You yourself have remained unacquainted with sin all the days of your life, and you have had nothing to do with people around you—how should you know what sinning is?" Faith—faith in God, faith in Judaism, faith in its strictest and purest sense and not merely in the religious forms, cults, and rituals which go by the name of religion—is the core and essence of the Besht teaching. The fundamental rule of piety, he said, is to seek to know God, to enter into active relationship with Him, to transcend the bounds of human existence and experience and live with Him face to face, so to speak. The laws and injunctions of religion are important adjuncts to faith in God, and the Besht would not abjure or abrogate any one of them; but he regarded them as religion's outer garb, not as its inner sanctifying essence.

He considered the depth and intensity of faith to be not of the mind but of the feelings and emotions, begotten not of books and study but of the naïve and, if you will, blind and unreasoning belief and trust in God. The Besht held faith to be more than learning, and a good and holy life more pleasing to God than excessive intellectualism. The joys and delights of heaven, he assured his followers, are reserved not only for the scholars who spend their days and nights poring over their books but for all those who are of a pure heart and upright spirit. One needs not, therefore, be vexed and troubled in his mind because he is not learned and versed in the words of the Torah if his faith in God is strong and unflinching. When the Besht was told of a man who was a great scholar, his remark was, "I envy him his scholarship, but what can I do? I have no time to study, because I have to serve my God."

Without actually repudiating or discouraging the study of the Talmud he decried making it one's lifelong occupation which, he said, should be the service of God. He considered the Law to be holy and its study meritorious, but it must not supersede but be subordinated to the service of God. Thus, while the rabbis of his day regarded the study of the Torah *lishmah,* for its own sake, as the highest form of religious activity, the Besht enjoined upon his followers the study of only those portions of the Talmud that engender the religious spirit and lead to the service of God, by which he meant piety, prayer, and the practice of good and holy deeds.

Contrary to the teaching of the Lurian Kabbalah, which regards a morose and melancholy disposition conducive to piety, the Besht taught that he serves God best who serves Him cheerfully. The highest value of a *mitzvah,* he said, is when it is performed with a glad and happy heart. Gloom and sadness are the work of Satan; far from stimulating piety, they thwart and hinder it. The true believer knows that God is good and life is good, and he will therefore serve Him with a free and untroubled spirit.

The joy and rapture of prayer is the keynote of everything the Besht taught and it flows naturally through every article of the creed he founded. He himself lived it, preached it, and demanded it of his followers. Prayer is an intimate personal experience with God and establishes communion with Him. By means of prayer man rises above the perils and pressures of life, sunders the veil between him and God, and achieves his moral and spiritual regeneration. "All that I have achieved," the Besht remarked, "I have achieved not through study, but through prayer."

But in order that prayer may have its transforming effect it must not be cold and barren nor must it be a list of requests and petitions which we expect to be answered. Instead it must be a stirring, ecstatic experience—a feeling of *debekut* in which man sheds his individual existence and is merged into God. Such worship of God *abotat ha-bore* is the outpouring of all of man's spiritual powers and faculties. It is fresh and spontaneous, fervent and impassioned, inspired by *kawannah,* complete and undivided concentration on God, and aglow with *hitlahabut,* the kindling flame of devotion to Him. In such worship, the words, language, time, and place of prayer do not matter; it is the spirit alone that counts. When Israel was reproached for disregarding the legally appointed time for prayer, his reply was, "Can a child be told when he may approach his father?"

The Besht not only taught the limitless power and influence of prayer but he advocated the employment of physical contriv-ances, such as motions of the body, shouting, shaking, and clapping of the hands, in order to bring about the prayerful state of mind. The highest form of prayer, the Besht said, is the one which not only moves the soul but sets all the limbs of the body in motion, as described by the Psalmist: "All my bones shall say, Lord who is like unto thee?" (Ps. 35:10.)

An important element in the ethical teachings of Baal Shem Tov is his insistence on *shiflut,* best rendered in English as humility, as one of the greatest of virtues. The true test of prayer, he taught, is the feeling of humility it leaves behind. He looked upon pride and vanity as the most seductive agents of sin. Even disparagement of learning was due to the pride and haughtiness it engendered.

He condemned the high and lofty attitude of the rabbis, but he combated even more vigorously the *maggidim* (itinerant preachers) who habitually made the assumed sinfulness of the Jews the sub-ject of their harangues. When it was reported to the Besht that one such preacher, while haranguing an audience of whom he knew nothing, indiscriminately abused them for their sins, he fiercely turned on the preacher: "Woe upon thee who darest to speak evil of Israel! Knowest thou not that every Jew when he utters ever so short a prayer at the close of the day, is performing a great work before which the angels of heaven bow down?"

Because of his great love of Jews, he would not allow in his presence a harsh word or critical remark to be passed about one of them. He had faith in his people—faith in their goodness, piety, and virtue. Certainly few men of his time had as intimate and accurate knowledge of the Jews as did the Besht. He met Jews of every kind and description. He observed their ways and was touched by their deep, and often unrestrained, piety and faith in God. He never tired of saying that, in times of trouble and persecution, the simple and ignorant Jews gave their lives for their faith more readily than their more educated and scholarly brethren.

He conducted himself as a simple man who had never left his native village. He lived in great poverty. He preached charity and exemplified his doctrine by his own practice. Though large sums of money passed through his hands, he distributed what he had among the poor. His generosity to his disciples was overflowing and not a few of them subsisted on his stipends. One day when he was returning with his son from a visit to a rabbi who lived in fine style and had costly furnishings in his house, he said to the son: "Thou must have envied the style and luxury of his living; but were the things thou hast seen belonging to me, I would have sold them and distributed the money among the poor." He entertained small respect for the established conventions of the time. He admitted women into his entourage and assigned to them not only a position of social equality but of high religious importance. "All Jews," Solomon Schechter quotes a Hasid to have remarked, reflecting the views of the Master, "even the uneducated and the women, believe in God."

The Besht's mission was completed: he had inspired a great movement; he had deepened the religious consciousness of the Jews. He had raised many disciples to carry on his work. But, even so, his last days were darkened by the saddest episode of his life. It was the part he played, together with the Polish rabbis, in the public disputation with the heretical Frankists, who presumed to expose the so-called anti-Christian teachings of the Talmud. The Besht stressed the religious spirit rather than the minutiae of the rabbinic precepts. Nevertheless he regarded the Talmud as sacred and inviolate and he was shocked by the danger threatening it at the hands of the infidel Frankists. Gladly he joined in its defense.

After the disputation, which was conducted with great bitterness on both sides, hundreds of Frankists allowed themselves to be baptized to prove their sincerity and devotion to Christianity. The rabbis rejoiced to be rid of the infidels. But the Besht was greatly disturbed by their defection, and exclaimed: "I heard the Lord cry out and say: 'As long as the diseased limb is joined to the body, there is hope that it may be cured in time, but when it has been cut off, it is lost forever'."

The incident proved fatal to the already failing Besht. Following the disputation and its tragic aftermath in 1759, the disciples noticed their master's lowered vitality and feared his approaching end. But the Besht continued his strenuous devotional duties in his usual way. When his followers urged him to discontinue some of his activities his answer was, "I want to busy myself with my God a bit longer."

When he was no longer able to leave his bed and as his disciples stood about his couch, he comforted them: "I have no worries with regard to myself, for I know quite clearly that I am going out at one door and I shall go in at another door."

His strength was ebbing fast, but those disciples who were nearest to him heard him murmur in a fading voice, "I shall surely return; but not as I am now." With these words on his lips Israel Baal Shem Tov died on the first day of the Feast of Weeks in the year 1760.

Rabbi Elijah Gaon of Vilna

WHEN RABBI ELIJAH of Vilna, whom an admiring Jewish world crowned with the title "Gaon," was born in 1720, Israel Baal Shem Tov, the founder of Hasidism, was an obscure young man of twenty, with little or no indication of his future greatness and influence. Moses Mendelssohn, another man who opened up a new era in Jewish history, was destined to be born nine years later. Thus the three greatest figures in modern Jewish life, who by their wisdom, learning, and leadership were to influence the intellectual and spiritual life of the Jewish people for many a generation, were contemporaries. Not only that, but they lived in such close proximity to one another that they were almost neighbors. Even in those days of slow and difficult travel, the countries in which the three lived were sufficiently near to each other that, had they wished it, they could have met and conferred together.

It is interesting to imagine the historic significance of such a meeting and the influence it might have had on the dark and troubled times in which the Jews were living. What more dramatic episode in Jewish history than a conference between men of such conflicting views and outlook upon Jewish life and thought as the Hasidic saint of Medziboz, the master of rabbinic learning of Vilna, and the gentle sage of Berlin! They were all men of great spiritual integrity and magnetic personality and each wielded authority and influence over great masses of Jews. Had a meeting of these three leaders taken place and had their conflicting religious views been composed in a grand synthesis of the mystic faith of the Baal Shem, the stupendous scholarship of the Gaon, and the worldly culture and enlightenment of Moses Mendelssohn, what a different turn modern Jewish history might have taken!

It was in a narrow but comfortable and wholly integrated Jewish

278

world that Elijah, surnamed the "Gaon," was born. The Jewish world of his time was small and it belonged almost entirely to the scholar. Jewish communities in those far-off days prided themselves not so much on their economic wealth and prosperity as on their intellectual and spiritual attainments. The scholar was more highly honored than the merchant, the man of letters than the man of wealth. When denied active participation in Jewish scholarship himself, it was the highest ideal of every Jew of old that his son be a rabbi or his son-in-law a scholar learned in the law.

The cultural atmosphere of the Jewish people of Vilna, the capital of Lithuania and the birthplace of the Gaon, was an inspiring example of the Jew's love for Torah. There may have been older and larger Jewish communities in the Diaspora, but what city in the world is more warmly and tenderly remembered for its piety and learning, for its saints and savants, than the city proudly overlooking the Wilja River? For centuries Vilna has been a city of proud and noble traditions, steeped in legend and learning, with famous synagogues and celebrated talmudic academies—a city, indeed, where even the merchants, hucksters, and shopkeepers are not without a taste for the finer things of life.

When Napoleon, at the head of his *grande armée,* entered Vilna and saw her bustling, busy life and her many synagogues and schools of learning alive with the warmth of prayer and study, he is credited with having nicknamed her the "Jerusalem of Lithuania." Actually, however, the description is said to have been used long before Napoleon's time; there is a legend that when the Jerusalem of the Holy Land was destroyed and the Jews were in desperation, the Holy One bade them not to grieve, for He was creating for them another Jerusalem—Vilna—to take her place. But it was not until the time of her greatest son, Rabbi Elijah Gaon, that Vilna attained her pre-eminent position and reached the zenith of her fame and glory in the intellectual and spiritual life of the Jewish people. "Even if Vilna had never produced any other Jewish scholar and writer," says a historian of Vilna and an admirer of Rabbi Elijah, "the fame of the Gaon alone would have conferred upon it eternal luster."

He was the incarnation of Jewish learning, the symbol and embodiment of talmudic scholarship. He not only towered head and shoulders above his contemporaries but was intellectually the superior of most of the Jewish scholars who preceded him. Scholars readily submitted to his authority and men learned in the sacred lore were silenced in his presence. The vast rabbinic literature of more than two thousand years, the complete studies of the Palestinian and Babylonian schools, were accurately preserved in his mind.

He was a faithful steward of Jewish learning. The atmosphere of his study was pure and holy. No infusion of alien thoughts and ideas disturbed his mental and spiritual serenity. His world was the Torah and the things that sharpened and deepened his knowledge of Torah. Any other studies he devoted himself to were merely instruments for making the words of the Bible and the Talmud better understood by him. He was a vigorous personality in spite of his innate modesty and humility. Greatly as he admired Moses Maimonides, he feared the influence of his *Mishneh Torah* and would have written a substitute for it; but "heaven did not permit," he explained.

His life was austere and simple, devoid of all wordly pleasures. He even denied himself the intimate joys of family life. He rarely emerged from his sanctuary of books and prayer and was seldom seen in public. He became intimately associated with but few people except his chosen disciples. He was not followed by crowds, as was Israel Baal Shem Tov; and unlike his younger contemporary, Moses Mendelssohn, he did not count illustrious gentiles among his friends. Yet the people felt themselves attracted to him and he dominated their lives and the life of Lithuanian Jewry by his sheer mental and spiritual powers. The most sacred of shrines in all Vilna before the Second World War was the synagogue where the great rabbinical luminary prayed and studied, which few people approached without the deepest awe and reverence. Few men personally knew the Gaon and fewer still were fortunate enough to come in close contact with him. Yet so great was their dependence on him that instinctively they felt that, with the Gaon in their midst, no evil could befall them.

Although Elijah Gaon's name and reputation are familiar to thousands of Jews, nothing is known about his life beyond the legends circulated about him. He is one of the instances in Jewish history of a man whose spiritual achievements and influence are deemed of greater importance than the events surrounding his personal life. The Gaon's only biography, *Aliyat Eliyahu* (Ascension of Elijah), except for Finn's brief sketch in *Kiryah Ne'emanah* (Faithful City), is written more in admiration for the Gaon than with regard to the real facts of his life. Like the authors of *Shibhe ha-Besht* (Praises of the Besht), presuming to be a biography of the founder of Hasidism, and its almost exact Christian counterpart, *Lives of the Saints,* the Gaon's biographers are seemingly incapable of detecting the line that separates the logical from the fantastic.

Yet, legendary as many of the stories about the youthful Elijah undoubtedly are, not all of them can be dismissed as imaginary. There actually were youthful geniuses in the now-vanished Jewish communities of Russia-Poland who accumulated in their early teens a wealth of rabbinic lore which made them the pride and envy of scholars many times their age. But even judged by that standard, the wonder youth of Vilna was the marvel of his age. He was an intellectual phenomenon the like of whom had not appeared in many a generation. He seems to have come into the world equipped with a greater capacity for learning than that of most other men.

No one could claim the honor of having been Elijah's teacher for any length of time. Almost unaided, he groped his way along the path of Torah. His father and the celebrated Moses Margalit attempted to teach him, but he soon dispensed with their instruction. At an age when children normally are learning to read, Elijah was already fighting intellectual duels with masters of talmudic learning of his native town, and at that stage he delivered a scholarly discourse with such skill and depth that he left his hearers surprised and puzzled. At the age of thirteen, when Jewish children ordinarily are just attaining their religious maturity, Elijah was in sober fact a Gaon, having mastered the entire Torah, consisting of the Bible and the Talmud, their numerous commentaries and super-commentaries, the law codes of every land and age, together with such "incidentals" as the Kabbalah or mystical writings of the Palestinian, Babylonian, Spanish, and German schools.

If there is any doubt that this represents a stupendous achievement for a youth still in his early teens, let the reader please remember that his knowledge covered the vast literary activity of the Jews from the time of Ezra the Scribe to the sixth century of the common era, including the Babylonian Talmud with its six thousand folio pages, the Palestine Talmud of somewhat smaller size but a staggering work nonetheless, the Midrashim and the geonic literature, quite a sizable library in themselves, to say nothing of the scores of learned tomes that had accumulated through the centuries.

The question naturally arises as to how all this was possible to one so young? Physical endurance has its limits and the ascetic life he followed from his childhood—eating and sleeping little and rarely venturing out into the open—is not calculated to support such strain. All the greater is one's surprise at reading that the Gaon was never subject to physical or mental fatigue, was always genial and cheerful, and lived to the age of seventy-seven without having recourse to doctors and medicine. He found his play in study and in solving knotty talmudic problems, and his diversion in the intellectual and spiritual conquests he made. When he felt the shadow of mental fatigue creeping over him he was wont to send for Jacob Krantz, famous as the Dubner Maggid, who amused him with his great wealth of stories and anecdotes. Once only was Rabbi Elijah known to have been sick; at that time, when a difficult Mishnah had puzzled him, he lay despondent, without food and sleep for several days. But he soon rallied and was cheerful again when, with the aid of his favorite pupil, Rabbi Haim Volozhin, he arrived at its correct meaning.

The Vilner Gaon, as Rabbi Elijah was known, disclaimed miraculous powers for his achievements. He used to say humorously, "If you only will you will be a Gaon." He was an assiduous student. He repeated every passage he studied hundreds of times.

He is said to have spent more than six months on a single Mishnah. He never spared himself. The injunction of the rabbis, "The Torah cannot be possessed unless a man is prepared to give his life for it," was carried out by him to the letter. He had a logical, razor-keen mind, able to cut through the most difficult and involved problem to its essentials. With his vast knowledge of rabbinic lore he was in a position to make contrasting passages, however involved, explain each other.

His prodigious memory was another help in making his immense scholarship possible. He never forgot anything. After reading a book once he could recite it from memory the rest of his life. He remembered not only the thoughts and ideas but the very words of whatever he read. It was said of the Gaon that, if by some catastrophe the whole rabbinic literature were to be destroyed, he could restore it from memory without the loss of a word. Equally phenomenal was his quick understanding. In a flash he caught the meaning of the most tangled problem. When still a young boy, he is said to have gone through and mastered in a single night *Zebahim* and *Menahot,* consisting of two hundred and thirty pages and regarded by scholars as among the most difficult tractates of the Talmud.

He was a tyrant with himself, a tyrant with his time, a tyrant with his family, with whom he took his meals only on the Sabbath and on holidays. He husbanded his every minute so frugally that no one passed unused. His two hours' sleep a night, he did not take consecutively, but in half-hour periods. He lived in great poverty. He and his famliy subsisted on a small stipend from a fund left by an ancestor, Rabbi Moses Rivkes, which was doled out to him in weekly installments, and when a dishonest official diverted the money to himself, Elijah let his wife and children go hungry rather than denounce the culprit and expose him to shame and humiliation, which, according to the rabbis, is a sin.

The Gaon's piety was equal to his learning. He was a harmonious personality. His love of Torah was more than matched by his love and fear of God. Study was to him more than merely an intellectual exercise it was a religious and ethical discipline. As Solomon

Schechter observes, "It must be understood that to learn Torah meant for the Gaon more than mere brain work for the purpose of gaining knowledge. To him it was a kind of service to God." While in the scholarly circles he was held in greatest reverence as the "Gaon," the unsurpassed master of rabbinic lore, his utter love for and devotion to God and His holy precepts gained for him what was perhaps his noblest title, "Hasid," (Saint). The greatness and completeness of Elijah's life and character were due to the fact that in him heart and mind, learning and saintliness, were perfectly fused.

The Gaon-Saint of Vilna was far from having been the chilly ascetic or wholly spiriualized being he is sometimes made out to have been. He spent much time in his study but he also felt a deep concern for his fellow men. His mind was acutely keen and sharp but his heart had not lost its throb. There was a spiritual chasteness about him that made him idolized by all classes of men, scholars and simple folk alike. He was severe with himself, but kind and gentle toward others, especially the poor and unhappy. While maintaining his family on a pauper's mite, he was reckless in emptying his pockets to the destitute. Once, when he was penniless, he sold his furniture—such as it was—and distributed the proceeds to the indigent.

He was admired for his knowledge of the Torah and loved for the purity and magnanimity of his character. He was not the walled-in hermit contemplating only himself and his books. He was never so happy as when he performed a *mitzvah* (a good deed) for an individual or for the community. Poor as he was, he could not be prevailed upon to accept a salaried position as a rabbi. What he accomplished, with the resulting fame and glory for his city and people, he did as a private individual. He shrank from public office, and would under no circumstances consider any emolument for what services he rendered but had the Board of Charities set aside a sum of money for distribution among the poor under his direction.

Rabbi Elijah lived his life from within and was consistently successful in the kind of existence he chose for himself. He took from life only as much as he absolutely needed for his undisturbed study of Torah. His wife, Hannah, whom in all likelihood, in accordance with customs of the time, he married at a very early age, was not only no hindrance to him but even helped him in the attainment of his ambition. An understanding woman and hailing from a family of learning, she troubled her great husband with the material cares and worries of her household as little as possible. Details about her life are lacking, but it is known that she blessed her husband with two sons, who also became great scholars, and at least one daughter, who became the wife of a distinguished rabbi. When the children were young and there was no bread in the house for them, rather than upset her husband, Hannah had them visit the neighbors, who, seeing that they were hungry would feed them.

The Gaon was scarcely twenty years of age when, although unaccustomed to the ways of the world and speaking no other language than that of the Bible and the Yiddish vernacular, he left his seclusion and made the rounds of the Jewish communities of Poland and Germany. What impelled Elijah to leave the security of his home for the dangers and hardships incidental to travel more than two hundred years ago, remains an unsolved mystery. Was it to get acquainted with Jewish life and scholars outside his own town and province or was it prompted by the piety that made so many learned Jews subject themselves to voluntary exile as atonement for their real or imaginary sins?

Did he meet in his wanderings with the rationalist tendencies which already had made themselves felt among the so-called more advanced Jews of Germany, or with the revivalist Hasidic movement active in the Polish communities he visited? The Gaon kept no diary and left no record of his travels. But if in his roamings abroad he came in contact with one group or the other, he could not have been impressed with either. At any rate, there was no visible influence of his travels abroad on his life and conduct, which, as before, remained in strict conformity to the requirements of Torah, down to its smallest precepts.

Rabbi Elijah had hardly given himself time to relax from his

travels when he set out again, this time for Palestine. The Holy
Land was to the Gaon-Saint of Vilna a kind of unrealized dream, as
it had been to Jewish saints and scholars of all time, whose passion
and longing were for the City of David and her historic associations. He longed to pray in the ruins of the Temple, at the graves of
Israel's kings and prophets and likely, to spend his life in the land
where the Bible came into being. Fate, however, decreed otherwise;
he did not get far beyond Germany, and he returned home soon
afterward. Various reasons are assigned for his change of mind,
the most probable one being the impossibility on board ship to
observe strictly the Jewish dietary laws.

From Koenigsberg he wrote to his family a letter which became
a classic and which was reprinted many times under the title, *Alim
li-Terufah* (Leaves of Healing), dealing principally with his family's
conduct during his absence. The Gaon reveals himself in the letter
as an excellent pedagogue, for while he enjoins upon his wife to
deal severely with their children he is at the same time not lacking
in the softer and gentler graces. After admonishing her not to spare
the rod when necessary, he also writes: "Let your words be tender
and caressing." Addressing his children's teachers, Elijah writes:
"Instruction is only efficient when it is conveyed easily and agree-
ably. Give them small presents of money, and the like, to please
them; this will help their studies."

The Gaon was irritated by the lack of decorum in the synagogue,
by the chatter of the men, the prattle of the women, and the
display of fineries, the latter a source of chagrin and envy to the
less fastidiously dressed female worshipers, and he pleads with his
wife and daughter, "It is better to pray at home, for in synagogue it
is impossible to escape envy and the hearing of idle talk. . . . The
more so on Sabbaths and festivals, when people assemble to talk,
it would be better not to pray at all." It is also better for your
daughter," he writes to his wife, "not to go to synagogue, for there
she would see garments of embroidery and similar finery. She
would grow envious and speak of it at home, and out of this would
result scandal and other ills." After which follows a list of biblical
books, with special reference to the Books of Proverbs and Eccle-

siastes, which he recommends for their reading in lieu of going to synagogue for divine worship.

The letter concludes on its noblest note as the writer entreats his wife to deal kindly with her mother-in-law and, conversely, begs his mother "to live harmoniously with my wife, each bringing happiness to the other by kindly intercourse, for this is a prime duty incumbent on all mankind. . . . Let there be no dissension of any kind among all the household, but let love and brotherliness reign. In case of offense, forgive each other, and live for God's sake in amity." The Gaon directed the letter "to be read every week, particularly on the Sabbath before the meal."

When the Gaon returned from his travels he gathered about him a group of disciples whom he instructed in the little synagogue which was also his study. What he taught them was greater, deeper, and more fundamental than the teaching of most other scholars, for he taught them how to think and how to study, what was primary and what was secondary in the study of the Torah. For a long time, especially in the Polish schools, the Talmud was studied not critically but piously. A halo of holiness developed not only about the spirit and content of the Talmud but about its smallest details. Mistakes, corruptions, and copyists' errors fell into the text but they were not to be changed or corrected, for had not the Oral Law come direct from heaven together with the Written Law? Out of their great love for the Talmud and the reverence they bore it, the Jews surrounded it with a kind of infallibility that was tantamount to book worship. A school of learning came into being which went by the name of *pilpul,* which, more subtle than logical, more brilliant than intellectually tenable, undertook to resolve all difficulties and reconcile all contradictions by a set method, however far-fetched and fantastic.

It was the Gaon's great service to talmudic learning that he abhorred such spurious cleverness, that he set simplicity above subtlety, and correct understanding of the thought and words of the rabbis above the keen-witted manipulations of the dialecticians. He frankly admitted that the printed text of the Talmud was imperfect and that it needed correction. Slight as this observation may seem today, it was a tremendous admission at the time, and it paved the way for a critical-scientific study of the ancient sources of Jewish literature which not many years after the Gaon had died was taken up by the high-spirited founders of the *Wissenschaft des Judentums.*

The Gaon's devotion to truth and his insistence on independent judgment were exemplified in a striking manner when he refused to accept as conclusive the decisions of the *Shulhan Aruk* (Prepared Tables), a work which had guided the religious life of the Jews for nearly two hundred and fifty years and whose authority had never been questioned, without previously examining the sources on which its opinions were based. "Do not regard the views of the *Shulhan Aruk* as binding if you think they are not in agreement with those of the Talmud," he cautioned his disciples. It was a bold statement, indeed, and only a man revered as saint and Gaon could make it without inviting the censure of his fellow scholars.

In the Gaon's time the ghetto festered with stagnation. Worldly knowledge and the sciences were nonexistent. Tradition alone was honored and filled the minds of the Jewish people. Rabbi Elijah was unique for the fact that he alone among the Russian-Polish scholars harked back to the Spanish tradition of enlightened Jewish scholarship. While he was leagues behind the cultural advancement of his Spanish brethren—neither his time nor environment offering him the opportunities which were at their disposal—he nevertheless went far in their direction when he indicated to his scholarly con-temporaries that there was no way to escape misunderstanding of the words and meaning of the Talmud if one neglected the auxiliary sciences. In his own words, "If a man is ignorant of secular sciences, he is a hundredfold ignorant of the Torah." This was for his time an epoch-making, almost revolutionary, assertion—one which must have shocked the Russian-Polish scholars who loftily sneered at any knowledge outside the Talmud. What need, they argued, was there of learning derived from foreign sources when all they wished to know, and all that was good for them to know, was contained in the Bible and the Talmud?

The Gaon not only did not disdain the secular sciences but

exemplified his approval of them as an aid to Torah by his own devotion to them. Frugal as he was with his time, letting nothing divert him from his sacred occupation, he perfected himself in mathematics, astronomy, geography, and anatomy insofar as material on these subjects could be found in Hebrew books. He would have taken up the study of music, botany, and medicine, the first two for the understanding of the Bible and the Talmud and the latter for the ministration it offered to suffering humanity, if it had not been for his father, who feared an accompanying neglect of Torah. Some time later, at his behest, Baruk of Shklow, his disciple, translated Euclid into Hebrew for the use of students of the Talmud, and in an introduction he recorded his master's opinion of the subject. The Gaon would have liked to see Josephus rendered into Hebrew, for the light it would cast on the historical portions of the Talmud. Philosophy alone was objectionable to him and, much as he esteemed Moses Maimonides (he spoke with the greatest admiration of his *Mishneh Torah* and his Commentary upon the Mishnah), he was less happy with his philosophical attitude toward the Bible and Judaism generally. It is generally assumed that the Gaon was familiar with no language other than that of the Bible and the Talmud—a supposition contradicted by his letter from abroad to his family on his way to Palestine. In that letter, already referred to, in which he entreats his wife and children not to profane the Sabbath with idle thoughts, he writes explicitly: "I possess many moral books in the German language; let them read these regularly; above all on the Sabbath—the holy of holies—they should occupy themselves with these ethical books exclusively." That Rabbi Elijah should house in his library books written in a foreign language, although in Hebrew characters, side by side with his holy tomes, is surprising enough; that he should have deemed them worthy of perusal on the Sabbath, "the holy of holies," testifies both to his unprejudiced attitude to language other than that of the Bible and the Talmud and to a broad-mindedness that was truly extraordinary, considering the time and environment in which he lived.

Solomon Schechter used to warn against imputing thoughts and ideas to scholars and thinkers against which if they were alive, they would rise in protest and indignation. But there is no mistaking the impulse the Gaon gave to the cultural development of his people, for his was the kind of character and personality from which influence radiated in many directions. A devotee of the rabbinic tradition from which he never moved an inch, he was at the same time tolerant of the secular sciences and spent considerable time in cultivating them; a rabbi of impeccable piety, he nevertheless wrote a treatise on mathematics and wished to see works of general knowledge translated into the Hebrew language.

Rabbi Elijah cannot by the widest stretch of imagination be labeled a "liberal," nor did the Haskalah, the Enlightened Movement, originate with him, as is sometimes claimed. He had too keen and profound a perception for the abiding value of tradition for one thing, and too conservative a view of Jewish historical development, for another. His own attitude was clear and consistent. It was the advancement of the Jews and Judaism through knowledge of the Torah and devotion to God. Nevertheless, by demanding a critical and useful knowledge of the Torah in place of the casuistry and aridity which dominated the scholarship of his time, and by opening new horizons of Jewish education by insisting that children be taught to make their way into Jewish knowledge easily and naturally, through the study of the Bible and Hebrew grammar, before plunging into the mazes of rabbinic learning, Rabbi Elijah Gaon contributed to the intellectual and spiritual enrichment of the Jews of his age sufficiently to deserve Isaac H. Weiss' tribute that he was "the first sower of enlightenment upon the soil of Russia."

There are few experiences more sad and tragic than those that occur when lives spent in peace and quiet end in storm and confusion. It is almost inconceivable that such a fate should have overtaken the Gaon-Saint of Vilna, who confronted the world with no gesture other than one of peace and good will. The man who lived his life barricaded against strife and struggle, who hated nothing so much as to be drawn into disputes on any account, found himself at the height of his career the principal figure in a controversy which set nearly all Jewry aflame. We refer, of course, to the part Rabbi Elijah played in 1772 in the campaign against the spread of the Hasidic movement.

As noted above, the Gaon lived a secluded and retired life. He would not on any account meddle in public affairs. Although the recognized spiritual head of his community and, indeed, of all East-European Jewry, he consistently refused to accept a position which would deprive him of the time he needed for the study of Torah. In his early thirties, and already famous for his learning and saintliness, he was approached by the celebrated Rabbi-Kabbalist Jonathan Eybschutz to arbitrate the latter's controversy with Rabbi Jacob Emden, another renowned scholar, who accused Eybschutz of secretly harboring heretical Sabbatian tendencies, the Gaon declined. "Who am I," he wrote excusing himself, "from a far-away land that people should hearken to my voice?"

His own community seethed with strife and conflict. A controversy of unusual bitterness raged about the head of a spiritual leader of the city, Rabbi Samuel ben Avigdor. Irregularities said to have been discovered in his office as rabbi and arbitrator in business disputes developed into an agitation demanding his resignation. The Gaon refused to interfere and use his authority, when a mere word from him would have spared the Jews of Vilna much shame and humiliation.

What, then, moved this man, in every respect so serene and gentle, to head the crusade against the followers of the Hasidic sect with such fire and fury? What made Rabbi Elijah, from whose mouth an angry or bitter word was rarely heard to issue, exclaim in one of his pronouncements against the Hasidim, "Had I the power, I would punish the infidels as the worshipers of Baal were punished of old"?

Admirers of the Gaon find it quite difficult to understand and condone the severity with which he proceeded against the adherents of the young Hasidic sect. Consideration of the time and circumstances of the struggle, however, will prove how inevitable it was that the Gaon should have joined in the conflict; how inevitable that, with the example of Sabbatai Zebi and Jacob Frank before him, he should have used what power and authority his name carried to check the progress of a party which, to all appearances, bore the earmarks of a new sectarian movement or a recrudescence of the old sectarian movement in a new guise.

It could not have been a matter of indifference to the Gaon, the spiritual leader to whom almost all Jewry looked for guidance and instruction, that the Hasidic influence took hold most strongly in just those areas of Polish Jewry where the Sabbatian heresy still lingered, and that the latter likewise went by the name of Hasidim. "Those groups of Polish Jewry," writes Gershom Scholem, "which already before and at the time of the first appearance of the Baal Shem called themselves Hasidim included many Sabbatians, if they were not indeed wholly crypto-Sabbatian in character, and it took some time before the difference between the new Hasidim of the 'Baal Shem' and the old ones became generally appreciated."

Despite his all-embracing genius, his wisdom and learning, the Gaon may not have been aware of the difference nor conscious of the spiritual implication of the neo-Hasidic movement and the faith, hope, and courage it brought to thousands of dismal Jewish lives. In all likelihood, in the solitude of his study and the atmosphere of scholarship in which he lived, he had never even as much as heard of Israel Baal Shem Tov, and, if he had, the latter's name could not have inspired him with much respect and confidence since it was not listed among the learned.

There was considerable difference between the emotional world of the Besht and the form Hasidism took under some of its latter-day "saints." The former was inner and mystical, the fervent product of a mind attuned to God; the other was an indecorous exhibitionism supposed to coax the spiritual powers into activity. Thus it was not the inner emphasis of Hasidism but the outward unconventional display many of the Hasidim made of themselves in public while praying—their shouting, stamping, clapping, and facial contortions—that aroused the ire of the more conservative Jews and invited their opposition.

While the Besht lived he was on tolerable terms with the com-

munity. He sponsored the spiritual element of religion but did not
introduce radical changes. But after he died the Hasidim did almost
everything to widen the gulf between the Mitnagdim, as their
opponents were called, and themselves. They withdrew from the
established synagogues and organized places of worship of their
own; they changed the traditional prayer book for the Sephardic
ritual of Isaac Luria, the kabbalist-saint of Safed; they disregarded
the fixed hours of worship and prayed when their hearts were
moved; they assumed an attitude of moral superiority over their
opponents; they held traditional Jewish learning in light esteem;
they introduced a new method in the ritual slaughtering of animals
for food, and, to cap their deviation from the orthodox tradition,
Sheneur Zalman, the celebrated Hasidic rabbi of Ladi, even ven-
tured to rewrite the *Shulhan Aruk,* a religious code by Joseph Caro
(1488–1575), to suit the changed customs and practices of his sect.

It was quite natural that Hasidism, which made sensational headway in Galicia, Podolia, and the district of Kiev, should have been
regarded with something less than sympathy in Lithuania, the bastion of Jewish learning and the home of its greatest representative,
Rabbi Elijah Gaon. When, therefore, in the year 1772, after the
death of Rabbi Dob Baer, the famous preacher of Meseritz,
the favorite disciple of the Besht, and later his successor, plans
were made by the Hasidim to extend their empire further
north, even to Lithuania, the war was on in all its heat and passion.
It was perfectly natural that the power and authority of the Gaon
should be appealed to against the advancing "heresy" and that he
should have answered the call as the performance of a religious
precept, as he saw it. Indeed, he would have been a leader unworthy
of his responsibility had he kept his peace and not answered the
summons.

The situation was aggravated when it was discovered that Hasidic
societies had already secretly penetrated into Lithuania and that
members of the "godless sect" had dared to raise their heads in
the very city of the Gaon. The usually retiring Gaon-Saint was in a
warlike mood. For the first time voices other than those of prayer

and study were heard issuing from his chamber. They were angry and bitter voices that called for strife and battle.

There was open and bitter war between the two groups. The struggle against Hasidism was prosecuted with the utmost vigor and determination. The signal was given from Vilna, headquarters of the campaign, and it was faithfully carried out in all places where the name of the Gaon was honored. Pastoral letters were dispatched by the Gaon against "the dishonorable followers of the Besht, the destroyer of Israel." Hasidic books were condemned and burned; no social or business relations were permitted with members of the "blasphemous sect"; their leaders were to be excommunicated and their rites and ceremonies placed under the ban. A children's epidemic, which broke out in Vilna and resulted in a number of deaths, was quite naturally attributed to the neglect of Torah and the departure from the true faith.

To placate the Gaon and appease his outraged feelings, Rabbi Shneur Zalman, founder of *Habad,* formed from the initial letters of the Hebrew words *hakmah, binah, deah* (wisdom, understanding, knowledge), an intellectual movement within Hasidism which sought to put it on a philosophical basis, rushed to Vilna, accompanied by another Hasidic leader, for an interview with the Gaon. No worse ambassador of good will could the Hasidim have chosen. Although a man of unquestioned learning and piety, Rabbi Zalman outraged the orthodox by his revised edition of the *Shulhan Aruk* and the new prayer book containing many Hasidic additions he had introduced. The Gaon personally objected to him because of the alleged pantheistic heresies the Gaon discovered in his principal Hasidic-philosophical work, *Tanya.*

As might have been foreseen, the mission was a complete failure. The Gaon refused to see its members. He not only declined to receive the Hasidic delegation but, to escape the pressure of friends who urged a more compromising attitude, he left the city and would not return until he made sure that the representatives of the Hasidic movement had departed.

The part the scholar-saint of Vilna played in the campaign against Hasidism makes a sorry chapter in his otherwise great and luminous life. While under the circumstances described the clash could not very well have been avoided, he could have done much to obviate the scandalous developments of the controversy. He insisted on complete surrender when compromise might have softened the harshness of the struggle. As it was, it did little credit to the Gaon that he permitted his name to be dragged into a conflict which not only divided almost all Jewry into two warring camps but which gave the Russian police an opportunity to meddle in its religious affairs.

It was fortunate for the Gaon that he did not live to see the full tragic consequences of the forces of hate and bitterness that were unleashed and which he did little to control, It was fortunate for him that he died before seeing with his own eyes the gentle teacher of Ladi denounced to the Russian government as a dangerous agitator and dragged to St. Petersburg in chains. And, lastly, unequivocally opposed as he was to the theory and spread of Hasidism, it was fortunate for Rabbi Elijah that he did not live to see the utter futility of his opposition. For it would have grieved him to know that he not only had failed to check its progress but that shortly after his death there was scarcely a community in his beloved Lithuania where the Hasidic sect had not struck roots and obtained a following.

Someone once characterized the Besht and the Gaon of Vilna as the heart and the head of East-European Jewry. But Jewish historic characters cannot be so sharply and dogmatically differentiated. In Rabbi Elijah of Vilna the qualities both of heart and of mind were perfectly balanced. He was both Gaon and Hasid, the head and heart of his people. If by reason of his great learning he particularly appealed to the scholars, his piety, modesty, and humility made him equally adored by other classes of men. Loath as he was to be disturbed in his studies, he rarely failed to attend a meeting of the *kahal* when a question involving the poor was on the agenda.

In his person endless goodness and generosity were combined with steadfast firmness. He did not shrink from battle when in his opinion the discipline of the Law was being transgressed, but his heart was with the poor and the suffering. He was the idol of the masses no less than the subject of admiration of the learned. When he appeared in public, he was greeted by a love and affection given to few other men. His scholarly achievements, consisting of brief critical notes and observations written in an unpolished style, are understood only by the scholars; but the image of the Gaon as a vivid human personality had remained a legacy of the ages. Thus one of the familiar pictures of Jewish celebrities that adorned the walls of Jewish homes in pre-war Russia and Poland was that of the Gaon of Vilna wrapped in his *talit* and *tephilin,* with a writing quill in his hand.

He became a legend to his people. The stories circulated about him indicate the depth of love and admiration in which he was held. One such legend is that when the army of Catherine, the Russian empress, had besieged and stormed Vilna, the Jews besought the Gaon to pray for them. The seventy-two-year-old man repaired to the Great Synagogue and led his wailing congregation in the recital of the psalm, "The Lord will answer thee in the day of thy distress." The prayer was no sooner concluded than a cannon ball came crashing down upon the roof of the synagogue without damaging the building or injuring any of the worshipers.

He was the very ideal of the talmudic conception of a scholar— the man who studies Torah *lishma* for its own sake. He burst the bonds of the old stultifying method of study by showing the way to a systematic approach to the Bible, the Mishnah, the Gemara, the Codes. He was modern in his frequent use and application of ancient sources. He was among the very few of his generation who made use of the Palestinian Talmud, then all but neglected by the scholars, for the light it shed on its Babylonian counterpart. By comparing similar passages in these two rabbinic sources, he was able to easily resolve seemingly difficult problems.

Scholarship was to the Gaon a sacred occupation worthy of one's greatest efforts. He knew no easy road to learning. He stood for no docile acceptance of authority, no matter how high the source, except what was proved and tested by one's own painstaking labor. Thus, somewhat naïvely, R. Haim Volozhin, Rabbi Elijah's favorite disciple, tells that "From his own lips I heard that one of the heavenly envoys pleaded with him again and again to reveal to him the profoundest secrets; his reply was, 'I do not desire to penetrate the secrets of the Law of God through an intermediary. . . . Whatever cannot be acquired with my own toil and the exertion of my own mental faculties—that I gladly forego.' "

The man who read and studied so many books himself contributed a list of works that would do honor to a man with much greater leisure than the Gaon had. He contributed commentaries in the form of notes, glosses, and learned observations, on every book of rabbinic literature he read. Rabbi Abraham Danzig, a pupil of the Gaon, who delivered the eulogy at his teacher's death, stated that the master had composed no less than seventy books, all of which were written before he was forty years old. He wrote on the Bible, the Mishnah, the Tosefta, the Gemara, Pirkei d'Rabbi Eliezer, Seder Olam, the prayer book, the Passover Hagadah, and the classical works of the Kabbalah, to say nothing of such secular subjects as chronology, geography, geometry, astronomy, etc.

Notwithstanding his secluded and ascetic life, the Gaon was in good health almost to the very end. Although he got almost no physical exercise, he was of a buoyant temperament, always cheerful and happy in the service of God and the study of Torah. When he was overcome by weakness or fatigue he found relaxation in switching his subjects of study. When, therefore, on the Day of Atonement in the year 1797, at the age of seventy-seven, he became seriously ill, he knew that the end was near, and he sent for his children in order to bless them, his wife having preceded him by several years. He died on the third day of the festival of Tabernacles with the *lulab* and *etrog* (the palm branch and citron), symbols of the holiday, clutched firmly in his hands.

The death of Rabbi Elijah Gaon was a signal for universal mourning and lamentation. Jews everywhere felt their loss and gathered in their synagogues to mourn his departure. In Vilna where the Gaon had lived and died, the whole city turned out to pay tribute to the man who had made it famous among the Jewish communities of the world. The funeral was said to have been so great that in all Vilna, with its multitude of synagogues and schools of learning, there was not a *minyan,* or quorum of ten men, to be found for the regular *minha,* or afternoon services.

The Gaon's greatest bequest to his generation and those to follow was not his scholarship nor the learned works and annotations he left behind, precious as they are to this day to students of the Torah. His greatest bequest was his rich spiritual personality, an ennobling and inspiring life spent in the service of God and his fellow men— this and the Volozhin Yeshiva, founded at the Gaon's behest by his friend and disciple, R. Haim Volozhin, which for more than a hundred years was a kind of talmudic Oxford from whose halls of learning some of the finest Jewish scholars and men of affairs emanated.

Moses Mendelssohn

I<small>T IS ONE</small> of the ironies of history that a man who all his life loved peace and shunned controversy became one of the most controversial figures of his time. Moses Mendelssohn was a gentle and tender-hearted man who loved peace and lived on good terms with the world. Yet about few other men has there been a greater variety of critical evaluation, running all the way from excessive praise to equally excessive censure—and this about the man who was hailed by his countrymen as the "German Socrates" and by his Jewish admirers as the "Third Moses." Between the historian Graetz, one of Mendelssohn's greatest admirers, and Perez Smolenskin, the Hebrew editor-novelist who was his severest critic, the German-Jewish philosopher was ridiculously overpraised and absurdly overblamed.

Moses Mendelssohn was a novel type of Jew for his time and environment. In his day the only kind of Jew who had access to the world outside the ghetto was the so-called *Hofjude* (court Jew) who acted as financial agent for an extravagant royal ménage or a costly military organization. He was one of the most widely known Jews of his day, and his admirers maintained that he had introduced a new period in Jewish history. He was the foremost spokesman and advocate of his people at a time when the Jews enjoyed little respect and consideration from the world. He loved Jews and Judaism deeply and sincerely. His soul was hurt by their humiliating condition and he attempted to evolve a philosophy that would make Judaism compatible with the world and prepare the Jews to take their place in the life of the state and society.

Mendelssohn pioneered in many fields and was active in many directions. He was esthete, philosopher, literary critic, leader in the German Aufklärung Movement, and Bible translator, and he achieved considerable fame in all these fields. He lived in an age that abounded in great men—Kant and Jacobi, to say nothing of the lesser lights, were among his contemporaries—yet he maintained his own position as one of the influential creative spirits of his time. If he did not bring about the so-called Jewish emancipation— the fall of the Bastille came three years after Mendelssohn died— he did much to speed its coming. He worked for the education and refinement of his people, hoping that by these assets their condition would be improved and the baseless prejudices against them removed.

Like other men of his stature, he was dominated by contradictory urges and impulses. He beheld glimpses of a new world and was passionately attached to the old; he was a rationalist who believed in the supremacy of reason, yet his roots were strongly imbedded in the Torah and in the rabbinic tradition, and he faithfully observed their every precept. He was a fervent advocate of the Jews, but on one occasion when their rights were in jeopardy he lacked the initiative to interfere personally on their behalf, but handed the matter over to a Christian. Wilhelm Dohm, a Prussian councilor of state. "Dohm defended the Jews," A. Roback wittily remarks, "much as a Southern humanitarian colonel would speak in behalf of the Negro." Mendelssohn was dissatisfied with Dohm's "defense" and had his friend Marcus Herz, a distinguished Berlin physician-philosopher, translate Mennasseh ben Israel's famous *Vindiciae Judaeorum* instead, to which he supplied an illuminating introduction.

Moses Mendelssohn was the younger member of a trio of Jewish personalities who, through their wide influence and the great movements they inspired, made the eighteenth century, in which they all lived, memorable in Jewish history. Rarely have there been three contemporary figures, living at no great distance from one another, whose lives and teachings were more radically opposed to each other; yet each one of them became a symbol of his time and environment. Israel Baal Shem Tov, living in the depths of Southern Poland, where the soil was virgin and life was more or less primitive entered the field of faith and created Hasidism, which still warms and inspires the hearts of millions of Jews. Rabbi Elijah, in more enlightened Lithuania, born and brought up in an atmosphere of books and learning, saw the genius of the Jew in his intellect, and thousands revere him as the Gaon of Vilna. Moses Mendelssohn, the very symbol of Western Europe, on the other hand, tried to prepare the Jew for making contact with the world.

Moses Mendelssohn was a child of his age. His virtues and faults, his merits and defects reflected the time and environment in which he lived. The eighteenth century, in which he was born, was one of the most important times in modern history and one of the most crucial in the life of the Jewish people. There was a new vision and a new spirit abroad and an unexampled change in the social and political order of things. It was the Age of Reason, with its demands for the inherent rights of man, his dignity and importance in the general scheme of life. It was also the age of intellectual endeavor, of research and scholarship, of science, literature, and philosophy. It was a revolutionary age in which obsolete ideas were banished, knowledge assumed the seat of authority, and scientific investigation displaced blind credulity.

The Jews did not remain ignorant of or indifferent to what was happening in the world about them, and they responded to the changed conditions with alacrity. The walls of the ghetto did not fall, but the changes wrought an upheaval in the inner life and consciousness of the Jews. Suddenly, like Rip Van Winkle, they awakened in a new and strange world. They did not realize how long they had slept and they were heartily ashamed of the rags and tatters of their old thoughts and antiquated ideas. From the point of view of the Jews and Jewish survival, the awakening was a rude, indeed a shattering, one. Many of the things they had been taught and had loved lost importance and interest for them. The books they had read, the ideas and ideals they had cherished compared poorly with the new knowledge.

The new spirit infected the sacred precincts of the yeshiva, where the folios of the Talmud were still pored over but not with the same zeal and passion as before. Books more interesting and absorbing than the Talmud competed for the attention and devotion of the students, and the more refined modern languages appealed more to their taste than the ancient Chaldean. Because of the resemblance between the Yiddish and German languages, students of the yeshiva devoted hours intended for the study of the Talmud to the reading of the German classics. Even the slightly fanatic Gaon of Vilna made concessions by allowing the study of the sciences, and had Euclid translated into Hebrew—on the pretext, of course, that thereby the knowledge of the Torah would be advanced.

The lure of the new spirit penetrated the small town of Dessau in the Duchy of Anhalt in Germany, and invaded the poor home of Mendel, a transcriber of the Holy Law on parchment, where his child Moses was born in September, 1729. Not much hope could be held out for the future of the deformed little child, who added a distressing stammer to his misshapen, stunted body. But there was no lack of love and affection on the part of the parents for their luckless child. They could give him only what their scanty means allowed, except for the love of Torah, which was the possession of even the humblest Jewish home. At the local Talmud Torah an unusual talent was discerned in the sickly boy which more than made up for his physical deficiencies to his happy parents.

He was fortunate in his teachers, for when his primary education was over he came under the tutelage of David Fränkel, a man who combined great talmudic learning with an interest in philosophy. After his Talmud lessons, he read with his favorite pupil *The Guide for the Perplexed,* and he even let the boy take the book home with him. The young student, barely in his teens, was delighted. He fell greedily upon Maimonides' masterwork and spent many happy hours in its company. Early in the morning and late at night he pored enthusiastically over the philosopher's abstractions, puzzling out every difficulty. This book, which grown men find sufficiently deep study, the youthful student read and reread until he fully absorbed its contents. Vistas of a new world opened up before him. He caught glimpses of things that lay beyond what he read and studied, beyond the Bible and the Talmud. He was fascinated by Maimonides and dared dream of his own latent possibilities. Later

Mendelssohn—Mendels-sohn, the son of Mendel—romanticized his deformity and attributed it to his devoted study of the *Guide*, "Maimonides," he said, "is the cause of my deformity. He spoiled my figure and ruined my constitution. Yet, I bear him no grudge for, if he has been the unwitting cause of my physical weakness, has he not amply compensated me by invigorating my soul with sublime knowledge?"

At the age of thirteen the boy presented a problem to his parents. He was too frail and weak for a trade, and as for preparing himself to become a rabbi, the times were not too favorable for that profession. But study the lad would, and he cried his eyes out at the threat of being denied his books. Just then there was an additional crisis in the young student's life. Rabbi Frankel accepted a call to the Chief Rabbinate of Berlin and, for the moment, with his teacher gone, the boy's hopes of studying and becoming a scholar, seemed dashed to the ground. A story tells of little Moses watching his teacher's departure for Berlin with tearful eyes. His parents were laying plans for a workaday occupation for their son not too taxing on his frail health. But the boy was clear and obstinate about his vocation. He would follow his teacher to Berlin, study and become a great scholar. Long and tearfully he pleaded until his parents agreed, and gave him their parting blessing.

The story of Moses Mendelssohn is an epic, closely resembling that of Hillel in his effort for an education. He covered the thirty miles that lay between Dessau and Berlin on foot, and when on the fifth day he arrived at the gate of Berlin, footsore, tired, and hungry, he was not quite sure that he would not have to tramp back. Only the mention of the name of Rabbi Frankel proved the sesame and opened the gate to him. What was the rabbi, himself poor and living in cramped quarters, to do with the penniless boy? But he could not turn away his former student and let him shift for himself, neglected and uncared for by anybody. There was a room in the garret of the rabbi's home and his table could provide for the lad a meal or two. As for the rest, God would help. The youngster, on his part, showed his gratitude to his benefactor by copying in his fine, clear handwriting—the only legacy from his father—the Rabbi's commentary upon the Jerusalem Talmud.

He made friends easily. He was awkward and ungainly looking; but he was modest and warm-hearted, which made people fond of him. One man, a scholar and mathematician, and as penniless as the boy, taught him mathematics; another man introduced him to the sciences; and through a third friend he acquired an elementary acquaintance with the classical languages. He found his greatest difficulty with the German language, chiefly because of the Yiddish dialect to which he had been accustomed since infancy. He was anxious to perfect himself in the knowledge of the German language, its diction, phrasing, and nuances. Language was to Mendelssohn more than a mere medium of speech; it was to him an index to life, a mirror to one's character and personality. Faultless speech bespoke to him a delicacy of taste and feeling, a sensitivity to the higher and finer things of life. Mendelssohn worked relentlessly to acquire the German idiom, until, not many years later, he became the most famous German writer, a master of German diction, the arbiter of German literary style and taste.

Seven years of poverty and privation passed. Mendelssohn lived the Rabbis' prescription for the scholar to the letter. He made the few marks he earned by copying go a long way. He marked his loaf of bread into accurate portions, lest his appetite should outrun his purse. The good Rabbi Frankel made him welcome at his table for a Sabbath and holiday meal and he had an occasional dinner at another good-hearted Jew's home. He accepted the kindnesses shown to him in a spirit of humility and a feeling of his unworthiness—not as a claim on the generosity of his benefactors. "Because I would drink at the well," he wrote in his picturesque fashion, "am I to expect every one to haste to fill my cup from their pitchers? . . . I have no claim save my desire to learn, and what is that to others?" To preserve his self-respect and independence he preferred to work out his own destiny, no matter what hardship it imposed.

Moses Mendelssohn's fate and fortune were fixed when through Aaron Solomon Gomperz, a wealthy Berlin Jewish medical student, he met Gotthold Ephraim Lessing, a young German journalist, poet, playwright, and uncompromising foe of every racial and religious prejudice. Shortly before their meeting, Lessing had scandalized all Germany by a comedy, "The Jews," in which, much against the standards of his time, he argued that a Jew is possessed of the same feelings, sentiments, and honor that characterize other people. The play met with an uproar of resentment and protest, but Lessing held to his view; and when he was invited to meet a Jew who would vindicate his viewpoint he gladly consented.

Other men, bound by the bias and prejudices of that time, must have found it difficult to understand what this dashing young German dramatist, in the flower of genius and manhood, could find in the utterly unattractive Moses Mendelssohn, with his thick lips, grizzly hair, hooked nose and humped back, who spoke not quite perfect German with an embarrassing stammer. But the poet-playwright, sensitive to an inner excellence hidden behind an unlovely façade, recognized the great potentialities of the young man before him. He saw them in the nobility that shone from his eyes and hovered over his lofty brow, in his quick wit and humor, and in his balanced critical judgment of men and books.

They met at a chess game in a cafe frequented by writers and students of the liberal arts. Both Lessing and Mendelssohn were skillful at chess, the latter probably having played the royal game in his early youth. While Jewish authorities of the Middle Ages were stern in their opposition to games of chance, they were more lenient in the case of chess, which Jews played even on the Sabbath. At any rate, the two men, one already famous and the other still to win his spurs, met at the chess board and became fast and inseparable friends. It was the fortune of Moses Mendelssohn—or was it his character and genius for making friends?—that most people to whom he was introduced became his lifelong friends. One wonders whether Lessing's famous play, *Nathan the Wise,* with Mendelssohn as its hero, did not evolve during their hours of companionship at the chess table.

In the meantime, perhaps prior to his acquaintance with Lessing, Mendelssohn's material circumstances had greatly improved. After years of privation he obtained a position as resident tutor to the children of a wealthy Jewish manufacturer, Bernhardt, a man of fine and cultivated tastes. After several years of tutorship, his employer, in recognition of Mendelssohn's fine penmanship, promoted him to the position of bookkeeper at his factory and later offered him a share in the business. Fortune had smiled on Moses Mendelssohn, and now that he was wealthy and independent he could afford to think of a wife and home. What made Mendelssohn turn to Hamburg for a wife at the age of thirty-two when many Berlin girls would have been only too glad to be courted by the successful merchant and budding philosopher, with his growing reputation in literary circles, is not quite clear. In Hamburg in 1761 he met Fromet Guggenheim, the daughter of a not-too-successful trader, and fell in love with her. Berthold Auerbach, the German novelist, wove a pretty legend around the philosopher's wooing of his fiancée. They were married two years later and lived happily in their modest little house. Mendelssohn's only regret was that, in the rearing of their family, Fromet did not live up to the piety her name would suggest.

Lessing and Mendelssohn were kindred spirits and stimulated and influenced each other no little. Notwithstanding their difference of background and early circumstances, they acted as a leaven upon one another. They were almost of the same age—Lessing was a few months older than Mendelssohn. Lessing was a poet and master of German diction, and he was his friend's godfather in the intricacies of the language he was struggling so hard to master; while Mendelssohn, in return, his mind sharpened on *The Guide for the Perplexed,* spurred Lessing on to philosophic studies. It was an ideal relationship, this friendship between the giant of German letters, the happy warrior for religious toleration, and the young man but recently emerged from the obscurity of his early life and environment. Lessing was Mendelssohn's teacher and mentor in the circle of cultured spirits that was Berlin society. Mendelssohn's philosophical writings began as a result of their friendship. When they read together and discussed a philosophical essay by the Earl of Shaftesbury, Mendelssohn remarked that he could do as well.

Lessing challenged him to do so, and some time afterward, Mendelssohn brought his composition to his friend for his criticism. When, after a long while, Mendelssohn became anxious about his manuscript, Lessing appeared and presented the budding young philosopher with a volume of the latter's maiden work published under the title, *Philosophical Discourses,* with a small fee from the publisher.

Moses Mendelssohn had made his debut; he had arrived. He definitely established himself as a citizen in the Republic of Letters. He gained composure and spoke and wrote in the enlightened German style. His maiden venture brought him great prominence. His slim volume was widely read, and even appeared in translation. The Prussian capital buzzed with the fame of the twenty-five-year-old, who but eleven years before had arrived apparently with none of the brilliant qualities that now made him a celebrity in the cultured circles of Berlin. His fame rose steadily, adding ever fresh laurels to his reputation. When Nicolai, a book dealer and one of the advanced spirits of Berlin, edited a publication devoted to the sciences and the fine arts, Mendelssohn was one of its principal contributors. It was in the *Literatur Briefe,* a journal on science, art, and literature, cast in the form of correspondence, that Mendelssohn was emboldened to gently rap his royal master on the wrist and playfully criticize him for his contempt for the German language and his preference for writing his verses in French. It was a presumption for which the king might have packed him off back to Dessau. It was only Mendelssohn's delicate treatment of the matter that prevented the storm from breaking out. Indeed, so impressed was Frederick by the daring of his Jewish critic that shortly afterward, at the petition of a mutual friend, he conferred upon Mendelssohn the "privilege" of a *Schutz-Jude* (protected Jew)—the right of living anywhere unmolested. The most remarkable philosophical triumph of Mendelssohn was his victory over Kant in the prize contest of the Prussian Academy for an essay on the subject of Evidence of the Metaphysical Science. Immanuel Kant, the senior of Mendelssohn by five years and by far the greater and deeper thinker of the two, came out second, with honorable mention, largely because of his rival's easy and persuasive style of writing; or, as Graetz gracefully puts it, because of Mendelssohn's art of plucking the thorns from the flowers of philosophy.

It was, however, *Phaedon* (the Immortality of the Soul), patterned on Plato's dialogue of the same name, that earned for Mendelssohn his greatest fame and distinction not only in his own country but abroad. It went through three editions in less than two years, and was read almost as a sacred writing by all classes of men —young and old, statesmen, philosophers, and theologians. In style and warmth of thought and feeling, it surpassed every other contemporary work. "The Berlin Sage" became a familiar title in thousands of homes. The book had no sooner appeared than it was translated into all European languages, including the Hebrew. Many who had read and were edified by his book wanted to meet its author, and Mendelssohn's modest home in the suburbs of Berlin became a mecca for scholars, poets, and high-ranking noble-men, who came to exchange a few words with the German Socrates —another title bestowed upon Mendelssohn.

But his fame was not without its price. For among Mendelssohn's foreign visitors was a young Swiss evangelical pastor, Caspar Lavater, who came all the way to Berlin to meet and pay homage to the author of *Phaedon*. Being a physiognomist and claiming to be able to read character and inner motives from facial features, he pretended that Mendelssohn was inwardly a Christian and required but little persuasion to become one in fact. He, therefore, sent him a copy of his translation of Bonnet's French work, *Evidence of Christianity,* with a dedication to Mendelssohn requesting that he read it and refute its arguments, or do what "wisdom, love of truth and honesty would naturally dictate."

Intending to embarrass Mendelssohn—Lavater cannot possibly have believed he could convert the Berlin Jewish Sage—the cunning Swiss fanatic succeeded only in adding to Mendelssohn's laurels. Mendelssohn was too shrewd and clever to fall into his challenger's trap. He, therefore, neither publicly refuted Bonnet's book, as Lavater had solemnly adjured him, nor did he defend his own re-ligion. Instead, he so cleverly phrased his reply that it turned the tables on his pious Swiss antagonist and made him the laughing stock of all Europe. Mendelssohn hated controversy; he was a man of peace and good will to all men. He held that no good cause, certainly no religious cause, is ever advanced by controversy. His only answer to Lavater was really that he owed no answer, that no one had a right to ask him why he was a Jew. His religion was his personal, private concern, for which he owed no explanation or apology to any man. Mendelssohn knew that he was treading on dangerous ground and that he could not defend Judaism without affronting Christians. He therefore refrained from being drawn into a discussion of the merits of Judaism and, instead, limited himself to declaring that Judaism was not a proselytizing religion, that it seeks no converts, and that it is binding only upon members of Jewish households. The Rabbis of the Talmud, he said, not only discouraged conversion of non-Jews but laid up difficulties for one seeking admittance into Judaism. "I am so fortunate," he wrote, "as to count among my friends many a worthy man who is not of my faith. Never yet has my heart whispered, Alas! for this good man's soul. . . . Suppose there were among my contemporaries a Confucius or a Solon, I could consistently with my religious principles love and admire the great man, but it would never occur to me to want to convert him, since my religious laws were not meant for him. Do I think there is a chance of his being saved? I certainly believe that he who leads mankind to virtue in this world cannot be damned in the next."

In the end, the controversy was concluded with complete victory for Mendelssohn. His modesty, wisdom, and moderation were as universally applauded as the young Swiss theologian's arrogant impetuosity was deplored. Lavater regretted, and was thoroughly ashamed of, the grief and annoyance his rude importunity had caused the gentle and peaceful Jewish philosopher. Not only did Lavater apologize to Mendelssohn but Bonnet, too, regretted the literary commotion his German translator had caused. Indeed, so sincere was Lavater's repentance that he remained unflagging in his admiration for Mendelssohn, and was instrumental in preventing a decree of expulsion of Jews from Geneva.

Moses Mendelssohn was a proud and keenly sensitive Jew. He bore his Judaism with dignity and distinction, and he would not let any one trifle with it in his presence. He not only never apologized for his religion but did not care whether his friends approved or disapproved of it. He was deeply rooted in the religious and national consciousness of his people. He disdained to accept honors and privileges for himself that were denied his brethren. It was only after considerable hesitation and persuasion by his friends that he submitted to the indignity of being singled out as a *Schutz-Jude* by the philosopher-king of San Souci. He had a keen sense of the responsibility of his position with regard to his people, and he never shirked an opportunity to be of service to them no matter how distasteful it was. When an order was issued by a ruler of a German dukedom that Jews refrain from burying their dead at once and wait three days, to avoid the danger of premature interment, the Jews were horrified as if the violation of a Sinaitic law were at stake. They appealed to Mendelssohn to avert the "evil" decree. Although Mendelssohn had before him testimony of physicians that there had been cases of premature burial, to pacify the aroused Jews he petitioned the authorities to modify the decree.

While Mendelssohn was liberal in principle, he was conservative —indeed, strictly traditional—in practice. There was a warm Jewish atmosphere in his home. The minute regulations of Jewish law were rigidly observed. There was no tampering with any of the Sabbath and holiday observances, no matter what high-ranking friends happened to be present. A friend left a touching account of a visit to the philosopher's home on such an occasion. "It was a Friday afternoon," he writes. "We were sitting and chatting on diverse matters over our coffee, when Mendelssohn, shortly before sundown, rose from his chair, and excusing himself, he said, 'Ladies and gentlemen, we must leave you to receive the Sabbath; we shall be with you again presently.' He and his wife, joining the family, retired for the consecration of the Sabbath by lighting the candles and reciting the appropriate prayers. At the end of half an hour, Mendelssohn returned to his wonted place, his face flushed and radiant with the joy and sanctity of the Sabbath devotions."

Mendelssohn's attachment to Judaism was sincere and genuine. He never broke with the hallowed things of the Jewish past. The Law, he declared in his masterwork, *Jerusalem,* may be defined, and even modified, to suit the circumstances of changed times and environment, but it cannot and dare not be abrogated. He was a bridge between the past and the present, as were Philo and Maimonides in their times. He was the last man to favor novelties or innovations in Judaism. Whether to his credit or not, the impact of the new age did not seriously shake his stand with regard to traditional Judaism, rationalist though he was. He was, of course, for the civil and political emancipation of the Jews, and in his own quiet way, he worked to bring it about. But he would have disdained to accept it had it in any way compromised the Jews' inherited faith. His declaration on this point is quite clear and definite and is not subject to misinterpretations." "If," he wrote, "civil rights cannot be obtained on any other terms than those of departing from the Law, we are heartily sorry for what we deem necessary to declare that we will rather renounce civil rights."

Perez Smolenskin notwithstanding, if Mendelssohn was not the savior of Judaism, as his overenthusiastic admirers maintain, he was certainly not its destroyer and perverter. It was not from him or his influence that the blight of the German *Taufen Bewegung* sprang and brought about the revolting scene of mass desertion from Judaism by a people seized by a mania of wholesale religious and national self-destruction. Had he foreseen it his soul would have cried out in anguished protest. Freedom for Jews meant to him freedom to live as Jews and practice their religion freely. Judaism was his very breath to Mendelssohn. It was no mere empty rhetorical flourish when he called upon the Jews of his country to repudiate emancipation if its acquisition was to be at the cost of their religion. His own life is the best guarantee of the sincerity of his words. He never compromised with his conscience or accepted an "enlightenment" that negated his religion. His Judaism was clear and strong, if not defiant, in the face of all challengers.

Fortunate for Mendelssohn he did not live to see the debacle of

German Jewry and Judaism with which Smolenskin associated his
name. He did not witness the birth of the radical Reform Movement, which sabotaged the traditional ritual, removed from the
Hebrew prayer book every historic national memory and aspiration,
and made the synagogue resemble a Protestant church as closely
as possible. Man of sentiment and emotion that he was, he was
deeply stirred by the old synagogue ritual and was keenly alive to
the beauty and poetry of the Hebrew language. He was a master
Hebrew stylist himself, and *Kohelet Musar,* a Hebrew periodical
edited by him and his associates, marks an era in modern Hebrew
literature. His metrical translation of the Psalms, almost reflecting
the magnificent lyricism of the original, indicates how deeply
saturated he was with the letter and spirit of the Hebrew language.

At no time did Mendelssohn reduce Judaism to a religion only,
minimize the national Jewish consciousness, or deprecate the ages-
old hope of a Jewish national restoration in Palestine. How could he
have done so, in view of the almost innumerable national symbols
and memories of Zion and Jerusalem which he saw observed in his
own and his parents' home, and which remained indelibly etched on
his mind? Zionism as a philosophy of Jewish national redemption
was a thing unknown in the days of Moses Mendelssohn; indeed the
very word "nationalism" had not yet appeared in the vocabulary of
human speech. People were identified as belonging to a group by
the factors of language, territory, and religion; but "nation" and
"national consciousness" were cryptic words that would have
needed much explaining. Yet Mendelssohn was acutely aware of
the Jews as a national entity, and declared their restoration to the
Holy Land as one of the principles of his religious faith. He pen-
sively looked forward to the "nuptial bliss, when Israel, and the
history and language of Israel, shall be restored to their pristine
glory in the Land of Israel."

Not a year passed in Mendelssohn's life but that he was of some
service to his people, either personally or through his friends.
Sympathetic with the intellectual aspirations of young Jews of the
early eighteenth century, he was active on behalf of their educa-

tional and cultural advancement. He felt that their neglect of secular knowledge was responsible for much of the stagnation that had crept into the life of the Jewish people and that was preventing their keeping pace with the advancing march of civilization. At the beginning of the eighteenth century the Jews really had no language. Hebrew was the literary and ritual language of the Jews, but the idiom they spoke was an incoherent gibberish, a mixture of foreign dialects. Mendelssohn was acutely conscious of the linguistic disability of the Jews. He knew what the acquisition of the German language did for him, and he was anxious to share the boon with his co-religionists. He, therefore, set himself to the task of translating the Bible into the German language in Hebrew characters, in order to make the language accessible to those who were unacquainted with the German alphabet.

He began with the Pentateuch, most frequently read and studied by Jews. Seven long years he labored at the task, setting aside all his other literary and philosophical work. To assure scientific and linguistic accuracy, he called on one Solomon Dubno for assistance, an educated and accomplished Hebrew scholar. It was a gigantic task—no less enormous than were the previous translations of the Bible into foreign tongues. To make the German version of the text not only available to the readers but to make its difficult words and passages comprehensible, Mendelssohn supplied the translation with a running commentary, which became familiar as the *Biur*. After the Five Books of Moses were successfully completed, Mendelssohn paraphrased in German the Psalms of David, rendering in metrical form the linguistic beauty and elegance of the original. After Mendelssohn's death, his German version of the Song of Songs was found and published in 1788. Mendelssohn published his biblical translation privately, but it was not long before it evoked great enthusiasm in certain circles, both Jewish and non-Jewish.

Translations of the Bible into the current vernacular had appeared from time to time through the centuries but, with the exception of the Aramaic version, they were not always graciously accepted by the authorities of the synagogue. They correctly felt that translations of the Torah put a premium upon ignorance of the Hebrew text. The Rabbis of the Talmud showed their disapproval of the Septuagint, or Greek version of the Torah, by complaining picturesquely that the day it appeared there was a tremor of the earth over an area of four hundred miles. A thousand years later, when Saadia translated the Bible, he called his Arabic version *tafsir,* signifying that his was not so much a translation of the Scriptures as an explanation of them.

Mendelssohn's German translation of the Torah was certainly no exception to the general rule, for it no sooner appeared than, while it received an enthusiastic reception in some circles, it met with passionate opposition in others, chiefly the rabbis of Germany, Austria, and Poland. They called it a "Germanized Torah," forbade its use, and put it under a ban, without, however, excommunicating Mendelssohn personally, in recognition of his fame and prominent position. The opposition of the orthodox authorities is understandable in view of the results that followed the translation. For not only was the Hebrew Torah neglected by the study of the "Germanized Torah" but soon, also, unforeseen by Mendelssohn, the study of the German language superseded nearly all other Jewish studies. Mesndelssohn himself, it was argued, was the best living proof that no translation of the Bible was necessary to acquire knowledge and mastery of the German language.

Mendelssohn, however, was not dismayed by the storm of opposition to his translation of the Torah. He was prepared for the opposition and replied to it by remarking, with complete good humor, "If my version had been received without opposition, it would have been superfluous. At first, I had intended it for ordinary people, but now I find that it is much more needed by the rabbis." It should be noted, that Mendelssohn had first intended the translation for his children, and it was not until Solomon Dubnow saw it and was convinced of its excellence that Mendelssohn agreed to publish it for the general good of the Jews.

If Mendelssohn was not the father of the Haskalah Movement, he was certainly its godfather. His extraordinary success on behalf of enlightenment in Germany, his translation of the Pentateuch, and, above all, the establishment of modern schools to replace the antiquated *hedarim* in Berlin and other German-Jewish communities, found a resounding echo in cities and countries beyond the borders of Prussia. There were lively business and intermarriage relations between the Jews of Russo-Poland and their brethren-in-faith in Germany. The inspiration and instruction the former carried away from the Berlin mentor acted as leaven in ordering their own moral and intellectual life.

Mendelssohn's personal contribution to the Hebrew renaissance was considerable. His Hebrew was clear, pure, and dignified, without the *melizah*, or florid style, of the post-medieval Hebrew writers. His preface to the *Biur* and commentary to Maimonides' treatise on logic, are good Hebrew writing, as is *Alim Leterufah* (Leaves of Healing), the prospectus and plan of his Bible translation. In 1750, he edited *Kohelet Musar* (A Collection of Ethical Essays) in the style of the English essayists, the first Hebrew periodical. In 1784–5, a group of Maskilim published a magazine called *ha-Measef* (The Collector). The enterprise was under the auspices of Mendelssohn and Hartwig Wessely, his collaborator on the Pentateuch translation after Dubnow had left him. Entirely in the spirit of Mendelssohn was the declared purpose of the publication, as stated by Nahum Slouschz: "To promote the spread of knowledge and the modern idea in the Hebrew language . . . and the purification of Hebrew, which had degenerated in the rabbinical schools." If Mendelssohn did not himself contribute to the *ha-Measef*, he did regard Hebrew as the only language available to all Jews, and he stimulated its cultivation. Thus the sparks ignited by Mendelssohn spread in almost all directions. It is the fate of many books that are much read and talked about at the time of their appearance to be neglected and forgotten by posterity. Moses Mendelssohn's work is as good an example as any of such a fate. His *Phaedon* was the literary rage of its time, not only in Germany but in several other countries. It was read, admired, and cherished by countless men and women. But it was forgotten as if it had never existed in less than a decade after its appearance. A like fate befell Mendelssohn's *Morgen Stunden* (Morning Hours). The book, which in reality was a polemical answer to Jacobi's attack on Lessing as a Spinozist, was made up of a course of lectures on the Deity which he delivered before a select group of young men of the Berlin intellectual aristocracy. Among the privileged auditors were the two Humboldt brothers, later distinguished as scholars, scientists, travelers, and statesmen. Philosophers apparently are poor prophets, for the book which the great Kant pronounced as a finished example of dogmatic metaphysics "whose value will never wane," so completely disappeared from notice that hardly an allusion to it is ever found. In the heyday of its fame translations of it appeared in Italian, and, later, in Hebrew. It is well to note that the *Morgen Stunden,* which was practically the last of Mendelssohn's philosophical testimony, was composed a year before the author died, when he was a sick man.

It is, however, the disappearance from circulation of *Jerusalem,* Mendelssohn's masterpiece, that is most to be deplored. For nothing the German Socrates wrote displayed to greater advantage his varied talents as a Jewish scholar and a philosopher, as a liberal and a conservative, as a pragmatist and an idealist, as a theologian and a statesman, as a dogmatist and a rationalist, than does this work, the product of his mature life and thinking. It is the most compeling statement on religious tolerance ever penned, and is far in advance of the time in which it was written. It is also an extraordinary defense and exposition of the Jews and Judaism, written with warmth and conviction.

So impressed with *Jerusalem* was Immanuel Kant, then at the height of his fame, that he forthwith wrote to David Friedländer, a friend of the Königsberg philosopher and a cooperator with Mendelssohn in the work of enlightenment: "I consider the book the herald of a great reform, which will affect not only your nation but also others. You have succeeded in combining your religion with such a degree of freedom of conscience as was never imagined possible, and clearly demonstrated the necessity of unlimited liberty of conscience in every religion, that ultimately our Church will also be led to reflect how to remove from its midst everything that disturbs and oppresses conscience, which will finally unite all men in their view of the essential points of religion." Israel Abrahams tells that in a long talk he had with Professor William James he discussed Mendelssohn with him. Professor James admitted that his own pragmatic theories were paralleled by *Jerusalem*, and he promised to write on the subject; but unfortunately death overtook him too soon.

Jerusalem is, so to speak, a Magna Carta of religious tolerance. It defines the respective functions of the state and church and the position of the individual vis-à-vis them both. Their functions with respect to the citizen are completely separate and distinct, their tasks are different. While the business of religion is spiritual, that of the state is temporal; the concern of religion is the promotion of human happiness and spiritual well being, the role of the state is the maintenance of order and public as well as political security. The function of the church, being wholly spiritual, Mendelssohn would deny her the right to own property, for property corrupts. Thought is free; let no government set bounds to one's conscience or interfere with one's manner of worshiping God, the gentle Mendelssohn cried out in an age in which, for independent thinking and beliefs, men were proscribed and persecuted. It was a novel, indeed a revolutionary, doctrine preached by this man, a stranger in the country and a *Schutz-Jude* only by the grace of the king and the intercession of friends. "How far in advance of his age!" Abrahams exclaims. It took a full century after his *Jerusalem* for England to abolish theological tests at the universities.

In the second part of *Jerusalem*, Mendelssohn discusses the subject of Judaism as it was conceived and taught by him. Mendelssohn's principal declaration—one which involved him in controversy with both his own people and with contemporary Christian scholars—was that Judaism is not a revealed religion but a revealed legislation. It does not tell man what to believe and what not to believe but, rather, what to do and what not to do. Judaism has no dogmas; it contains no binding articles of faith. It recognizes freedom of religious consciousness; everyone may think, believe, or err as he pleases.

Judaism being a religious legislation, its laws and ceremonies, its rites and rituals, not only those of the Torah but also of Tradition, are binding upon the Jews. There being no dogmas, there are no rewards and no punishments. With the destruction of the Temple, the Jews had lost or surrendered the authority to penalize religious transgressors. He nevertheless recognized the permissibility of proceeding against offenses such as atheism and epicureanism, which he regarded as dangers to both religion and state. He opposed energetically the ban and excommunication by the synagogue, which in his day were employed quite freely.

Rationalist though Mendelssohn was, he defended, and even vigorously insisted upon, the strict observance of the ceremonial laws, not alone because they are part of the divine legislation but because they help to preserve and solidify the Jewish people. The so-called ceremonial law, he said, is of divine origin, and its obligatory character must continue until it pleases the Supreme Master to abrogate it as plainly and publicly as it was revealed. He strongly believed in immortality, but he made its attainment conditioned upon a pure life and conduct and strict conformity to the dictates of reason. He did not, however, believe in miracles as evidence of eternal truths, nor did he believe in formulation of articles of faith. When he published a schoolbook for children, he included Maimonides' Thirteen Articles, but instead of the formula, "I believe," he substituted, "I am convinced."

He believed in the harmonious religious coexistence of the Jews with the state in which they live. The Jews have their own religious legislation which in no way conflicts with legislation of their country. Judaism, he maintained, is not a missionary religion; it does not impose its faith upon others. It does not claim that its path is the only road to salvation. But one born a Jew remains one for life and can on no account renounce his religion. The world may not accept Judaism but the Jew may never reject it. "I do not see," writes Mendelssohn, "how those who were born in the house of Jacob can, in any conscientious manner disencumber themselves of the Law. We are allowed to think about the Law, to inquire into its spirit . . . but all our fine reasoning cannot exonerate us from the strict obedience we owe to it." To the faint-hearted, the gentle but stern Mendelssohn cries out: "Hold firm and remain strong and unfaltering in the post which Providence has assigned to you, whatever may befall you."

Mendelssohn's last years were filled with chagrin, pain, and anxiety. He had lived a full and satisfying life, this man who had conquered poverty, privation, and deformity to become one of the famous men of his generation, with his secure place in society, his position in German letters and philosophy, his companionship with the most brilliant men of his day, and with Lessing in his immortal *Nathan the Wise* raising up a monument to him during his lifetime. He had also fought the good fight for his people. He had not spared himself, either in safeguarding their faith, their rights, or their enlightenment.

Yet, as the shadows closed in about him, there were things that grieved and distressed him. Nothing was as distasteful to Mendelssohn as pantheism, which he regarded as subversive to religion and contrary to the spirit of Judaism. When, therefore, after Lessing's death Jacobi disclosed in a pamphlet that the playwright-philosopher had secretly been a Spinozist, Mendelssohn was shocked to learn that Lessing had entertained convictions of which he, his lifelong friend had been kept in ignorance. His children's future, too, caused him grave anxiety. His wife bore him six children. When they were young he did his best to instill into their hearts the principles of the faith that was dear to him. It was for them, he wrote to Herder, that he translated the Pentateuch into German, and it was for them, too, that he planned his *Morgen Stunden* lectures.

But they had grown up and the future was not bright for their faithfulness to the religion he had taught them. They were studying French and reading Voltaire and the works of other French free-thinkers. Shortly before his death Mendelssohn was seen walking gloomily up and down the street before his home. A friend accosted him: "You look troubled, Mr. Mendelssohn." "And so I am," the philosopher replied. "I am thinking what my children's fate will be when I am gone."

Mendelssohn had good reason to be troubled about his children. But fortunately he was personally spared the tragedy of witnessing the fulfillment of his fears, for death mercifully intervened on January 4, 1786.

Solomon Schechter

IT IS IMPOSSIBLE to convey to a generation that did not know Solomon Schechter the living image of the man. His stupendous learning, sparkling wit, and the other varied gifts of his genius are known to all who read his books and studies. But his striking appearance and magnetic personality—as perfect a harmony of physical and mental powers as the rabbis of the Talmud would seek in a Jewish sage—are best known to those who retain a personal recollection of him.

The inner traits of his character, both severe and gentle, excessively kind and sometimes absurdly intolerant, were housed in a physical frame so fine and noble that he attracted attention everywhere. When he appeared on public occasions, his broad shoulders wrapped in his crimson Cambridge academic robes, his shaggy white hair covering a massive head, with his gray beard, his delicate features, his blue eyes flashing behind his spectacles, one was conscious of a great presence, a man "higher than any of his people from his shoulders upward." He was easily the most identifiable man of his generation; he could not escape attention. Interested glances followed him wherever he went. He mastered every occasion and dominated every gathering.

Like many other men of genius, Dr. Schechter was a curious combination of contrasts and contradictions, a fusion of grandeur and simplicity, of lovable faults and delightful inconsistencies. He could be brusque or gentle, as tame as a lamb or as uncontrollable as a lion. Both scorn and tenderness were parts of his peculiar make-up; he combined the loving kindness of a saint and the wrathful indignation of a zealot. The charm of Hillel and the impatience of Shammai were blended in equal measure in his nature. He was unique and original in his failings and virtues. A warm stream of

321

tenderness followed his every outburst of temper. He was kind and gracious to all, even to those with whom he differed explosively. He was the most sociable of men, a congenial companion, concerned with all human interests.

There was a vein of humor in his tempestuous outbreaks which, like a heavenly balsam, quickly healed the wounds he inflicted. He was witty and scintillating in conversation; impromptu quips, epigrams, and sparkling observations flashed from him as unexpectedly as lightning. He was incapable of dullness and regarded the bore as a most intolerable nuisance. It is a pity that he had no Boswell to record his spontaneous sayings and sallies, deplores Bentwich, his biographer.

His tastes were cosmopolitan, his knowledge encyclopedic. He was a romanticist whose enthusiasm was for anything that was not ordinary, banal, or commonplace. Although all his life he burrowed in books and manuscripts and made one of the greatest literary finds of a thousand years—The Cairo Geniza—his passion was for the luminous figures in history, their romantic lives and adventurous careers. The Bible and the Talmud, great though his achievement in these fields were, did not exhaust Dr. Schechter's literary interest and he had more than a passing acquaintance with other forms of literature, not always of the conventional kind. He was an indiscriminate reader of contemporary fiction and it was not unusual for him to be found stretched out on his couch with the latest Hebrew, English, French, German, or even Yiddish, novel in his hand.

On the best available authority, Solomon Schechter was born on December 5, 1850, into a large family of children, in Focsani, a Roumanian town of 24,000 people, one fourth of whom were Jews. In Schechter's time Focsani, situated hard by the Carpathian Mountains where a hundred and fifty years earlier Israel Baal Shem Tov mused over his great dream and where Hasidism was born, was a small and insignificant community, far off the highway of Jewish life and learning. Nevertheless it is not without its niche in Jewish cultural history, because of its learned rabbis and scholars, not the least of whom was Nathan Hannover, who was an eye-witness of the massacre of Jews during the fatal decade of 1648-1658 and who gave a striking description of it in his historical *Yeven Metzula* (1653).

Isaac Schechter was his gifted son's first teacher, partly because of the scarcity of Hebrew teachers in Focsani but mainly because his meager income as the community *shohet,* ritual slaughterer (hence the adopted name "Schechter"), did not permit the luxury of a trained teacher for his children. The elder Schechter was a scholarly and saintly man and a devout and warmhearted Hasid of the Habad school of Hasidim founded by the famous Shneur Zalman of Ladi, after whom he named his son. He supplemented his instruction with an outpouring of Hasidic feeling and sentiment that accompanied his son throughout his life. In later years, when the political and cultural upheaval produced so many tragic defections from Judaism, Solomon Schechter ascribed his Jewish steadfastness to the influence of his father and the high moral and ethical principles he imbibed from his teachings.

The uncommonly precocious young student of the Torah learned to read Hebrew at three; at seven he knew the Five Books of Moses, and when he was ten years old he vindicated his love for study by running away to a near-by talmudical school from which his father brought him home in disgrace but not in repentance. He was past his Bar Mitzvah when his parents recognized his irrepressible love for learning and they sent him to Lemberg to the celebrated talmudical academy of Rabbi Saul Nathanson, a man of great scholarship and erudition and the author of numerous learned works. Solomon Schechter had at last attained his goal; he studied with unflagging zeal and industry. He not only thoroughly mastered what he read and studied of rabbinic literature but when there were not enough books for all the pupils he committed their contents to memory. It was a remarkable gift and one which was of inestimable service to him in later life. He developed such a memory that at any time, without the aid of dictionaries and concordances, he could summon any passage in the Talmud he needed and recognize from a single scrap of manuscript its relation to some great lost work.

Solomon Schechter returned to Focsani in what should have been a jubilant mood. He had slaked his thirst for knowledge of the Torah. His great teacher was generous in his praise and admiration for the zeal and originality of his student and predicted a shining future for him as a scholar and a great man in Israel. But inwardly Solomon did not share the happiness of his parents. Indeed, there were unuttered longings and ambitions secretly tugging at the strings of his young heart. Lemberg was a great city with Hasidic saints and scholars of ancient Jewish lore; but it was also a great center of modern culture and enlightenment, a strange and foreign world of which he had caught but a tantalizing glimpse through the window of the Bet Hamidrash. In his early childhood Solomon Schechter had not had the advantage of a regular school education and was largely self-taught. Jewish children who attended the Focsani primary school were pelted with stones and were called ugly names by their Christian schoolmates. This outraged young Solomon and he gave up the attempt. He longed for an academic education, but he had neither the preparation nor, as a Jew, the possibility of attaining one in anti-Semitic Roumania.

He was already a man of twenty, but as yet his life lacked a definite plan or purpose. He was an erudite student in almost all branches of Jewish literature and culture, but his scholarship was poorly organized. He read and studied voluminously, including works not approved of in his orthodox environment. His mind vacillated, his tastes varied, his thoughts wavered between the mystical yearnings of Hasidism, the rationalistic Haskalah, and the traditional loyalties of the past to which his life was anchored. He had his moments of doubt and skepticism. In the course of time, the Hasidic influence of his environment weakened, even to the extent of his writing disparagingly of the Hasidic mode of life and some of its teachings. In later years he regretted his youthful hostile attitude and sought to atone for it by his magnificent essay on Hasidism, his first literary venture which was translated into English by Claude Montefiore.

Vienna, the capital of the old Austro-Hungarian empire, started

Solomon Schechter off on the distinguished career that was almost fabulous in the annals of Jewish scholarship. It was lucky for the young stranger in a city of many races, tongues, cultures, and interests that he was not seduced by any of its diverting influences but came under the care and tutorship of such men as Meir Friedmann and Isaac Hirsch Weiss, the two greatest masters in their respective fields of Jewish learning. Lector Friedmann pioneered in the art of critical editions of rabbinic literature and became a model for other workers in the same field, while Isaac Hirsch Weiss was the first to write a comprehensive history of Tradition. Written in Hebrew and consisting of five great volumes, Weiss's work was titled *Dor Dor v'Dorshov*. Schechter's sojourn in Vienna was decisive to his future because of its influence over him. From Friedmann the young scholar acquired the scientific treatment of rabbinic texts, which in later years stood him in good stead in his own grappling with similar tasks, and from Isaac Hirsch Weiss he derived the conception of Judaism as a living and evolving tradition, which was of inestimable service to him in his formulation of the policy of the Jewish Theological Seminary, over which not many years later he was called to preside. He was fortunate in his association with Adolf Jellinek, the third faculty member of the Bet ha-Mdirash, a modernized theological school in Vienna. Dr. Jellinek was a remarkable character who combined the learning and scholarship of Weiss and Friedmann with a poetic, mystical temperament which made him a brilliant writer and a great preacher. Through his long and intimate association with them, Solomon Schechter reflected some of the qualities and characteristics of all three of his teachers. He adopted the historical method of Isaac Hirsch Weiss; he imbibed the deep humanity and irrepressible kindliness of Lector Friedmann, and what Bentwich calls the "spiritual flashes" of Adolf Jellinek. It would have fared ill with the impecunious Roumanian scholar in the Austrian capital if it had not been for Lector Friendmann, who employed him as instructor and companion of his children, and Adolf Jellinek, who appointed him as custodian of his great library. Schechter spent six years under the tutelage of these great masters of learning.

Roumania had given him the foundation for his Jewish culture, and in Vienna it was scientifically organized and systematized, so that it became a tool ready for use should the occasion arise. When, therefore, Schechter felt that he had exhausted all, or nearly all, his teachers had to give him, he left for Berlin.

Berlin, where the roving Jewish scholar found himself next, was in direct contrast to Vienna. Berlin was the capital of the German empire but was Prussian in spirit—proud, insolent, and domineering. It was also the capital of the destructive Bible criticism, where Wellhausen and his satellites occupied the center of the stage and lectures on the cultural inferiority of the Jews were delivered in the august presence of the German kaiser. Schechter watched the German critical treatment of the Bible with deep concern and apprehension. He was the first Jewish scholar to sense the meaning of the pogrom that was being prepared in the German academic circles against the Jews and Judaism. He was the first to detect in the German disparagement of the Jewish culture a menace that would one day end in political anti-Semitism with consequences he dared not speak of. When years later a bill was introduced in the German Diet calling for the appointment of a commission to examine the Talmud, he noted in a letter to Dr. Cyrus Adler, "the commission has been sitting in unbroken session since the days of Pfefferkorn in the fifteenth century."

Yet notwithstanding its rampant anti-Semitism, Berlin was a center of modern Jewish learning, the city where the *Wissenschaft des Judentums* was born and where one could meet and converse with some of the most stimulating and creative Jewish spirits. In 1879, when Schechter arrived in Berlin, Leopold Zunz, the Nestor of Jewish learning and culture, was already an old man and not easily accessible; but Moritz Steinschneider, whom Schechter called "the Urim and Thummim of every Jewish student," likewise advanced in years, was still burrowing in the depths of neglected Hebrew manuscripts bringing up pearls with which he adorned his famous *Catalogue*. But it was to Israel Lewy, the great scholar whose critical studies covered the whole range of talmudic knowledge, whom Solomon Schechter felt himself specially related to and who exerted the greatest influence upon him. Neither at Vienna nor in Berlin had Schechter written anything, although he was at the height of his physical and mental vigor. He began to work on his edition of *Abot de Rabbi Nathan,* but it was not completed until some years later.

Solomon Schechter was one of the most fortunate of young Jewish scholars. He won friends and attracted attention wherever he went. Was it his single-hearted devotion to learning or that indefinable something in the man which, for want of another term, is described as personality? A photograph made in his early manhood shows him as a very handsome man—tall, erect, full-bearded, with clear and finely formed features. There were energy and moral firmness in the man, besides his attractive physical appearance. His posture was not that of a rabbi or a scholar who spent years stooping over his folios. One might well have mistaken him for a scientist or an artist, which, indeed, temperamentally he was.

Although he spent three years in Germany and formed many deep and lasting friendships, he never fully adjusted himself to the Prussian Teutonic spirit. Roumanian anti-Semitism was obnoxious and hateful to Schechter. He remembered the many times he ran home from *heder* bleeding from wounds inflicted by Christian ruffians. But it did not compare with the academic hatred of Jews in Germany, which was intense, deep, and fanatical. It was, however, in Berlin that Schechter met young Claude G. Montefiore, a great-nephew of Sir Moses Montefiore, who dedicated his rich gifts to the study of the Jewish religion and literature and who attended lectures at the *Hochschule,* a liberal school of higher Jewish learning in the German capital. When he wished to continue in England the studies he had auspiciously started in Berlin, Schechter was recommended to him as the man he was looking for. The arrangement was historic in its results. For if, through Schechter, Claude Montefiore gained an insight into ancient Jewish life and literature, through Montefiore, Schechter's impact on England changed the religious and cultural character of the Anglo-speaking Jewries of two continents.

Under the patronage of Claude Montefiore and with the help of his own charming personality, it did not take Solomon Schechter long to feel at home in the British capital. Indeed, he loved and admired England long before it occurred to him that he would one day become a citizen of the great empire. He loved England for her atmosphere of freedom, for the respect and honor in which the Bible was held there, for the conservative spirit of the Anglo-Jewish community, and for its gratifying reawakening of Jewish learning and scholarship. But what made the young scholar's heart tremble with enthusiasm were the almost fantastic treasures of Jewish books and manuscripts in the great libraries of the British Museum and the Bodleian Library. For some time prior to his coming to England, Schechter was already working on a critical edition of *Abot de Rabbi Nathan,* a minor ethical tractate of the Babylonian Talmud. He postponed publishing it, however, until after he had exhausted the priceless treasures of the British libraries and convinced himself that there was no more valuable manuscript material on the subject. In 1887, after Schechter had resided five years in England, his book appeared, replete with the learned treatment appropriate to the subject, and the work was generally regarded as a superb example of critical scholarship and a model for all who work on scientific editions of ancient Hebrew texts.

The Roumanian-born scholar, who had come to London without knowledge of the English language, was received by the insular Jewish community with a cordiality rarely accorded to a foreigner. Instinctively it was felt that this man, with his halting English but tantalizing mind and personality, represented an unusual source of power and wisdom. Under the tutorship of Claude Montefiore and Joseph Jacobs, the latter an Australian-born fountain of knowledge and no less a romantic figure than his Roumanian friend, Schechter acquired the English language rapidly, although his accent remained markedly foreign. Schechter had no sooner mastered the intricacies of the English language than he began to turn out a veritable stream of learned articles, popular essays, book reviews, and literary comments on Jewish and general subjects. When Israel Abrahams and Claude G. Montefiore founded and edited the *Jewish Quarterly Review* in 1888, Solomon Schechter led off the first number with "The Dogmas in Judaism," which was the beginning of that extraordinary series of articles which comprised the three volumes of his celebrated *Studies in Judaism* and his even more important *Some Aspects of Rabbinic Theology.* Of the twenty volumes of the *Quarterly,* appearing in England there was scarcely a number that was not adorned by a contribution from the man who but recently was introduced into the mysteries of the English language and who, according to his own testimony, had battled with every English word as with the devil.

His writings were stimulating and inspiring. But even more effective than anything he wrote was the character and living personality of the man. He was not long in England before he attracted the attention of a young group of Jews who called themselves "The Wanderers," partly because they had no permanent meeting place and partly because of the rambling nature of their discussions, which jumped from subject to subject as the spirit moved them. To this group belonged some of the choicest young Jewish spirits of Anglo-Jewry, each one of whom became in time an ornament to Judaism and the Jewish people. Israel Zangwill, the critical but affectionate lover of the *Dreamers of the Ghetto;* Ashel Myers, editor and publisher of the widely read and influential *Jewish Chronicle;* Lucien Wolf, historian, diplomat, and publicist; Moses Gaster, a compatriot of Schechter, a distinguished scholar and passionate expounder of Judaism; Israel Abrahams, a tutor at Jews' College and one of the most brilliant of Anglo-Jewish scholars, and, of course, the most amazing and loquacious of them all, Joseph Jacobs, essayist, folklorist, historian, editor, and master of almost all literary and scientific activities.

Into this charmed circle of writers, thinkers, and scholars—men who had won, or were about to win their spurs in the manifold fields of Jewish learning and culture—Solomon Schechter, at the height of his physical and mental vigor, Jacobs recalls, "burst upon us as a blazing comet in the intellectual sky. . . . It is impossible to convey an adequate idea of the genial radiance and *èlan* of Schechter's personality at this period." According to English standards, Schechter was unconventional. He hailed from an atmosphere of depth and sincerity but often lacking in the small niceties society demands. To the conventional type he could appear uncouth, for he paid slight attention to his appearance. He was frankly outspoken, with no inhibitions. Truth rather than tact or diplomacy governed his utterances. He was impetuous and given to sudden outbursts of temper. He defended his views with insistence, often noisily shouting his opinions. But he was irresistible because he was so direct, fearless, and inflexible.

The newcomer, sponsored by Montefiore, who had discovered Schechter and brought him to England, fell like an explosive bomb on "The Wanderers." He attended their meetings and took part in, or rather dominated, the discussions with intellectual brilliance and persuasive eloquence. His knowledge and experience were deeper than most of the distinguished company. He had behind him the training of the schools of Berlin and Vienna, with their contrasting and conflicting currents of thought and influence; and the still deeper foundation laid by the talmudical schools of his native land, with their rich wisdom and holy atmosphere. In the presence of such a man, sometimes shaken by outbursts of indignation, when, according to Jacobs, he would pace up and down the room like a wounded lion roaring his retorts, sometimes eloquent with enthusiasm, but always charming and lovable, they could do nothing but nod assent or quietly mumble their disapproval.

After "conquering" London, he "conquered" Cambridge University, in which he held a lectureship in Rabbinics. A brilliant company of England's best minds—scholars, writers, and men of wit and learning—gathered about him. They forgave much where there was so much to admire. He often hurt and lacerated, but they had the utmost respect for his solid learning and original views. He showed as little restraint with his Christian as with his Jewish friends. They admired him, none the less, and he was the most popular faculty member on the campus. His imposing figure gave him the appearance of Zeus descended from Olympus. Admiring women pointed to him as "the wild man of genius." The scholar who had never had a formal school education was awarded by

Cambridge University the degree of Master of Arts and Doctor of Letters *honoris causa*. He formed close friendships with a number of friends who recognized the prodigality of his genius and his new approach to scholarship. The most distinguished of his friends at this period were Sir George James Frazer, author of *The Golden Bough*, and Charles Taylor, who devoted a lifetime to post-biblical literature and who published a scientific edition of *Pirke Abot* (The Sayings of the Fathers), a mishnaic ethical tractate on the Talmud, in the second edition of which he paid generous tribute to Schechter's "learning and acumen."

But what made Solomon Schechter universally famous and guaranteed his immortality in the world of scholarship was his discovery of the Hebrew original of *Ben Sira*. The author of the book, Simeon the son of Sira, was a native of Jerusalem about two hundred years before the common era. His book, greatly resembling the *Book of Proverbs*, was written in Hebrew. Disputes about its holiness arose and the book was not deemed worthy of inclusion in the Hebrew Canon. Although it is frequently referred to in the Talmud and in the Midrashim under the name *Ben Sira*, with quotations, the original text was lost and forgotten. Only the Greek translation, under the Latinized title *Ecclesiasticus*, remained. In the sacred graveyard of Hebrew books and parchments in the basement of the Ezra Synagogue in Cairo, Egypt, known as the Genizah, Jews had for centuries deposited their "dead" books, among which, unknown and unnoticed, reduced almost to powder by time, lay the pages of *Ben Sira* in its original Hebrew.

Regarded as one of the greatest literary discoveries in a thousand years, the find came about by sheer chance—another of the lucky accidents that attended Solomon Schechter throughout his life. The discovery, which was the high-water mark of Schechter's career and which revolutionized our knowledge of Jewish history and literature, originated through Solomon Schechter's acquaintance with two Christian ladies. Mrs. Agnes Lewis and Mrs. Margaret Gibson, two sisters, had recently returned from Egypt, bringing with them fragments of two faded parchments, which they submitted to their learned friend for examination. Schechter's scholarly curiosity was immediately aroused. After painstaking study of the tattered sheets, he discovered that one fragment was part of the Palestinian Talmud and that the other unmistakably belonged to the lost Hebrew original *Ben Sira*. In such a fever of excitement as an astronomer experiences "when a new planet swims into his ken," Schechter called out to his wife in great agitation, "As long as the Bible lives my name shall not die."

Dr. Schechter decided to go to Cairo to learn for himself what the Genizah contained, little dreaming of the treasure-trove he was to discover. In the windowless, doorless basement of the synagogue housing the Genizah he found a "battlefield of books," numerous "injured" fragments struggling for living space for their stories, sometimes tragic, sometimes comical, of the shifting life recorded in their pages. The numerous trophies he carried off proved to be the most fantastic collection of Jewish antiquities ever beheld. *Ben Sira,* or the six chapters of the book Schechter rescued from oblivion, was his most impressive and sensational find. "It may be said without exaggeration," writes Alexander Marx, "hardly any other single scholar has enlarged our knowledge of the past to the same degree as Dr. Schechter. He has changed our whole view of conditions in Babylonia, Palestine and Egypt in the tenth and eleventh centuries. . . . By no stretch of imagination can the importance of the discovery of the Genizah be overestimated." Summing up the results of his findings, Dr. Schechter remarks: "The work is not for one man and not for one generation. It will occupy many a specialist, and much longer than a lifetime."

Although Solomon Schechter worked on the Genizah finds throughout the remaining years of his life, he did not limit his interest to them. Following the promptings of Claude Montefiore, who sensed Schechter's great power of expression and urged him to write on lighter themes, he wrote a series of essays on the Bible and the Talmud, and sketches of Jewish leaders of past centuries, including "The Saints of Safed," and "Jewish Saints in Medieval Germany." In his essays he re-created life-like images of his subjects in all their glamor and greatness. When collected and published in three volumes under the title *Studies in Judaism*, the series met with an enthusiastic reception seldom accorded to Jewish works. Had he done nothing more his *Studies in Judaism* would have entitled him to the admiration and gratitude of the Jewish world.

Solomon Schechter united in himself something of the romanticism of Israel Baal Shem Tov, the love of learning of the Gaon of Vilna, the mystic piety of Nahmanides, and the gentle skepticism of Nahman Krochmal. As a writer, Dr. Schechter conceived of everything in terms of life and action. He gave a humanizing touch to every subject he treated, no matter how apparently dull and dry. What subject, for instance, is apt to be less interesting to the general reader than theology? Yet, for its freshness of style and treatment, with flashes of rare humor enlivening its pages, his *Some Aspects of Rabbinic Theology* turned out to be one of his most popular books. It not only met with universal acclaim but it may be said to have paved the way for a more sympathetic understanding of the Rabbinic Tradition on the part of Christian scholars. Many hoped that the volume would be followed by still further "Aspects," but death overtook him soon after the book appeared.

There was nothing shy or timid about the Roumanian-born "gypsy-scholar." He challenged the Jews and he challenged the Christians. In his *Epistles to the Jews* his farewell message to English Jewry, Schechter bitterly scourges the "encyclopedic ignorance of the highly uneducated," their attempt to occidentalize the Jewish religion, and their ignorance of Jewish life and thought which made them susceptible to every fad of the moment. He pleaded that they rediscover themselves as Jews, repossess themselves of their scriptures, revive the Hebrew language and Hebrew literature, and redeem the soul of the Jewish people. In a note on "Spiritual Religion Versus Spiritual Men," one of his choicest bits of irony, he contrasts the so-called spiritual and ceremonial religion of the Western Jews with the religion of the Eastern Jews.

In a classic passage characteristic of Schechter, he caricatured with exquisite sarcasm those Jews who prattle about spirituality while themselves living unspiritual lives. "If you refrain from food and drink on the Kippur, walk to the Synagogue, and spend the day there reading your ancient liturgy, and listen to an exposition by your preacher of the lesson from the Scriptures, then you are a worshipper of the common type, a slave laboring under the yoke of the letter. But if you ride to the temple after an ordinary breakfast, pass an hour or two there listening to an oratorio and following a sermon on the merits of the last novel of Hall Caine, or on the more subtle subject of the intellectual relations between Master Grieve and Reverend Robert Elsmere, and employ the rest of the day in looking after your affairs and taking your other two meals as a rational being should, then you have acted as a spiritual Jew and have worshipped your God in truth."

A Hasid whose Judaism was based on feeling and emotion, Solomon Schechter was more than slightly suspicious of the Jewish historical school whose attitude toward religion may be defined as an enlightened skepticism. He was himself on the side of mystical religion, declaring its roots to be imbedded deep in the Bible and the Talmud. "Those," writes Schechter, "who are at all familiar with the old rabbinic literature hardly need to be told that the 'Sea of the Talmud' has also its Gulf Stream of mysticism which, taking its origin in the moralizing portions of the Bible, constantly commingling with the icy waters of legalism . . . communicating to it life, warmth, and spirituality."

The inventor of "Catholic Israel" hated nothing so much as "geographical Judaism." His plea was for Jewish solidarity. Israel was to him one and indivisible. East and West had no meaning for him. The Torah was to him the sum and substance of Jewish life, and for its preservation all the forces of the Jews must unite. In his *Epistles to the Jews* he said: "Whatever our political destiny may be, our religious destiny can never be worked out by the West in isolation. The religious energies of all our brethren of the West and of the East, in close communion, will be required for its consummation."

Schechter was himself the most striking living symbol and embodiment of the fusion of forces and energies he advocated. Gathered together in his own being was a synthesis of currents and influences of almost every kind. He bore within himself the whole process of Jewish development, from the *yeshiva bahur* to the modern scholar. He was a product of the Roumanian ghetto and a citizen of England; a Talmud student and a teacher at Cambridge; a religious enthusiast and a follower of scientific methods. He was indeed one of the greatest Jewish spirits of his time.

He protested vehemently against the bias with which Christian scholars treated Jewish subjects and against what he called the "vivisection of the Bible"—particularly the distortion of the religious and ethical teachings of the Rabbis of the Talmud in order to establish the moral and spiritual inferiority of Judaism and the Jewish people. His indignation rose to a crescendo when he took up the cry of "legalism" with its implied legend of the "burden of the Law" raised by Christian theologians. He scoffed and raged at this distorted view of the Jewish religion. As one born and brought up under the discipline of the Torah, he had no difficulty in dispelling this wrong impression and proving that the fulfilling of a *mitzvah* was not a burden to a Jew but his highest joy. He reminded the disparagers of rabbinic Judaism that Rabbinism was synonymous with Judaism for two thousand years. He called on the Jews to write their own commentaries to the Bible, for, having created it, they are its masters and understand it best.

Nevertheless, Dr. Schechter was not an obscurantist, and he interpreted Judaism as a progressive religion, which, indeed, it was in all the creative periods of Jewish history. While he deplored and fought vehemently with all the caustic wit at his command against the radical tendencies of Reform Judaism and the non-Jewish despoilers of the Bible, he was at the same time unalterably opposed to the position of stereotyped, static Orthodoxy which, in his opinion, had no future in the modern world. His scientific conscience led him to accept the critical study of the Bible, but such study, he insisted, to be fruitful and helpful, must be undertaken by Jews, who alone fathom its spirit and can interpret correctly its meaning. In a letter to Judge Mayer Sulzberger, Solomon Schechter explained his position: "I am not a 'possumus' man. I admit that there is a good deal where reform would be desirable; but this reform can be done with the authority of the Bible and the Talmud, which are elastic and wide enough for all reasonable purposes. This will be Jewish reform."

England was Solomon Schechter's proving ground. There he developed, matured, rose to fame and position. There his epoch-making work was done, his academic honors won. There, too, he met and married Matilda Roth, justly described by Norman Bentwich as an "ideal helpmate for the scholar genius." Schechter loved England with a deep and strong love. Certainly few men owed as much to an adopted country as he did. It stood in marked contrast to the lands he had known and turned his back upon. Like their fellow citizens, the Jews of England were liberal in their outlook and conservative in their religion, culturally cosmopolitan yet faithful to the laws of Moses and the Rabbis.

But, inwardly, he was far from happy. He felt himself fettered to a mode of life that gave him neither present satisfaction nor hope for the future. He longed for the company of Jews, great masses of Jews. He longed to live and act and work with them. "In Cambridge," he wrote to Richard Gottheil, his erstwhile student in Berlin, subsequently professor in Columbia University, "there is no community and no synagogue. . . . I want to be a Jew and bring up my children as Jews." It was a point that greatly exasperated Schechter and made him hope for a change.

While Dr. Schechter was gloomily contemplating his prospects he attracted the attention of the conservative Jewish circles in America anxious to stem the tide of radical Reform Judaism, with its program verging almost on utter assimilation. To combat its extreme tendencies, the Jewish Theological Seminary of America was organized in the year 1886 by the saintly Rabbi Sabato Morais. But it was a feeble and timid attempt, and to cope with the situation stronger and more determined leadership was needed.

It was but natural that all eyes should be centered on Solomon Schechter, whose reputation had reached these shores.

Leaders of the American Jewish community, among them Judge Mayer Sulzberger, Dr. Alexander Kohut, Dr. Cyrus Adler, Dr. S. Solis-Cohen, and Rabbi Sabato Morais, became interested in the matter, and it was decided to invite Dr. Schechter for a course of lectures at Gratz College in Philadelphia. This was in March, 1895. The impression he made—the man no less than what he said—was striking. Recording his own reaction, Dr. Schechter wrote: "The hall was crowded, and I hope that at least a *minyan* understood my English, and that I shall be saved for the sake of the ten."

Several years were spent in correspondence and negotiations. Dr. Schechter made no attempt to conceal his desire for a change. He wrote to Gottheil, "I believe that the future of Judaism is in America." To Cyrus Adler he wrote, "America has ideal attractions for me, offering me, as it does, a large field of activity which may become a source of blessing for future generations." And to Herbert Bentwich, a London friend, who tried to dissuade him, he said: ". . . in New York I may become a great power for good through the Seminary and my public position. I may become—if I am deemed worthy by God—the saving of conservative Judaism. I can see that even the Reformers promise themselves a revival of Judaism if I come." It was, however, not until the close of the year 1901 that the discussion came to a successful conclusion with Judge Sulzberger's and Solomon Schechter's mutual announcement that he had agreed to accept the Presidency of the Jewish Theological Seminary of America.

To Professor Schechter the move from England to the United States was only a geographical shift; spiritually he may be said to have always belonged to America. His infatuation with America began early in his life when, as a boy, he eagerly read all he could find about the marvelous land far beyond the seas, and about its great President, Abraham Lincoln, who, like Moses, had freed the slaves and, like Hillel, had in his youth been a rail-splitter. He was better read in the history of the United States, especially that pertaining to the Civil War, than many a native American. He revered

Lincoln as one of the greatest men of all time and he regarded the abolition of slavery as one of the few great ethical triumphs in modern times. To Solomon Schechter, America was a vision and a hope—a vision because of the millions drawn to its shores from all parts of the world, and a hope because of its great moral and spiritual potentialities.

Schechter not only possessed a genius for religion but he had a deep sense of practical Jewish piety. Religion was not to him a vague and ethereal thing, falsely described as "spiritual," without demands and mandates, but a positive discipline of life, with definite demands and prohibitions. Sympathy, tenderness, and loving kindness are part of it, but also the sterner duties Judaism exacts of its believers. He believed in the vitality and validity of Judaism, in the permanence of its faith and of the moral and ethical discipline of its rites and ceremonies. He preached loyalty to the Torah and tradition as essential to Jewish survival. His love was not only for God but for the laws and institutions of Judaism, the disregard of which was to him a matter of deep concern. "The source of inspiration for Jews," he wrote, "must remain the Torah in all its ramifications and conceptions." And, again, "Only a gypsy camp is possible without institutions, ceremonies and symbols."

He was perhaps the greatest, certainly the most eloquent defender of what, both within and without the Jewish fold, is stigmatized as "rabbinical legalism." With what artful humor and devastating irony he descended upon his opponents! The passages are too numerous to quote—they are strewn throughout his books. He pointed to the beauty of the law, the joy of the commandment, the *simha shel mitzvah,* the holy rapture Jews experienced in carrying out the precepts of the Torah. With hasidic ecstasy he cried out, "For me the *tephillin* are my banner, the *Sepher Torah* our Magna Carta, the Synagogue our Parliament. The Dietary Laws are consequences of holiness. Greece aimed at manhood; we at saintliness and holiness."

In his inaugural address he spoke of the seminary as a place of learning and research and a training school for the Jewish ministry.

But that training, he insisted, "must be specifiically Jewish, without any alloy or adulteration. . . . Those who are entrusted with carrying out the purpose of this institution which aims . . . at the perpetuation of the tenets of the Jewish religion, both pupils and masters, must faithfully and manfully maintain their loyalty to the Torah. There is no other Jewish religion but that taught by the Torah and confirmed by history and tradition, and sunk into the conscience of Catholic Israel." And, again, "Any attempt to place the center of gravity [Judaism] outside the Torah must end in disaster."

He was particularly emphatic on the ceremonial observances of the Jewish religion. "Judaism," he said, "is not a religion which does not oppose itself to anything in particular. Judaism is opposed to any number of things, and says distinctly 'thou shalt not.' It permeates the whole of your life. It demands control over all your actions, and interferes even with your menu. It sanctifies the seasons and regulates your history. . . . It insists upon the observance both of the spirit and of the letter. . . . In a word, Judaism is absolutely incompatible with the abandonment of the Torah."

There was something grand and prophetic in his magnificent vision of the seminary as a unifying force serving all classes and sections of the American Jewish community. Paraphrasing the Midrash and telling of the Voice that descended from Sinai and reached all stations of men according to their own level, Dr. Schechter said: "All that I plead for is that the voice should come from Sinai, not from Golgotha; that it should be the voice of Jacob, not of Esau. The Torah gave spiritual accommodation for thousands of years to all sorts and conditions of men, sages, philosophers, scholars, mystics, casuists, schoolmen and skeptics; and it should also prove broad enough to harbor the different minds of the present century."

The impression made by his inaugural address on November 20, 1902, was electrifying. Like a breath of fresh air, what he said cleared the American Jewish atmosphere, and many a man that night sat brooding long and deep. Never before in this land had a man spoken thus, and with such fervor and eloquence. In the glory and vigor of his fifty-two years, with his massive head and graying beard, he was indeed like a Prophet-Sage out of the pages of ancient Jewish lore. He was witty and penetrating, his address was a masterpiece of choice quotations from ancient and modern literature—a Midrash in which the Rabbis of the Talmud fraternized congenially with Abraham Lincoln, Walt Whitman, and George Eliot. One man who saw and heard him on that occasion, recorded his impression: "One felt with certainty that there stood a man whose every word, agree with it or not, was packed with personality, impressive by reason of him who uttered it."

Dr. Schechter was not a cloistered scholar. For a man of his age, he worked with unwonted zeal and enthusiasm. He was determined to make the seminary a center of learning and bastion of Conservative Judaism. He assembled and co-ordinated a distinguished faculty, collected a great library, and fired the imagination of his students with a spirit of loyalty and devotion to the Torah. Writes Professor Alexander Marx in his memoir of Solomon Schechter: "The Seminary became the center of all his thoughts: he absolutely identified himself with it to the exclusion of anything else, and looked at every question from the angle of the Seminary. . . . it accompanied him on his vacations and on his travels, it even took precedence over his scientific work." He initiated the United Synagogue of America as an instrument for the preservation and dissemination of the faith and ideals of the seminary. He regarded this, one of his last activities, as his greatest bequest to the seminary and to American Israel. Unfortunately, he did not live to see its full growth and development, for he died not long after its organization.

The love and devotion Dr. Schechter bestowed on the seminary was extended in a large and generous measure to his students. He surrounded them with that impulsive love and affection of which his Hasidic spirit was capable. He remembered his own student days and the encouragement he received from his teachers. He was his "boys'" friend, helper, and mentor; and they, in turn, adored him. They regarded him with a feeling not so much of awe as of love. Their relations were not limited to the classroom, for he took a warm personal interest in everything pertaining to their private life and problems. He was the safest refuge from their exacting teachers, their dependable advocate at the faculty meetings. The door of his study was wide open to them. They had unrestricted access to his presence without the formalities of secretaries and appointments. He taught more by his personality than by his lectures, which, though never dull or boring, he read from large sheets of paper covered with undecipherable notes.

He had an extraordinary capacity for friendship and a deepening influence on institutions and cultural movements besides those of the seminary. The man who felt himself stifled in England was ready for any and every challenge in the largest Jewish Community in the world. He served on the board of the Jewish Publication Society, worked as one of the editors of the new Bible translation, projected a series of Jewish classics, and played an active part in the agitation for the abrogation of the treaty with Russia because of her persecution of the Jews. He was a member of the Board of Directors of the Educational Alliance, from which, however, he resigned when he became uneasy about its religious program.

He won his greatest popularity among the Jewish masses by his "Zionism: A Statement," which brought him into controversy with Jacob H. Schiff, one of his greatest friends and a generous supporter of the seminary. The storm his address aroused was so painful to Schechter that, in his own words, "It gave me many sleepless nights and more mortification than I care to speak of."

Emotionally, Schechter was a Zionist, perhaps more of the Ahad Ha'am than the Herzl variety. "Zionism," he said, "was, and still is, the most cherished dream I was worthy of having." He regarded Zionism as "the greatest bulwark against assimilation . . . bringing back into the fold many men and women . . . who otherwise would have been lost to Judaism. . . . Only then when Judaism has found itself, when the Jewish soul has been redeemed from galut, can Judaism hope to resume its mission in the world."

"But this dream," he wrote, "is not without its nightmares. For in their struggle to revive national sentiment, some of the Zionist spokesmen, calling themselves by preference Nationalists, manifested such a strong tendency to detach the movement from all religion as can only end in spiritual disaster. There *is* such a thing as the assimilation of Judaism even as there is such a thing as the assimilation of the Jews, and the former is bound to happen when religion is looked upon as a negligible quantity. When Judaism is once assimiliated, the Jew will surely follow in its wake, and Jew and Judaism will perish together. All this is a consequence of preaching an aspect of nationalism more in harmony with Roman and similar modern models than with Jewish ideas and ideals. However, nightmares are fleeting and evanescent—the vision as a whole still remains glorious. The aberrations will, let us hope, be swept away quickly enough as soon as their destructive nature is realized by the majority of the Zionists whose central ideas should and will remain God and His people Israel."

He never ceased toying with the thought of settling in the Holy Land, where his twin brother had gone in 1882. When wooing Matilda Roth, Schechter is reported by Alexander Marx to have said to the hesitating young lady: "If you will not take me, I shall be a farmer in Palestine; if you will take me, I shall become something of a scholar." A farmer in Palestine Schechter did not become, although shortly before coming to America he wrote, "I am prepared to go to the Holy Land whenever I could reckon to have bread to eat and raiment to wear, in spite of my doctorship and professorship." At one time he expressed the wish to die and be buried in Palestine for fear that "some rabbi may pray over me if I am buried in America."

Schechter's American career was crowded with almost incredible activity. Few men ever worked for an ideal with greater enthusiasm or achieved a greater measure of success than he. He came to America with a great hope in his heart and he lived to see it realized. The expansion of the radical Reform Movement was in many respects checked; there was a renaissance of Jewish learning; Zionists found moral support in his emphasis on the national aspect of Judaism; the ferment of the new ideas he introduced worked in almost all directions. Talented young Jews and Jewesses, whom the gilded precincts of the reform temples ceased to attract, found themselves quickened and stimulated in his company. He preached a defiant Hebraism, a militant conservatism, a "Catholic Israel" without adjectives and adverbs.

It was, therefore, no vain boast when, after a little more than a decade in America, he wrote to Mr. Louis Marshall, Chairman of the Executive Board of the seminary: "The conservative influence is not confined to our students. It extends also to the Reform section of the community which fell under its appeal and began to look at Judaism from a point of view differing widely from that prevalent before. . . . It is no exaggeration to say that the last ten years saw more books of the substantial learned order published by American Jewish scholars than all the two hundred years and more since Israel began to dwell in this country."

But was Schechter happy and satisfied that he had heard the call and followed it? Perhaps restless natures like his never are happy; they grow impatient with the progress their work is making. At any rate, in the same letter to Marshall in which he gives an account of his stewardship of the seminary there are intimations of dissatisfaction and frustration which are in striking contrast to his usual Hasidic cheerful disposition. As the years wore on he grew less enthusiastic and more doubtful about the success of his American mission. Three years before he died, with the fumes of incense still strong about him, he confided to Dr. Cyrus Adler: "The last few years of my life could be better spent than in the financial cares of the institution and the bickering all around. If I had the means today, I would resign and devote myself to scientific work exclusively, and finish the two or three things I have on my mind."

What, then, discouraged and embittered Schechter to a point where he wanted to resign after ten such seemingly brilliant years as president of the Jewish Theological Seminary? The "financial cares" of the institution were, no doubt, a contributory cause of his unhappiness; but that is not the whole story. For deep in his mind were cares and frustrations which affected him more seriously—

which, indeed, almost made the continuation of his work unbearable.

On assuming charge of the seminary Dr. Schechter was confronted with the embarrassing situation of preaching a Judaism "specifically and purely Jewish, without any alloy or adulteration" while having to work with an Executive Board that was but remotely sympathetic with his ideal of Judaism. With few exceptions, the financial sponsors of the seminary were Reform Jews, members of Reform Temples of the assimilationist fringe who had neither sympathy with nor understanding of what the man they called from England had set out to do. They had profound respect for his personality and his reputed scholarship, and they were even ready to tolerate his "conservative tendency," but they were hardly prepared for the revolutionary force which his teachings had let loose upon the Jews of America. They had listened to his inaugural address, in which he declared that the seminary would be "all things to all men," and they took comfort in that. But when they saw him emerge as the blazing symbol and leader of a counter-Reformation, repudiating everything which from their childhood they had been taught to believe and think, and teaching a doctrine they heard branded by their rabbis as "Ghetto Judaism," their enthusiasm for the man and the cause he represented shrank almost to the vanishing point.

In their mental and spiritual outlooks, Schechter and the financial backers of the seminary were worlds apart. They were philanthropists, he a religious enthusiast with a mystic bent; they were for the Americanization of the Jewish immigrants, he for their Judaization; they were anxious to see them shed their religious rites and customs, he as strong for their retention; they were for reason and sanity in religion, he for the unchecked and unbridled outpouring of one's religious feelings and emotions. The hope entertained by some members of the Board that in Schechter's hands the seminary would evolve a kind of delicate technique of Americanization and would "refine" the religiously "unruly downtown Jews," was rudely dispelled by Dr. Schechter in his letter to Louis

Marshall in 1913: "I must take it out of their minds," he said, "that I came to this country for the purpose of converting the downtown Jews to a more refined species of religion." When the Union Prayer Book was about to be introduced into the Hebrew Orphan Asylum he vehemently remonstrated at the attempt "to force the new ritual on children of parents the majority of whom came from the old country and were orthodox. The support which the Reform Jew extends to the institution does not justify him to force his theological views on others."

But Schechter had his difficulties with the Orthodox Jews as well—indeed, more than with their Reform brethren. Although he constantly preached loyalty to the Torah, observance of the Sabbath and the dietary laws, the maintenance of the traditional character of the liturgy and the retention of Hebrew as the language of prayer, it availed him little as far as the Orthodox element of the community was concerned. They refused to accept him, no matter his professions. They accused him of temporizing with the old faith, of being a reformist in the guise of a conservative Jew. One militant Canadian Rabbi even went so far as to call for a "Protestant Israel" to protest against "Catholic Israel."

In no small measure opposition to Schechter was sharpened by his open disregard of the Orthodox element of the Jewish community and the not very exalted opinion he was known to hold of its lay and spiritual leaders. While he fraternized on intimate terms with Reform Jews and conferred an honorary degree upon one of their radical rabbinical spokesmen, he was rarely seen in the company of Orthodox Jews nor had any of them ever received any honors at his hands. His presence and the address he delivered at the dedication of the new buildings of the Hebrew Union College at Cincinnati and the number of seminary graduates who served as rabbis in Reform congregations did not escape the censure of his unkindly critics.

The Yiddish press and the Yiddish reading public maintained an attitude of hostility toward Schechter from the very beginning of his coming, for he was unfriendly to the Yiddish tongue, spoke of it as an "unfortunate necessity," and would not admit it as a language of instruction in the seminary. He regarded Yiddish as a mark of the ghetto, without historic value or significance. Ahad Ha'am maintained the same attitude toward the folk language of the Jews, and advised that the best in its literature be retained by translation into Hebrew. But Ahad Ha'am was a pioneer of the Hebrew Renaissance, while Schechter was a trainer and teacher of rabbis who were to lead and instruct the Jewish masses. But despite his lack of enthusiasm for Yiddish he was well read in the classical Yiddish literature and was deeply impressed with it. He was profoundly moved by the high moral and spiritual tone of the *tehinot,* a collection of women's prayers and meditations in the Yiddish language, and he regretted that it was so little known to modern Jewish women.

Dr. Schechter lived in the splendid isolation of Upper Manhattan, which in his day was remote from the throbbing life of the largest Jewish community in the world. As in England, his personal influence, aside from his teaching, although wide-spread, was confined largely to individuals—scholars, thinkers, intellectuals, and literary men more or less like himself—the great masses of the Jews remained almost unconscious of the man, his great learning and magnetic personality. While Hasidically democratic, Schechter was temperamentally an aristocrat. When he was in England he romantically longed for contact with Jews; but when he found himself living in the midst of the largest community of Jews in history he all but spurned association with them. He rarely met with them and was little more than an observer of the religious, cultural, and fraternal activities of the majority of his people. Yet, while he did not make himself a part of the tumultuous life of his city and country, he was generally respected and his words excited more than passing interest.

Literary man and scholar in England, seldom leaving his study for the rough and tumble of everyday life, Schechter surprisingly became a man of action upon coming to the United States. In his thirteen years in America he attempted and accomplished more than most others could achieve in a much longer time. As though sensing that his years would not be many, he crowded into the few remaining years of his life all the devotion and energy he could command. He presided over the destinies of the reorganized Jewish Theological Seminary; acted as recognized spokesman of American Jewry; attended meetings and delivered lectures at important national Jewish conferences; was instrumental in promoting an intensified Jewish education; inspired a healthy development of traditional Judaism; represented the Jews of his country on all important ceremonial occasions; and participated in their cultural and communal activities.

Dr. Schechter was physically a well-preserved man. He had a strong constitution, was sturdily built, and walked erect to the end. The dust of the ages which he had breathed while he worked in the Cairo Genizah evidently did not affect his magnificent physique. He used glasses, but they were more often on his forehead than on his eyes. He had the typical professorial forgetfulness and was subject to writers' cramp, which made his script illegible not only to others but to himself. He would often stop in the middle of a lecture and ask his secretary to read what he could not decipher for himself. His lectures and public addresses, which were carefully and painstakingly prepared, were revised over and over until the final form bore little resemblance to the first draft. Dr. Schechter was at his best in his home, when he could rage and storm with only his students or his confidential friends around. When his speech waxed unconventional on the telephone Matilda, his wife, would rush to the rescue to "interpret" what the Professor "meant" to say. Dr. Schechter smoked incessantly, and he enjoyed a glass of wine at dinner. He belonged to the Hasidic school, which put no restraint on alcoholic beverages.

Dr. Solomon Schechter lived a full and good life. He had few regrets and disappointments to complain of except those already mentioned. He had a host of friends and admirers and practically no enemies. Even his idiosyncrasies were accepted as a mark of his genius. While, no doubt, much of his success was due to his own genius and accomplishments, there was an element of luck which never deserted him in all the great moments of his life. He might have spent his life as a frustrated scholar in Germany, as did many of his kind, had it not been for Claude G. Montefiore, who brought him to London, taught him to write English, and stimulated his superb gift of communication. Likewise, *Ben Sira,* might still be moulding in the musty grave of the Cairo Genizah if the English ladies had not chanced to bring mutilated pages of the manuscript to Schechter.

He captured America, as he captured England, with his great learning, brilliant wit, and magnificent personality. He was the spokesman for Judaism as he was spokesman for the Jews, both of whom he represented with great dignity and distinction. His leadership in Jewish learning was recognized by Harvard University, which conferred upon him an honorary degree of Doctor of Letters, and by New York University, which elected him a member of the University Senate—both honors following the appearance of his *Jewish Sectaries.* While Dr. Schechter's major literary work was done in England, his American publications include *Some Aspects of Rabbinic Theology, Seminary Addresses and Other Papers* (the latter of which he arranged for publication but did not live to see in print), and the third volume of his *Studies,* which was edited after his death by Dr. Alexander Marx. His "Lincoln Address," delivered at the seminary in Febraury, 1909, on the occasion of the one hundredth anniversary of Abraham Lincoln's birth, aroused much interest and admiration because of its novelty of style and conception.

He was aged and broken by the World War and the havoc and devastation it wrought among the Jews in the warring countries. It was the severest ordeal of his life. He bore his nation's sorrows in his heart, and they hastened his death. His connections in Europe were so many, his relations with its scholars, libraries and institutions so long and intimate that he could not think of their destruction without the most poignant suffering. His heart was strained to the breaking point. Upon his return from a trip to Europe with his wife he was not the same Schechter. But he still performed his duties to the seminary faithfully, and even laid plans for new books and learned articles, not realizing how serious his condition was—or, if he knew, he kept it from his family and friends. On Friday, November 20, 1915, while lecturing to his students he suffered a heart seizure and died the same day, on the eve of the Sabbath.

I. L. Peretz

ONCE IN A great while a writer appears who is not only a literary phenomenon but a great moral and spiritual force as well. Such a man was I. L. Peretz, or, as he preferred to be called, Yitzhok Leibush Peretz. He is referred to by his various admirers as "Literary Colossus," "Father of Yiddish Literature," the "Voice of East-European Jewry," and similar terms of adulation. Peretz may not have been all these things, but he certainly was an artist who could express himself equally well in almost every form of writing. He was at once poet, dramatist, allegorist, short-story writer, and essayist. On every one of these forms he left the imprint of his moral and spiritual personality, which is still honored and recognized nearly forty-five years after his death.

There are, of course, other writers of moral and spiritual force besides Peretz. It radiates from the works of Mendele Mokher Sefarim through the mute struggle and helpless suffering of the men and women he describes with fierce, almost savage, realism. But Mendele is the preacher, the reformer—a man who bitterly though subtly cries out against the tyranny and oppression of the small-town political bosses and their sycophantic flunkeys. It is, however, chiefly with the outward lives and lot of his characters that he is concerned, rarely with their inner being, which remains unexplored and unknown. Shalom Aleikhem, one of the most prolific of Jewish writers, required no less than twenty-eight volumes to give play to his amazing versatility. He wrote on almost every subject and excelled in theim all. His stories, legends, and monologues are still so fresh and vivid that they are indelibly impressed on the minds of thousands. He is particularly brilliant as a humorist. He wrote for the masses, and it is by them that he is best loved and admried. He neither delves nor quibbles, neither probes nor instructs, but finds jolly and zestful moments in tragic situations. In other words, he is the revealer and interpreter of the Jewish character, which laughs amid tears and jokes and banters with a sorrowful heart.

Peretz, on the other hand, is a moral and spiritual force in Yiddish literature without precedent or equal. More than any other writer he strives to reveal the deep and enduring qualities of his men and women. He works from within. He floods everything with inner light and warmth. And the visions he captures and the magic with which he makes his characters come alive stem from the spiritual qualities of his genius. He was a man of boundless sympathy and tenderness. He was depressed by the shocking poverty and wretchedness of his people no less than Mendele and Shalom Aleikhem were. But what mattered most to him was the yearning heart, the conquering spirit of love, faith, and devotion. Hence he saw beauty underneath ugliness and dignity in sordidness; and he revealed the real men and women behind his subjects' outward forms. He divined their joy in God, their love of Torah, their devotion to the eternal values of their faith and their people. He plumbed the depths of character and spread an aura of holiness over the crude and shoddy. He was not the sociologist whose concern is with groups and masses of men but the poetic artist and revealer of the individual human soul.

There is no single literary standard by which the genius of Peretz may be judged or measured. He was an artist who brought to his writing the painter's insight and imagination. The writing styles and fashions of his day did not interest him; instead, he strove to perfect a tool that suited his own craftsmanship. He knew the Russian, Polish, and German literary masters, but what he imbibed from them was negligible. He went to older and deeper sources and derived his insights from the fabled wealth of the Talmud and the Midrashim, from the mysticism of the Kabbalah, from the romanticism of the *Bet ha-Midrash* and, above all, from the living faith and life of the people with whom he was in active daily contact. It was from these things that the magic web of his tales and legends was woven.

I. L. Peretz was one of the most original of Jewish writers. At the same time, there is not an alien element in any of his folk tales. His concern is with a particular faith and tradition and people, and he invites his readers to share with him the same unified mood and feeling. Some of his stories have been translated into foreign tongues, but one wonders how "Love in a Basement," "Bontche the Silent," and "If Not Higher Still" come off in alien garb. Peretz was incurably Jewish. He wrote of Jews and for Jews, and in the language which is characteristically the folk language of the Jews. He began to write in Hebrew, the classical language of his people, but he realized, as did Mendele before him, that the great masses of Jews did not know Hebrew, and he accordingly communicated in their folk idiom.

Yitzhok Leibush Peretz was one of the most original of Jewish writers, and a pathfinder. He belonged to no school and acknowledged no literary tradition. A. A. Roback makes the interesting observation that the writer's name Peretz denotes in Hebrew "breaking through," symbolically signifying the poet's creative position in Yiddish literature. For Peretz was both a creator and an inventor. He created both a literary style and form of his own and coined the very words with which he shaped his images. When he began writing Yiddish was a crude and shapeless medium of literary expression. The language of Glupsk and Kabtzansk and the folk idiom of Shalom Aleichem's stories were not suitable stuff for the more subtle and delicate themes he had in mind. He was depressed and disappointed, and in *Monish,* the ballad with which he made his debut in Yiddish literature, he expressed his frustration in words which read, in paraphrase: "My song would sound quite differently were I to sing to Gentiles in their language, not to Jews in jargon." He felt himself checked and hindered by a language so limited that it lacked even such words as "love" and "sweetheart." Simon Frug, a talented poet, was likewise discouraged by the linguistic barrenness of Yiddish and wrote his songs in Russian, although he later returned to the language of the ghetto. But Peretz, poetic genius that he was, plodded along and fashioned his own mode of expression, with the result that in the numerous songs and stories he composed there is not a mediocre line, an imperfect word, or an expression that mars the high level of his thought, despite the shortcomings of the language.

Yitzhok Leibush Peretz was spared the poverty and loneliness which were the lot of many other Jewish scholars and writers. He was born almost in the middle of the nineteenth century in Zamosch, Poland, also the birthplace years before of Alexander Zederbaum, a pioneer Hebrew and Yiddish publicist. Peretz's father was a well-to-do and scholarly merchant. He was considered a liberal for his time, but he brought up his son in the rigid orthodoxy of his environment. It was, however, really Yitzhok Leibush's teachers who most influenced him and initiated him in the study of the Torah and molded into his youthful mind the intricacies of the Talmud. In other words, his early training did not differ much from that of most other Jewish children of the time who were prepared for lives of Torah and the performance of good deeds.

Yitzhok Leibush was a prodigy—a phenomenal child. Indeed, what Jewish youngster in those days who knew his Bible and mastered folios of the Talmud was not something of a genius? But of Yitzhok Leibush there could be no doubt—he was out of the ordinary, even in such company. He had an extraordinary memory and what he heard and learned remained indelibly etched in his mind. But like so many other talented children of his age, he was spoiled, and he made the life of his teachers miserable with all kinds of mischievous tricks and deviltries. When no teacher would longer put up with him, bright though he was, because of his impish ways, his father packed him off to a neighboring town for the completion of his education.

His mischievous behavior toward his teachers in no way suggests a trace of rebellion against the education he was receiving. On the contrary, young Yitzhok Leibush loved learning and was exemplary in his devotion to and passion for books and study. He supplemented what he received from his teachers with other books which he found in his home and in the synagogue. In olden times the synagogue was not only a house of prayer but a Torah-center as well. In their leisure time Jews would go to the synagogue for a word of intellectual and spiritual refreshment. There were libraries in the synagogues, with books of almost every kind and description —devotional books and books of study, the portentous volumes of the Talmud and the sacred tomes of the mystical Kabbalah. And sometimes, when one was particularly assiduous in his search, he would even find a much-fingered copy of Maimonides' *Moreh Nebukim.*

Yitzhok Leibush immersed himself in the study of these books. He pored and brooded over them. The more incomprehensible they were to him, the greater was his desire to grasp their inner meaning. The mystical books he read were to him a particular source of puzzlement. What, for instance, did he know of the subjects they vaguely and subtly alluded to, such as soul, death, transmigration? His education had prepared him for none of these things. He had to find out for himself. He became interested in moral and metaphysical problems. The question of sin and evil was much in his mind. He delved still deeper, and God became the subject of his questioning thoughts. He became conscious of the need of an education that would straighten out and clarify all these things in his mind. Of course, the Talmud itself was an education beyond which some Jews would not go. It was indeed a whole university. But it was so fragmentary and unconnected that it required another kind of education—modern secular training—for its understanding.

This training came to him in a curious and most extraordinary way. The story goes that there was in Zamoshch a lonely old man, a musician, who was keeper of a roomful of books stored away in an attic. The books were on all kinds of subjects and in several European languages. The mysterious old man took a liking to the young student, and before his death he entrusted Peretz with the key to the library. Yitzhok Leibush was both pleased and puzzled by what he found. For before him, in row after row, sprawling on the floor and tightly packed in boxes, was the recorded thought of Europe, both in languages he knew and in those he could not read. Russian and Polish books hobnobbed with French and German volumes; works of history and the sciences fraternized with philosophical and theological treatises; and the Code of Napoleon, so to speak, rubbed shoulders with the Code of Maimonides (Yad ha-Hazakah).

But what was even so omnivorous a reader as Yitzhok to do with them? He answered that question by devouring them all, row after row, shelf after shelf, to the last page. He knew Russian and Polish, and German was but a stepsister of Yiddish. As for French and English, he learned them with the aid of the dictionaries he found in the garret. Young Peretz spent many days and nights in the loft—days and nights that belonged to the synagogue and the *Bet ha-Midrash*. When it was dark in the windowless room he perused his precious volumes by the dim light of a lantern he himself had made. "This history of his education," writes Leo Wiener, "is also the history of his genius. There is reflected in it the subtleties of the Talmud, the wisdom of the ancients, the sparkle of Heine, the transcendancy of Shelley, the mysticism of Hauptmann."

Peretz was married when he turned nineteen. It was not a love match but one that had been arranged by his father, and unfortunately it went on the rocks. His father-in-law was a maskil who wrote Hebrew poetry, and his daughter was an admirable young lady in every respect and well-educated; but she was fanatical in her religion, a trait that did not meet with sympathy from the man who had just digested a whole library of the best liberal thought in Europe. They remained together for five years in this unhappy marital state, and two children were born to them. But their rift was irreconcilable and their marriage came to a bitter end when Peretz showed his displeasure with his wife's religious zeal by casting into the fire the wig that strict orthodox Jewish women wear after their own hair is clipped before marriage.

At slightly under twenty-five years of age Peretz was in the unhappy position of a man without a home, without a trade or profession, and without any visible means of self-support. He was a student and a scholar, but how could he put his scholarship to profitable use? He mastered the Hebrew and Polish languages, and tried his hand at tutoring, but the financial returns were meager. A business venture turned out to be even more tragic, as he lost in the enterprise his small savings. But Peretz was not the kind of man to yield to desperation. He faced the world with faith and confidence in the final outcome of his financial problem.

Was it the codes of Maimonides and Napoleon that Peretz found and studied in his garret library, that aroused his ambition to become a lawyer; or was it that his thought hearkened back to the days of his youth, when his mind was sharpened on the legal niceties and technicalities of the Talmud? Whatever the answer, his decision was indisputably a fortunate one. How did Peretz, the poet, identify with Peretz the attorney; the man with an exquisite sensitivity for words and phrases meet the prosaic demands of his legal profession? The fact is that Peretz had an abiding interest in the moral values of life, in human acts and motivations, and in the law he found an excellent opportunity to put his ideals of right and wrong to practical application.

Contrary to what might have been expected of the incurable idealist, Peretz proved to be a successful lawyer, with a large and profitable practice and half a dozen clerks. His personal integrity and his solid common sense won for him the trust and confidence of both the Jewish and Polish population of Zamoshch. At the same time, he did not permit the poet and the man of letters in him to be stifled by his extensive law practice. His superbly creative mind, which was later to establish his reputation as one of the great writers of the day, had not yet fully flowered, but intimations of it were evident in a number of stories and poems in Hebrew publications. When *Ha-Ugov* (The Harp), a slim volume of poems, appeared, critics detected in it a fresh note in Hebrew poetry and predicted a great future for the writer. A great future was, indeed, in store for Peretz, but not as a writer in the Hebrew language.

I. L. Peretz lived in comparative affluence from his law practice for a decade, from 1877 to 1887, and could afford to remarry. He married a certain Helena Ringelheim, and established a home fitting to the dignity of his profession. But unfortunately his law career did not last much beyond ten years. He was falsely denounced to the Russian government as a radical socialist, and not only was he debarred from the practice of law but he was sentenced to three months in jail, as well. The prison penalty was not of serious consequence to Peretz, for in czarist Russia a prison sentence was the price liberal spirits of the country were expected to pay for their political courage and idealism. But his disbarment, which ruined him financially and deprived him of the means of earning a livelihood, was a different matter.

With the loss of his law practice there was nothing to keep Peretz in Zamoshch, and he settled in Warsaw, until her destruction by the Nazis the largest and intellectually the most creative Jewish community in the world. When Peretz went to Warsaw it was a cosmopolitan city, with a vast diversity of Jews swarming in her streets and boulevards. There were integrated Jews and Hasidic Jews, pietists and agnostics, Hebraists and Yiddishists, Zionists and Bundists—what a variety of colorful Jewish types and characters to inspire a man of talent and imagination with a gift for writing! Peretz found in Warsaw the kind of contact with the world he longed for. After Zamoshch, with her antiquated atmosphere of religious fanaticism, the Russian-Polish capital, with her cosmopolitan spirit and cultured life, was certainly a city to warm any one's heart with visions of achievement. There was something about the man and his vigorous personality, notwithstanding his comparatively small literary background, that soon attracted to him talented young men eager to discuss with him their own literary ideas. For Peretz was a brilliant conversationalist who fascinated his listeners with his eloquence.

His financial affairs were in a precarious condition and he lived with his wife in a one-room apartment. He still wrote poems and short sketches in Hebrew, which appeared in periodicals published by Perez Smolenskin and Nahum Sokolow; but the income from this source was too meager for even his barest subsistence. It was at this time that he was invited by a certain Jan Bloch to take charge of a statistical survey of Jews in a certain area in Poland, being conducted in an effort to disprove the economic accusations against them. Peretz's report on his journey was, no doubt, an important document and it made impressive and absorbing reading; but Peretz was not a sociologist, and, in any event, whatever value the report may have had was nullified by the destruction of the towns and villages through which he had passed. But his *Travel Pictures,* an album of psychological observations on the lives of the men and women he met and studied on his expedition, is of lasting interest. When the purpose of his investigation was accomplished and he found himself again without a position, he accepted a clerkship in the mortuary office of the *gminah,* the Jewish community of Warsaw, a job he held to the end of his life. The task to which he was assigned—keeping a list of the dead—was not particularly appealing to a person of Peretz's poetic temperament, but it afforded him economic security and some leisure for his creative work.

There were many social and political movements among the Jews in Peretz's time. The streets and boulevards of Warsaw were filled with their followers, but Peretz did not belong to any of them. He wanted to be free. He hated nothing so much as to be tagged and labeled. He loved the common people and made himself one of them. His sympathies were with the masses and he was against every form of oppression. His *The Sewing of the Wedding Gown* is a mighty poetic cry against exploitation of the poor. He had little liking for the capitalistic system but neither was he a revolutionary or a Marxist. He could not honestly and conscientiously be either. When, therefore, the Bundists with their revolutionary tendencies mistook Peretz's affection for the poor and the downtrodden and proclaimed him as their banner bearer, he was quick to disillusion them. "I am with you in your struggle," he wrote; "My eyes rest lovingly on your flaming flag; my ear does not tire listening to your mighty song, and yet, I fear you. . . . I fear lest you lower the cedars to the level of the grass. . . . There will be no empty stomachs, but souls will starve, and the eagle, the ringing human spirit, will stand with broken wings at the crib along with the ox and the cow. I hope for your victory, but I fear and dread it."

It was the same with the Yiddish language, to which he turned his hand and became one of its leading exponents. Peretz was one of the creators of Yiddish literature. He gave shape and form to its language and established its claim as one of the cultured languages of the world. But he was not a fanatic Yiddishist who would sabotage the historic language of the Jews for the idiom which had not sprung from the life and thought of the Jewish people. Jarring as it must have been to the ears of his listeners, Peretz publicly declared in 1908 at the Czernowitz Yiddish Conference: "I have chosen jargon for my instrument because something like three million Jews understand no other language. But there must be no illusion about it. Jargon is not our national language. We want all Jews to know the Hebrew language so that the Bible may not be forgotten. . . . Abandonment of Hebrew is like lopping off a branch of the tree to which it belongs. It is the Jew's death sentence."

Peretz was an early devotee of the Haskalah, as were many of the intelligent young Jews of the time. He was versatile and prolific in the Hebrew language and contributed to almost all the current periodicals and, like Mendele, translated into Hebrew some of his Yiddish stories. But he did not join in the Hebrew revival. He was sentimental about the Hebrew language and did not take kindly to the idea of making the language of the Bible and the prayer book the language of the street and the market place. It was to him a sacrilege that he abhorred and would have nothing to do with. While in other respects Peretz held "no language *per se* is holy; no language is good or bad in itself . . . but is a means whereby human beings communicate with each other, and whereby the educated influence the uneducated," Peretz the romanticist preserved in his heart a special niche for the language of the Torah, which he would not willingly see lowered to the mundane affairs of life.

Peretz was a Zionist. He lived in the classical days of Zionism when its structure and ideas were being forged, so to speak, by the leading Jewish spirits of the time. Peretz was a Zionist long before he was anything else. Indeed, he could not help being a Zionist after the books he read, the culture he had imbibed, the influence of the environment in which he had been brought up. Yet Peretz never joined the movement which stirred the hearts and imagination of thousands of his people. He was as skeptical of Zionism as he was of the revival of the Hebrew language. He doubted the practical feasibility of Zionism, the soundness of its philosophy, the correctness of its concept of the fate and destiny of the Jewish people. He did not think that a narrow strip of land in Asia, be it ever so permeated with the life and experience of the Jewish past, squared with the prophetic ideal of Israel's redemption. He held to the missionary ideal of Judaism and looked upon the Jews as a messianic people suffering for the liberation of the world and the freedom of humanity. This, one might be led to believe, sounds something like the assimilationist philosophy, on one hand, and the Bundist attitude to the Jew, on the other—both of which, however, Peretz vigorously rebuked. "Not for this," he angrily remarked, "have we suffered these thousands of years that our civilization be forgotten and repudiated."

Peretz was the best loved of Yiddish writers, although while he was still alive a school of writers arose who were serious contenders for that honor. He made his appearance in Yiddish literature with *Monish,* a ballad, which tells the story of Satan's victory over a saint by tempting him with earthly love. The poem did not create any particular stir among the Warsaw literati; but when it was followed by his *Travel Pictures* and a host of other sketches and novelettes his literary standing was securely established. He was generous to his friends and encouraging to younger writers. He had a way of his own of getting to the roots of a story. "He had one great gift which helped him to discover new talent," writes Sholem Asch in his recollections of Peretz. "He seemed to sense the 'soul' of everything that was read to him. . . . And the moment he penetrated the intrinsic significance of a piece of writing, he was willing to overlook many external flaws."

His home was a mecca for young Yiddish writers, who came to him to be instructed, guided, and inspired. The older writers, recalls Mukdoni, were afraid of Peretz, and avoided him. With their fixed style of writing and their fixed ideas, they feared his power and influence. But with the younger men it was different.

They sought his advice and respected his judgment. They brought him their literary efforts, and patiently he had them read to him. He was both a severe and a friendly judge. He was as lavish with his praise as he was merciless in his criticism. When a piece of writing pleased him, when he detected in it a fresh word or a novel thought, his face glowed with satisfaction. The time and attention he gave to the young hopeful literati is all the more remarkable when one remembers the many other burdens he carried. To mention but one, as editor and publisher of *Die Yiddishe Bibliotek* he not only contributed the poetry and stories but furnished most of the articles, reviews, and editorials.

He was one of the most active and energetic of Jewish writers. He had such a reserve of energy that work came natural with him and he readily assumed new obligations and responsibilities. When he was not busy writing or engaging in public lectures or in any of the many community activities in which he was interested, he squandered his time on helping or visiting people, whom he barely knew. For Peretz loved people. He loved the excitement of crowds, the inspiration of living men and women. He hated nothing so much as to be alone, and he rarely was. He was one of the best known Jews in Warsaw, and crowds followed him everywhere.

He was much in demand as a public lecturer, especially among the Jewish working classes. His schedule of lectures covered a wide range of subjects, including religion, history, education, and economics. With these topics he had but the slightest formal acquaintance, a jumble of facts and theories which he had picked up in the course of his reading in his garret library; but he handled them with such fluency and adroitness that he was never nettled by questions from the audience. "As secretary of these question-and-answer meetings," writes A. Mukdoni, recording his impressions of 'Yal' Peretz, "I was frequently electrified by his flashes of thought and deep insight. Yes, insight, for Peretz did not possess great erudition. . . . And there were times when on hearing him expound and clarify some intricate philosophical problem of which he had but the vaguest knowledge, I did not believe my own ears."

Peretz was an intense and conscientious Jew with a warm-hearted love for Judaism notwithstanding his occasional outbursts. The spirit he had imbibed in his youth glowed in him undimmed all through his life. He was rooted in the soil of Judaism and his inner self remained Jewish despite the *gilgulim,* or transformations through which he passed. When he spoke before radical groups his lectures were more of a training in the eternal values of Judaism and the Jewish people than a harangue against God and religion. He made them feel that the universal spirit was embodied in the Jewish soul. He hated chains and shackles of any kind and those of religion most of all. He hated hypocrisy masquerading in the name of piety and fanaticism posing as religion. These things Peretz lashed out at with all the severity of his caustic pen. He was merciless in denouncing men who enslave and tyrannize over the people by reason of the outward insignia or symbol of their positions. In *The Streimel* (The Fur Cap), Peretz holds up to ridicule the man who inspires awe not through any inner virtue of his own but because of his enormous fur cap, without which he never appears in public. In other words, it is the cap and not the man, the cap and not the rabbi and scholar he may be, that gives him his authority over the people.

Peretz is the poet of the little man, of the meek and humble whose virtues are silent, whose piety is unostentatious, whose Godlike qualities are not on display. He is the poet of the gentle, suffering soul whose character is evolved through pain and suffering and a squalid existence, and he sang the song of *Bontshe Shweig.* Here on earth Bontshe made little impression. He was not of much consequence in the world, and suffered poverty, hunger, and humiliation without the slightest murmur; and when he died it was just like a grain of dust blown away by the wind. But in the other world it was different. White-winged angels welcomed him with silver trumpets, and great honors were done him. Terror befell Bontshe when he saw all the fuss that was made over him. His heart melted in fear and trembling when he heard the celestial court announce that, since all his life he had suffered quietly when he might have cried out and had been silent when he might have complained, he might now have for his reward whatever part of the heavenly splendor he chose. "That being so," said Bontshe, who never in life had known any greater delicacy than a crust of dry bread, "I want every morning a hot roll with fresh butter."

It was his search for the soul everywhere that attracted Peretz to Hasidism and made him one of its greatest poets and story tellers. Peretz himself may not have been a Hasid. He probably never saw a Hasidic rabbi, nor heard one "say" Torah. For Peretz was a Maskil nurtured in the best tradition of Haskalah. While Maskilim mocked and ridiculed Hasidism and saw in it nothing but crude and shoddy provincialism, Peretz penetrated into its inner spirit. They dwelt on its outward faults and failings, its uncouth ways and unvarnished simplicity; he sensed its depth and spiritual significance. Proud Polish Jew that Peretz was, solidly rooted in the centuries-old Jewish tradition in Poland, he regarded Hasidism as the finest product of Polish Jewry and destined for the enrichment and preservation of the Jewish spirit.

"Yal" Peretz was more than the creator of the Hasidic story—he was its greatest master. Nahman Bratzlav was a great Hasidic saint and a superb story teller. In his hands the story became an exquisite instrument of pure delight rarely found among Jewish writings. But Nahman Bratszlav's stories are surrounded by an aura of holiness and are intended to stress religious devotion. They are mystery tales, more imaginary than real, drawn not from life but from the poet's dream world. Peretz's tales, on the other hand, are concerned with the inner life of the Hasidim, their reservoir of hope and faith, and their unceasing striving for communion with God.

In a series of finely etched sketches and longer dramatic poems, Peretz portrays Hasidic saints and teachers, their kindling faith, burning love, and almost fanatical devotion to God and to their people, Israel. One of these tales, *If Not Higher,* is the story of the Rabbi of Nemirov, one of the exalted saints of the Hasidic tradition. He made it his habit to disappear on the morning of the Penitential Days—the days between the New Year and the Day of Atonement—when the hearts of Jews are particularly heavy with fear of the coming of the Day of Judgment. The Hasidim were not much worried about their rabbi's disappearance, for at a time like this where could the *zaddik* be other than in heaven pleading for the salvation of his people before the celestial tribunal? But what really happened was that, instead of ascending to heaven long before dawn, the Rabbi of Nemirov left his home unnoticed and, dressed in peasant garb, went with a rope and an ax to a near-by forest where he felled a young tree, which he chopped into faggots and carried to a hut of a sick and penniless old widow who was without kindling wood to warm her shack. Since she was too weak and helpless to light it herself, the great Rabbi of Nemirov made a cheerful crackling fire, after which he left and joined his congregation for the *selihot,* the Penitential Prayers. Thereafter, when the question whether the sage of Nemirov ascended to heaven was raised, the answer was, "If Not Higher."

The contrast between a cold and formal religion and a faith that is deep and stirring and that transforms life into a moving, ecstatic experience, is described by Peretz in *Reb Noah and the Rabbi of Brest,* renamed by Maurice Samuel *Between Two Cliffs.* The sage of Brest was a renowned scholar. "If the Torah were an ocean," says Peretz, "he would be a leviathan in that ocean. With a single stroke, he would swim the length of ten tractates of the Talmud with all its commentaries. He rumbled, surged, seethed and bubbled just as the ocean does. Indeed, watching him, one would become dizzy." But Noah, the most mystical of his students, with a love and rapture for the *living* Torah, rebelled against his teacher's dry and formalistic Torah and left him, later to become the celebrated *zaddik* of Biala. When years later, the two men met and the Rabbi of Brest asked his former pupil why he had left him, and what he had been seeking, the *zaddik* of Biala said, "What I sought was air. I could not breathe in your *yeshibah.* . . . Your Torah, Rabbi, is but an arid Law. It is without benevolence, without a spark of graciousness. . . . Your Torah is far too private—it is only for men of learning, only for the chosen ones. What can you offer *all* Israel? What have you for the butcher, the woodcutter, the artisan, the common Jew? Harsh is your Torah—harsh and dry. It is but the body of the Torah, not its soul."

The Golden Chain, which Peretz prized as the best thing he wrote, is a drama of extraordinary power and distinction. It portrays the conflict between realism and romanticism that was going on in the writer's mind. In other words, it poses the struggle of the light and reason of the modern spirit, against the fanatical mystical world of the Hasidim. Leah is the scion of a "golden chain" of *zaddikim* reaching back several generations. But the chain snaps under the impact of the new age, when link after link is broken off and disappears in a strange and alien world not dreamed of by the forgers of the chain. Leah finds the atmosphere of her Hasidic ancestors galling and stifling and goes out into the world and marries Dr. Bergman, an apostle of the light and reason for which she yearned. But she does not stay very long in that world but returns disappointed to her old home. "Light and reason, like snow," she says, "are clear, but cold and dead. . . . Man has a heart, a warm and feeling heart. The world, too, must have a heart, a pitying and compassionate heart. The world cannot live without God."

Peretz is the most musical of Jewish writers. He re-interprets the exalted place of the *nigun* in the religious life of the Hasidim. His characters live and move in the ecstatic mood of Hasidic song and melody. What learning is to the *talmid hakam,* the *nigun* is to the Hasid. It stands on the boundary between the carnal and the spiritual, between the pure and the impure. There are mansions in heaven, the Zohar teaches, which are approached only by song, and it is related of a *zaddik* that he attained more by the sound of the *nigun* than by the words of prayer. What is the hidden meaning of King David's words, "All my bones shall say, Lord who is like unto Thee?" Peretz makes the Kabbalist, Reb Yekel, ask. The meaning is that to be effective, to penetrate heaven with its song, the *nigun* must sound in the very depths of the soul, not merely from the lips, which are of flesh and blood. Peretz tells of the Nemirover who used to say, "All creation is a song; what lives must sing; death alone is silent. Every letter in the Torah is a musical note; its words are melodies, song and harmony are in its teachings."

Peretz was enamored of the Hasidic *nigun;* he idealized and spiritualized it and made it the subject of some of his best-remembered stories. The *nigun* is the Hasid's mystic communion with God, the key with which he hopes to unlock the gates of heaven. It uplifts him, it exalts him, it makes him forget the misery and poverty of his daily existence. When the Hasid sings his holy songs, the celestial choir of the *seraphim* is hushed still and listens. There is yearning and sobbing in the *nigun,* but also love and joy, and a happiness such as no mortal can describe. For there are no limits set to the *nigun*. It hymns merrily the festive songs of Passover and *Simhat Torah* and it sobs mournfully the dirges of *Tisha b'Ab;* it sings with flaming joy the wedding melody and sobs poignantly the requiem *El Moleh Rahamim*.

It is the greatness and mystery of the *nigun* that it is of many moods and motifs. It exalts and depresses, raises to the Throne of Glory and saturates with tears and melancholy. There is the *nigun* of the Hasid, fresh and rapturous, and there is the monotone of the scholar, uttered with cold and lifeless lips. It is only the Hasid— the Hasid who has risen to the *madregah,* the spiritual level of the *zaddik*—who has caught the secret of the *nigun* as an ecstatic instrument of the soul. In *The Metamorphosis of a Melody*, Peretz describes the various changes and transformations through which a *nigun* may pass. In the hands of a street comedian, it becomes a cheap and vulgar song; when played by a poor blind girl, it turns into a sorrowful plea for mercy and charity; but when the *zaddik* infuses into it his religious warmth and sanctity, it is transformed into a hymn fit for angels.

Peretz not only idealized the *nigun* but he classified it, so to speak, into several grades and divisions. For a *nigun,* he said, differs not only in its effect and tempo but also in the means employed to produce it. A voice like a human being, says Peretz, is made up of body and soul. The *nigun* in just the same way, has its outward and inward elements: the words are the body, or the material part of the melody; but when someone feels something singing within him, singing without words, that is the highest type of *nigun*—it is his soul that sings. Says Reb Yekel the Mekubal: "There is the melody which needs words. That is the lowest degree.

There is a higher degree; the melody which is sung without words—pure melody still needs a voice and it needs lips from which the voice can issue. And lips, you understand, are only flesh . . . and the melody which is brought forth by the voice and depends upon lips is not completely pure—it is not completely spiritual. True melody is voiceless; it is expressed within the heart, in the secret place of one's being."

I. L. Peretz may be said to have died with a song. It was in the first year of the First World War, when, driven by the victorious German armies on the one hand and the defeated Russian troops on the other, thousands of Jews fled to Warsaw. The city was overcrowded and the Jewish institutions were hard pressed to cope with the needs of the sufferers. Among the most pitiful victims were the children who, in the horror and confusion of the war, became separated from their parents. With the leading Jews of Warsaw, Peretz was active in founding a children's home. But poet and warm-hearted friend of children that he was, he set to work on the third of the intermediary days of Passover of the year 5675 (April 3, 1915) to compose a children's poem. But the song which was to brighten the lives of the little ones was not finished. Peretz was found dead at his desk before it was completed.

Solomon Jacob Abramovich
(Mendele Mocher Seforim)

MENDELE MOCHER SEFORIM'S place in Jewish literature is unique and significant. For more than two generations he was king in a realm in which he had few, if any, rivals. He represents a departure and an epoch—a method and style of writing he himself invented and made popular. Even writers who derided and flouted his work could not escape its influence. Mendele was the longest lived of Jewish writers. He died at the age of eighty-one. His stories and novels are to this day the most treasured gems of Yiddish and Hebrew literature, the two languages in which he wrote. While his real name was Solomon Jacob Abramovich, he wrote under the pen name of Mendele Mocher Seforim (Mendele the Book Seller), but to the thousands who loved and admired him he was known simply as Mendele.

Authors and their works have their times and vogues; but the changing literary fashion has done little to affect Mendele's fame and popularity. He was a prolific writer; until his death the creative urge did not leave him for a moment. In his long literary career he put his talented hand to almost every kind of writing. He wrote poetry, drama, novels, allegories, satires, a thinly veiled autobiography, and even translated scientific works from the German and Russian languages. He was a moralist, rebel, and social reformer, a keen observer and accurate recorder. As though with camera in hand, he swept through the Jewish scene, taking snapshots of its varied types and moods without missing a single point or detail. He commented upon everything he saw—nature, animals, people, the rich, the poor, the corrupt, the exploited, the saints and sinners.

It is impossible to measure Mendele Mocher Seforim against the background of the Jewish literary tradition of his time, for there was no such tradition. He took nothing from his contemporary writers; he was not influenced by any school; he had no master to follow or imitate. What he was and what he did were completely his own. Every one of his creations, the very language in which he clothed them, bears the stamp of originality. He was one of the first to discover the force and vigor of the everyday Jewish vernacular. He took the dialect of the common, illiterate masses and made of it an instrument of vivid literary expression. In other words, Mendele was not only the creator of the Yiddish novel but, in a sense, the revealer of the Yiddish language as well, in his exposition of its style and diction. Mendele was fastidious to a fault. He was finicky about his personal appearance, and he carried the same care over into all his literary efforts. Words were to him not merely a tool but were almost an end in themselves, and they had to be accurate and beautiful.

No other Jewish writer was as pedantic about style and diction as was Mendele. He not only wrote and rewrote, revised and polished, until his words shone like glistening jewels but he weighed and sounded them to make sure that they were accurate and reliable. When visitors came he liked to read to them what he had written, not so much for their judgment or approval as to enable him to get the feel and sound of his own words. He was one of the first Hebrew and Yiddish writers to go to the Talmud and the Midrashim for the pungent word and pointed expression and, invariably, the results were striking and lent character and picturesqueness to his writing. Indeed, so steeped are his stories in the homely guise of the ancient past that one feels as if he were perusing a bit of Midrash or a marvelous passage of Rashi.

Mendele stood at the end of one period and the beginning of another in Jewish literature. The Romantic Movement had ended with the death of Abraham Mapu, who was its greatest champion, and the time for realism had come. Perez Smolenskin was a realist of a sort. He was stormy, courageous, and volcanic, a writer of contagious enthusiasm. He attacked the obscurantism of his time with an unsparing pen. He exposed mercilessly the sham and hypocrisy that masqueraded under the guise of piety. He was also deep and penetrating, particularly in his polemics against the reformers of the post-Moses Mendelssohn school. But Smolenskin was more of a pamphleteer than an artist, more of a propagandist than a novelist. He lacked the detachment and poetic temperament of either the novelist or the artist. Mendele, too, was far from a neutral observer of the Jewish scene of his time. He scolded and lashed with a sharp and caustic tongue. But there is humor in his lash—that quaint and unique Mendelian humor that makes one forget the sting it inflicts.

Mendele Mocher Seforim introduced a new technique in Jewish literature. He copied from living models. His characters are not idealized creatures; they are not wax figures dressed up and painted to make them look natural and alive. They are living human beings with feelings, sentiments, and emotions characteristic of their time and environment. They are awkward or easy, grotesque or refined, loquacious or reserved, just as they came from the hand of their Creator. Their speech is the speech of the home, the street or market place, or the talk one hears wherever hungry Jewish beggars get together.

Mendele not only sketched his men and women—their faces and movements down to the batting of an eyelash and the curl of a lip but he delved deep into their barren, corroded, and exhausted lives. He is the one writer in Jewish literature whose every book is a self-portrait. There is more of Mendele in his stories than he himself was willing to admit, more of him in the episodes and adventures he described than in the formal biographies of him. His heroes and victims are extensions of his own self, fragments of his life, pages and incidents from his diary, as it were.

He is the painter of the humble folk—the poor, downtrodden, lowly masses. He is their spokesman, their mouthpiece, their advocate and pleader. The great, the rich, and the powerful rarely appear on his canvas, except for censure and criticism. But although Mendele was at home with the poor and the scorned he did not sentimentalize or glamorize them. If there is meaning in his work, if his message remains true and vital, it is because he makes clear that there is nothing beautiful or lovely about poverty and hunger, but that instead it is hideous and loathsome, something to be fought and uprooted.

Mendele is the spokesman for Russian Jewry, its mirror, its photographer, its poet. Its men, women and children, its cities, towns, and villages, its bigotry, fanaticism, and superstitions are all part of the panorama he knew so well and described so masterfully. His canvas is crowded with good and honest folk, but also with shams, scoundrels, and vagabonds. In his album there are purse-proud Jews who ruled their townsmen with a coarse and heavy hand. For, to repeat, Mendele was a realist. He wrote from life and not from imagination. And what he saw on his travels or beheld in the homes of his characters was not always pretty or edifying. Other writers, too, saw the same thing, but made their written pictures more idyllic.

Mendele was better at diagnosing than at curing. He had a dynamic, emotional, one might almost say prophetic, attitude toward evil, a real enthusiasm for humanity; but he was not sure of the cure. There were rebellion in his heart, challenge and defiance in his soul, but they did not stir him to action. He saw the crippling and corrupting influence of poverty, the defeated and wasted lives, though he lacked the theory, the formula, the philosophy to cure them. He saw the disease and recognized and described it with such accuracy that none could help but be moved by it.

The terrific struggle for bread—this is the principal theme of Mendele's stories and novels. There are different degrees and shades of poverty among the Jews he describes. There is the stark, naked, ugly poverty that makes a person fight like an animal for a crust of bread; and there is the outwardly more dignified poverty dressed up on the Sabbath in shining satin, that, in its quieter way, also makes life joyless beneath its outer show. Yet their poverty has not made Mendele's characters bitter or unhappy. They bear their lot with good humor and are never in want of reasons for gratitude. Thus, when in *The Travels of Benjamin the Third* someone approaches a Jew of Batlon and asks him what is his business or his means of support, he for the moment feels embarrassed and stammers, but then answers in a cheerful voice:

"God's name be praised, as you see me, I have really nothing to complain of. The Holy One favored me with a precious gift—a voice to sing with, and I am thus called out to officiate on the High Holydays in a synagogue in one of the neighbourhood communities. I am likewise an excellent Mohel and an expert Matzah baker. Besides, I have quite a reputation as a matchmaker, and sometimes make a little money that way. As you see me, unworthy as I am, I have a permanent seat in the synagogue. And let it remain a secret between you and me, I have a little whiskey hidden away in the house, which brings me in a little, and a goat, may no evil eye befall her, which contributes a little milk to the family upkeep. I have a relative not far from here, who, willing or not, sometimes helps out in time of need. But, besides everything, the Lord God is good and merciful, and Jews are merciful children of the Merciful. So why should one complain?"

There are of course, other notes than poverty in Mendele Mocher Seforim's works. For instance, his most popular book, *Die Klatche* (The Mare), is an allegorical narrative in which the author wrestles with the eternal Jewish problem and satirically criticizes some of its proposed solutions. It was a daring work for the time and place in which it was written, but was also a charming and touching book, full of humor and pathos, with passages of rare lyrical beauty —as complete a picture of the Jews' universal tragedy as was ever penned. Although the political conditions symbolized in *Die Klatche* have since changed, the book is still read with the same pleasure it gave nearly ninety years ago, when it was written.

The parable or allegory is a well-known Jewish method for conveying thoughts they dared not write or speak openly. It is found in the Bible and was used extensively by the Rabbis of the Talmud. Perhaps the best-known biblical example of the allegorical method is that of the trees choosing a king. In *Die Klatche,* probably taking his lead from Balaam's talking ass, Mendele symbolized suffering Israel by a lean, persecuted, half-starved and homeless mare, which is pursued by the "bosses of the town" and is stoned and set upon by the street urchins, who would not let her graze on the common pasture land with the other "town cattle."

Yisrolik, whose pity was aroused for the poor mare, appeals to the Society for the Prevention of Cruelty to Animals, meaning the Russian government. But the latter cannot quite make up its mind whether to grant the mare equal grazing rights with the other horses, and the matter is referred to a special commission. After long deliberation the commission concludes that the mare may be altogether without fault, but that, to attain equal rights, she first must be cleansed and educated—a gentle satire on the Haskalah advocates. The mare, however, protests that her woebegone condition is due not to lack of education but to lack of nourishment. As in most of Mendele's stories, there are in *Die Klatche* episodes within episodes. In this instance, the most interesting are those dealing with King Solomon and his fabled Ashmodai (the prince of devils). The work, which was written with great artistry under much nervous tension in three days and nights of acute mental strain, created a sensation and was read by thousands. It appeared in many translations, but when attempts were made to render it into the Russian language its circulation was forbidden.

Mendele did not leap into fame at once. His ascent was slow and painful before he reached the top. He was past thirty when his first work, a Hebrew novel, under the Haskalah influence, appeared. It proved a failure, but a natural history *Toldot ha-Teba,* in four volumes, which he translated from the German, won for him considerable fame, chiefly because of the Hebrew nomenclature he ingeniously invented for the zoological terms of the book. Still there was nothing to betray the future master, the exquisite artist, the subtle and admirable portrayer of characters and episodes.

When once he was accepted, however, books seemed to flow from his pen. And after a time they were read widely and were sold by the thousands of copies. The young and the old, the discriminating and the poorly educated—they all read them. There was scarcely a home in which "Mendele" was not a familiar name. Because of his realism and his exceptional gift of characterization, he was acknowledged as one of the greatest Jewish writers of his day. In his introduction to Mendele's collected works, David Frishman tells of Polish writers who made a study of the Yiddish language so that they could read Mendele's stories in the original and translate them.

The epic of Mendele's own life is perhaps stranger and more fascinating than any of the stories he wrote. He was born to the poverty and sordidness of a small Lithuanian Jewish village community in the Province of Minsk in the year 1836. His father, a gentle, saintly scholar himself, was eager for his child's education, and he placed him in the care of an expert teacher who introduced his talented pupil at a tender age to the wisdom and learning of Jewish lore and tradition. The Bible with its marvelous stories of kings and prophets and heroes made a deep and lasting impression upon the youthful scholar's poetic mind which later colored his stories and novels, as did the exciting debates and dialectics of the Talmud. It was, however, the fields and meadows, the haunting quiet beauty of the forest with its many-colored birds twittering their love songs in the night, and its lazily flowing river, that cast a spell upon the future poet and remained as treasured memories in his mind. Time and again he recalled them, time and again he vividly relived and described them.

It was, however, a paradise in which he was not destined to tarry long. He was barely thirteen when his father died, leaving his wife and family to fend for themselves the best they could. From then on Mendele repeated the struggles and experiences of many a Lithuanian Jewish boy bent on an education. To lighten his widowed mother's burden, he left Kapuli and became an itinerary student, wandering from town to town, wherever he could find a noted teacher. His odyssey eventually led him to Sluzk, celebrated for her school of talmudic learning. Possessed by a prodigious spiritual hunger, Mendele plunged voraciously into his studies, ate what the good and pious Torah-loving Jews of Sluzk could spare of their own meager substance, and made the hard bench of the Bet ha-Midrash his bed. In his later years Mendele, describing this phase of his childhood, wrote of his hard bench as the stone on which his namesake, the Patriarch Jacob, had laid his head when heavenly visions were revealed to him. Heavenly visions had indeed been revealed to Mendele, too—visions of fame and greatness which he was not to recall until many years later.

Mendele did well in Sluzk. He was a serious and diligent student and he atracted wide attention as a future shining light in Israel. But he was restless and set his heart on still greater centers of learning. His wandering led him to Vilna, the "Faithful City," famous throughout Jewry as the Jerusalem of Lithuania. There were schools of learning there, and a Jewish community of almost legendary origin. But what most fascinated Mendele about Vilna was its fabled Gaon, Rabbi Elijah, about whom, although he was long dead, stories and legends were still circulating. Mendele remained in Vilna for some time, studied in the Goen's *Klaus,* and fervently prayed that his spirit might rest upon him.

But the lonely student of Torah became restless again, and at the age of sixteen he returned to his mother and the lovely countryside of his childhood. What he found there changed the whole course of his life. His mother had remarried, and she lived with her husband on a small farm not many miles from Kapuli, Mendele's native town. The farm was located amid the simple loveliness of woods and brooks and open sunshine, which made his heart thrill and quicken. It was there that a grotesque relationship began, which, like the finger of providence, pointed the way to his destiny. He met a professional Jewish beggar, Abraham the Lame, who excited Mendele's imagination with odd and fantastic stories of his adventures as a wandering beggar and of the fabled wealth and strange sights of the towns and provinces he visited. He persuaded the young *yeshiva bahur* to join him and his company of mendicants. Moreover, Mendele's aunt, an *agunah,* deserted by her husband, agreed to come along with them, in the hope that she might find her spouse. What a well-laid plan it was on the part of the scoundrely beggar to enrich himself! With the young scholar to spice his plea for donations with quotations from the rabbis and the unfortunate woman to add pathos, what heart could withstand their appeal to contribute generously? He might even succeed in

palming off his learned young mendicant as husband to some rich
Jew's daughter and collect customary marriage commission. After
some time, when Mendele was weary of the company he was
keeping and made plans to escape, the wily beggar frustrated him
by stealing his passport, without which in czarist Russia one could
not move about freely. (Ultimately he did manage to escape, however, and made the acquaintance of Abraham Gottleber, a pioneer
of the Haskalah, under whose auspices he wrote his first and only
Hebrew novel, *Fathers and Sons.)* Hideous as the journey and his
association with the beggar were—he was dragged along with his
despicable companion in a rickety cart drawn by an emaciated half-
starved nag—they were not without their rewarding influence on
the budding poet and novelist. For his experiences and impressions
were stored up in his mind, to emerge later in *Fishke the Lame,* the
most realistic epic of Jewish beggardom in literature. Only a man
who himself had gone through such an ordeal and had lived in
intimate relationship with the dregs of society he described could
masterfully reproduce their speech, their actions, their morals—or
want of them.

There are bits of *Fishke the Lame* in almost all Mendele's writings—the same gaunt melancholy figures, the same restless faces
and eyes, and, with local variations, the same vexatious problems
that Mendele observed in the towns and villages which he traversed.
From Mendele's first Yiddish novel, *The Little Man,* through his
more mature works, including *The Mare, The Travels of Benjamin
the Third,* and *In These Days,* his last and one of his most finished,
we see the same Mendele, puddling through the crooked muddy
streets and alleys of the Volhynia and Ukraine ghettos in his mendicant years, taking note of all he heard, saw, and experienced. In
The Little Man Mendele strikes out against the unscrupulous
flunkeys who, by fawning and flattery, manage to establish themselves in high places of authority for the oppression of the poor
and the helpless. The subject was a timely one in the middle of the
nineteenth century, when just such men were the plague of many
Jewish communities in the old Russian Pale of Settlement. Likewise, in *The Meat Tax,* Mendele made his stay in Berdichev in-

secure by going after the representatives of *Kahal* (the Jewish community) for what Mendele branded their rascally imposition of a heavy meat and candle tax that worked great hardship on people to whom meat and candles were luxuries they allowed themselves only on the Sabbath. The tax imposed nominally for the support of the communal institutions, actually went to the enrichment of the men who were commissioned to collect it. The *Travels of Benjamin the Third*, an entertaining story written with poetic artistry and the typical Mendelian humor, was probably suggested by the adventurous travels of Eldad Hadani and Benjamin of Tudela. It is a narrative about a man who made up his mind to go to Palestine and, incidentally, to visit the land of the Ten Tribes and the mystic river Sambation, which flows turbulently all week and rests only on the Sabbath, and about his failure to get any farther than Berdichev and its dirty river Guilopyat. The story proved popular, and its author was dubbed the "Jewish Cervantes." *In These Days*, an idealistic picture of Jewish life in olden times, with brilliantly written echoes of the author's life and experiences and childhood memories of his home and studies, is the most mature and best remembered of his writings.

But a writer may possess great and rare literary gifts, even genius, yet fail because of a lack of harmony between his personal viewpoints and the spirit of the time in which he lives. Likewise, many an author who scores brilliant successes in the beginning, may find himself neglected and forsaken by the very admirers who first hailed him. The literary form and the ideas they thought so novel and striking not infrequently lose their power and challenge under the impact of changed conditions.

Many of the world's greatest minds have suffered from neglect and desertion. Their thoughts and ideas were unfamiliar and too radical for their compatriots, their demands too high, their pace too fast for the timid and the conservative. But Mendele was not one of this class. At no time was he so far ahead of his time, his stride so rapid, or his thoughts and ideas so unconventional that they could not be followed by his contemporaries. On the contrary, if there is any complaint to be registered against Mendele, it is that he was always careful and cautious, always playing the part of "grandfather," content to follow rather than to lead.

Mendele might have been a prophet and a liberator, as were other men of his generation much less equipped than he. For he was peculiarly gifted. He had a keen mind and a sharp eye and he knew from his own experience the life of the masses. As few other men of his time, he knew the tales they handed down; he knew their toil and the deep aching sadness that tore at their hearts. He saw the misery and suffering of the Russian Jews, their poverty and squalor, the boycotts, expulsions, pogroms, and butcheries. He saw a Jewry of millions of lives given to despair and despondency, on the verge of moral and physical dissolution. He might have cried out, he might have protested, he might have given vent to his outraged feelings in flaming, searing words. He did raise his voice once, in *Die Klatche*. But how mild was the voice, how timid the rebuke—a faint, veiled, hardly audible whisper, when it should have been strong and thunderous.

Fully thirty-seven years, the most creative of his life, were spent in Odessa, a city which, for its far-reaching influence, might well have been regarded as the cultural and spiritual center of world Jewry. From that city thoughts and ideas went forth which had a galvanizing effect upon Jews the, world over. It was the city of Pinsker, Ahad Ha'Am, Bialik, Lilienblum, Ussishkin, and many others. Like them he might have probed the cause of his people's misery and he might have become guide and prophet of its national destiny. More than any one of his group he had the ear and heart of his people.

There was great Zionist activity in Odessa during the latter part of Mendele's life. The air was electric with expectation, the horizon rosy with national hopes. Dr. Pinsker published his famous brochure; Ahad Ha'Am wrote his celebrated essays; Bialik sang his great songs. Dr. Theodor Herzl appeared upon the scene, electrifying thousands with his daring dream of "The Jewish State." Zionist congresses made the Jewish atmosphere tense and excited as it had not been for a thousand years. But during all this time Mendele was as silent as the grave. His heart was not warmed, his imagination was not kindled by what was going on around him. The noise and thunder of the times had passed him by unnoticed.

Mendele was not opposed to Zionism. Indeed, how could he be? How could anyone as fanatically devoted to Jews and "Yiddishkeit" as he was, be opposed to Zionism? Is not Zionism Eretz Yisroel, and is not Eretz Yisroel "Yiddishkeit?" Jews are Jews, he argued, and, being Jews, how could they be indifferent to Palestine? And as for himself, does not Palestine occupy a prominent, indeed, a substantial place in his stories? What of Reb Nahman, the vagrant Jew with his long caftan, beard, and earlocks, who made his periodic leave-taking tours of the Jewish towns and villages, was wined and dined by the poorest of the Jews and made away with their last *kopeka,* all because he pretended to be on his way to Palestine? And what of the Palestine dates, and Rachel's grave, and the Western Wall—such well-remembered episodes in Mendele's novels?

No, Mendele was not opposed to Zionism. It was only that he did not lift a finger to advance its cause, to further its aims, to hasten the day of Zion's restoration. He even laughed cynically and poked fun at Zionism and had many a good-humored quarrel with Menahem Mendel Ussishkin because of the latter's "crazy notions" and "wild" dreams! Mendele was a firm believer in the ghetto. Its life had a certain poetic attraction for him. It had left with him memories which he loved to contemplate and describe. It was part, an unforgettable part of his "Yiddishkeit." Was it not because of the ghetto stories that he became great and famous?

He stood nearer to Dubnow than to Ahad Ha'Am or Herzl. He was not as deep a thinker or philosopher as the great historian. But like him, he stressed the futility and impossibility of the Jew's escape from the ghetto. That thought he intimated in *Die Klatche* (The Mare). Pursued and persecuted, it would many a time have abandoned the wagon and escaped except that it found itself surrounded by impassable swamps, with every route of escape cut off. With Dubnow, Mendele believed that the future of the Jews lay not in escape but in endeavoring to make their life more tolerable in their native lands by the amelioration of their economic and political condition.

Mendele was not a philosopher; he was not even a social re-former, although his stories revolve around the social and economic life of the Jews. His books are more of a projection of the author's own experience than a balanced outlook on the Jew's position in the world. He had no philosophy of Judaism, no faith in the Jewish national hopes and aspirations, no faith or confidence that by their own will or effort the Jews could ever force their way to freedom. In this respect he did not differ from the most fanatic orthodox Jews, to whom Zionism was heresy and a blasphemous attempt to force the hand of God. The *galut* was to him something fixed and definite; it was contrary to his conception of *"Yiddishkeit"* to rebel against it. In all his stories there is not a single character who rises in definance against the chains and shackles.

He was, of course, a good Jew and passionately devoted to Judaism, with all its traditions and practices, and, in his later years, he was the most scrupulous of his group in his religious ob-servance. His most orthodox townsmen could find no flaw in his religious conduct. But he did not waste any time on the problem of survival; indeed, speculations of this kind irked him. Of course, the Jews and Judaism would survive; they will survive without them-selves lifting a finger—for is it not part of the divine plan, an axiom of history?

Few men understood better the mental and spiritual nature of Mendele, his moods, his whims and caprices, than Chaim Tchernowitz. He was both friend and admirer, follower and gentle critic. In his *Masekhet Zikhronot* (Book of Memoirs), he devotes to Mendele what is perhaps the most penetrating study of the Sage of Odessa. In one of the passages in the book Tchernowitz reveals what made Mendele so strange and involved a character. He writes that Mendele confessed to him that at times he felt as though two Mendeles were living within him—that, like the legendary Mohammed's coffin, he was suspended between two worlds, drawn by two forces, pulled hither and thither, not knowing which way to go.

The implication is clear. Mendele, the great lover of Israel, was touched to the very core of his being by his people's sorrow. Sensitive artist that he was, he was overwhelmed by his nation's tragedy. Under the spell of his agony he even decided at one time to stop writing altogether. In a letter to a friend he laid bare the cry of his heart: "Unhappy is the life of the Jew. In my agony, I have lost all desire to write. I am stunned by the blow." He lacked the courage, the faith, and the conviction to make himself the torchbearer of a new day. And so, when he sufficiently roused himself to resume writing again after a brief interlude, he came back to his people not with a new clarion call but with still another story of the recent past, *Fishke der Krumer* (Fishke the Lame).

He felt that his labors belonged to the simple instead of to the intellectual elite. Like his younger contemporary I. L. Peretz, he pondered which language was more effective for educating the people. He concluded that the future lay in the spoken idiom of the masses. Hebrew was a language with more writers than readers. It was limited primarily to the Bible and the prayer book and, of course, the *Gemara,* all of which are more edifying than "entertaining." He wrote Yiddish in a loquacious and amusing style which captivated many readers. His choice diction, a panorama dyed in fascinating, breath-taking hues, and pages teeming with characters that move the reader alternately from tears to laughter, made Mendele Mocher Seforim the most popular writer of his time. In his own words: "I observed the ways of the people and desired to give them tales in the holy tongue from the sources of Israel. But most of them do not know Hebrew and speak Yiddish. And what has the author for all his toil and thought if he does not profit his people?"

Here speaks the realist; also the social reformer, whose principal ambition is to "profit his people." Here, too, is the Jew who speaks, the Jew Mendele, whose highest love is for the "sources of Israel," a love, indeed, from which he never wandered far. And toward the end of his life, when Mendele was sated with years of success and popularity, he did what few other Jewish writers had done before— he translated his own works from Yiddish, the language in which they were originally written, into Hebrew. What made him undertake this long and arduous task when he might have written new books and created new stories? Was it that his creative genius had exhausted itself, or that, upon arriving at an age when many a man begins to think of *olam haba,* he was anxious to link his name for posterity with the language of the Bible and the Prophets? If posterity's judgment was Mendele's concern, he succeeded equally in both languages, for he is as much read today in Hebrew as in Yiddish.

Mendele's world is destroyed—not a shred of it is left—the world of the covered wagon, the beggars, the vagabonds, the *hekdhesh* (lodging place for the transient poor and sick), the bath house, the lean, lame, half-starved mare, the world of Kabzansk, Glupsk, and Tuyadevka. Many another Jewish writer's world has been destroyed, also, but no one's as utterly and as completely as his. Flames and ashes have buried his world. It belongs to the past. Its humor and pathos, its sights and insights. It was the world of the grandfathers; the grandchildren no longer know it.

When Sholem Aleichem dubbed Mendele "Grandfather," he was more critical of him than flattering. The keen penetrating eye of the master humorist discerned weaknesses in Mendele which took others years to recognize. Hardly had Sholom Aleichem begun to write when he noticed that Mendele was getting old, perhaps never had been young. In other words, he was a Grandfather whom the future might respect and honor but hardly follow.

I. L. Peretz was more candid and outspoken in his appraisal of Mendele. The man who appeared upon the literary scene like a knight in shining armor, courageous and unafraid, gave vent to his feelings about Mendele in an article he wrote as early as 1894. "He who is a stickler for fine words," he said, "will find them in Mendele's *Stormy Days,* and in *In Those Days,* but he who looks for ideas will not find them there. It is sickening to see the great eagle descend into the gutter of *batlanut* for just idle, garrulous talk which neither helps nor serves anyone. One wonders what would become of Mendele were he suddenly deprived of his mare and wagon!"

Peretz's disparagement of Mendele may be harsh, but it is not far from the truth; for the great eagle's garrulousness is among his greatest faults. His garrulousness may be pleasant and entertaining while it flows on, but it is barren and empty in the end. Mendele may have been an artist, but his artistry lay more in the realm of observation and expression than in that of thought and ideas. He had a keen and delicate feeling for words and language, but the impression is that he sacrificed almost everything else to his worship of style. The typical Mendelian novel is not a provocation to thought or a trumpet call to action; it is not even an artistically woven unit of design and plot but a series of loosely connected episodes, held together by the most tenuous of threads.

Mendele saw the Jewish world through its poverty and ugliness, its contortions and convulsions; but one wonders how much he beheld of its inner beauty and greatness. He was a photographer of the Russian Jewish ghetto, not its philosopher. With *Fishke der Krumer* he made a pilgrimage to the towns and villages of the old Pale of Settlement. He puddled through its muddy streets, dark alleys, and swarming crowds. He slept in its synagogues, cemeteries, and cowsheds, and met and conversed with almost everybody. But all he brought back was a picture of a hopeless and helpless beggar-people, without spirit, without hope, without a future.

Peretz, too, knew the pain and the misery of the Jewish home and street. His *Travel Pictures* is a panorama of Polish Jewry in travail and suffering. But Peretz looked beyond its wretchedness and frustration to its qualities of heart and soul. He looked to the moral core of his men and women, their passionate faith, their lofty idealism, their spiritual greatness, with the result that under his hand the careworn, ghostlike creatures, never living beyond the shadow of their personal material wants, became transformed beings with something of the divine within them.

What made Mendele the favorite of the masses was that they found in him a friend and master they could understand. He did not soar too high above their comprehension. His instrument was conditioned to the popular taste and understanding. He was descriptive rather than imaginative. They discovered in his stories facts, faces, and incidents they knew very well. And he did not disdain to write in the language that many of his colleagues scornfully dubbed "Jargon." It was largely due to Mendele that the Yiddish novel, at that time crude and primitive, was raised to a work of high artistic merit.

When, late in life, Mendele visited Lodz, he was received like a national hero. Writes David Frishman of that visit: "Thousands crowded around the house where Mendele stayed, and waited. Men and women of all classes, children, and girls dressed in white and carrying flowers, stood and waited. For many hours they stood and waited. Thunderous cheers went up, 'Long live Mendele!' 'Long live the Grandfather!' The window panes and the very walls of the house shook and rattled. Mendele and his assembled friends did not dare leave the house. When by a ruse they hoped to pass unnoticed, Mendele was quickly recognized. Then there was pandemonium. What I saw then, I may never live to witness again. Thousands mobbed the carriage. It could not move a step. Unnumbered hands were stretched out toward Mendele. Wild cheers again went up, 'Long live Mendele!' 'Long live the Grandfather!' The carriage was lifted high above the heads of the people. And as Mendele was lifted up, it seemed to me that I, too, was lifted up with him."

Mendele is one of our most famous writers. He is notable for his style, his diction, and his comprehensive pictures of the *galut*. But he belongs to the past—more antiquarian than modern, more entertaining than helpful. Jews struggling for their national existence received little support or encouragement at his hands. Had he lived longer, even lived to see this day, it is doubtful whether he would have helped to hoist the flag of Zion.

Yet, with his contradictory qualities of strength and weakness, Mendele is a striking figure—perhaps the greatest from a world that has passed. In his pathos and his humor, and in the vast variety of characters and types that crowd his pages, future generations will catch a glimpse of a faded and vanished life. For Mendele was more than a writer. He was in his own personality a symbol of his people as they used to be.

Saul Tchernichovski

SAUL TCHERNICHOVSKI was a striking and novel figure in modern Hebrew literature. A creative artist of unusual gifts, he was a poet by divine grace, a man of primitive instincts who wrote and sang in a fresh and vigorous style rarely equaled by any other poet of the Hebrew Renaissance. Had he written in any language besides Hebrew he might have taken his place among the great poets of his time. But writing in the language of the Bible he joined the company of a great many other Hebrew poets whose talent and reputation cannot be measured by the size of their reading public.

Tchernichovski was striking not only for his talent but for his imposing physical appearance, which matched the massiveness of his poetic genius. He was a tall man with a powerful frame, a great head, a bushy mustache, an imposing forest of hair, and half-closed but keen and penetrating eyes—a veritable physical giant who could have given a good account of himself in any test of strength and muscle. He was an attractive figure after whom passers-by often turned for another look. Place Tchernichovski's picture in a gallery of the great poets of the world—Italian, French, English, Russian, *especially* Russian—and he would be among his own. But the weak-eyed, sunless Hebrew bards of the ghetto would never know him as belonging to their company.

And this incongruity of Saul Tchernichovski, who sang and wrote in the language of the Hebrew poets but was not, in his appearance and the universality of his creations, one of them, followed him all through his life—and in death. He was poor and lived amid material hardship all his life. The only economic security he enjoyed was during the last eight years of his life, when his strange odyssey brought him to Palestine—and then not as a poet but as an attending physician in the public schools in Tel Aviv. "He

385

occupied," writes the late Max Raisin, who visited him, "a tiny office with a conglomeration of books thrown about in disorder, and mixed in among them were bottles filled with medical fluids and surgical instruments." When Bialik died he was mourned by the Jews almost as a beloved son, a great national hero and poet, not unlike the way the death of Dr. Theodor Herzl was greeted. The death of Tchernichovski, on the other hand, as far as the great masses of the Jews were concerned, was passed over almost in silence; he was deeply mourned only by those who stood near him and recognized the magnitude of his poetic genius.

Why this difference between the two Hebrew poets? Why was the popularity so freely accorded to Bialik denied to Tchernichovski? The reason cannot be the difference in the quality of their genius, for it is not unlikely that of the two Tchernichovski was the greater technician, the more finished artist, the more enduring and universal poet. It is possible that with changing conditions of Jewish life in Israel Tchernichovski will be sung and read with no less love and admiration than was accorded to Bialik.

Tchernichovski himself was often depressed by the indifference of his people to him, by their coolness and aloofness. He did not for a moment doubt his strength or importance; nonetheless, he took his disappointment bitterly. To his closest friends he even complained about his people's neglect of him. He searched his mind and tried to account for it. He poured out his plaint in a bitter ironical poem, "A foreign plant art thou, a strange shoot to all." He came to ask the question, "Have I not been before my time, or has God not delayed my coming?"—a vain and conceited idea of himself, one might say, but one which in truth contains the key to the Tchernichovski riddle.

Saul Tchernichovski was indeed a "foreign plant," a "strange shoot" in the poetry of the Hebrew Renaissance—strange and foreign for his time and environment. He was born before his time in the sense that he belonged to the class of poets who do not follow in the traditional footsteps of their age or people. He was an originator and not an imitator, a creator and not a follower. He created his own style, fashioned his own tools, devised his own method and manner of writing. Everything was new; for him the world had just come into being. He took nothing from the past but left every-thing behind—the conventions, the practices, the traditions of his time.

It was a new song that he sang to his people—a song of strength, life, and beauty. Nature bewitched him, love encircled him; trees, mountains, flowers, glistening dewdrops filled him with delight and rapture. His heart pulsed with life and movement. "I write," he said, "because I live, because at this very moment I feel the song of life in my heart. It is the song of triumph over chaos and void." He was aware of the flaming sun, the paling moon, the star-studded sky, the brook, the lake, the sea in its storms and calm, the warb-ling bird, the speckled butterfly, and the thousand changing moods of nature. To all these things he felt himself related; his eyes, his ears, his heart saw them, heard them, felt them. Not a thing in the vast panorama of earth and sky escaped him. His soul roamed over the wide expanse of nature. He was part of it and it belonged to him. He thrilled to its every whispered secret. And it was of these things that he made his songs, that he spun and wove and fashioned his loveliest poems.

He hated poverty, ugliness, depression and tried to keep himself unconscious of their existence. Tears and sighs evoked wrath and anger in him. The only struggle he recognized was to realize him-self, to fulfill himself, to remain true to his pagan joy of life. Joy of life! This is the secret of Tchernichovski, his task, his mission. No one preached it with a clearer voice. He was the joy-intoxicated singer of his people, their first and their greatest. The joyous song of Israel which had lain dormant many a generation was revived in him. It became renewed in him in all its old-time strength and beauty. Once again, after its millennial sleep, one could hear it, feel it, experience it as it had once flowed from the lips of the bard of the Song of Songs.

It was a song to which the ears of a people living for hundreds of years in the gloom and poverty of dismal ghettos had grown unaccustomed. They were not trained for such songs but rather for the wail and dirge of the poets of lamentation. Their eyes were blind to the beauty and their ears deaf to the song of the things they had never seen or heard in the darkened life of their miserable existence. To be sure, Hebrew poets occasionally wrote of love and nature, greeted the arrival of spring and summer, and composed neat little lines in the approved biblical style to the mistress of their heart. But it was not from inner compulsion, from a deep instinctive intoxication with these things, but from a desire to follow the fashion.

When Tchernichovski's first book of collected verse, *Hesyonot u-Manginot* (Visions of Songs), appeared in 1889, when the poet was twenty-six years old, it was received coldly, even with astonishment and resentment, by the few who read it. His poems represented a strange departure from the conventional tradition of the Hebrew poets, and critics attacked the singer for doing violence to the language of the Bible by making it serve such "trivial" themes as nature, love, and the like. What a jarring note to his early contemporaries must have been lines like:

> Let us joy and exult in our love, dear,
> Let us shout and sing gladly today,
> While our skies are o'ermantled with glory
> Ere the clouds lower dark on our way.
> While our cheeks are still burning with blushes,
> While my heart and thy heart are aflame,
> While youth tide and joy tide are still with us
> Ere they pass and then nought can reclaim.
> Ere the shadows of even have fallen,
> Let us breathe of life's frolic, be gay,
> We'll have joy and exult in our love, dear,
> We'll shout and we'll sing while we may.

It was Reuben Brainin, perhaps the first "European" in Hebrew literature, always on the alert for the new word and promising talent, who not only went to the defense of the young poet but hailed him as a new star in the Hebrew literary firmament.

Saul Tchernichovski broke with the literary tradition of his forebears in still another and graver way. He came to Hebrew literature with no shackles on his mind. Unlike many other Jewish writers and poets, he had not brought with him the heritage of the synagogue or the yeshiva. He was a stranger to that tradition which Bialik so magnificently extolled in his poem *Ha-Matmid*. He never knew the discipline of the *heder*, the rigorous life of the Talmud student, the grinding days and dismal nights of study. His childhood memories contained none of the things that cramped and confined one's spirit. On the contrary he looked back to a sunny childhood in his parents' home, a life free from the fears and inhibitions that rendered the existence of most of his fellow poets a prolonged agony.

He was born in 1873 in a small country town in the Crimea, where intercourse between the Jewish and peasant children was normal and natural. Together they romped and played, without the least restraint or hindrance. He loved his native land with the joy and devotion of a Russian peasant rooted in his ancestral soil. There are many allusions in his poems to the early history of South Russia, and the Scythians and the Khazars both find a place in his long folk-poem *B'rit Milah* (Circumcision).

His parents were moderately well-to-do people and the family had a background of bodily vigor and fairly good education. While his parents observed more or less punctiliously the ceremonial rituals of their religion, there was no fanaticism in their home. Indeed, youthful Saul studied the Russian language before he acquired even a reading knowledge of the Hebrew prayers. While he did not have the training of a *heder*, he learned Hebrew from travelling teachers who knew better how to win the affection of the budding young poet for the language and literature of his people than the traditional *melamed* did. The results of his education are perhaps the best proof, if any is needed, that the heder is *not* necessarily the indispensable instrument for implanting love and devotion to their faith in the hearts of the young that so many think it to be.

He learned quickly and thoroughly. Before long he was reading the Bible, the romances of Mapu, the stories of Mendele, and whatever other books came his way. He also read Hebrew translations of the classics of other languages, among them the transla-

tions of Kalman Schulman and the *Vale of Cedars,* by Grace
Agular. "I remember," he writes, "how I sat and wept over the
Vale of Cedars. It was the first Hebrew book I read. How I hated
Rashi—that man who found difficulties at every corner when the
Bible text was so clear and beautiful."

It was, however, the strong, the heroic, the adventurous, that
he loved in the Bible, not its laws and precepts. From his youth he
was on the side of the winner, the victor, the conqueror. In his
veins flowed the blood of the heroes of Israel, the conquerors of
Canaan—Joshua, the Judges, the Maccabees, Bar Kochba. His
hero was not Moses, for whom he had slight regard, but his disciple,
Joshua, the stormer of Jericho, the slayer of the thirty-one kings,
the winner of the Holy Land. He wasted no sympathy on the defeated. In one of his first poems he sings the song of the sword. "My
sword, my sword! Where is my sword, my avenging sword?" he
cries.

When a poet who hates the common and the ugly becomes
acquainted with the pain and misery of the Jewish ghetto life one
of two things happen: he will either be subdued by it or he will
struggle against it and attempt to overcome it. There was no
thought in the mind of Tchernichovski of letting himself be
crushed by the dismal lot of his people. He was too young, too
confident, too high-spirited. What he saw and experienced when
he left his father's home and went out into the world failed to
quench the fire and song that was in his heart. The nightingale is
not discouraged by the storm. Tchernichovski's reaction to the
pain and misery of his people was:

> Life is round me, light is round me,
> Magic songs and songs of glee,
> Melodies from Eden's garden,
> Songs of the prisoner set free.

This, however, does not mean that Tchernichovsky was blissfully
ignorant of his nation's fate or that he failed to sympathize with
his brethren. Quite the contrary is true. He felt their sufferings
deeply, both in a personal and in a national sense. Bitterly he

raged against their enemies in language that is rare for its wrath and anger. He contemplates his nation's heroic record and shudders at the spectacle of its present impotence. Thus, in a poem, "Hanukah Night," he protests:

> Over the housetops on the wings of the
>   wind
> Hover dark hosts—the shadows of the night,
> Lifeless and still, that were a mighty
>   band.
> Staring with sockets that were anguished
>   eyes:
> 'Lo! These are the Maccabees! These
>   heaps of bones,
> These shrivelled hands, these bloodless
>   arteries,
> These blighted brains—'tis a miracle
>   they live,
> Who live and live not, aged ere their
>   time—
> Sans strength or power, but with
>   craven cowardice
> Bent double like a willow o'er the
>   brook;
> They have not seen God's light, their
>   life's a coin,
> Their hapless soul knows not what
>   beauty is;
> In chains of the king's law, dogma and
>   its bonds,
> These errant plod on and sin for bread.

Some time before the appearance of Tchernichovski there were similar cries of protest against the atrophy of the spirit that made the Jews an enslaved people, powerless against their enemies. One remembers J. L. Gordon's last historical poem, "King Zedekiah in Prison." But whereas the tragedy of King Zedekiah, according to Gordon, was due to the age-old conflict between the synagogue and the state, something similar to the German *Kulturkampf* at the time of Bismarck, the tragedy of the Jews, in Tchernichovski's judgment, lay in the people's own inner decay, in shutting themselves in behind fences and dusty walls, in exchanging the sword for the book, life for the synagogue. To him the tragedy of the Jews in the Diaspora is that a great and heroic people had become old, weak, and submissive, and that their God, as they conceived him, had grown old like them.

It is this attitude that makes Saul Tchernichovski so bold, so unique a spirit of the Hebrew Renaissance. Unlike Bialik, he rails against his own people rather than against the world. They fill him with bitterness, protest, and revolt. He directs stinging words against them. It is not that the world had betrayed the Jews but that the Jews had betrayed themselves. They are untrue to their past, to their tradition, to the heroic example of their forefathers. Why were there such valiant men in those days? Why only in those days could Jews fight, conquer, triumph? Had the Jew's arm lost its cunning or his hand forgotten how to wield a sword?

There had been rebels in earlier days, rebels against what they called the enslavement of the Jewish spirit, and Tchernichovski, though of a later time, may be said to have been the stormiest of them all. Hebrew literature, the literature of the Haskalah, was conceived in rebellion and born in protest. Almost all its greatest spirits, with such exceptions as are typified by Mapu, with his idylls, were apostles of revolt. Smolenskin waged war against small-town fanaticism; Lilienblum struggled against the rule of rabbinism; J. L. Gordon against talmudic "despotism," Berditchevski against the supplanting of the Jew by Judaism, and Brenner against the Jew's nostalgic infatuation with the past. As against one Ahad Ha'am, who preached an abstraction, holding out to his contemporaries the unsurmised wealth of the old values, there were any number of voices that cried for change and clamored for revision.

Saul Tchernichovski was the flaming sword of this rebellion. If there is any value in his work it lies in his resistance to the past, to things as they are, to the taming and shackling of the spirit of his people by an "outlived" tradition. He was a revolutionary through and through. There was not a drop of conservative blood in his veins. Somewhat younger than some of his fellow soldiers in the holy war of liberation, he went faster and farther than most of them. Whereas Berditchevski drew a line between the biblical and the post-biblical tradition, the first of which he honored and the latter scorned. Tchernichovski was not satisfied with even this distinction. For in many of his poems there is an undercurrent, strong and fervent, which is neither biblical nor talmudic, having as little to do with the prophets as with the rabbis, trumpeting a new faith, announcing amid the thunder and lightning of his most striking and original lines the descent of a new deity.

What is the origin, the dwelling place of this deity whom Tchernichovski proclaimed with so much noise and clamor? He did not descend from Sinai. Israel knew him not. He is a stranger to the Jewish tradition. Indeed, their prophets and sages had spent many long generations in waging war against him. Pious Jews turned away from him as an abomination. He is Apollo, the gay and lusty Apollo, the Greek sun god, a god renowned in battle, skilled in the use of the bow and arrow, a god who slew Titans; and his dwelling place was Mount Parnassus.

It was this jolly deity of ancient Hellas, whose marble brow is untroubled by the pain and misery of a groaning world, that inspired Tchernichovski to some of his most vigorous lines. After seeking in vain, in the miserable state of his people, a sign of the old Jehovah, God of the ancient Hebrews, the conqueror of Canaan whose garments were red with the blood of his enemies, he turns in desperation to the "god of might and giants on earth."

> Thou eyest me astonished! For I have
> come
> Farther than all before me; on the road
> Behind me men wander, chained to
> death.
> I am the first to come to thee again,
> This instant, weary of the age-long
> moan,
> I rend the shackles bound about my
> soul;

My soul is living and it clings to earth.
The people have grown old—their God
    with them
I bend the knee to life, to beauty,
    power,
To every form of grace—these have
    subdued
Man's body and the soul corrupt of
    men,
And rule o'er life in place of Zuri
    Shaddai,
Lord God of the deserts which no eye
    hath seen,
Of the conquerors of Canaan in the
    storm—
But they bound him up in straps—
    phylacteries.

It was certainly as unconventional a theme as any Jewish poet had ever made the language of the Bible serve. But he went even further than this. He would burn with his scorching breath everything that had gone before, so that from the destruction of the old values new life might emerge. He longed for the outer world, for the witchery of strength, beauty, and song—the world that was shut to the Jew by the "catastrophe" of the spirit. His standards were more Nietzschian than Jewish. He searched the Bible and Jewish history for strong Jews rather than pious Jews, for Jews who were loyal to the commands of life rather than to the commands of God—pre-Torah Jew he was called. These he found among the followers of the so-called false prophets. In a poem, "Of the Visions of the False Prophets," he castigates the prophets of the Bible for their having misled and deceived the people by their impossible vision of other-worldliness. He plowed under the millennial tradition of his people and composed songs to Bel and Ashtarta, the very heathen deities against which the Bible spoke with scorn. In a rollicking song Tchernichovski bewails the death of Tammuz, the Babylonian god of Spring and fertility:

Go, daughters of Zion
And weep you for Tammuz,
For Tammuz, the beautiful Tammuz,
    is dead;
And days dark with clouds and eclipse
    of the soul,
Autumn days endless, dull days are
    ahead.

What dance shall we dance
Around the high altar?
What dance shall we dance for Tammuz
    this day?
To the left, to the right, and sevenfold
    seven,
We shall bow to him, calling, "return
    to our play."

But always, always, the motif is the same. The life-intoxicated poet roams over the whole wide world seeking the life force he cannot find in the wail and lament of his people. When, however, he apotheosizes Apollo or sings to the pagan deities it is not because they are heathen gods but because they are symbols of light and life, the very qualities the God of the Hebrew, conqueror of Canaan stood for, and because he feels that there are things more lasting than parchments, more enduring than laws and commandments. Even in his later poems he never wearies extolling strength and beauty as the greatest of gifts given to man.

He lived for some time in Odessa, the beautiful city on the Black Sea. There he met and mingled with the leading spirits of the Hebrew revival and the Jewish national movement. For Odessa was to the Jews what Weimar, in the days of Goethe, was to the Germans. Mendele, Ahad Ha'am, and Bialik were the major luminaries of that group of men, but around them revolved no lesser lights than Lilienblum, Klausner, and Ussishkin. Dr. Pinsker was already dead, but his influence was still a living force. It was the springtime of *Hibat Zion,* and modern Zionism was being born under the inspiration of Dr. Herzl.

The company in which he found himself in Odessa had a powerful effect on the young poet. He naturally became a Zionist and vied with Bialik to be the Poet Laureate of his people. Bialik, however, won out, for Tchernichovski's muse could not be restrained, but still broke forth in one disapproved form or another. He still sang of strength, might, and will to conquest—a far cry from the gentler spirit of his brother poet. When Ahad Ha'am preached the "spiritual center," Tchernichovski sang:

> Towards Zion your banners, O strong
>   ones of Judah,
> Our God, O my brothers, is fortress
>   and all,
> If bulwarks be lacking, our bosoms are
>   ready
> Our hearts linked together will serve
>   as a wall.

He sang the song of hope but also the song of wrath and anger. But by now, however, not against his own people but against their persecutors and tormentors. Whereas Bialik is made almost impotent by his rebellion against injustice, uttering laments instead of resolves and threats, Tchernichovski, in unrestrained exuberance of youth, girds his sword and rides forth to put his enemies to rout.

To his Jewish national songs, written in his later years, belong some of the most beautiful of his poems. They are gentle and soothing, winning the heart with their almost unbelievable splendor of style and rhythm, as if the influence of the Holy Land, where he spent the last eight years of his life, had softened and mellowed some of his wonted harshness. There is fire in them, but it is a fire that warms and inspires. His muse is still secular, but it almost reaches the intensity of religious conviction. What can be more gentle and bewitching in its effect than the new dawn he describes as breaking upon the ancient land and dispelling its ancient gloom? Or his tender, almost caressing, greeting to the returning exiles? Or the dialogue between the young Jew and Rabbi Akiba, the one master of the Jewish tradition upon whom the poet lavished his love:

Peace to thee, Akiba!
My teacher, peace to thee!
Where are all the hallowed?
Where the Maccabees?
Answers thus Akiba,
Thus he answers me,
"All Israel is hallowed;
You are the Maccabee! "

When Tchernichovski greeted with silence the storm of pain and agony that followed the Kishinev slaughter—the agony so bitterly and graphically described by Bialik in his two poems *Al ha-Shehitah* (On the Slaughter), and *B'ir ha-Regah* (In the City of Slaughter), the Jewish world felt disappointed. Was it possible that Tchernichovski had deserted his people, that the strings of his lyre were not responsive to his nation's pain and sorrow? Had he no balm for their wounds, no burst of anger for their enemies? And, indeed, Joseph Klausner, Tchernichovski's most intimate friend, rebuked him for his baffling reticence. But the poet, wounded and smitten though he was, remained silent. He did not rise to the occasion and do what was expected of him. In a revealing letter to his friend, the poet wrote: "All life around me is steeped in a sea of tears. . . . All poets should by right be poets of conquest, but the ugliness of life, poverty, oppression and evil, make many of them poets of defeat. I am a poet of conquest, but, as a Jew it is my destiny to be a poet of defeat. And against this fate, I struggle, and even as a Jew, I am the bearer of the song of conquest. But when I really feel defeated, I am silent, for the conquered have no songs but dirges."

This was typical of Tchernichovski, typical of the man who would not allow depression to master him and who, even when he wrote of defeat, wrote not as one vanquished but victor. There is perhaps no more striking illustration of this than his long poem, "Baruch mi-Magenz," written shortly before the Kishinev massacre, and which as a historical narrative stands unequaled in Hebrew literature. In this poem, almost too poignant to read, are gathered all the pain and agony of his people's sufferings. One may detect in it the voices of the past, the anguish of the present, the stifled cries of a thousand pogroms, massacres, and destructions. Yet there are neither tears nor moans in the moving and touching drama, no attempt at arousing the world's sympathy or compassion for the victim. Indeed, Baruch moves about the stage not as the victim but as the hero of the story.

In a massacre of the Jews of Mayance, Germany, during the First Crusade, Baruch loses his wife. That his two daughters might not be ravished by the blood-intoxicated rabble, he slays them with his own hands, and then, in order to execute the revenge he has planned, he allows himself to be carried off to the church and baptized. Alone in his cell in the monastery he sees an oil lamp swinging before a holy image. Ah, his opportunity for revenge— the sweet, longed-for opportunity he had dreamed of through half-crazed days and nights! He quickly gathers all the inflammable stuff he can lay his hands on, soaks it well in the oil from the lamp, and sets it afire. How his greedy heart leaps for joy as his eyes watch the bursting flames lap the altar, the holy images, the walls, the ceiling, everything in the monastery, as it crackles and snaps with a musical sound! From the monastery the flames spread to the town hall, to the whole city. Soon everything is a mass of flaming red, with men, women, and children victims of the conflagration. At last Baruch has his revenge. That he might not miss a detail of his work of destruction, he runs frenziedly through the debris of the smoking streets secretly enjoying the devastation his act of revenge had wrought. Nay, more: he goes to the cemetery to tell his wife how he has avenged her and their children.

"Baruch mi-Magenza" represents the high-water mark of Tchernichovski's poetic genius, although he wrote many other things which reveal the artist and the almost perfect architect of style and composition. This phase of his work cannot properly be disposed of without making mention of at least a few more of his longer poems distinguished for their poetic insight and narrative style. Almost at random one thinks of *B'rit Milah* (Circumcision), *L'bibot M'bushalot* ('Pancakes), *Hatanuta shel Elkah* (Elka's Wedding), *K'hom Hayom* (In the Heat of the Day), *Ma'aseh b'Mordecai v'Yoakim* (Story of Mordecai and Joachim). There is pathos in them, as well as humor and an almost unbelievable mastery of detail. But there are also resignation, faith, and struggle for existence—struggle without outward evidence of tears and suffering.

He is the first Hebrew-language poet to sing of the everyday life of the peasant, the farmer, the shepherd, the coachman, the black-smith, and the first to make room on his canvas for men and women not of his people—the Russian muzhik, the Tartars, the Cossacks, with whom Jewish writers for the most part had less than a passing acquaintance. But Tchernichovski knew them from his childhood and there was in his nostrils the hot breath of their labor and their soil.

Although not deeply religious, he could not resist the romance and beauty of the Jewish holidays as he had seen them observed in his parents' home, and in his poetry he left touching pictures of them. What could be more surprising than that Tchernichovski, the great humanist, the pantheist—one might say the man who merged his life with the life of every living thing, animate and inanimate—should sing with such rapture and such an intense warmth of feeling of such themes as *Leil Hanukah* (Hanukah Night), *Moze Shabbat* (Departure of Sabbath), *Hakafot* (Rejoicing of the Law), *Olat Regel* (Pilgrim Festival)?

Saul Tchernichovski was unquestionably the most cultivated and accomplished of Hebrew poets. His milieu was not the ghetto but the world. While others had depth in varying degrees, he had both depth and breadth. What he lacked of Talmudic learning he amply made up for by his knowledge of the arts, the sciences, languages, and universal literature. He studied at several universities, specializing in mathematics and the natural sciences, with courses in philosophy and literature. He read and absorbed the best that was written in German, French, English, and Russian. He excelled in the latter particularly, and, aside from Hebrew, refused to speak any other language. Gorky remarked to a friend that Tchernichovski was so thoroughly Russian that, had he chosen to write in that language, he might have become one of the great Russian writers.

He may be said to have been the first European to breathe into

Hebrew literature the modern spirit and the first to introduce into it the classical wealth of other nations. Until his appearance Hebrew literature was an artificial thing—a hot-house plant, as it were, feeding on itself, impervious to the currents of the outer world. Tchernichovski modernized it by bringing into it the cross currents of the thinking and history of other men and other ages. His translations, including those of Shakespeare, Byron, Shelley, Burns, Molière, Alfred de Musset, Goethe, Dehmel, and Longfellow, also included ancient writings extending backward to the hymns of Egypt, the myths of Babylon, the epic poems of Homer, and the dialogues of Plato. The Finnish White Rose was awarded him for his Hebrew translation of the Finnish epic *Kalevala*.

He was also the most widely traveled of Hebrew poets. He visited and lived in many lands, in both the Old World and the New. He studied in Germany, France, and Switzerland; he visited in Finland, the United States, and the Argentine, and was in Palestine at least once before he made his home there. After he took his medical degree he practiced his profession in small Russian village communities, where months sometimes passed without his seeing the face of a Jew—he, the singer of his people! He also knew the horrors and dangers of war. He served at the front in the First World War, and afterward, as a doctor, in the hospitals of the Russian capital.

Through all the vicissitudes and experiences of his strange destiny his nature remained cheerful, his spirit gay, his heart young, never despairing for a moment. His love for every living and breathing thing, his feeling of kinship with the great Universal Spirit that quickens and animates all things down to the lowest blade of grass, was the buoyant force that kept his heart from sinking when he had every reason to feel the neglect and ingratitude of his people. He was the great virtuoso who kept the lyre of his people alive with melody to the very last, when, in 1941, a cruel disease stilled his fingers on its strings, and he died at the age of sixty-eight.

Asher Ginzberg (Ahad Ha'am)

TO THIS DAY, seventy-three years after his name first appeared in print and more than thirty-five years after his death, one still cannot think of Asher Ginzberg, who wrote under the pen name of Ahad Ha'am, without the same awe and reverence he inspired when he lived and labored on this earth. His impact on his time was more than that of a great thinker, a great teacher, a great writer and editor who trained a whole generation of Hebrew writers. For he was a great and exalted soul, a man of prophetic stature and vision, closely related to the great Jewish spirits of the past.

Many exceptionally gifted men in the days of Ahad Ha'am made their mark as writers, thinkers, poets, and leaders; but Ahad Ha'am influenced and dominated them all. They accepted his leadership, and when they differed with him at all, as sometimes they did, they did so meekly and humbly, as when one finds himself at odds with a beloved and venerated master.

Ahad Ha'am was the most original of Hebrew writers. Everything about him was new—ideas, style, and diction. A high seriousness and deep sense of responsibility dominated the man and everything he wrote. He spent more time in studying than in writing. He wrote with exceeding moderation and reserve, never using two words where one would do. He realized the importance of his work but was oblivious to flattery and was not given to lofty self-appraisal. Indeed, he was a meek and modest man, always conscious of, if not weighed down by, his inborn sense of responsibility.

Asher Ginzberg was not a prolific writer. His literary career was comparatively brief and, in point of quantity, not very productive. His greatest and most lasting work was confined to the *Hashiloh,* which he edited. But as comparatively meager as his literary output was, every word that came from his pen was judiciously weighed and balanced—a model of logical thinking and reasoning. His essays were read and reread with undiminished interest by a constantly growing following, both in translations and in their original language. The late Israel Friendlaender, who translated Ginzberg into German and English, very properly observed that Ahad Ha'am was the first to bring into the Hebrew movement the spirit of truth-seeking, good manners, and rigid ethical standards.

He was the first great moral personality in modern Hebrew literature. Not a few Hebrew writers, untrained in the ways and amenities of the world, writes the late Max Raisin, were wont to regard each other as competitors for a seat in the temple of immortality—which was about all they aimed at in their scholarly labors. There was little friendly feeling among them, little of the spirit of camaraderie and the feeling that they were working for the same high purpose. Ahad Ha'am taught his colleagues to be human toward each other even as he taught them to write clearly and precisely, with the result that there is hardly a Hebrew writer whose style has not been refined and whose attitude has not been influenced by him.

In his youth in the "benighted village" in which he was born Asher Ginzberg was lacerated by the same religious doubts and uncertainties that plagued his young contemporaries. In his lonely study he kept in close touch with the intellectual life of Europe through the books and periodicals which he read and studied. He was conscious of the cleavage between the old and the new, between Judaism and the world. He, therefore, watched sympathetically as the young Jewish intellectuals emerged from the *yeshiva* restless and impatient, angry young men vacillating between Nietzsche and the Bible, between Schopenhauer and Hillel. There was rebellion in their minds. They cried out for a change, for a transvaluation of the old Jewish traditions. They saw decadence in Judaism, decadence in the Jewish people. The Talmud, they maintained, had encoffined both Judaism and the Jews, had stifled their energies and smothered their creative spirit. Mordecai Eherenpreis and

Jacob Thon, accomplished Hebrew writers and scholars, were in the shock brigade, with Mivah Berdichevski, the most brilliant and radical of them all, leading in the controversy.

Asher Ginzberg, or as he was best known in the Hebrew literary world, Ahad Ha'am, was like a torch in the night. He agreed with the dissenters that somehow the cleavage must be healed. But, deeper student of Judaism and Jewish history that he was, in the words of Leon Simon, Ahad Ha'am's latest biographer, he formulated the theory that "Judaism, which he identified with the creativity of the Jewish people, was not an old-fashioned system of beliefs and practices, antithetic by its very nature to modern thought and progress. It was itself a part of humanistic culture; it was the Jewish people's distinctive way of expressing universal, human ideas, which other nations expressed each in its own distinctive way." The first requirement, he said, for those who thirst for western culture is "to delve into the past of their own people, to rediscover and revivify the humanist element in the Jewish tradition. That once done, it would again be possible for a living Judaism, developing in accordance with the law of its being, to meet other cultures on equal terms, and to give as well as receive in the commerce of ideas and ideals."

Asher Ginzberg, who was born to Hasidic parents on August 18, 1856, was not a product of the *yeshiva*. Indeed, there were no *yeshivot* in the unenlightened Hasidic area of the Ukraine, in southern Russia, where his childhood was spent. The heder, the old-fashioned educational establishment where young Asher received his first lessons in the Hebrew language, lingered long in his mind, and he recalled it with no special pleasure. Learning and piety were the twin ideal of Jewish education, and the youthful student applied himself to both with great devotion. He was an exceptionally gifted boy, docile, studious, and quick to learn. He showed a special aptitude for talmudic studies; so that, when he was at the age of sixteen, recognised authorities reckoned with his proficiency in rabbinic learning. This naturally delighted his father, who, himself a scholar, had hoped his son would be a rabbi. In this Isaiah Ginzberg was disappointed, for his son's avidity for knowledge

turned to other fields of learning than the Talmud. But his greatest
disappointment was that Asher refused to join him on his annual
pilgrimage to the "court" of the famous Sadigora Zaddik, to whose
Hasidic brotherhood he belonged. The boy naturally was brought
up to revere the holy man as a near-divinity and when he was
approaching Bar Mitzvah his father took him to the saint of Sadigora for his blessing. But that was the first and the last time that
Asher Ginzberg allowed himself to be regaled by the wild and unruly crowd of Galician Hasidim, dancing and shouting ecstatically
around their man-idol, the Zaddik of Sadigora. His sensitivity was
hurt by and disgusted with all he saw, felt, and experienced at the
"court" of the celebrated Rabbi, and he vowed never again would
he be seen in its precincts. At the age of thirteen, Asher Ginzberg,
much to the chagrin of his father, became a *Mitnaged,* an
Oppositionist.

Asher Ginzberg, an only son of well-to-do parents, spent his
boyhood years in a large, well-appointed, even luxurious, house of
many rooms and a staff of servants, with a flower garden, orchard,
and a river near-by in which he could swim, float sail boats, and do
many of the things children of his age enjoy. But Asher did none
of these things. In fact his boyhood was not a particularly happy
one, and in his reminiscences, brief and casual, he rarely dwells
upon his childhood. Nature had little attraction for him; he was
more of the *talmid hakam* than the poet. There is not a lyrical line
in any of his writings. His relation to his parents was more correct
and dutiful than affectionate. There was little intimacy between his
parents and himself—indeed, there was little intimacy with anybody around him. He had no brother and no playmates on the big
estate on which he lived. His father was proud of the progress his
son was making in his studies but never encouraged him by a
tender word or a flattering remark. "There can be little doubt,"
writes Leon Simon, "that he was emotionally starved"—which
may be responsible for his shy and cold demeanor in his later years.

Isaiah Ginzberg could not have been the bigoted person one
would imagine a fanatical follower of the Hasidic Sadigora saint
to be, since he permitted such works as those of the medieval

Jewish philosophers and the books of the Haskalah in his library. The budding Ahad Ha'am saturated himself with the philosophical and ethical treasures he discovered among his father's books. He read and studied them till they became part of him. But it was Maimonides who had the greatest attraction for his maturing mind. Strangely he thought he had found many of his own ideas reflected in *The Guide for the Perplexed*. He pored and lingered long over its pages. He subordinated all other books to the study of this work, which somehow he sensed would one day play an important part in his life and thinking. It was out of this youthful preoccupation with Maimonides' philosophy that many years later emerged Ahad Ha'am's brilliant essay, "Sovereignty of Reason," with a penetrating analysis of Maimonides' philosophy and his thoughts on religion and the Bible. To this period of his life may also be ascribed his germinal thoughts on Moses, which later matured in his article on the Lawgiver, whose image, he said, enshrined in the hearts of the Jewish people, is a more correct testimony of his historical existence than the results of biblical scientific criticism.

Unfortunately, Asher Ginzberg's reveries did not remain long undisturbed, for there was a change in the family's circumstances, and the young man, who by that time had a wife and two children, was compelled to grapple with the hard realities of life, for which he was ill prepared. His father had lost his lease on the estate he managed, and he looked for some other means of subsistence for his family and himself. Isaiah Ginzberg would have taken to farming or gone to Palestine as an agriculturalist, but he was dissuaded by his son, whose opinion by now his father seriously considered. They drifted for some time from one place to another, until, in 1886, they finally settled in Odessa. There, too, fortune failed to smile on them. In a succession of business enterprises, in which Asher acted as manager, Isaiah lost his money and the family was plunged into poverty.

To Asher Ginzberg, soon to emerge as the world-famous Ahad Ha'am, apart from his financial position the "escape" from the village to Odessa was like a flight from darkness to light, from frustration and despair to opportunity and hope. To be sure, his years in Gopitshitza were not idle ones. He had become an accomplished Talmudist, had read and thought a great deal, and stored away ideas which he later molded into brilliant essays. But he was starved for books and intellectual companionship—books above all things. Odessa, an important port on the Black Sea, gave him everything he needed for his mental and spiritual growth and development. It was a beautiful city with a large Jewish population and many high-minded and profound scholars and idealists. Zionism, under the banner of *Hibbat Zion,* the Love of Zion, was greatly in vogue there, with Dr. Leo Pinsker, whom he later immortalized in his famous essay, "Pinsker and his Brochure," at its head.

Asher Ginzberg did not immediately reveal himself. He was modest and retiring and not quite sure of himself. He read and studied, devouring whatever books and ideas, from both Jewish and foreign sources, he could lay hold of. He continued his investigations in medieval Jewish and modern Hebrew literature, and he familiarized himself with the works of the outstanding Russian, French, and English writers. What he read passed through the crucible of his mind and not infrequently influenced his own thoughts and ideas. His intense diligence, immense learning, and deep insight began to attract wide attention, and a coterie of friends and admirers gathered about him. They knew they had a genius in their midst, a trail blazer in the Jewish renaissance. In the confusion and turmoil of the Jewish world situation he was looked to for leadership; but he would rather listen than speak, and his scholarly caution and his reticence disqualified him for leadership. Nevertheless there was little that affected Jewish life on which he was not consulted.

For his first three years in Odessa, eventful and critical years in the life of Russian Jewry, Asher Ginzberg, who impressed every one with his fine intellect and great learning, was not moved to raise his voice on the issues and problems with which the Jews of the world were confronted. Was he not concerned with the tragic fate of the Jews, their shocking poverty and homelessness? It was not long after the savage pogroms of 1881, in which hundreds of Jews were murdered and thousands driven from their homes. Asher Ginzberg's own family were victims of the May Laws which followed the pogroms and which forbade the leasing of estates to Jews. Shaken by the outrages and seeing no future for the Jews in Russia, Dr. Leo Pinsker, a prominent physician in Odessa, wrote his famous pamphlet *Auto-Emancipation,* long regarded as the first modern Zionist manifesto, in which he advocated the emigration of the Jews to other lands where they could acquire land for colonization and thus pave the way for their self-emancipation. Pinsker laid his finger on the root of the malady from which the Jews were suffering. There will always be anti-Semitism in the world as long as there are Jews, he said, notwithstanding appeals, complaints, and campaigns against it. For anti-Semitism is a congenital fear of ghosts, and since the destruction of their state Jews have been little more than disembodied spirits without a national existence. The only means of liberation, according to Pinsker, is the creation of a national state by the Jewish people on their own land.

Pinsker's brochure electrified the Jewish world. It was widely read and translated into many languages. It became the grand text of the "Lovers of Zion" and a challenging summons to action. The brochure and the agitation of the *Hoveve Zion* for rapid colonization in Palestine created so great a stir that a number of Jewish university students organized themselves under the banner of **BILU**, formed from the initial letters of the Hebrew *Bet Ya'akov leku v'nelka* (House of Jacob, come and let us go), and left for Palestine as pioneers, to colonize their ancient homeland. Unfortunately, however, there was more valor and idealism in the enterprise than practical wisdom and knowledge of the land. The young men and women were poorly equipped to cope with the difficulties and hardships the undertaking entailed. Were they ever so strong and willing and ever so dedicated, they could not with their bare hands drain the marshes, clear away the rocks, and make livable the land, despoiled and neglected for two thousand years. The inevitable result was that those who did not die of malaria returned to their Russian homes, disappointed and heartbroken.

The debacle of the BILU and the doldrums into which the Zionist movement had fallen shook Asher Ginzberg out of his retirement, and for the first time, much to his reluctance, he permitted his writings to appear in public print. It was not, however, without the pressure of his friends and the insistence of Alexander Zederbaum, the redoubtable editor of *Hamelitz,* a Hebrew publication, that he was prevailed upon to contribute an article to the paper. It was his first serious contribution and it contained in essence the whole philosophy of Zionism which he developed throughout the forty years of his literary career. The article appeared in the *Hamelitz* in the year 1889, under the title, *Lo Ze Haderek* (Such is Not the Way), and was signed Ahad Ha'am (One of the People), a pen name which became a household word in cultured Jewish circles all over the world and which to this day is held in deepest respect and reverence.

As the title implies, it was a polemical article written with all the freshness and vigor of the author's young manhood—he was then thirty-three. It was also a courageous arraignment of the Zionist principles and methods of colonizing the Holy Land. The zealots were for immediate and rapid colonization of Palestine, whereas Ahad Ha'am, the sober evolutionary thinker, was for slow growth and development; to them every dunam of land won, every new colony, every house, even every goat, strengthened the Jewish position in Palestine; to him the winning of hearts through a process of propaganda and education meant more in the long run than the acquisition of colonies, houses, and goats. He sought to inject a new spirit and new life into the Lovers of Zion, to interpret anew and reveal to his readers the inner principles which motivated the old Hibbat Zion. He pleaded not only for set objectives but for a revival of national sentiment and consciousness by which the objectives would be attained. The malady of Zionism that made Hibbat Zion lose its original inspiring momentum, he said, was not external but internal and spiritual. Therefore the remedy also must be internal and spiritual. He argued that a people long in exile cannot be re-established in its ancient homeland under the pressure of a moment. Confining itself to material remedial efforts, Zionism will not succeed. A score of colonies in Palestine will not stem the spiritual decay of both the Jews and Judaism, will not save the Jewish soul, will not even save the Jews, since the great majority of them are doomed to remain in the Diaspora.

What, then, is to be done? Israel Friedlaender interprets the philosophical theoretician of Zionism as meaning that every goal must be preceded by a desire, and that the greater the goal, the keener and greater must be the desire. "If you desire, then it is no fairy tale," Herzl's motto of his Altneuland, coincides precisely with Ahad Ha'am's conviction. There is no aim that cannot be reached if it is but strongly and energetically willed. Zionism as an ideal is surrounded with innumerable gigantic difficulties; therefore the desire for its attainment must likewise be boundless and gigantic. Such desire, he characteristically maintained, can be brought about by what he called *tehiyyat ha-levavot* (revival of the hearts) of the Jews, by developing all the spiritual means at their disposal to strengthen the Jewish religion, Jewish literature, Jewish history, Jewish art—in short to strengthen all those manifestations of the Jewish spirit which we compress into the word "Judaism," or, in modern times, into the words "Jewish culture."

This Jewish culture of which Ahad Ha'am spoke, cannot be created, cannot even be maintained, in the Diaspora, where the Jews are a minority, and where perforce they are bound to be influenced by the civilization and culture of the nations in whose midst they live. In the Middle Ages, especially in Spain, the Jews did create, and for a long time maintain, a culture of their own which produced many of the Jews' finest minds. But that was at a time when the Jews had a solidarity which centuries later was broken up by Jewish emancipation, with its well-known tragic spiritual results. The only thing, therefore, for Jews to do, if they are to maintain the uniqueness of their religious and national life, is to create a cultural center in Palestine, where Jewish culture had its birth and its most glorious development, and where, too, it will be free from the intrusion of foreign ideas and influences Such a center, for which Ahad Ha'am coined the happy name *merkaz ruhni* (Spiritual Center), will minister not only to the cultural needs of the Jews in Palestine but will serve as a cultural beacon for their brethren in the Diaspora, invigorating their Jewish life and making them one united Jewish community.

It was quite natural that, with the high ideals he conceived for the Zionist movement and the new spirit he wanted to see breathed into it, Ahad Ha'am should be thinking of a training ground for leaders, where in company of like-minded men they would in the course of time succeed in winning other self-dedicated men for the Jewish national and spiritual revival. Indeed, in an article, *Derek ha-Hayyim* (The Way of Life), he suggested the formation of just such an association. The idea was quickly taken up by friends, and the brotherhood B'nei Moshe (Sons of Moses) came into existence. The name of the organization was not haphazardly chosen but expressed Ahad Ha'am's feeling that Moses was the protagonist of the highest prophetic outlook developed in the Bible—the man of truth, the extremist, the example of righteousness in word and action—an estimate of the Hebrew Lawgiver which he later worked out in his famous article.

The B'nei Moshe, writes Leon Simon in his recent volume on Ahad Ha'am, was patterned after the Order of Freemasons, with *lishkot,* lodges, solemn ritual, and secret membership. Applicants for membership in the society had to pass a rigid test of their moral and spiritual character and were to be at least twenty-five years of age. They were not to divulge the purpose and proceedings of the meetings. At the outset the quasi-religious character of the society was stressed, but in course of time a tendency to secularization asserted itself. The oath taken by new entrants originally began with, "In the name of the God of Israel," but later it was changed to, "With heartfelt conviction of all I hold precious and sacred." The association called for self-dedication, not excluding self-sacrifice, to the service of the Jewish national revival. For the object of the society, Leon Simon quotes Ahad Ha'am's introduction to its rules and regulations: "The supreme object of our Society . . . is the rebirth of our people in our ancestral land. . . . The attainment of our national object demands a national effort carried out by the national resources both material and intellectual, and involving an inner moral unity. This effort must be a prolonged one, and there must be no indiscipline, no haste, no beating of drums, but circumspection, moderation and patience, guided always by good organization and settled rules of procedure. . . ."

During the eight years of its existence, from 1889 to 1897, B'nei Moshe exercized a strong appeal to many of the so-called Jewish elite in various countries, although at no time did its membership exceed one hundred and fifty. Founded by Ahad Ha'am, who for a time was both its guiding spirit and leader, the Order had a comparatively short life. Internal dissension and the handicap of secrecy, no less than the onslaught of religious and secular groups, were responsible for its dissolution. Ahad Ha'am was alternately attacked as a heretic and a religious fanatic, as an enemy and destroyer of religion and as a builder of a priestly cult. But the most damaging attack on the society and the one which caused it to be disbanded was the ridiculous fabrication that the notorious Protocols of the Elders of Zion was the work of Ahad Ha'am, whose aim, it was claimed, was to bring the whole world under Jewish domination.

The B'nei Moshe broke up, but not until it had contributed to the Jewish world men of great moral and spiritual stature who, in official and unofficial capacities, served the Jewish cause with great devotion and dedication. So deep and lasting was the influence of B'nei Moshe, that for many years it was still spoken of with a kind of religious awe.

In his approach to the Jewish problem and in the solution he proposed, Ahad Ha'am differed widely both with the orthodox Jews and with the author of *Auto-Emancipation*. The orthodox Jews, while the restoration of the Jewish nation in Palestine is a treasured principle of the synagogue, held that its consummation must come about by a sudden miracle without human intervention. And he differed with Dr. Pinsker, who in a measure broke with the religious aspect of restoration by maintaining that the self-emancipation of Jews need not depend upon their acquisition of Palestine but might be effected in any land where they might settle. To

Ahad Ha'am the Jewish state could come into being only in the land bound up with the Jewish national spirit and historic associations. It goes without saying that he could have nothing but scorn for the so-called emancipated Jews of Western Europe—the *Wissenschaft,* antiquarians, who were primarily concerned with the Jew's honorable past and gave no thought to their present or future.

Ahad Ha'am was not much more satisfied with the remedy of the Jewish problem through political Zionism, as preached by Dr. Theodor Herzl. The difference between the two men—Herzl and Ginzberg—was not merely a personal disagreement but one arising out of diverse views, cultures, and outlook upon Jewish life. To one the malady of the Jews was external—poverty, oppression, the lack of freedom. To the other, it was internal— national and cultural, and connected with the fatal alienation of the Jews from their language, literature, and religion. "The only means to revive the heart of the Jewish nation and prepare it for the gigantic task of Zionism," the late Israel Friedlaender states Ahad Ha'am's position, "is to make first the Jews—Jews, not negative Jews, who are Jews only because they are not allowed to die, but Jews with a positive ideal for which they are ready to live and struggle. We have to develop all the spiritual means in our possession in order to influence the Jewish soul."

Ahad Ha'am attended the first Zionist Congress at Dr. Herzl's personal invitation, but he went away sad and disappointed. He regarded himself as "a mourner at a wedding feast" in the delirium of excitement and demonstrations that accompanied the opening and closing of the Congress. He heard little about Judaism, about Jewish culture, about the things that made Zion a sacred hope and memory to Jews. Whenever these things were referred to, the declarations sounded to him hollow and empty. Assimilated Jews, to whom Judaism had ceased to have any meaning, were in command of the Congress. The Jewish masses were to them poor and unfortunate kinsmen, whom they genuinely tried to help but for whose lives and needs they had little understanding. How could Ahad Ha'am, a Russian Jew, square his philosophy with that of the dandified gentlemen of Western Europe in their high hats and frock coats? He felt himself a stranger in their company. At their very first meeting an antagonism developed between him and Dr. Herzl which the years did not efface. And, indeed, considering their respective viewpoints and positions, how could it be otherwise? For, while Herzl spoke of diplomacy, Ahad Ha'am believed in prophecy; one was for charters, loans and credits, the other for the intangible things of the spirit.

On the surface there seemed every reason that Theodor Herzl and Asher Ginzberg should be friends. They had many things in common. They were both journalists and brilliant stylists in their respective languages, and both had unbounded love for and devotion to their people. But their differences were equally numerous. They grew out of the differences in their respective backgrounds, culture, and personal lives. Herzl was led to Zionism by external circumstances; to Ahad Ha'am it was an inherited gift, an inner compulsion. To Herzl, Ahad Ha'am was an adroit pilpulist, a man of lofty but impractical ideas. To the sage of Odessa, the creator of modern Zionism, was a man suffering from grandiose illusions, if not altogether a deceiver of the Sabbatai Zevi pattern. He attacked the Basle program; he ridiculed Herzl's *Altneuland;* he opened the pages of *Hashiloah* to a savage attack by Reuben Brainin on the New Ghetto; he heaped scorn and ridicule upon the Uganda project and joined the "weepers" when it was introduced to the Congress. He remained implacably hostile to every suggestion of political Zionism, regarding it as a heresy and a betrayal of the idea of the Jewish National Renaissance, until the eve of the Balfour Declaration, when he relented sufficiently to join Chaim Weizmann and Nahum Sokolow in the negotiations.

Ahad Ha'am was more successful as a writer, thinker, and editor than he was as a leader. He lacked the warmth and temperament necessary to rouse and influence masses of people. He was by nature quiet, reserved, and retiring, modest and exact of speech to the point of pedantry. With the financial assistance of Kalonymus Wissotzky (1824–1904), a Russian Jewish magnate, he founded the *Hashiloah,* a unique Hebrew monthly, which under his guidance compared favorably with the best contemporary European publications. Previous attempts to create a Hebrew periodical produced a coterie of romancers, poets, and essayists of high standing. But it was not until the emergence of *Hashiloah* that a fresh and vital medium for cultured literary expression appeared. Ahad Ha'am was the editor, leading writer, and high priest of *Hashiloah*. He was also the sentinel who kept a watchful eye on what was going on in the Jewish world. He aimed at truth, clarity, and accuracy of thought and expression. His style was unusually precise and balanced. Writing was to him a holy occupation, and he devoted himself to it with the utmost care and sense of responsibility. He avoided both the elegant style of the Haskalah and the ornate mystical jargon of the rabbis.

Through *Hashiloah,* Ahad Ha'am trained a generation of Hebrew writers. He laid out the path followed by some of the best-remembered names in modern Hebrew literature. Men like Neumark, Ehrenpreis, Thon, Joseph Klausner, and Shmarya Levin, to mention but a very few, who later themselves became leaders in their respective literary and public activities, passed through the crucible of *Hashiloah* experience and the criticism of its editor. If Bialik and Tchernichovski did not need Ahad Ha'am's inspiration to ignite their native poetic genius, *Hashiloah* provided them with a podium from which to sing songs that were listened to by the whole Hebrew-reading world. Ahad Ha'am, the man whose every essay was written with meticulous care and sober reflection, admitted to the pages of *Hashiloah* radical barn-storming writers like Berditchewski and others, who threw their heresies right in the gentle teacher's face. He corrected their errors, reproved their rashness, and quieted the storm of alien thoughts and ideas in their minds.

When Ahad Ha'am in 1904 relinquished the editorship of *Hashiloah,* the longest-lived Hebrew periodical, after the issuance of its twelfth volume, and turned it over to H. N. Bialik and Joseph Klausner, he accepted the managing editorship of *Ahiasaf,* a publishing house in Warsaw which issued books in Hebrew for the dissemination of Jewish and general culture. The editor assembled a staff of writers that included such writers as Dr. S. Bernfield and S. P. Robinowitz, who contributed a number of volumes of outstanding literary and historical merit. Under the imprimatur of *Ahiasaf* appeared Ahad Ha'am's own first volume of collected essays, *Al Parashat Derakim* (At the Crossroad), in 1895. Following the example of *Ahiasaf*, two other Hebrew publishing houses, *Tushia* and *Ben Abigdor*, made their appearance, and all three of the publishing firms contributed mightily to the Hebrew National Renaissance.

Ahad Ha'am did not write many books. From the time he began to write to the time of the "great silence," due to his illness, he wrote so little that all his essays were collected in four modest volumes. In addition, there were six volumes of letters, which he himself arranged and edited. He wrote on the philosophy and ethics of Jewish nationalism, and, although he did not write a systematic philosophy, his sporadic essays on these subjects in *Hashiloah* and other publications add up to one. A very lucid and comprehensive analysis of Ahad Ha'am's thought is presented by Leon Simon in his Introduction to *Selected Essays by Ahad Ha'am*. Briefly stated, at the core of Ahad Ha'am's teaching regarding the essential character and function of the Jews and Judaism in the world lies the thought that the Jews have a moral and spiritual mission; that they received their religious and ethical personality from Moses and the Prophets; that they rejected the human cult of power and violence; that they were destined to make the ideals of justice and righteousness triumphant in their own life and in the life of the world.

This, however, the Jews could not realize in the ghetto, because of its stifling and crippling environment and "the mountains of minute regulations and prescriptions which threatened to smother the underlying spirit." Nor could it materialize in their so-called lands of freedom, because of foreign cultural influence. Ahad Ha'am was very strong on this latter point, and he spoke out bitterly against the enormous price the emancipated Jews had to pay for the niggardly rewards of political freedom dealt out to them by their patronizing countrymen. Ahad Ha'am used this situation as evidence that they needed their own land if the Jews were to live their own life, to act in freedom, to realize those moral and spiritual aspirations that are peculiar to their being. Even the *galut,* with all its bitterness, was made bearable to the Jew because of the hope that some day there would be a restoration, an ingathering, a working out of the moral and spiritual destiny which constitutes the real significance of his national history. Emancipation, says Ahad Ha'am, has not solved the Jewish problem; it only complicated and worsened it. It loosened bonds which once united the Jews and erased allegiances and loyalties that had once made them one family. Even in times of their deepest misery there had been among the Jews a feeling of solidarity—a solidarity based on religion, habits, customs, and national hopes and aspirations. This solidarity was broken up, and the Jews, both physically and spiritually, were scattered. They participated in the cultures of all the countries of the world, enriching them with their talent and genius, while their own culture was neglected and forsaken, as a thing of no value. Our nation, writes Ahad Ha'am, has only expenditures but no income; it scatters the sparks of its genius in all directions; it constantly increases the wealth and glory of its enemies but itself receives no benefit from its labors. He calls for an awakening that the Jewish people may fulfill its destiny and be a light unto the nations and lead them in the path of righteousness.

Ahad Ha'am, then, put the accent on *Zarat ha-Yahadut,* the "plight of Judaism," (or of Jewish culture), which in his opinion was the fundamental problem of Zionism. The hearts of the people must be revived, their spirit raised, their national consciousness resuscitated. There must be an inward change before redemption is achieved. In other words, Zionism was to Ahad Ha'am a cultural historic process, with Palestine as *merkaz ruhni,* a spiritual center, for its goal. He dismissed political Zionism as an error and a delusion, contending, as indeed do the majority of orthodox Jews, that it ran counter to the stream of Jewish tradition. In a letter to a friend he wrote that he would not be a Zionist if he believed that the Jewish spirit could be developed in the Diaspora.

Ahad Ha'am's six volumes of letters, collected at the suggestion of his friend J. H. Ravnitzki, present an aspect of his personality but faintly revealed in the four volumes of his published essays. Whereas in the latter we see the scholar, teacher, thinker, and Zionist theoretician, in the letters we behold the man, the editor in his easy chair, the prolific correspondent, the friend, the critic, the commentator upon the Jewish and the world scenes. Snatches of his literary autobiography are disclosed to us. We see him as editor of *Hashiloah,* as managing director of *Ahiasaf,* as the great moral and spiritual personality of self-consuming zeal and earnestness whenever the question of right and truth were involved. Writers did not find Asher Ginzberg an easy editor to get along with. He was austere in his views, severe in his judgment, stern in his demands. He would not forgive his best friends a wrong word or an indelicate expression. Thus he chided Frishman and rebuked Bialik for such literary lapses. Although in their ideologies they were far apart, Ahad Ha'am had great admiration for M. J. Berditchevski's literary genius; but when the rebel novelist got himself involved in un-Jewish pagan novelties, the editor of *Hashiloah* reprimanded him and would not publish his stories.

There are few better histories of Zionism or of the modern Hebrew renaissance than that scattered through Ahad Ha'am's collected letters covering a period of nearly twenty-five years, from 1896 to 1920. Through the pages of this voluminous correspondence the principal figures of both movements pass in review. Ahad Ha'am was in touch with them all and corresponded with them all. They wrote to him, asking for his advice and opinion, and he answered in his own straightforward, unequivocal way. He criticized, admonished, and exhorted, but never on personal grounds. As revealed in his letters, his criticism was characterized by moderation, his opposition with due regard to the feelings of those involved.

The turn of the century brought about a change in Asher Ginzberg's life. The deterioration of his own and his father's fortune in an unfortunate business venture compelled him to look for a more dependable source of income for his family and himself than his literary activities afforded. For some time he acted as agent for the Wisotzky Tea Company in Russia; but in 1901 he was transferred to London, as general manager of the company. It was a prosaic occupation for the man who had reigned over the literary world of his people; but he discharged his duties with his customary care and diligence. Inwardly, however, Asher Ginzberg was not happy. He missed Odessa, he missed Warsaw, he missed the friends and associates with whom he had spent the many years of his literary life. They were all, of course, in constant correspondence with him and were guided by his wisdom and authority; but he missed the faces and voices which had faded into the past.

In a way England was Asher Ginzberg's intellectual and spiritual home. For years he had feasted his mind on the works of her writers and thinkers. Asher Ginzberg was self-taught; he had no regular academic training and what general culture he had acquired was largely gained through the philosophical writings of German and English scholars, especially the latter. But living in the English capital was something different. He found the noise and bustle of the great city annoying, her interminable fog intolerable, and the time spent in traveling between his home and his office wasteful. London was indeed a far cry from the city on the Black Sea, with her quiet streets and ordered life. Nevertheless, Ginzberg kept his hand on the pulse of Jewish life, and when Claude Montefiore's book, *The Synoptic Gospels,* which advocated a more sympathetic appreciation of the New Testament by Jews, appeared, he roused himself and wrote one of his most significant essays, warning of the consequences of the Reform Movement to the Jews once it led them to diverge from the Jewish national spirit.

It was, however, the last flicker of his genius before the long dark night set in. His physical decay was rapid and steady. Moroseness and long periods of silence became frequent. When friends and admirers crowded his study, he not only did not lead but he rarely joined in the conversation. Then a creeping paralysis set in which made creative work impossible. Nevertheless, he kept up his voluminous correspondence, and the old spirit occasionally shines through. But, on the whole, both the man and his letters make a painful impression. What one beholds is a giant in chains, a great mind struggling to express itself held down by an invisible hand. He yearned to spend his last years in Palestine. This boon was vouchsafed him, and he lived there amid the adoration of friends and admirers. Greater honor and respect came to few other men than were shown to the shriveled and shrunken Ahad Ha'am. Only a few people were allowed to see him, and, so that he might not be disturbed, traffic was rerouted from the street where he lived. Still, he was not happy. His days and nights were spent in physical discomfort and loneliness of spirit. Astonishing as it may seem, he longed for "London and its thoroughfares," the very things he so utterly abhorred when he lived there.

He wrote to Simon Dubnow from Tel-Aviv: "I am surrounded by intimate and devoted friends; respect and affection are shown me on every hand . . . and all this in Palestine, which has been my dream for years and years. And in the midst of all these blessings, I long for London, yes, for London—not for the friends I left there, but literally for London, for its busy streets and thoroughfares, for the dark city in which I spent so many hours without light or air, for the choking fog." Sick at heart and in body, he looked even more shrunken than he actually was. He lived with little hope of seeing his condition improve, but he retained his interest in the world through his correspondence with his friends. Shortly before he died, he wrote to Max Raisin, an American rabbi: "What shall I write you, aside from thanking you for your good wishes? Would they came true if only in part. At present my condition is still bad and my hope of regaining my strength is growing ever smaller. But what is one to expect from a sick old man? . . . Do inform me from time to time about your affairs and activities, and be not too exacting about the letters you get from me in reply to yours."

The death of Asher Ginzberg in 1927, at the age of seventy-one shook all Israel. Even those who were unfriendly to his philosophy stood in awe of the man who was truly Ahad Ha'am, the Only One of His People. His passing, like that of Dr. Theodor Herzl, was mourned as a national loss. Such a throng of mourners as Tel-Aviv never before saw accompanied his remains, which were laid at rest in Tel-Aviv's old Jewish cemetery.

Many years after his death, with the stupendous changes, both tragic and happy, they have wrought in the life of the Jewish people, it is plain who won the battle of words between Dr. Herzl and Asher Ginzberg. Despite his wisdom and understanding, Ahad Ha'am failed to see many things. He failed to recognize that the overwhelming mass of the Jewish people were on the side of Dr. Herzl; that it was his image that took root in their hearts and minds, and that without Herzl Zionism might have continued as the beautiful dream it had been for centuries. Ginzberg failed to see that the people, in their desperation and bitterness were not in a mood to play with words and theories, however finely spun, but wanted a quick solution of their misery.

Much of what Ahad Ha'am had stood for was realized in Palestine during his lifetime, and much more after he had died. On the other hand, much of what he had bitterly opposed and fought against was achieved by the strange, almost messianic, turn of events. He fought against Jewish Statehood, and Jewish Statehood in Palestine became a reality; he sneered at diplomacy, and it was through diplomacy that the United Nations voted the Jews a legally assured home in a considerable part of Palestine; he was against large-scale immigration to the Holy Land, and the spare quarter of a million Jews there during his lifetime later rose to approximately eight times that number; he feared the ebbing of the pioneering spirit of the Halutzim, and their spirit, instead of weakening and declining, has been almost miraculous for its energy and achievement. The "Spiritual Center" Ahad Ha'am had advocated has been more than realized in Israel's university and libraries, in its scholars, poets, and novelists, in its showers of books, magazines, and studies, which are of tremendous interest to men of the spirit everywhere.

Although Ahad Ha'am erred in many things, his image stands clear and sharp against the background of time. He was a great writer, a thinker of unusual force and distinction; his philosophical essays shaped and molded the literary style and thought of a generation of Hebrew writers. Modern Hebrew literature may be said to have begun with him. Magnet-like he attracted the scattered energies of Hebrew writers and directed them on the path of literary fame. Although much of his Zionist philosophy has been invalidated by the process of time and the extraordinary course of events, he acted as a ferment without which the Jewish national renaissance would have been much slower and of narrower scope and character. Ahad Ha'am still retains his position as a vital and challenging figure both in Hebrew literature and in the Jewish national revival and Hayim Nahman Bialik's tribute is as appropriate today as it was in 1903, when it was written:

> Since first thy light broke in on us, we behold
> Master! in the paladin of truth,
> And champion of the spirit, clear of vision,
> Modest and pure in every thought and deed;
> Secure in thine own truth, caring naught
> How others judge, treading thy chosen path
> With firm step and unflinching gaze, as one
> Who carries in his soul the sacred flame
> And guards the last spark of heavenly fire.
> So shines some focal star that wheels his course
> On high, and draws his satellites around him,
> Masters them from afar, and forces them
> Into his orbit by some hidden power.

Simon M. Dubnow

SIMON M. DUBNOW, publicist, historian, philosopher of Jewish nationalism, and one of the leading spirits of his age, was slain in December, 1941, at the age of eighty-one. He was among the Jewish martyrs of Riga, where he spent the last years of his long life.

Even in those days of poignant suffering for the Jews, when losses by violence were so enormous that the death of one individual scarcely seemed to count any longer, the passing of Dubnow could not be overlooked. For he was indeed a great and outstanding figure among the celebrated men of his time and the greatest historian the Jews of eastern Europe have produced—one whose works, in the original and in many translations, are read by thousands.

He was a friend, intimate, and collaborator of most of the leading Jews of his age. Hardly anything happened in the social, political, and cultural life of his people for almost two generations but was reflected in his life and writings. While not himself an active leader, he blazed the trail for many of his younger contemporaries in Russia—aye, and in other lands as well. For he was not a cloistered scholar who divorced or segregated himself from his people. On the contrary, they were close to his heart; all his life he fought with them and for them, and nothing that affected them was indifferent to him.

He was a child of two worlds. In him the old and the new had met—the learning and saintliness that characterized the traditional Jewish way of life, and the hunger for Haskalah, enlightenment, which in his time filled the hearts of thousands of the Jews of Russia and Poland.

He was born in 1860 in Mstislavl, a typical small town of the old Russian Jewish Pale of Settlement. His youth was spent in the old world, with its holy books of the Bible and the Talmud, under the guidance of his grandfather, Ben Zion, a man truly remarkable for his learning, piety, and wisdom whom Dubnow never mentions without a touch of genuine warmth and affection.

But, simultaneously, he became aware of that other world—the world of books that one read clandestinely only when there were no spying eyes around. Yet they were harmless books—Mapu's idylls, Smolenskin's romances, M. J. Lebensohn's poems, Kalman Schulman's Hebrew translations of Eugene Sue's *Mysteries of Paris,* and the like—all incapable of unsettling the mind of a child even as young as he. And inasmuch as these books were written in Hebrew, neither his mother nor his grandfather—his father was almost always away from home on business—would have objected much if they had knwn he read them.

Even so, they were not without their effect upon him, for they helped to open up for him a world still stranger and more forbidden —the world of the Russian language with its books, literature, and culture. Those were days when the so-called Jewish men of Enlightenment were carried away by a frenzy of Russification. All the Jews needed for their social and political emancipation, they naïvely thought, was to make themselves more intimately at home in the Russian environment; learn its language, copy its manners, and acquire its culture, and all would be well with them.

The reveille was sounded by poets like Gottlober and J. L. Gordon, indeed by everyone who wielded a pen, however imperfectly. What followed was similar to the Hellenic craze during the period of the Second Commonwealth. Suddenly Jews began to "progress" rapidly. Russian schools were opened, under government auspices, in almost every town and hamlet where Jews resided, and Jewish children flocked to them in numbers out of proportion to their population.

The little town where young Dubnow lived boasted just such a school. After many vain attempts on his part to enter the school his grandfather finally yielded and consented to his registering, but only after Simon had promised that he would continue to attend his lectures on the Talmud in the synagogue. This presented no difficulty, for the lectures were given in the morning, before school hours.

The young student was eager and quick to learn. The enthusiasm he had formerly devoted to his Jewish studies he now lavished on his secular education. In a very short time he learned to write clear and vigorous Russian, besides distinguishing himself in history. His leisure time he devoted to reading. He digested the works of Gogol, Turgenev, Dostoevski, Tolstoy, and the poems of Pushkin and Lermontov. He also read translations from foreign languages. Boerne's *Letters from Paris* and Solomon Maimon's autobiography made the deepest impression upon him—the first because of its revolutionary spirit and the other because of the stirrings of rebellion toward the traditional Jewish way of life it set in motion in his mind.

He absorbed the spirit of his time and environment only too well. While he still attended his grandfather's discourses on the Talmud, he began to look with disdain upon his former "unenlightened" education and regretted bitterly the time he had spent in the dismal atmosphere of the Heder. Indeed, his first literary effort, which also proved to be his last for some time, was a tempestuous attack on the Heder method of education, which he dispatched to the *ha-Zefirah,* a Hebrew publication in Warsaw, but which, no doubt for sufficient reasons, remained unpublished.

Then began his odyssey—the typical quest of a small-town Jewish youth for an education. His dreams were of the gymnasium, a Jewish boy had to surmount almost insuperable difficulties before he could enroll. He had to study twice as hard and know ten times as much as the ordinary Christian student, and even then he was not always sure of success.

Young Dubnow studied with all the zeal and energy of his devoted nature. He plunged into the classical languages and became proficient in Greek and Latin; he took up the modern languages and mastered English, French, and German. Mathematics and the sciences presented no difficulties, although he made less progress in drawing. But after making the rounds of the schools in Vilna, Dunaburg, and Molhilev, he gave up his ambition in despair.

His enthusiasm for knowledge was not dampened, however. Failing to enter a school, he prescribed for himself a private course of studies. He was only eighteen years of age, but minds trained in the Bible and the Talmud mature early. He was still in his adolescence when he became a devotee of the positivist school of thought and read and absorbed the works of Buckle, Spencer, Draper, Lewes, and John Stuart Mill, besides the principal writings of the French and German thinkers.

As a result, he became skeptical of religion, and no longer believed in theology and supernaturalism. As for Judaism, while he admired its ethical teachings he repudiated its rites and rituals. Positivism demanded practical, useful knowledge, while in the Talmud the youthful philosopher beheld a system that crippled the Jew and unfitted him for life.

What followed was not religious nihilism but a demand for religious reform. He joined the company of his many contemporaries who felt that the tragedy of the Jew lay in his faulty education, in the Talmud, in the Heder, in his clinging stubbornly to an antiquated method of living. He began his career by joining the ranks of the extreme liberals, by tilting his lance against so-called reactionaries, by demanding a rejuvenated and regenerated Judaism based on instructed minds instead of pious hearts.

He felt himself drawn to St. Petersburg, the capital of the Russian empire, where, legally, Jews were not supposed to live, but where, nevertheless, some of the finest Jewish minds resided. It is difficult to exaggerate the influence of this city upon the cultural life of the Jews of Eastern Europe. Although living there clandestinely, mostly on the pretext of fictitious occupations, they developed a degree of cultural activity that made itself felt everywhere. Baron Günsburg, a friend and patron of Jewish scholars, lived there and the Society for the Dissemination of Knowledge among Jews and almost all the great Russo-Jewish publications and, later, the Hebrew *ha-Melitz*, were located there. A large number of Jewish poets, writers, critics, and scholars—Frug, Gordon, Harkavi, Kantor, Landau, Zimberg, Zederbaum, and many others, lived and labored there.

St. Petersburg marked the end of Dubnow's odyssey. He had

more than arrived. He found an atmosphere congenial to his spirit among rebels and intellectual warriors like himself. He was accepted as an equal in a company of men twice and three times his age. He was barely twenty-one; but he was full of ideas and enthusiasm and possessed no small amount of learning—a safe passport in a society of men where these things counted above everything else.

His first serious literary steps were taken in *Razsviet* and *Russki Evrei,* two influential periodicals which began to publish his articles on a great variety of subjects. But he soon afterward went over to the *Voshod,* a unique monthly publication, counterpart of the Hebrew *ha-Shahar,* and later, the *ha-Shiloah,* influential among scholars and laymen alike. The *Voshod* was both literary and popular, scholarly yet widely read, under the surveillance of the Russian censorship, yet liberal and almost independent in its editorial policy and political views.

Once Simon was thrown into this exalted circle there was not a voice in St. Petersburg more often heard or listened to with greater respect than was his. He was prolific; articles flew from his pen with amazing rapidity. He had no special assignment, but wrote on literary, historical, political, and critical subjects, besides book reviews, always with care, insight, and penetration. Writing was to him a kind of spiritual exercise, which he discharged with the greatest devotion.

He was brilliant, he was thorough, he was effective; he became a celebrity in a city of noted writers. He wrote from wide learning, sincere conviction, and in a style that was both vigorous and popular. Studies were tossed off by his fertile pen which afterward went into books and saw many translations. Editors and readers alike forgot his age in the depth and freshness of his contributions. He became the heart and conscience of his people, with hardly anything happening anywhere that didn't echo in his thought and writing. He wrote in Russian and for Russian readers, but noted every quickening of the Jewish pulse. He did much to popularize Solomon Jacob Abramovich, universally known and loved as "Mendele," among non-Yiddish readers, and Sholem Aleichem acknowledged his indebtedness to him. When, in addition to the Hebrew *ha-Melitz,* Zederbaum proposed to issue a Yiddish newspaper, Dubnow hailed it as a step toward the education and enlightenment of the Jewish masses.

He lived in poverty, often on the verge of starvation; for, while his editors lauded his work, their recognition rarely took the form of proper remuneration. What money he managed to collect went into books, and a coveted German, French, or English volume was not infrequently the *ersatz* for a much-needed meal. Still, he was happy—happy in his work, happy in his boundless love for his people, happy beyond measure that the woman he loved and married was willing to share with him his poverty and his dreams.

But in the early eighties his heart was lacerated by the pogroms which spread almost everywhere. The Jews of Russia were called upon to endure their worst ordeal in a long history marked by suffering. Dr. Pinsker wrote his celebrated *Auto-emancipation,* and in Odessa a little group of Hebrew nationalists preached Jewish colonization in Palestine. But Simon Dubnow remained the positivist, the realist, the cosmopolitan, refusing to budge an inch from his youthful illusions. He fought for auto-emancipation all his life, but for emancipation within, not without, the galut. He was stubborn, he was adamant, he was unyielding in his convictions. An older brother who lived as an early Haluz and colonist in Palestine, reprimanded him for his obstinacy in a letter: "You have allowed your devotion to humanity to blind you to the fate and future of your people." But all in vain.

Yet Dubnow was far from an assimilationist. His clear and keen mind pierced through the confusion, prejudice, and cowardice of the Jewish assimilationists, both abroad and in his own country. He did not happily look forward to the disappearance of the Jews as a people, and their too-rapid Russification often filled him with fear and apprehension. Indeed, one of his severest ordeals as associate editor of the *Voshod* was to read in the German exchanges of the servility and self-contempt of his Western brethren. He was only thirty years old, but already a program or philosophy was maturing in his mind to bring redemption to his people without the blessing of Zionism, which was to him an unattainable ideal.

He was much less than thirty years old when he projected what was perhaps his greatest work, the *History of Hassidism*. "There is only one key to the present," remarked a celebrated scholar, "and that is the past." What time, therefore, he had left from his work on the *Voshod* and other publications, he devoted to the more abiding things of Jewish life and thought. His researches in Jewish history led him to the mystical movements of the seventeenth and eighteenth centuries. He wrote and published several sizable essays on Sabbatai Zevi and Jacob Frank, but it was the movement set ablaze by Israel Baal Shem Tov that fascinated him most.

The book was an ambitious and daring undertaking in a field not known or exploited before and largely hidden in manuscripts, family traditions, and personal experiences heretofore inaccessible to anyone. Readers of Dubnow's memoirs will remember the difficulties, the hardships, the almost insuperable obstacles he had to surmount to get at these sources. He went to Warsaw and spent days and weeks in bookstores and private libraries. He had to plead, beg, cajole, and bribe for the mere permission to be allowed to read or copy a priceless manuscript. The possessors of these treasures were wary and cautious of him because of his unsavory reputation among the orthodox. It took all the suaveness and diplomacy of Nahum Sokolow, co-editor of *ha-Zefirah,* to overcome their prejudice and permit the zealous scholar a glance at a rare book, a faded manuscript, or a lovingly-treasured family paper. It was several years before the work was finally completed, but in 1887 he was already deep in his masterly introduction to the book.

What could have attracted Simon Dubnow to mysticism—he the skeptic, the rationalist, the man whose yardstick of knowledge was that it should be useful and attainable? Was it that, keen observer that he was, he saw his people's future to be so desperate and hopeless that there was no balm for them except their ancient faith? Or was it that he was beginning to long for that other life that his grandfather, in his wisdom, had sensed long ago? Dubnow tells in his reminiscences that when the wise old Ben Zion beheld his grandson departing from the ways of his fathers he neither scolded nor upbraided him but, quoting the words of Hosea, merely said,

"My child, a time will come when you too will say, 'I will go and return to my first husband, for then was it better with me than now.'"

The time came even sooner than might have been expected. Discouraged by his many vain attempts to legalize his residence in St. Petersburg, Dubnow decided to move his family to Odessa. As far as the Jews of that time were concerned, Odessa and St. Petersburg were not merely two different cities but, in their views and outlooks on Jewish life, were in sharp contrast to each other. St. Petersburg was Russia's most westernized city, copied, as Peter the Great, its founder, had meant it to be, after Prussia, Germany, and France and resembling Berlin and Paris in almost everything except language and government; while Odessa, situated on the Black Sea, had a more eastern outlook, toward Turkey, Egypt, and Palestine.

The Jews of St. Petersburg, if not assimilated, were westernized, in almost everything. The very cultural movements that arose there were intended, subtly and slyly, for their Russification. Between the Haskalah of the St. Petersburg type and the German *Aufklährung,* the difference was only in name—not in their aim and content. On the other hand, Odessa from her very beginning was the home and center of the Jewish national renaissance. As if drawn by an invisible magnet, many of our greatest men, heroes and prophets of the Jewish revival, flocked to the southern metropolis, creating an atmosphere that was world-wide in its scope and influence.

Dubnow immediately felt himself at home in his new environment. He found there a company that was congenial to his spirit. When he arrived the city was in the full glow of her cultural aspirations. Prosperous in business, the Jews lavished money on their schools, to the end that their educational system surpassed all others in the Russian Empire. The effects of the wave of enlightenment had been felt there, but it did not produce the unfortunate results it had in some places. To be sure, the old garment had many patches, but it was still worn proudly and with dignity.

The city was a rendezvous of the brightest Jewish spirits of the time. The people Simon met were stimulating in every sense. While not agreeing on all points, they had much in common. In his diaries Dubnow preserved touching sketches of many of the men whose names are landmarks in Jewish history and literature. One finds there the wise though detached Ahad Ha'am, the gifted though reserved Bialik, the astute though obstinate Lilienblum, the silent though competent Ravnitzky, the energetic Druyanov, the resourceful Dizengoff, the popular Lewinsky, and the dazzling though terrifying "wonder child" Jabotinsky. But crowning this rare and distinguished company of the Sages of Odessa was the unique and extraordinary figure of Mendele, loved by all, sought by all, towering like a giant above his contemporaries.

Those were the most fertile and productive thirteen years of Dubnow's energetic life, expanding his genius in almost every direction. Odessa provided the creative spark for the mind that was never at rest. He continued his work on the *Voshod,* but his thoughts were busy with other plans. He had a passion for study, a huge appetite for work, an amazing memory, and an almost fabulous capacity for concentration. He could read, think, and write in the midst of company and confusion. He read greedily, storing away in his mind anything that might one day serve his purpose. He rarely gave himself time for rest, for leisure, or relaxation. He loved nature and was fond of walking, but the broad streets, the fine parks, the promenades of Odessa rarely saw him. He had tremendous energy, a vigorous constitution, and was almost never sick except for an eye ailment, which, however, was soon cured by Dr. Max Mandelstamm, the famous oculist and Zionist leader of Kiev.

His mind was sharpened by contact with other minds as clear and alert as his own. The only time he borrowed from his books and the inkpot was Saturday night, which he spent in the company of his friends and intimates at the home of Mendele. Those were unforgettable hours, and Dubnow dwells lovingly on them in his diaries. The atmosphere was glowing with the heat of discussion. Everybody seemed to be talking together, except Ahad Ha'am, the priest and prophet of Odessa, who quietly walked up and down the spacious room, as was his habit, with a lighted cigarette in one hand

and a steaming glass of tea in the other. When he did pause to speak, an awed hush fell upon the gathering, so that not a word of the oracle might be lost. He was listened to with the esteem and deference due his exalted position.

Political Zionism was in the making. Dr. Theodor Herzl's *Judenstaat* had just appeared, to be followed shortly afterward by his *Altneuland*. The Jewish world was astir. Odessa was seething with excitement, and there was almost no other topic than the redeemer who had come out of Vienna. Ahad Ha'am's strictures on the new trends in modern Zionism fell like a bombshell in the camp of the infatuated lovers and admirers of Herzl. It called forth opposition and deep grievous regret. To many it was as if Zion was being destroyed for a third time.

In the midst of this controversy and excitement Simon M. Dubnow penned his now celebrated *Letters Concerning Judaism, Old and New*. It was memorable for its clear thinking and novel approach and established for its author a reputation as a philosopher of Jewish nationalism. By rejecting Zionism, especially political Zionism, he came nearer to Ahad Ha'am's conception of spiritual Zionism by affirming the principle of Jewish nationhood, but in a way which proved acceptable neither to Ahad Ha'am nor to Herzl.

The Jewish people, he wrote, are a nation. They manifest special habits, characteristics, and a mode of life which set them apart from every other group of individuals. But their nationhood is different from the nationhood of other peoples in its independence from land, statehood, and other such outward bonds. In other words, the Jews are a historical-cultural nation capable of maintaining its separate existence in the diaspora as though in a land and with a government of its own. Indeed, all the Jews need for their national and cultural regeneration is not a return to Palestine (the past is Israel's cradle, not its prison) but the right of citizenship in the lands where they now live and local autonomy for the free exercise of their religion, schools, language, and unique life and culture.

It was a clear and forceful statement of a point of view that brought him into conflict with almost every known shade of Jewish opinion. Everyone found in it much to accept but also much to reject. It laid the foundation for a new theory that regarded the Jews as a nation but as a nation within other nations. Zionists naturally rejected it and even followers of Ahad Ha'am frowned upon it; but it quickly found many adherents and gave rise to the Jewish People's Party in Russia in 1906, thus spreading Dubnow's philosophy of political rights, which became the basis for the demand for minority rights for Jews at the Peace Conference of World War I.

Many other studies occupied Dubnow's mind during his Odessa period, principally the subject of Jewish history. So vast was the field and so little of it was known! Krochmal, Rapoport, Jost, Zunz, Geiger, and Weiss had done their work, important and necessary work in its way; but their books were histories of Jewish tradition, idealogical conceptions of history as found in books, schools, and institutions. But where was the group life, the collective consciousness of the people, the common, ordinary broad masses who were not scholars, wrote no books, and founded no schools but who merely lived, struggled, and died? He felt the need of a re-evaluation of Jewish history, of changing its approach, of shifting its emphasis. In the life of the Jewish people, as in every other living and active group, there were social and economic forces, struggles not necessarily of an idealogical-metaphysical nature, that produced changes and affected the course of its history. Of these things there was no echo, no mention, no sign or indication, in the books he read.

Graetz's monumental *History of the Jews* had appeared, and Dubnow fell under its influence. It was just the kind of work to appeal to his fancy, written with imagination, conviction, and sentiment. He decided to have the volumes translated into Russian and went so far as to write an essay on the subject "What is Jewish History?" in order to clarify in his own mind the explanation of the unique life and continued existence of the Jewish people. The essay eventually grew into a sizable book that saw many translations and is widely read to this day.

But his enthusiasm faded as he continued reading volume after volume. What particularly angered him at the German-written history of the Jews was their almost complete indifference to the Jews of Eastern Europe. Modern Jewish history was written as if it began with the French Revolution or with Moses Mendelssohn. A Jewry of six million souls, with their heroes and martyrs, their ideals and aberrations, was as if it had never existed. Anything that was not in the pattern of German thinking was treated patronizingly or with open contempt. While many long pages were devoted to Moses Mendelssohn and his school, which brought nothing but confusion and division into Judaism, saints and mystics like Israel Baal Shem Tov and his disciples, were given scant and contemptuous attention.

As a result of his dissatisfaction the idea of writing a history of the Jews took root in his mind—a herculean task, but Dubnow was not dismayed. He was energetic and ambitious and had the learning and preparation necessary for the work. He began by filling in the gaps in the works of Graetz and his fellow historians. First of all, however, he set out to make the Jews of his country history-conscious by a series of articles in a number of publications —no small task in itself in a land where Judaism was a matter of faith instead of history. He then called upon his people to send him any material in their possession that threw light on the history of their respective communities. He was quickly deluged with an enormous mass of manuscripts, transcripts, and *pinkasim*. It seemed almost the work of a lifetime to examine, sift, arrange, and place in their proper order the enormous quantity of material that was before him. But he who seemed to have been born for work, glowing with enthusiasm with every passing hour, kept steadily at his task until after many years, he gave to the world the moving drama of the *History of the Jews in Russia and Poland,* covering a period of almost a thousand years—or, more precisely, from the kingdom of the Khazars to World War I.

Dubnow concludes his history with words that are singularly appropriate and prophetic. "What may the World War be expected to bring to the World-Nation? Full of agitation, the Jew is looking into the future, and the question of his ancient prophet is trembling on his lips: 'Ah, Lord God, wilt Thou make a full end of the remnant of Israel?' Let the entire past of the Jewish people serve as an answer to this question, a people which, in the maelstrom of human history, has succeeded in conquering the two cosmic forces: Time and Space."

He was continually turning out for the publications to which he was a regular contributor sketches, articles, book reviews, and longer or shorter studies, besides assuming responsibility for *Yevreiski Starina* (Jewish Antiquities), a scientific periodical which he both founded and edited. He had such a reserve of energy and work came to him so naturally that every new obligation only hardened his nerves till, like tempered steel, they became proof against exhaustion. In less than two years he not only issued a Russian adaptation of the German histories by Samuel Baeck and Marcus Brann, with a few original chapters of his own, covering the history of the Jews in Russia and Poland, but wrote a textbook of Jewish history for school use, which enjoyed such popularity that it appeared in several editions and translations. He not only wrote and translated these books but, working without the help of secretaries, he supervised their printing, read the galleys, made corrections, revised and corrected again, until he was completely satisfied.

His growing reputation as a historian served to sharpen his ambition to undertake the major work of his life—a *Weltgeschichte des Judischen Volkes* (World History of the Jewish People). The title *Weltgeschichte* is significant, for he was the first Jewish historian to consider the Jews as part of the general stream of world history instead of the curiously isolated phenomenon they were heretofore conceived to be. He consideres them such an integral part of the life of the world that he often devotes more space to the impact upon the Jews of such factors as the rise of Christianity and Mohammedanism, the writings of the church fathers, the emergence of new cities, countries, and civilizations than he does to the intricacies of the talmudic schools, which he considers of minor importance. He subordinates the purely theological and metaphysical disputations to the political and sociological factors—the so-called social tissue of the times of which he was writing. He allowed himself to think that what the people in the mass said and thought, their beliefs, their superstitions, their ideals, their habits—yes, even their habits—were of far greater consequence than the learned discussions of the scholars.

He had not completely abandoned the method of Zunz and Graetz; the literary and spiritual achievements of his people made great claims on his attention, and the ten bulky volumes of his history plainly testify to it. But it was with the collective consciousness of the Jewish people, their group life, as it were, with their pains and struggles, with that unique something that makes up the soul of the Jew, that he was primarily concerned. He is not always consistent and does not always succeed; we get often allusions and intimations instead of a consistently worked-out program. After reading his work one gets the impression that the definitive social history of the Jews is still to be written. But he was the first to recognize the social and economic forces in Jewish history; the first to perceive, however imperfectly, the operation of natural law in the pattern of Jewish life; the first to seek for the secular trends in the Jew's universal struggle for existence instead of the theological-metaphysical cobweb with which it was heretofore surrounded; and, lastly, the first to attempt to humanize a history that was thought too grand, too noble, too sacred for ordinary human hands to tamper with. All these things required courage, daring, imagination, a mind unusually equipped. Simon Dubnow possessed all these things, in addition to extraordinary erudition and the unique temperament of the historian.

He had already completed the manuscript of the first two volumes of his *Weltgeschichte* when he suddenly decided to leave Odessa and move to Vilna—Vilna, the city of Jewish traditions, with the halo of Elijah Gaon about her, the *Kiryan Ne'emanah,* the Faithful City, as S. J. Finn called her, although, alas, in the days of Dubnow, there had already been many defections. He decided to move, partly because Odessa no longer had anything to give him, since he had exhausted everything there that was of interest to him and was now hungry for new pastures, but primarily because he felt the need of the company of the kind of Jews he had known in Mstislavl, the root of Jewish life, however much he had once enjoyed the company of the sophisticated Jews of St. Petersburg and the highly intellectual Jews of Odessa.

But his stay in Vilna was not destined to be very long. He remained there only a little more than three years, from 1903 to 1907. And they were years of pain and anger, of political reaction and the plague of the "Black Hundred," when pogroms increased and Jewish blood flowed freely in Kishinev, Homel, Bialistock, and other cities. He gave some time to his *Weltgeschichte,* revising, improving, correcting, even writing a few new chapters; but those were not times for concentrated literary activity—not for one like Simon Dubnow, whose heart and soul were seared by the afflictions of his people. They were days when the true patriot, the real lover of his people, laid down his pen and took up the sword, as Dubnow did.

Never had he been so busy with the affairs of his people as during those three years. He called meetings, attended conferences and secret gatherings, consorted with all kinds of people, even Bundists, with whose political programs he otherwise had little sympathy. It was no time for division; only in united action lay what hope there was. He gathered around him a group of men famous for their Jewish activities and such leaders in the Zionist movement as the Goldberg brothers and the eloquent and brilliant Shmarya Lewin.

He secured the cooperation of Maxim Winawer, a colorful figure if there ever was one. From his position as a great jurist, Winawer became entangled in politics and was a member of the first Russian Duma; but on account of his radical views he was in and out of prison any number of times. He was a senator during the brief provisional government, but died in exile in Paris after the Bolshevists assumed power. He was the founder of the Society for Obtaining Political Rights for Jews, and during the pogroms he took a hand in organizing for self-defense.

When, however, Dubnow realized that for the present nothing could be accomplished, he accepted a call from St. Petersburg to lecture on Jewish history and kindred subjects at the Institute for Oriental Studies, which was founded by Baron Günzburg. He returned to the scene of his youthful activities—but with what a changed heart and chastened spirit! But he threw himself into his work with his wonted energy, wrote many articles, delivered many lectures, and was active in every cultural movement, while in his "leisure hours" he worked on his *magnum opus*. Because of these activities he was as contented as any man of his temperament and devotion to his people could be in such a time of stark tragedy.

Then came the First World War, with its swiftly moving events and its frenzy of slaughter and massacre of Jews. To read the tenth volume of his history or, better still, his unadorned diary, written in flaming wrath and pain, is to realize the full extent of the agony and suffering of the Jews during those satanic years. A few excerpts from *Mein Leben*, the greatly abridged German edition of his autobiography, will suffice.

March, 1915: We 'celebrated' the *Seder* at the Winawers. We ate our *Matzoh* in tears and silence. We read the *Hagadah* and tried to chant its songs, but the mood was lacking. Winawer's question, *Ma Nishtanah*, remained unanswered. There was no answer. We are just slaves given to shame and slaughter.

December, 1916: The Hanukah lights burn and sputter in my study. I lighted them for my grandson Alja, who loves them so. He comes around every Hanukah to watch them burn. But my soul is weary and tired like the sputtering tapers. Soon they will be exhausted and die and everything will be dark.

February, 1917: I see no end to these frightful days. I spend my days and nights in silence. I cannot even think, I dare not think. I take up the Talmud, Tacitus, the Church Fathers. I try to read, but in vain. I cannot concentrate. My soul is not moved by what I read.

March, 1917: Spring is in the air. The sun shines, but it does not warm. Nothing seems to warm any more. Everything is chaos and confusion. No Mirabeau among the conservatives, no Danton among the radicals. What will be the end? But, hold! Someone has just burst in with great news. The provisional government has swept all inequalities away with one magic stroke. Winawer and Grusenberg are named senators in the government. Our suffering, Jewish suffering, is at an end. The dream, the hope of a lifetime, is fulfilled.

Unhappy, deluded Dubnow! His joy was but of the night—the morning brought terrible changes. The provisional government was swept away, and everything was confusion and anarchy again. He saw St. Petersburg, his St. Petersburg, dying from utter weariness and exhaustion. "Around me," he writes, "everything is falling as if in a flood. For me the revolution came too late. My strength is ebbing. Yet, there is work to be done. My history must be written. It cannot end so."

No, indeed, it was not to end so. His life work was to be done, his history was to be written and given to the world in ten great volumes. But under what terrible circumstances! Only a soul as strong, as heroic, as unflinching as that of Dubnow could master the pain, the suffering, the hunger, cold, and loneliness, and save the work he had set his heart upon completing.

A few more excerpts from *Mein Leben:*

December, 1917: The capital is freezing. No coal, no wood anywhere. . . . I sit in my coat. . . . I attempt to write, but my fingers are numb with cold. . . . There is no light in the house. . . . The electric current is turned off. . . . No kerosene in the lamp. . . . What little there was I used for writing. . . . The history at all events must be written. . . . My wife went for wood. I came out to meet her. . . . My heart sank when I saw her coming with the basket empty. . . . I work with my fingers frozen. . . . The pen is dropping from my hand. . . . Now the last kopek is spent, and no food, no wood, no lighting material. . . . We moved into the kitchen, where, by shutting off the other rooms, we might keep from freezing. . . . We are all there and I am trying to work. . . . Cold and hunger. . . . My thoughts whirl around madly in a circle. How can one work? . . . How often in my despair have I thought of Zionism and Palestine! Perhaps I was wrong; perhaps I have sinned. . . . How happier I might have been in the Holy Land together with my own! . . . Yet, how could I? How could I leave and desert my people in their degraded and fallen position? I shall end my days in the wilderness, perhaps never to see the Land of Promise.

And so on and on in touching and tragic words. His position was slightly improved by a grant Maxim Gorky was able to obtain from the Soviet Government for scholars and intellectual workers like Dubnow. Can one imagine this man Dubnow, approaching sixty, his health greatly impaired by the burden of his experiences, trudging through the slush and sleet of Leningrad's neglected streets groaning under the weight of the provisions he had to carry weekly to his home?

Yet, even in those dark and dismal years, there occurred a flash of satisfaction. His colleagues and co-workers, remembering Dubnow's forty years of service to Jewish scholarship and the Jewish cause, assembled to honor him at a reception at which speeches were more abundant than food. It was the only cheerful note in a drama that for five long years had contained nothing but sadness and bitterness.

He nursed hopes of escaping the "Soviet hell," as he called his Russian prison. Some of his friends did escape and found refuge in other more hospitable lands; but how could he, whose anti-communist views were well known, who had never made any attempt to conceal them, get away? An invitation came to him from the University of Kovno to fill the chair of Jewish history, which was created especially for him. After many vain attempts, he at last succeeded in obtaining the desperately hoped-for passport. But his books and papers, especially the latter, among which were many incriminating documents—how could he smuggle them out of a country where every scrap of paper was meticulously examined and scrutinized? Luck, however, which had long passed him by, was with him this time; for in April, 1922, the doors of his Soviet prison were unlocked and, together with his wife and his precious papers—his children already lived abroad—he was set free.

He could not have been in Kovno very long, for shortly after his release he was in Berlin, capital of the Weimar Republic and meeting place of almost all the bright spirits he knew in his younger and happier days in Odessa. It was a joyous reunion, and in the depths of his still-active mind plans for new work were maturing. But suffering had blunted his creative genius and he devoted himself, instead, to completing his *Weltgeschichte*—no small task for a man like Dubnow, so critical of himself and punc-tilious in everything that came from his pen. He wrote, and revised, and rewrote his manuscripts, and when he was in doubt about the smallest detail he consulted experts.

The work he wrote in Russian for the instruction of his brethren there was destined to appear first in German and afterward in several other European languages, as well as in Hebrew. It was in the year 1929, when Dubnow was almost seventy years old, that his ten-volume history appeared under its full title, *Geschichte des Judischen Volkes von Seiner Anfange Bis zur Gegenwart*. It was an occasion for rejoicing and celebration among Jewish scholars everywhere, and a *Festschrift*, hailing both Dubnow's seventieth birthday and the appearance of his master work, was edited by the late Professor Ismar Elbogen (Berlin, 1930).

Simon Dubnow had another eleven years to live but, unfortunately, they were years darkened by fresh sorrow and suffering. Soon after his triumph of his history the Weimar Republic was destroyed and the Hitler plague appeared on the scene. Dubnow, now past seventy, had again to look for a new domicile; but where could he go to escape the Nazi scourge? Friends urged him to settle in Switzerland or in France where, they thought, he would be safe. But Simon Dubnow with his inborn passion for Jews and Jewish community life, chose Riga, then an intelligent and enlightened Jewish community—a fatal blunder that shrouded his few remaining years in disaster which ended in martyrdom.

He was in the midnight of his career, but work still obsessed him, and he busied himself with arranging his papers and documents—precious manuscripts he had carried with him through all the years of his exile because of their bearing on the latest drama of his people. He lived in solitude, but in comfort, in a pleasant house in the outskirts of the city. Then came the Nazi satanic hordes and ordered him into the ghetto to share the fate of his stricken and fallen people. Never was he so serene and calm, never so brimful of love and pity for his sorrowing and suffering brethren, as during those frightful months when he shared their fears and dangers. One thinks of Jeremiah following his people into captivity, or Don Isaac Abravanel comforting his brethren on their hard and bitter road to exile. To be with the Jews he loved to the end, to live and perish with them, was his dearest dream. He would have wished himself no better fate. And when the last bell tolled and he, together with his fellow captives, was ordered to his final martyrdom, one can almost see this man of eighty-one, the living symbol of the heart and conscience of his people, walking proudly to his doom as had walked those martyrs of Mayance and Worms whom he had so lovingly described in his history.

It is difficult to take leave of Simon Dubnow without a final word of appreciation. For he was indeed a great man, a colossal figure of his generation. He united in himself so many elements of greatness that for any one of them history would have accorded him a niche in its hall of fame. He was a great Jew, a great historian, a great writer, an impassioned lover of his people, a man with an unbiased judgment of the past, and a vigilant observer of his time —in his person and achievement one of the noblest products of his people. Indeed, there is not a blemish on his record. Through a long and distinguished life he served the cause of his people with such singleness of purpose, with such Hasidic devotion and utter forgetfulness of self, as to earn their undying and reverent gratitude.

There were other great men in his day whose names still ring out in the pages of Jewish history and literature But Simon Dubnow was perhaps the greatest and best loved of his contemporaries. He was not a scholar born for the ivory-tower but a warrior who fought for justice toward his people with all the weapons at his command. And the battles he waged, covering a period of almost two generations, were many and heroic. He fought the enemies within the Jewish camp and the foe without—fought to the very last, when death took the sword from his hand.

His loss created a vacancy in the life of the Jewish people. For he was the kind of man—scholar, thinker, and doer—whose place will not easily be filled. With all the sorrow and suffering it endured, his generation still was fortunate to have lived in the shadow of so great a man.

Louis Ginzberg

PROFESSOR LOUIS GINZBERG belonged to the classical age of scholarship, to that world of Jewish learning which produced the profoundest minds and warmest hearts. He favored the modern method of education yet looked back fondly to the old-time *heder* where the spirit of piety and the Jewish atmosphere prevailed. A product of the *yeshiva,* he is almost lyrical in his praise and admiration for its curriculum, its method and manner of study, and the pious and learned men who presided over it. Modern scholar though he was, and himself a practitioner of the most approved scientific methods, he nevertheless paid glowing tribute to the Polish masters of talmudic learning—to such men as Solomon Luria, Moses Isserles, and Shalom Shakna. He had even a good word to say in favor of the pilpulistic, or dialectical, method they introduced in the study of the Talmud.

Dr. Ginzberg lived up to the highest requirements of Jewish scholarship. The talmudic definition of a *talmid hakam* as one who replies satisfactorily to all questions concerning any subject of *halakah,* applied with greater accuracy to him than to most other scholars. For he was the master of Jewish learning, a man of great erudition and unrivaled scholarship who knew the whole Torah, both the revealed and the esoteric lore, with all their commentaries and supercommentaries. His radiant spirit, impressive learning and unusually attractive personality made him one of the best loved and most admired Jewish scholars of our time.

Dr. Ginzberg was the *Matmid* of whom the poet Bialik sang. There was no room in his life for idleness. His tremendous energy and industry were astonishing. The passing years stimulated rather than impaired his remarkable creative powers.

442

High up in an apartment building overlooking the campus of Columbia University this unwearied and keen-eyed scholar sat in a room lined with books of all sizes and in almost all languages from early morning until late at night—and sometimes all through the night—adding one by one to the pile of sheets which he had covered with the thoughts of his busy mind. All day long noises from the street below and the sound of voices and hurrying feet of students late for their classes intruded upon the quiet and calm of the study; but, undaunted, the tireless worker kept at his task. There was no time to be wasted. The huge folios of the Talmud, as it were, begged to be explained, interpreted, and clarified for future generations. He was the watchman of his people, the keeper of a treasure to which only he held the key. Sometimes he paused for a moment and drew deeply on the cigar that was always in his hand when a knotty problem disturbed the smoothness and evenness of his thought. It might have been a problem in the history or philology of the old text. Quickly other editions, cross-references, and standard dictionaries were consulted, until the table literally groaned beneath the weight of books. Then a smile came to his eyes. The problem was solved, the mistake corrected, and everything was tested and molded into shape. He could now resume his work.

He was one of the most prolific scholars and writers of his age. Scarcely a year passed but that he contributed a volume or essay of the deepest interest and importance. "Search it and search it again, for everything is in it," that ancient adage which the Palestinian sage applied to the Torah, was peculiarly applicable to Professor Ginzberg, for there was not a subject he had not exhausted nor a field of learning he had not explored. He established the origin and editing of the *Mishnah;* he made a survey in two volumes of the Gaonic *Halakah* and *Responsa* literature; in another two volumes he edited fragments from the Schechter Genizah collection; he expanded into an 800-page volume his series of studies on *An Unknown Jewish Sect.*

The student of *Halakah* was also master of *Haggadah,* the folklore of the Jews as found in their literature over two milleniums.

The agility with which the writer switched from one subject to the other, from the intricate and complicated legal disputations of the Rabbis to their lighter or imaginative side, is almost incredible. But in the comprehensive mind of Ginzberg, *Halakalah* and *Haggadah,* law and legend, precept and story, were all one, deriving from the same source and intended for the same purpose—the glorification of God and His holy Torah.

He was as noted for his acquaintance with Christian and Islamic religious and philosophical literature as for his unrivaled knowledge of the biblical, post-biblical and post-exilic literature of his own people. Indeed, he was one of the few men of whom it may be said that there was hardly a field of knowledge he had not invaded, not a branch of learning, sacred or secular, he had not mastered. And what he read or heard remained stored away in his marvelous memory, so that nothing was lost. It was literally impossible to mention in his presence any book or article on any subject in which he was interested that he had not read or seen, no matter how long ago it might have been published. He would refer to a book or magazine he read in his student days as if he had seen it only the other day.

He did not loiter in the halls of learning or superficially toy with the knowledge he acquired, but was the premier master of almost all matters pertaining to Jewish and general learning. And whatever he touched was transformed into shining gold, for Dr. Ginzberg was not merely a skillful scholar but an imaginative one. He combined clarity of vision with a high poetic temperament; he possessed the scientist's precision and the insight and penetration of the artist. He published old manuscripts and annotated obscure texts; but always he peered between the written lines into the soul of the writer. He made the dim and obscure fresh, vivid, and luminous. Solomon Schechter was master of this style of writing and Ginzberg, particularly in his *Students, Scholars And Saints,* had more than inherited his talent.

He served every field of Jewish learning, for he was a *ben bayit,* at home everywhere—in Bible, Talmud, history, philosophy, theology, liturgy, philology, to say nothing of the commentaries of the Palestinian, Babylonian, Spanish, French, German, and Slavic schools. Besides his books, great and learned works embodying the Jewish wisdom and culture of the ages, he contributed a steady flow of papers, essays, and articles to periodicals, encyclopedias, and tribute and memorial volumes in Hebrew, German, French, and English. He wrote with ease and with unrivaled knowledge and acumen.

While still a young man and a student at German universities Dr. Ginzberg embarked on one of the most ambitious ventures of his career. He conducted researches in the works of the Christian church fathers for traces of Jewish folklore, and what he discovered both surprised and astonished him. For he found that not only did they contain a considerable number of stories and legends of the Jewish talmudic-Midrashic literature but also a good deal of Jewish folklore material not recorded in the writings of the synagogue. He found the same to hold true of Islamic literature, in which he found embalmed many a Jewish legend that one would seek in vain in Jewish books.

It was a find that warmed the young student's heart—a discovery, indeed, in which he sensed his future career. The literary artist in him was stirred by the enormous wealth of legendary material in almost all languages and literatures regarding the important episodes and personages of the Bible, from the creation of the world to Queen Esther. It was virgin soil, a fabulously rich and fertile territory yielding undreamed of treasures at every thrust of the spade. He issued two monographs on the Haggadic elements in the works of the church fathers which, for their originality and novelty of approach, were immediately seized upon by scholars as an important contribution to the study of comparative folklore. But only the beginning had been made, for the mind of the writer evolved the more ambitious plan of a vivid, coherent, and systematically arranged survey of Jewish legendary literature as found in Jewish and non-Jewish sources.

The Legends of the Jews appeared as one of the crowning achievements of Dr. Ginzberg's life and a red-letter day in Jewish scholarship. It is a book for the layman and for the scholar, both a popular and a strictly scientific work. While the average reader will enjoy the hundreds of fascinating stories and legends, presented in a charming and entertaining manner, the expert eye will look to the scaffolding, the colossal labor, and the almost unimaginable craftsmanship which went into the sifting and arranging of the material, assembling bit by bit the widely separated myths and fables scattered through not one literature but many. The uninitiated reader will probably rush breathlessly through the four narrative volumes, paying little attention to the thousands of notes in the other two volumes which reveal the author at the height of his genius as a scholar, thinker, and historian of Jewish folklore. It was indeed a Herculean task—one which only the mind and stupendous learning of a Louis Ginzberg could have accomplished. One can well understand the universal enthusiasm with which the work was received. It was succinctly expressed by Dr. Boaz Cohen, the noted disciple of the master who supplied the index volume to the *magnum opus:* "Suffice it to say that this work represents the greatest single contribution to the study of the Agadah within a century. Its significance lies not only in its unsurpassed collection of materials from all out of the way sources but also in the fact that it paves the way for numerous monographs in the various fields of theology, folklore, superstition, customs and legends." The four narrative volumes of the *Legends* appeared in 1956 in a one-volume edition under the title, *The Legends of the Bible,* with an Introduction by Shalom Spiegel.

Had the *Legends* been Dr. Ginzberg's only achievement it would have sufficed to win for him the international fame that was his; but actually it was only one of his great accomplishments. For in close affinity with Ginzberg, the folklorist, stands Ginzberg, the Halakist, one of the greatest modern exponents of the enormous body of religious law which makes up the bulk of both the Palestinian and Babylonian Talmuds. Master of the legendary lore of the Jews that he was, he was frank to admit that it is only in the *Halakah,* as its meaning, "conduct," indicates, that we find the mind and character of the Jewish people clearly and adequately expressed. "The Halakah," Dr. Ginzberg insists, "comprises life f style and feeling for color and language that made him rare among scholars.

One need but read his *Students, Scholars and Saints* to appreciate the warmth and feeling which animate his writing. The book is a collection of lectures and addresses delivered on public occasions and sketches of great and holy men. So vivid and radiantly alive is the writing that the reader shares the writer's feelings and memories as if they were his own. He sees with the author's eyes the recreated images of the "Jewish Primary School" and the "Rabbinical Student." He finds himself among a gallery of glowing figures—Rabbi Elijah of Vilna, Rabbi Israel Salanter, Isaac Hirsch Weiss, Solomon Schechter, and David Hoffman—all of whom enriched Jewish life.

No better impression of this truly unusual volume can be given than by quoting a passage from his essay on Solomon Schechter. "The Dutch peasant of today," he says, "admires and appreciates Rembrandt not because this great painter tried to gain the popular appreciation, but because he had penetrated into the depth of the soul of his people, and in looking at a Rembrandt the Dutch people recognize themselves in it." It was to the end that the Jews might recognize themselves in the work of their great masters, that they might be inspired by their lives, informed by their lessons, and encouraged by their examples that Dr. Ginzberg has brought these outstanding Jewish leaders to life in this book.

Solomon Schechter declared that Leopold Zunz, founder of Jewish *Wissenschaft*, once said to Professor David Kaufman, "Those who have read my books are far from knowing me." The same may be said of Professor Ginzberg. While his books are known to the world and his reputation as scholar and thinker rest securely on them, Louis Ginzberg, the man, was wholly revealed only to those who were so fortunate as to know him in his private life and to enjoy his company and conversation. He did not isolate himself within the sanctuary of scholarship. He loved people and people were instinctively drawn to him. He was kind and gentle, gracious to everyone.

in all its manifestations—religion, worship, law, economics, politics, ethics, and so forth. It gives us a picture of life in its totality and not of some of its fragments."

Halakah, in Ginzberg's view of the rabbinic law, is not casuistry, not mere legalism, as the traducers and defamers of Judaism would have us believe, but the very essence of the Jew's being, the unfailing expression of his ethical and historic personality. Nor is *Halakah* that static and unchanging rabbinic legislation which fettered the Jewish mind and rendered it incapable of progressive development, as the detractors of Pharisaic Judaism maliciously represent it to be. "With unwonted lucidity and an abundance of erudition," writes Solomon Goldman, an adept pupil of Professor Ginzberg, "he has demonstrated . . . that the law had not been static but evolving, that it had not become petrified but continued sensitive to the exigencies of time and circumstances, and that the differences of opinion among the Rabbis were not formalistic, a kind of show of skill in pedantry, but concerned living issues."

It was to the defense of the historic development of Jewish tradition as manifested in *Halakah* and in everything else that proceeded from the Palestine and Babylonian rabbinic schools that Dr. Ginzberg devoted his vast erudition and expository powers. It was for this purpose that he explored the learning of all times and lands and brought back a harvest of knowledge and information commensurate with the greatness of his spirit. He made detours into *Mishnah, Gemara,* and geonic literature, into history, liturgy, and jurisprudence, into his *Students, Scholars and Saints,* and issued books and monographs on all these subjects which may be said to have widened and clarified the intellectual and spiritual horizons of Judaism.

Transcending in significance and more than fully measuring up to the literary and scholarly importance of the *Legends,* is the last published work of his scientific career—his commentary on *Yerushalmi,* the Palestinian Talmud. It is a historic achievement, although at the time of his death only three volumes, comprising two thousand pages had appeared. It is historic for his method and his unrivaled knowledge, historical insight and keen analytical powers. The work is more than a conventional commentary explaining obscure words and passages; it is a fresh and novel interpretation of the text, often resulting in discussions that in themselves are sufficiently extensive and important to be classified as substantial studies in the history and philosophy of *Halakah*.

Professor Ginzberg chose the Palestinian Talmud for the most triumphant achievement of his learned career because, of the two Talmuds, it has been the more neglected. The Palestinian Jews had not proved as successful in disseminating it as had their Babylonian brothers in spreading their talmudic literature, and many a famous rabbinic scholar was not even aware of its existence. The Babylonian Talmud had had its commentators. Rashi, through his celebrated commentary, had made it accessible to thousands, while the Tossafists, the Franco-German scholars of the thirteenth and fourteenth centuries, enriched and deepened it with their critical and analytical studies. But its Palestinian brother, outside the land of its birth and the North African schools of learning, remained neglected and forsaken. Dr. Ginzberg may not have restored the Palestinian Talmud to popular study but he certainly demonstrated that there are vast areas of Jewish culture which remain dark and unknown because of its neglect.

Professor Ginzberg was the most energetic and industrious of scholars. He worked under all conditions and circumstances, no matter how trying. Failing health did not deter him; he was a tyrant with himself and his time. He worked through the two global wars which set almost the whole world ablaze. Great parts of Europe— the Europe Ginzberg loved and so often visited because of its great libraries and scholars—were destroyed and reduced to a shambles. Millions of Jews were slain and the whole Jewish race was threatened with extinction. He felt their pain and anguish and his face was grim and sad; but he did not interrupt his work. So must Rabban Johanan ben Zakkai have felt when he pleaded with Vespasian for the school of Jabneh and its scholars while flames were reducing the Holy Temple to ashes. So, too, must have felt Rabbi Judah ben Babba when, in a crisis in the life of the Jews, he

continued to instruct and ordain his disciples. L... must have felt that the life and destiny of the ... in their books and their spirit, and that as long ... they need not fear the future.

In addition to the books he wrote and the l... contributed to various periodicals and memori... Ginsberg was a diligent author of scholarly notes. ... volumes published in recent years bear the stamp o... supplied his own *Legends* with thousands of note... volumes; he furnished Dr. Moses Gaster's edition of ... a work of Jewish tales and legends originating abou... century, with hundreds of notes; he annotated Dr. Isra... *Mahzor Yannai* with many critical observations; he ... special volume of notes to Professor George Foot Moo... work, *Judaism*.

In the approximately three years of his connectio... *Jewish Encyclopedia,* first as editor of the division o... Literature and afterward as contributor, he wrote 40... many of them of major importance and of monograph... bibliography of the known writings of Professor Ginzberg... Dr. Boaz Cohen, covers twenty-three pages, not taking int... the substantial number of volumes left in manuscript for... death.

Dr. Louis Ginzberg was a scholar blessed with artistic ... and his works are distinguished for their style. He hated t... and commonplace, and all his writings are marked by an u... freshness of approach and by lively observations. As a rule ... are the most wearisome of all writings, but Ginzberg's were ... with interest.

These stylistic gifts came to him from the poetic spirit of ... *yeshiva* and his immersion in the German classics. In his youth ... published a volume of poems, and Ginzberg told this writer that ... his student days he was a "first nighter" at German theatres a... contributed dramatic reviews and articles to the *Frankfurter Ze... tung.* This early writing also probably helped to develop that sens...

He was most patient and tolerant with all sorts of people, even those with whom he differed. Although he was aware of his place and importance, like Shammai, he greeted every man with a pleasant countenance. On Saturday and holiday afternoons, when his home was crowded with a diversified company of visitors, he was all congeniality and friendliness. A genuine spirit of *gemutlichkeit* pervaded the atmosphere. Everything was bright and cheerful and the entire company was made to feel at ease. He loved to recall his experiences, and fortunate was the man who touched the springs of his memory. What a wealth of observation and anecdotes on men and events would pour forth from his rich store of memories!

Dr. Ginzberg was not a party man and was rarely seen at public meetings. His only party label was that of the Torah, to which he subordinated every other interest. Whatever helped to further the interests of the Jewish people or Jewish learning he encouraged; whatever tended to degrade them, no matter what party was guilty of it, he scorned. He particularly abhorred sectarianism and refused to be drawn into religious controversy which might bring about division among the Jewish people. His own students who tried to gain his support for a particular religious issue found him unresponsive. He detached himself from the shibboleth or battle cry of the moment. He stood forth as the ideal scholar, the spiritual and intellectual sentinel of his people, guarding their treasures so that they might not suffer neglect.

He loved teaching and loved his students; and they venerated him. He taught up until two days of his death. He took a fatherly interest in his students, inquired after them when they left the seminary, and was never so disappointed as when he heard that one of his "boys" had been in the city and had not called to see him. He was not what is known as an eloquent public speaker, but his listeners were rewarded by his scholarship, depth of observation, and wealth of humor.

Although honorary degrees were conferred upon him by a number of institutions of learning, including Harvard University, and he was the first visiting Professor of Rabbinics at the Hebrew University in Jerusalem in 1929, he was actively affiliated with no institution other than the Jewish Theological Seminary of America, whose faculty he adorned for half a century, and the American Academy for Jewish Research, of which he was a founder and president.

To the best of the writer's firsthand knowledge Louis Ginzberg, unlike Solomon Schechter, did not publically declare himself a Zionist or take an active part in the Zionist Movement. Joshua Bloch, an old friend of Ginzberg, on the other hand, maintained from personal knowledge that "throughout the years that I have known Dr. Ginzberg, his faith in Zionism was at no time shaken. Moreover, he did declare himself publicly for Zionism and took an active part in promoting the Zionist cause prior to his coming to America. In fact, he is the author of an admirable presentation of Zionism in the Dutch language. It appeared under the title "Het Zionisme" in *Nieuwe Israelietische Weekblad,* Amsterdam (1899), where he then resided. Upon his settlement in this country at the beginning of the century, he became a frequent contributor to the *Maccabaean,* a monthly publication, which was for many years published in New York City as the organ of the Federation of American Zionists." It is certainly a fact that his writings reveal a deep faith in the awakened Jewish national spirit and the eventual restoration of the Jews to their national home. Thus, in a significant essay on Zechariah Frankel, Dr. Ginzberg applauded warmly the great German Jewish scholar for realizing that "Judaism possessed a far broader basis than that of a mere religious community," and referred derisively to "the spiritless superficiality which avoids any expression of national character." As though to clinch his argument, he declared: "Nationalism is the very air in which Judaism breathes."

From the number of books he wrote and the unnumbered volumes he read, one would imagine Dr. Ginzberg to have been a bookish individual. But in fact he was the least bookish of men. For he was more than a great scholar who annotated difficult texts and composed works bristling with the wit and wisdom of the ages. He was, above everything, a great and unique personality —genial, generous, warmhearted and spontaneous—a man of depth of feeling and tenderness who loved not only humanity but people as individuals.

Dr. Ginzberg was the most accessible of men. There was no formality in his presence, no stiffness of tone or bearing. He kept no calendar of appointments and people freely came and went at all hours without any show of annoyance on his part. He might have been studying an old manuscript in his room lined from floor to ceiling with books of all sizes and in almost all languages; his eyes may have been heavy for lack of sleep, for sometimes, being a poor sleeper, he worked all through the night; but he always welcomed an unexpected visitor in his customary bright and cheerful manner, seemingly unmindful of his interrupted work.

He was a man of feeling and warmth and his emotions were easily aroused. He wrote with a depth of insight and sympathy almost Hasidic in style and tone, although he came from a family that was antagonistic to the Hasidic way of life.

While Dr. Ginzberg's books are intended for a small circle of scholars, they nevertheless reveal the warm character and personality of the man. He was deeply affected by the death of a friend or colleague, and he once bitterly deplored to the writer, with tears in his eyes, that life was becoming empty with the passing of so many of his friends. Stored up in the writer's mind is the unforgettable episode of a *Tisha b'Ab* scene at a summer resort, where the master was surrounded by a number of his former students. It was a clear, cool, starry night when the teacher and his erstwhile pupils assembled for recital of *kinot,* the traditional lamentations prescribed for the occasion. Professor Ginzberg officiated, but he had no sooner read the first few lines than his voice became inaudible, choked by tears and sobs. It was the most effective Zionist propaganda the writer can remember. Who, after that incident, would venture to ask him if he were a Zionist and had faith in the national restoration of the Jews to their ancient homeland?

There is no blank page in Dr. Ginzberg's life; he was the epitome of the old-time *matmid* who gave himself to the Torah day and night. He had a great family tradition to live up to and he dared not default. He was a scion of an intellectual and spiritual aristocracy that extended over many centuries. His immediate forebears were men of great religious and scholarly stature and occupied leading positions in their respective communities. There was R. Moses Kraemer, one of the most learned men of his time, known as "shopkeeper" because he declined to take a salary as a rabbi and preferred to live on the meager earnings of a little provision store conducted by his wife; another was the famous Gaon of Vilna, of whom he always spoke with boundless awe and reverence. The love of learning and devotion to Torah that had come down to Ginzberg through the generations was never weakened or diluted, but grew in strength and intensity.

He was born in the year 1873 in Kovno, for hundreds of years a bastion of learning and piety. His father, R. Yitzhak, who had received his rabbinical ordination from no less an authority than Rabbi Itzhak Elhanan but preferred a mercantile career, was his gifted son's first teacher, since he was well versed in the Torah. But Levi, Louis Ginzberg's Hebrew name, advanced so rapidly in his studies that he soon outgrew his father's and other private teachers' instruction and was deemed sufficiently proficient for a *yeshiva*. The choice fell on Telzh, a new school of talmudic learning organized with the avowed object of stemming the tide of the rationalistic *Haskalah,* which took its toll of the young Russian Jews seeking secular enlightenment.

The young student was only sixteen years old, but he was already adept enough in talmudic dialectics to become famed in the learned circles as *illui,* a young prodigy. It was lucky for Levi that he was not subjected to the crushing poverty and heartbreaking loneliness that fell to the lot of so many other students of the law; for not only was his father able to maintain him in comfort but members of the Ginzberg family were so widely dispersed that, wherever the youthful scholar went, he could always depend upon finding a home with a relative.

in all its manifestations—religion, worship, law, economics, politics, ethics, and so forth. It gives us a picture of life in its totality and not of some of its fragments."

Halakah, in Ginzberg's view of the rabbinic law, is not casuistry, not mere legalism, as the traducers and defamers of Judaism would have us believe, but the very essence of the Jew's being, the unfailing expression of his ethical and historic personality. Nor is *Halakah* that static and unchanging rabbinic legislation which fettered the Jewish mind and rendered it incapable of progressive development, as the detractors of Pharisaic Judaism maliciously represent it to be. "With unwonted lucidity and an abundance of erudition," writes Solomon Goldman, an adept pupil of Professor Ginzberg, "he has demonstrated . . . that the law had not been static but evolving, that it had not become petrified but continued sensitive to the exigencies of time and circumstances, and that the differences of opinion among the Rabbis were not formalistic, a kind of show of skill in pedantry, but concerned living issues."

It was to the defense of the historic development of Jewish tradition as manifested in *Halakah* and in everything else that proceeded from the Palestine and Babylonian rabbinic schools that Dr. Ginzberg devoted his vast erudition and expository powers. It was for this purpose that he explored the learning of all times and lands and brought back a harvest of knowledge and information commensurate with the greatness of his spirit. He made detours into *Mishnah, Gemara,* and geonic literature, into history, liturgy, and jurisprudence, into his *Students, Scholars and Saints,* and issued books and monographs on all these subjects which may be said to have widened and clarified the intellectual and spiritual horizons of Judaism.

Transcending in significance and more than fully measuring up to the literary and scholarly importance of the *Legends,* is the last published work of his scientific career—his commentary on *Yerushalmi,* the Palestinian Talmud. It is a historic achievement, although at the time of his death only three volumes, comprising two thousand pages had appeared. It is historic for his method and his unrivaled knowledge, historical insight and keen analytical powers. The work is more than a conventional commentary explaining obscure words and passages; it is a fresh and novel interpretation of the text, often resulting in discussions that in themselves are sufficiently extensive and important to be classified as substantial studies in the history and philosophy of *Halakah*.

Professor Ginzberg chose the Palestinian Talmud for the most triumphant achievement of his learned career because, of the two Talmuds, it has been the more neglected. The Palestinian Jews had not proved as successful in disseminating it as had their Babylonian brothers in spreading their talmudic literature, and many a famous rabbinic scholar was not even aware of its existence. The Babylonian Talmud had had its commentators. Rashi, through his celebrated commentary, had made it accessible to thousands, while the Tossafists, the Franco-German scholars of the thirteenth and fourteenth centuries, enriched and deepened it with their critical and analytical studies. But its Palestinian brother, outside the land of its birth and the North African schools of learning, remained neglected and forsaken. Dr. Ginzberg may not have restored the Palestinian Talmud to popular study but he certainly demonstrated that there are vast areas of Jewish culture which remain dark and unknown because of its neglect.

Professor Ginzberg was the most energetic and industrious of scholars. He worked under all conditions and circumstances, no matter how trying. Failing health did not deter him; he was a tyrant with himself and his time. He worked through the two global wars which set almost the whole world ablaze. Great parts of Europe— the Europe Ginzberg loved and so often visited because of its great libraries and scholars—were destroyed and reduced to a shambles. Millions of Jews were slain and the whole Jewish race was threatened with extinction. He felt their pain and anguish and his face was grim and sad; but he did not interrupt his work. So must Rabban Johanan ben Zakkai have felt when he pleaded with Vespasian for the school of Jabneh and its scholars while flames were reducing the Holy Temple to ashes. So, too, must have felt Rabbi Judah ben Babba when, in a crisis in the life of the Jews, he continued to instruct and ordain his disciples. Like them, Ginzberg must have felt that the life and destiny of the Jewish people are in their books and their spirit, and that as long as these are secure they need not fear the future.

In addition to the books he wrote and the learned papers he contributed to various periodicals and memorial volumes, Dr. Ginsberg was a diligent author of scholarly notes. Many important volumes published in recent years bear the stamp of his genius. He supplied his own *Legends* with thousands of notes in two bulky volumes; he furnished Dr. Moses Gaster's edition of *Ma'aseh Book,* a work of Jewish tales and legends originating about the fifteenth century, with hundreds of notes; he annotated Dr. Israel Davidson's *Mahzor Yannai* with many critical observations; he contributed a special volume of notes to Professor George Foot Moore's standard work, *Judaism.*

In the approximately three years of his connection with the *Jewish Encyclopedia,* first as editor of the division of Rabbinic Literature and afterward as contributor, he wrote 406 articles, many of them of major importance and of monograph length. A bibliography of the known writings of Professor Ginzberg made by Dr. Boaz Cohen, covers twenty-three pages, not taking into account the substantial number of volumes left in manuscript form at his death.

Dr. Louis Ginzberg was a scholar blessed with artistic talents, and his works are distinguished for their style. He hated the dull and commonplace, and all his writings are marked by an unusual freshness of approach and by lively observations. As a rule notes are the most wearisome of all writings, but Ginzberg's were alive with interest.

These stylistic gifts came to him from the poetic spirit of the *yeshiva* and his immersion in the German classics. In his youth he published a volume of poems, and Ginzberg told this writer that in his student days he was a "first nighter" at German theatres and contributed dramatic reviews and articles to the *Frankfurter Zeitung.* This early writing also probably helped to develop that sense of style and feeling for color and language that made him rare among scholars.

One need but read his *Students, Scholars and Saints* to appreciate the warmth and feeling which animate his writing. The book is a collection of lectures and addresses delivered on public occasions and sketches of great and holy men. So vivid and radiantly alive is the writing that the reader shares the writer's feelings and memories as if they were his own. He sees with the author's eyes the recreated images of the "Jewish Primary School" and the "Rabbinical Student." He finds himself among a gallery of glowing figures— Rabbi Elijah of Vilna, Rabbi Israel Salanter, Isaac Hirsch Weiss, Solomon Schechter, and David Hoffman—all of whom enriched Jewish life.

No better impression of this truly unusual volume can be given than by quoting a passage from his essay on Solomon Schechter. "The Dutch peasant of today," he says, "admires and appreciates Rembrandt not because this great painter tried to gain the popular appreciation, but because he had penetrated into the depth of the soul of his people, and in looking at a Rembrandt the Dutch people recognize themselves in it." It was to the end that the Jews might recognize themselves in the work of their great masters, that they might be inspired by their lives, informed by their lessons, and encouraged by their examples that Dr. Ginzberg has brought these outstanding Jewish leaders to life in this book.

Solomon Schechter declared that Leopold Zunz, founder of Jewish *Wissenschaft,* once said to Professor David Kaufman, "Those who have read my books are far from knowing me." The same may be said of Professor Ginzberg. While his books are known to the world and his reputation as scholar and thinker rest securely on them, Louis Ginzberg, the man, was wholly revealed only to those who were so fortunate as to know him in his private life and to enjoy his company and conversation. He did not isolate himself within the sanctuary of scholarship. He loved people and people were instinctively drawn to him. He was kind and gentle, gracious to everyone.

He was most patient and tolerant with all sorts of people, even those with whom he differed. Although he was aware of his place and importance, like Shammai, he greeted every man with a pleasant countenance. On Saturday and holiday afternoons, when his home was crowded with a diversified company of visitors, he was all congeniality and friendliness. A genuine spirit of *gemutlichkeit* pervaded the atmosphere. Everything was bright and cheerful and the entire company was made to feel at ease. He loved to recall his experiences, and fortunate was the man who touched the springs of his memory. What a wealth of observation and anecdotes on men and events would pour forth from his rich store of memories!

Dr. Ginzberg was not a party man and was rarely seen at public meetings. His only party label was that of the Torah, to which he subordinated every other interest. Whatever helped to further the interests of the Jewish people or Jewish learning he encouraged; whatever tended to degrade them, no matter what party was guilty of it, he scorned. He particularly abhorred sectarianism and refused to be drawn into religious controversy which might bring about division among the Jewish people. His own students who tried to gain his support for a particular religious issue found him unresponsive. He detached himself from the shibboleth or battle cry of the moment. He stood forth as the ideal scholar, the spiritual and intellectual sentinel of his people, guarding their treasures so that they might not suffer neglect.

He loved teaching and loved his students; and they venerated him. He taught up until two days of his death. He took a fatherly interest in his students, inquired after them when they left the seminary, and was never so disappointed as when he heard that one of his "boys" had been in the city and had not called to see him. He was not what is known as an eloquent public speaker, but his listeners were rewarded by his scholarship, depth of observation, and wealth of humor.

Although honorary degrees were conferred upon him by a number of institutions of learning, including Harvard University, and he was the first visiting Professor of Rabbinics at the Hebrew University in Jerusalem in 1929, he was actively affiliated with no institution other than the Jewish Theological Seminary of America, whose faculty he adorned for half a century, and the American Academy for Jewish Research, of which he was a founder and president.

To the best of the writer's firsthand knowledge Louis Ginzberg, unlike Solomon Schechter, did not publically declare himself a Zionist or take an active part in the Zionist Movement. Joshua Bloch, an old friend of Ginzberg, on the other hand, maintained from personal knowledge that "throughout the years that I have known Dr. Ginzberg, his faith in Zionism was at no time shaken. Moreover, he did declare himself publicly for Zionism and took an active part in promoting the Zionist cause prior to his coming to America. In fact, he is the author of an admirable presentation of Zionism in the Dutch language. It appeared under the title "Het Zionisme" in *Nieuwe Israelietische Weekblad,* Amsterdam (1899), where he then resided. Upon his settlement in this country at the beginning of the century, he became a frequent contributor to the *Maccabaean,* a monthly publication, which was for many years published in New York City as the organ of the Federation of American Zionists." It is certainly a fact that his writings reveal a deep faith in the awakened Jewish national spirit and the eventual restoration of the Jews to their national home. Thus, in a significant essay on Zechariah Frankel, Dr. Ginzberg applauded warmly the great German Jewish scholar for realizing that "Judaism possessed a far broader basis than that of a mere religious community," and referred derisively to "the spiritless superficiality which avoids any expression of national character." As though to clinch his argument, he declared: "Nationalism is the very air in which Judaism breathes."

From the number of books he wrote and the unnumbered volumes he read, one would imagine Dr. Ginzberg to have been a bookish individual. But in fact he was the least bookish of men. For he was more than a great scholar who annotated difficult texts and composed works bristling with the wit and wisdom of the ages. He was, above everything, a great and unique personality —genial, generous, warmhearted and spontaneous—a man of depth of feeling and tenderness who loved not only humanity but people as individuals.

Dr. Ginzberg was the most accessible of men. There was no formality in his presence, no stiffness of tone or bearing. He kept no calendar of appointments and people freely came and went at all hours without any show of annoyance on his part. He might have been studying an old manuscript in his room lined from floor to ceiling with books of all sizes and in almost all languages; his eyes may have been heavy for lack of sleep, for sometimes, being a poor sleeper, he worked all through the night; but he always welcomed an unexpected visitor in his customary bright and cheerful manner, seemingly unmindful of his interrupted work.

He was a man of feeling and warmth and his emotions were easily aroused. He wrote with a depth of insight and sympathy almost Hasidic in style and tone, although he came from a family that was antagonistic to the Hasidic way of life.

While Dr. Ginzberg's books are intended for a small circle of scholars, they nevertheless reveal the warm character and personality of the man. He was deeply affected by the death of a friend or colleague, and he once bitterly deplored to the writer, with tears in his eyes, that life was becoming empty with the passing of so many of his friends. Stored up in the writer's mind is the unforgettable episode of a *Tisha b'Ab* scene at a summer resort, where the master was surrounded by a number of his former students. It was a clear, cool, starry night when the teacher and his erstwhile pupils assembled for recital of *kinot,* the traditional lamentations prescribed for the occasion. Professor Ginzberg officiated, but he had no sooner read the first few lines than his voice became inaudible, choked by tears and sobs. It was the most effective Zionist propaganda the writer can remember. Who, after that incident, would venture to ask him if he were a Zionist and had faith in the national restoration of the Jews to their ancient homeland?

There is no blank page in Dr. Ginzberg's life; he was the epitome of the old-time *matmid* who gave himself to the Torah day and night. He had a great family tradition to live up to and he dared not default. He was a scion of an intellectual and spiritual aristocracy that extended over many centuries. His immediate forebears were men of great religious and scholarly stature and occupied leading positions in their respective communities. There was R. Moses Kraemer, one of the most learned men of his time, known as "shopkeeper" because he declined to take a salary as a rabbi and preferred to live on the meager earnings of a little provision store conducted by his wife; another was the famous Gaon of Vilna, of whom he always spoke with boundless awe and reverence. The love of learning and devotion to Torah that had come down to Ginzberg through the generations was never weakened or diluted, but grew in strength and intensity.

He was born in the year 1873 in Kovno, for hundreds of years a bastion of learning and piety. His father, R. Yitzhak, who had received his rabbinical ordination from no less an authority than Rabbi Itzhak Elhanan but preferred a mercantile career, was his gifted son's first teacher, since he was well versed in the Torah. But Levi, Louis Ginzberg's Hebrew name, advanced so rapidly in his studies that he soon outgrew his father's and other private teachers' instruction and was deemed sufficiently proficient for a *yeshiva*. The choice fell on Telzh, a new school of talmudic learning organized with the avowed object of stemming the tide of the rationalistic *Haskalah*, which took its toll of the young Russian Jews seeking secular enlightenment.

The young student was only sixteen years old, but he was already adept enough in talmudic dialectics to become famed in the learned circles as *illui*, a young prodigy. It was lucky for Levi that he was not subjected to the crushing poverty and heartbreaking loneliness that fell to the lot of so many other students of the law; for not only was his father able to maintain him in comfort but members of the Ginzberg family were so widely dispersed that, wherever the youthful scholar went, he could always depend upon finding a home with a relative.

The Rabbis of the Talmud frown upon a scholar who receives instruction from but one master. Young Levi had spent two years at the Telzh *yeshiva.* They were fruitful years and he was at the head of a class of five hundred. But there was a mysterious longing in his heart to try his wings at the Slobodka *yeshiva,* not only because of its close proximity to Kovno, the place of his birth but primarily because of the spiritual personality of Rabbi Israel Salanter, founder of the *musar,* or moralist movement, which hovered over it. His deeply sensitive and ethical nature longed for a philosophy of Judaism that would combine learning with the practical conduct of life. The change to the Slobodka *yeshiva* profoundly affected his whole life and many years later resulted in his writing one of his most brilliant essays, on Israel Salanter and the movement he founded.

A crisis in Levi's life came when, for business reasons, his parents moved to Holland and his own health was undermined to the point of serious illness. After he had recovered his parents planned to send him to a Hungarian *yeshiva,* where he was to round out his studies under famed masters of Jewish learning. But the youthful scholar had formed plans of his own. Was it the influence of the rationalist *Haskalah* which he steadily imbibed while at Telzh or was it his desire to combine Torah with *hakmah,* sacred with secular learning? Be that as it may, he could not be dissuaded from the course on which he had set his heart—to matriculate at a German university for acquisition of the general or profane sciences.

"It is impossible to estimate," wrote Dr. Alexander Marx in his essay on Solomon Schechter, "how great a loss Judaism is suffering through the numerous defections from its ranks caused by the sudden removal of its most gifted sons from the Eastern Ghetto into the university life of the West. It requires great inner strength to withstand the influence of the new surroundings and to continue to value the heritage of the Jewish past so little esteemed in those circles." The truth of Dr. Marx's words was borne out by many gifted sons of Israel who, in their quest for the so-called wider world, had become estranged and alienated from their faith and people. But Louis Ginzberg did not desert the spirit and atmosphere of the *yeshiva,* and all the learning and knowledge he acquired was used for its glorification. It was for the purpose of enhancing and beautifying the tents of "Shem" that he sought out and dwelt in the palaces and halls of learning of "Japhet," whether at the university of Strassburg, Heidelberg, or Berlin. He brought to bear the method and scientific approach of the West upon the learning and culture of the East, and the result was a revival of Jewish study and scholarship unique in our time.

Dr. Ginzberg's life was divided between several countries. Russia, Germany, Holland, and America made up the odyssey of his life. But it was in the United States that he achieved his greatest fame and distinction as a scholar. He came to this country in 1899 as a young man of twenty-six, with a reputation for learning already familiar in the scholarly world but without a plan for the future. It was fortunate that at about that time *The Jewish Encyclopedia,* the first product of American Jewish cultural development, began publication and that Louis Ginzberg became one of its moving spirits, first as contributor and afterward in recognition of the high level of learning, as editor of the talmudic-rabbinic department. It was planned to publish his more enduring contributions in the *Encyclopedia* as an anniversary volume to mark his eightieth birthday. When death overtook him before that time, his contributions appeared posthumously under the title, *On Jewish Law and Lore.* The volume also includes "An Introductory Essay to the Palestinian Talmud," "Jewish Folklore: East and West," an address delivered at the Tercentenary of Harvard University, and "The Significance of the Halachah for Jewish History," delivered at the Hebrew University in Jerusalem.

It was an event of the highest historic importance to the religious and cultural life of the Jews of the United States—one might say of the world—when Solomon Schechter, with his usual insight, recognized the genius of the young scholar but recently come to this country and prevailed upon him to accept the professorship in Talmud and senior membership on the faculty of the reorganized Jewish Theological Seminary of America—a position which he filled with great distinction and service to the cause of Jewish learning for more than five decades, to the very end of his life, on November 11, 1953.

When a *talmudic hakam,* or scholar, departed this earth, the Rabbis tell us, his colleagues were wont to say: "Happy is he who has been brought up in the Torah, and devoted himself to Torah. He is a source of delight to his Creator; he acquired a good name, and departed this world with a good name." Professor Levi Ginzberg was not only brought up in the Torah and devoted himself to the Torah, but, through his teaching, example, and inspiration, he stimulated thousands of others to love Torah. He was a source of delight because of the harmonious symmetry of his life, in which feeling, sentiment, love of Torah, historical perception, and religious devotion in a high degree all blended. He was indeed a source of delight to his Creator, and his memory will remain a source of delight and affection to all who knew and loved him.

Chaim Weizmann

DR. CHAIM WEIZMANN, Zionist leader and first president of the State of Israel, is one of the most fascinating figures in modern Jewish history. The age in which he lived abounded in great and famous Jews, and Dr. Weizmann has a secure place among them. If he was not the originator of the Jewish State in Palestine, no other man did as much to bring it about. He was the herald and symbol of the Jewish national renaissance—its eloquent interpreter and advocate before the nations of the world. There was what was called a "holy restlessness" in him, a driving force which made him work for the ideal—to bring Jewish homelessness to an end—which seemed nothing short of messianic. From early youth the idea possessed him and it burned all his life like a sacred flame in his heart. To achieve it and attain his goal he strained every effort, marshaled all his talents and abilities, his persuasive powers, his scientific reputation, and his influence with the great and mighty men of a great empire. He was disappointed and disillusioned, betrayed by the empire he fanatically loved and trusted and by the impatience of his own followers. But internal discord and political betrayal did not deter him in his efforts. He had faith in the Jewish people, faith in the eternity of the ideal for which he was working. In his own words: "Everything which pertains to the building of the Jewish national homeland is a question of eternity. Therein lies the charm of our work."

Dr. Weizmann was ideally prepared for leadership of the Jewish people. He did not come from the distant outposts of Jewish life but from antecedents and an environment from which generations of Jewish leaders, sages, and thinkers had sprung. To this day Dr. Herzl's coming to Zionism—indeed, to the Jewish people—is a mystery still to be solved. He came from an assimilated environment in one of the most completely assimilated countries in Europe. There was nothing about him in his early youth, in his adolescence, in his highly gifted young manhood to foretell that the brilliant young man, the writer of amusing *feuilletons* and the much-talked-about correspondent of the *Neue Freie Presse* in Vienna, would one day emerge as the author of the *Judenstaat* and write a new chapter in Jewish history.

There is no such enigma about Chaim Weizmann. His Zionism was not the result of a crisis, a fierce struggle within himself and his environment. He was born into it, as were thousands of children of observant Jewish parents. He came into it as to an inherited tradition, an ancestral legacy that was passed on from father to son for generations throughout the *galut* life of the Jews. His love for the Holy Land was sharpened and stimulated by a hundred customs and ceremonies he saw carried out in his own home and in that of his grandfather's home near by. The love for Zion and the longing for her speedy restoration were spelled out for him in the prayers he was taught to recite and in the synagogue and home rituals.

Weizmann loved the Jews and the evironment in which he was born and brought up, and he never drifted far away from them. He was perhaps the most westernized Jew of his Zionist compatriots. The largest part of his life was spent in the West, and he absorbed its culture and assimilated its spirit more than his fellow Jews who were born and bred there. But his roots were deeply imbedded in Eastern Europe and his greatest love was for the oppressed and struggling masses of the country of his birth. To his very end Weizmann remained the typical East European Jew, with all his characteristics and peculiarities. He was never so happy as when he was among his own people. He spoke their language and understood their thoughts and feelings, and they in turn were devoted to him.

One of the very greatest Jews of the nineteenth century, Weitzmann was born under the most inauspicious circumstances in the year 1873 in Motol, a wretched hamlet in the old Russian Jewish Pale of Settlement, into a family of fifteen children, twelve of whom lived to grow up. Motol's sole claim to distinction is the fact that the future Zionist leader and statesman was born and spent his childhood there. Pinsk was Motol's nearest well-ordered Jewish community, but the muddy roads made the city almost inaccessible to travelers, so that there was little communication between the two communities.

Weizmann's mother, who lived to the age of 87 and who died in Palestine, was a hard-working woman, worn out by bearing and rearing so many children and taking care of her home, which resembled an institution more than a private household. His father was a rather remarkable man, for his time and environment. He was a kind, gentle, and loving parent, and was respected alike by the Jews and gentiles of the town. A lumber merchant, he worked with peasants in the forest, cutting and felling trees and floating them by rafts down to Danzig. His family saw little of him, but when he was home he exerted a great influence on the children. He was kind and tender, and almost never scolded or reprimanded them; but when he spoke his words carried great weight. He was something of a scholar of the traditional type, deeply religious; and when he found the time he steeped himself in the study of two widely dissimilar works—the *Shulhan Aruk* and *The Guide for the Perplexed*.

Young Weizmann's Hebrew schooling was not any different from that of most Jewish children of his time and place. He attended the squalid, primitive *heder,* a one-room so-called educational establishment, which also served as the rabbi's living quarters, where the students shared the space with the family washing and the family goat, which took shelter there in cold weather. To be sure, it was not an ideal training ground for the future Zionist leader and advocate of the Jewish cultural and national renaissance, and everything about the school, the teacher, and the method of instruction became obnoxious to Weizmann. Fortunately, he later came under the influence of a teacher of the modernized Haskalah type, a man of spirit and imagination who knew and loved the Bible and understood how to make it come to life unforgettably in the hearts and minds of his pupils. Paradoxically, it was through this teacher that Weizmann first developed an interest in chemistry. Surreptitiously and not without considerable risk to himself and his position, the teacher brought with him to school a Hebrew text book on chemistry, which he read to his favorite pupils. What the youthful Weizmann heard made such a deep impression on him that he made up his mind to learn more about the subject when he grew up.

For his secular education Weizmann went to Pinsk, where he entered the Real-Gymnasium, which devoted special attention to the study of chemistry. Geographically the town was not very far from Motol, but intellectually, and as far as the Motol Jewish community was concerned, the distance was astronomical. For Pinsk was a metropolis with a large Jewish population. There Chaim found Jewish schools and scholars and a flourishing revival of the Hebrew language and literature. Although Zionism was not allowed as a political movement in czarist Russia, it throve successfully in Pinsk and produced prominent figures in the Zionist Movement. For Weizmann it was a time of growth and development. Under the influence of wise and intelligent leaders his faculties deepened, his horizon widened, and his life assumed Jewish character and meaning.

An activity in which the eighteen-year-old Weizmann engaged, directly related to Zionism and with enormous bearing upon the cultural life of Russian Jewry, was his agitation for a *heder metukan,* a modernized Hebrew school. He remembered his own dismal experience and knew its crippling effect upon thousands of Jewish children, and he joined in the efforts of the advanced spirits of the Haskalah Movement for an improved primary system of Hebrew education. "A reform was badly needed," he writes in *Trial and Error,* "not only in regard to the accommodation, pedagogy and curriculum but in regard to the entire attitude toward the elementary education of young children. . . . It was extraordinary that the Jews, with whom the education of their children was a matter of profound concern, paid no attention to the first stages of that education. Any sort of luckless failure in the community was considered good enough to teach children their letters, and the word *melamed,* or teacher, was synonymous with *shlemihl."* Weizmann himself amplified the meager Hebrew training he received at the *heder* by devoting much time and effort to the study of the Hebrew language and literature. With his polyglot family he corresponded in several languages. While he wrote to his mother in Yiddish and to his sisters and brothers in Russian, to his father he was allowed to write only in Hebrew. And when Weizmann one day forgot and wrote to him in Yiddish, the letter was returned to him unread.

Weizmann's student years were cast in an atmosphere of *Sturm und Drang.* The ghetto of Jewish isolation became greater, their Pale of Settlement narrower. For a while there was surcease and hope, but soon the bitterness of disappointment darkened their expectations. The liberal reign of Alexander II raised high the hopes of liberation of the Jews of Russia and Hebrew poets sang their hymns to the dawn of the new day. The emperor emancipated the peasant slaves, revised the legal status of the Jews, extended their right of residence, abolished child conscription, sent back the child soldiers to their parents and relatives, and, probably not without missionary overtones, encouraged the fusion of the Jews with the Russian native population. Assimilation proceeded at a rapid pace, as was the case in the post-Mendelssohn period in Germany. Jews rushed blindly into the new life, unconscious of its spiritual danger to Judaism.

When, however, the emperor was assassinated in 1881, with suspected Jewish complicity in the outrage, the reaction under Alexander III was swift and terrible. Government-inspired pogroms broke out against Jews, with murder, rape, and looting. Jews were expelled from their ancient urban and village communities and a decree was issued limiting the admission of Jewish students to Russian colleges and universities to three per cent of the non-Jewish candidates. This would not have been so bad, considering the small number of Jews compared to the overwhelming Russian population, except for the fact that the ruling made no allowance for the much greater craving for knowledge on the part of the Jewish young men and women. The result was that scores of talented young Jews who could not satisfy their ingrained thirst for knowledge in their own country were compelled to leave their homes and attend the schools of learning in foreign lands, some of them going to Germany and some to Switzerland.

Weizmann was one of the venturesome spirits who left their native land for the great world of Europe. He later made his way to Germany, where no shackles were put on the spirit and Jews were free to enter the colleges and the professional schools. His objective was Berlin, at the very name of which the Jews of the ghetto pricked up their ears because of her historic association with modern culture and enlightenment. But he paused for some time in Darmstadt, where he attended the university, and in Pfungstadt, a short distance from the university town, where he occupied a position as a subordinate teacher at a kosher boarding school for his board and lodging. He was cast into a new world utterly unlike the one he had known. Everything was strange and unfamiliar to him—people, language, customs, and environment. What was particularly irksome to him was the excessive religiosity of the boarding school. Weizmann was himself deeply religious by nature and temperament. He loved the religious customs and ceremonies he remembered at home, the poetic feeling they aroused in him, and their historic associations. But the rites and rituals of the boarding school—dry, mechanical, without the warmth and feeling of Jewish national consciousness—made a dismal impression upon him. There, too, for the first time, he became acquainted with the assimilationist fringe of Jewish life—that is, Jews who renounced every form of Jewish national and cultural identification, calling themselves "Germans of the Mosaic Persuasion," and blindly ignoring their insecurity and the danger that the deluge would soon sweep over them.

At the time Weizmann attended the Berlin University the Prussian capital was the center of the creative Jewish spirit. Some of the best-remembered names in modern Hebrew literature, its poets, novelists and philosophical essayists, had lived and worked there. For a brief time it was a kind of literary and cultural Yabneh, from which vitalizing Jewish thought went forth and made the rounds of the Jewish literary circles in Europe. Ahad Ha'am was the magnet that attracted the Hebrew celebrities of Berlin, and around him revolved the younger spirits of the national Hebrew revival who made the city a center of Jewish life and thought. But there were also other men who, without a bridge between the *yeshiva* and the university and with the ghetto memories fresh in their minds, had gone to the extreme of abandoning faith in the Jewish future and espousing causes that were antagonistic to their faith and people. They were the Jewish revolutionary groups, who scorned Zionism, mocked Judaism, and regarded Jewish nationalism and the cultivation of the Hebrew language and literature as reactionary. They equated their persecution as Jews with the general fate of oppressed humanity. There were lively debates in the cafes and clubs between the two rival groups, the Zionists and the revolutionaries, which sometimes lasted until the small hours of the morning. Weizmann took part in these discussions and, excellent debater that he was, he often scored over his opponents.

Weizmann had no illusions about Germany. The temporary peace and prosperity the Jews enjoyed there did not blind him to the stored-up subterranean mass hatred of the Jews. German anti-Semitism was unlike the prejudice against Jews in other countries. It was a fanatic, brooding anti-Semitism which, once let loose, spread with lethal speed over the whole nation. It was the so-called scientific anti-Semitism, rooted in debased racial theories and ideas of Teutonic national superiority. Weizmann realized that his future did not lie in Germany. When, therefore, he was awarded his doctoral degree with high academic honors, he lost no time in leaving the country and settling in Geneva, Switzerland, a city both ancient and modern, with medieval memories and twentieth-century culture, an almost fantastic town of beautiful lakes and towering hills. It was not long before he was given a lectureship in chemistry at the university and he succeeded in patenting two chemical inventions which he sold to the German I. G. Farbenindustrie. In *Trial and Error*, Weizmann records the feeling it gave him to realize that he, like many an innocent foreign chemist, contributed to the power of the sinister instrument of German ambition. In Geneva he met the young woman, a medical student at the university at which he lectured, whom he converted to Zionism and later married, although in her home at Rostov-in-the-Don she had been reared more as a Russian than as a Jew.

At the second Zionist Congress Weizmann for the first time came face to face with Dr. Herzl, a man of majestic appearance, who stood like a king before the people in the splendor of his manhood. He was arresting and irresistible by reason of his great faith and his deep sincerity. His *Judenstaat,* which became a Zionist classic, had made an overwhelming impression in almost all sections of Jewry. It was as if the Jubilee Trumpet was sounded for dispersed Israel, and thousands heeded the call and rallied under its banner. When Dr. Herzl read its first draft of the book to Dr. Moritz Güdemann, the learned Chief Rabbi of Vienna was so moved that he rose and kissed Herzl and said, "Who knows, perhaps you are the one who has been called by God." The Reform and assimilated Jews alone were frightened by the *Judenstaat* and met its appearance with scorn and derision. They violently attacked and disowned it, afraid of the impression it would make among their German compatriots. To the Russian Jews, who knew their Hess and Pinsker, the *Judenstaat* did not come as a bolt from the blue as it did to the westernized Jews, and they admired the courage and sincerity of the man fresh from the boulevards and salons of the Austrian capital.

While Weizmann himself was deeply impressed by Herzl and saw in him a great and historic personality, he was critical of his Zionist policies. For, indeed, considering the differences between the two men in education and background, it would have been surprising if Weizmann's attitude toward the founder of political Zionism and his method of procedure had been other than it was. Herzl was a poet and a playwright and, as correspondent of a great newspaper, had his associations with the great and the near-great in the capitals of Europe, while Weizmann was a chemist whose training was in the laboratory and who was rooted in the warmth and idealism of the plain and humble folks of Eastern

Europe. Herzl spoke of Zionism in large terms of diplomacy and statesmanship, of charters and international agreements—terms hardly comprehensible to the great majority of the Russian delegates—and was looking for quick results. To Weizmann, on the other hand, Zionism was an ideal of an aroused national consciousness to be deepened and matured by slow growth and development. The East European Jews felt a lack of deep insight and understanding in Herzl's Zionism of the spirit of Jewishness which had kept the ideal alive through the centuries. Herzl's program was too cold and mechanical, making it appear more like a glorified philanthropy than a movement for the revival of the Jewish national spirit. More was heard at the Zionist Congress about the freedom of Jews than about the freedom of Judaism—more about trying to save the body of the Jewish people than about saving its soul. It was for these reasons that, as a kind of Loyal Opposition to the Western conception of Zionism, Weizmann with a few other Russian Zionists organized the Democratic Fraction, which gained the support of the Poale Zion and the Mizrachi, respectively the left and right wings of the Zionist Movement.

It was also in fulfillment of the cultural aspirations of Zionism, first and always insisted upon by Ahad Ha'am, that Weizmann, in collaboration with Martin Buber and Berthold Feivel, proceeded to press for the execution of a project for a Hebrew University in Jerusalem, as proposed at the first Congress by Hermann Schapiro, a professor of mathematics at Heidelberg University. It was not until the Congress at Vienna that the matter was placed on the agenda, and Weizmann was named to head a Commission to explore the practical and technical phases of the project. It was a tremendous undertaking. It called for great tact in approaching scholars with reputations that would lend prestige to the project. And it called for experience in organizing a school of learning, with faculties in the physical and biological sciences and departments in humanistic, Jewish, and Oriental studies; with museums and libraries—all these, not to mention the money required for such purposes. Weizmann was fortunate in that he lived to see the realization of his and his colleagues' pet dream with the laying of the cornerstone of the University in July, 1918, on Mt. Scopus—on the very spot from which Titus, the Roman general directed the destruction of the Second Temple 1840 years before.

The twentieth century was still young when it witnessed a crisis in Jewish life, in Zionism, and in Weizmann's personal affairs. The cry of the Russian Jews for freedom was answered by the government with an outburst of massacres in Kishinev. Scores of Jewish men, women, and children were brutally murdered and hundreds wounded and their homes and businesses looted and destroyed— all this with the knowledge and connivance of the Russian government. The Jews of the world were stunned and paralyzed by the catastrophe—all the more so because they knew that it was but the signal for further outrages. The Russian press was muzzled by a strict censorship which prevented full details of the tragedy from reaching even the Russian people. It was merely reported that "incidents" against the Jews had occurred. Not even Count Tolstoy's protest was allowed to appear in the press. Chaim Nachman Bialik's flaming poem "Ir ha-Harega (The City of Slaughter) had to appear under the disguised title, "The Burden of Nemirov."

When the atrocities became generally known, the press of the world was aroused to wrath and indignation, and condemnatory protest meetings took place in both Europe and the United States. The Sixth Zionist Congress was a scene of turmoil and excitement, and reached almost a delirium of agitation when Herzl announced the British offer of Uganda, an English colony in East Africa, for Jewish settlement and colonization. There was alarm among the delegates at the mere thought of Uganda replacing Palestine and, paradoxically, on the part of the very people most exposed to the terror of Russian brutality. Zionist leaders opposed to Herzl saw in his friendly reception of the British offer how little he understood the temper of the East European Jews, who were willing to wait and suffer, as had their ancestors for hundreds of years, rather than accept the temporary palliative of Uganda. In vain

Herzl pleaded that Uganda was not intended as a substitute for the Holy Land, and with a trembling voice he voiced anew the age-old pledge of loyalty to Zion: "If I forget thee, O Jerusalem. . . ." And Nordau characterized the place of Uganda as *Nachtasyl*. It did not help. The Russian lovers of Zion looked upon the Uganda project as a betrayal of Palestine, and left the Congress weeping.

Weizmann, naturally, was on their side. He admired Herzl, recognized that he was a force in Israel, and believed in his genuine devotion to the Holy Land; but he did not agree with his policy of panic as far as the Uganda project was concerned. Zionism was to him an ideal of eternity. As a realist he did not minimize the difficulties and hardships in the way, but said, "these are mere episodes which are shattered to pieces on the rock of eternity."

At the turn of the century England was the likeliest country in the world to attract the attention of a Jew searching for a new home. There was a greater freedom for Jews in England than in any of the European countries. The Jewish community was comparatively small but it was compact and conservative. Anti-Semitism, in the vulgar sense of the word, had not attained the dominance there it had in some of the other countries of Europe. When, therefore, after Germany and Switzerland, Weizmann took thought of his professional career as a chemist, it was natural that, in view of England's pre-eminence in the chemical industry, he should decide to make his home there.

England had something like a legendary reputation among Jews, and Weizmann remembered the stories his grandfather had told him about Moses Montefiore, a friend of the great queen, whose picture, with skullcap and high collar, hung on Weizmann's wall. There was a sentimental feeling among the English about the Holy Land; they were students of the Bible and had developed a sympathy for its creators. English poets hymned their Hebrew melodies, and the novelists, especially Benjamin Disraeli and George Eliot, struck notes of pathos and enthusiasm for the re-establishment of the Jews in their ancient homeland. The new life that was fermenting in the soul of the Jewish people found its advocates among the English poets, writers, and statesmen, and prepared the country for the role it was to play in the great Jewish drama.

Weizmann's long sojourn in England was the key to his political life and his career in Zionist leadership. Russia, Germany, and Switzerland were episodes in his odyssey; in England he felt himself at home. There were no impediments to overcome except that of the English language, which at thirty he had to work hard to master. He found the English congenial, friendly, and understanding. He did not feel himself an alien among them. The relations between the English and the Jews were sympathetic and intimate. A Jew did not have to disguise or hide his Jewishness to be accepted and respected by his non-Jewish compatriots. The image of Sir Moses Montefiore was always before Weizmann, as was also the legend of Benjamin Disraeli. What difficulties he experienced were not with the English Englishmen, but with certain Anglicized members of British Jewry.

Weizmann came to love and admire England; he became an almost fanatical Anglophile. He could see no fault in England, no iniquity in her dealings with her colonies. He found her officialdom kind, courteous, and affable—what a contrast to the officialdom he had known in Russia and Germany! There was, of course, no conflict between his loyalty to England and his loyalty to his own people and the ideal he carried in his heart. Weizmann speaks of his "flight" to England as mere "intuition." But, far-seeing politician that he was, he must have seen it would be England, the England he loved and admired, that one day would hold the key to Palestine and the Jewish national aspirations.

His beginnings in England were modest and inauspicious enough. He settled with his wife in Manchester and was appointed to a lectureship in chemistry at the university; but, although he knew himself to be a good chemist and did fine experimental work in the laboratory, he never achieved a professorship. But he had an affable, ingratiating personality, and he attracted the attention of P. C. Scott, the editor of the influential *Manchester Guardian* and a friend and long-time sponsor of Jewish national aspirations in

Palestine. The acquaintance turned out to be historic, for it was through the editor of the *Guardian* that Weizmann had his first meeting with Lord Balfour, and they became lifelong friends. Balfour was a philosopher and a statesman, and at the time of their meeting, he was almost twice Weizmann's age. But so interesting was the obscure young chemist that, instead of the fifteen minutes that was allotted for the interview, the British statesman kept him for more than an hour and a half.

The interview arranged by the editor of the *Manchester Guardian* during a general election was to be held in a hotel room. It was while Weizmann was still new to England, and his English was not easy to follow. It was also right after the Uganda offer was vehemently rejected by the Russian delegates at the Congress. When Lord Balfour led off the discussion by asking why the Uganda project was refused, Weizmann countered, probably not realizing his boldness, "Mr. Balfour, supposing I was to offer you Paris instead of London, would you take it?" Balfour looked up in astonishment: "But we have London." "That is true," Weizmann shot back, "but we had Jerusalem when London was a marsh." Weizmann was probably the first Jewish Jew Lord Balfour had ever met, and he not only did not resent his daring but he wrote to Mrs. Leopold Rothschild shortly after the interview: "I had a most interesting conversation with a young Russian Jew, a lecturer at the university."

His real opportunity came at the outbreak of the First World War. By that time Weizmann was a chemist of stature, with scientific contributions to his credit that materially helped in winning the war. He became the director of the Admiralty Laboratories, which brought him close contacts with such men as Lloyd George, General Smuts, and other leading English statesmen—contacts that gave him the opportunity to place before them the problem of Jewish homelessness and the age-old Jewish dream of a homeland in Palestine. There is no foundation, at least none that Weizmann himself provided, that in response to Lloyd George's question as to what he could do to reward him for his war effort, Weizmann replied for himself nothing, but everything for his people.

But there is good reason to believe that Weizmann sought no credit for himself but transferred what glory there was for him to Palestine and his people. There is likewise good reason to believe that during the war, when England wanted to make an idealistic gesture that would influence public opinion in the world in their favor, Weizmann put forward the idea of a Jewish national renaissance in Palestine—an ideal familiar to English statesmen for generations.

The Balfour Declaration of November 2, 1917, in agreement with France and the United States, is often compared to the edict of Cyrus, the Persian emperor, in 537 B.C.E., which granted the Jews permission to return to Jerusalem and rebuild the Temple. But the comparison is not quite accurate. For Cyrus was an absolute monarch who had neither a parliament nor a cabinet to consult nor public opinion to consider. Above all, there were no assimilationist Jews in his empire to impede and obstruct their fellow Jews' return to Jerusalem. These differences constituted factors to be reckoned with in England at the time of the Balfour Declaration. Indeed, so violent was the assimilationist Jews' opposition to Zionism and the Balfour Declaration that, at one of the stormy meetings of the cabinet, Edwin Montagu, later Secretary of State for India, broke into tears during his uncontrolled tirade against the Zionist project in Palestine. After the meeting Lloyd George confided to Weizmann: "I know that with the issuance of this Declaration I shall please one group of Jews and displease another. I have decided to please your group because you stand for a great ideal."

The Balfour Declaration was the high-water mark of Weizmann's diplomacy, although Weizmann himself scoffed at the imputation of diplomacy to him. "Where did I learn diplomacy?" he asked. "In Pinsk? Oh, no. . . . Eighty generations and thousands of yours speak through my mouth, and the voices of our wise men, our heroes, our martyrs who rest in the holy dust of Eretz Israel were heard through me. It is the voice of history that spoke through my mouth, and it is to this voice that the hard practical statesmen of our world lend their ears." All of which is no doubt true; the British are a sentimental people and the voice of history has a decided appeal to them. But to these factors must be added the uncanny force of Weizmann's personality to sway people to his purpose. "I was confronted with a personality," writes Richard Crossman of Weizmann, "who combined the fanaticism of Lenin with the sophisticated charm of Disraeli."

Still, the Balfour Declaration was not due to personality and sentiment alone but was the outcome of a hard and bitter struggle and of agitation that was almost world-wide in scope. While the center was London, the propaganda reached out to every Jewish community in the world, especially to that in the United States. In England the climate was favorable to Zionism and a Jewish National Home in Palestine. Not only such figures as Lloyd George, Balfour, Robert Cecil, Lord Milner, and General Jan Smuts, but practically the entire thinking public in Britain were unanimously in favor of the Declaration. Viscount Robert Cecil, one of the founders of the League of Nations, considered the Jewish Homeland to be of equal importance with the League itself. In the United States, Louis Brandeis threw the whole weight of his remarkable personality into the effort to win support in government circles for the Declaration. The only vociferous opposition in England to the Balfour Declaration came from the Arabs and the British Jews, the latter headed by the Board of Deputies of British Jews and the Anglo-Jewish Association.

The Balfour Declaration, the most dramatic event in Jewish history since the Declaration of the Persian Cyrus some 2500 years earlier, was to a great extent due to the Russian-Jewish chemist who did so much to win over Balfour, Lloyd George, Milner, and the other British statesmen. It was greeted with unequaled enthusiasm by the Jews of the world. For the second time in history the Jews' right to Palestine as a National Homeland was recognized by a great empire and, naturally, Weizmann was one of the greatest heroes of the hour. He had achieved what Herzl had failed to accomplish. Such an outburst of joy and exaltation broke out in every Jewish community in the world as must have welcomed the

Declaration by King Cyrus of Persia. Rhapsodic thanksgiving services in synagogues climaxed endless triumphal processions in the streets. Even Jews cool or indifferent to Zionism could not but be moved by the historic magnitude of the event.

Then came the long, painful years of the British Mandate for Palestine (June, 1922), with all its disappointments and failures, its retreats and frustrations, its misleading pledges and broken promises. There are but few examples in history of a great power so completely reversing itself as England did in the five years between the Balfour Declaration and the ratification of the Mandate in 1922. The ink had no sooner dried on the Mandate than there was an abrupt cooling off of English sentiment for the Jewish National Home. The lead was taken in the House of Lords and by the influential newspapers of Lord Northcliffe and Lord Beaverbrook. Transjordania was sliced off and made into a separate state, with a handsome British subsidy. By an artful distortion of the Balfour Declaration, the Churchill White Paper made the economic absorption of Palestine a condition of Jewish immigration into the country and tore to shreds Weizmann's demand that Palestine be made as Jewish as England was English. Of the touching faith in British promise to do "its utmost" to facilitate the establishment in Palestine of a Homeland for the Jewish people nothing was left but an aftermath of pain and unalloyed disappointment.

The Arabs took heart and defeated earlier in their opposition to the Balfour Declaration and the Mandate, now saw their opportunity to attack the Jews and extirpate the *Yishuv* (Jewish settlement) root and branch. Zionist fortunes were declining; there was little co-ordination between the Colonial Office in London and the Palestine Administration, whose officials, frankly anti-Zionist, scoffed at the Balfour Declaration and the Mandate. Churchill himself admitted to Weizmann that nine-tenths of the officials in Palestine were completely out of sympathy with Zionism. By appointing Sir Herbert Samuel as High Commissioner of Palestine, the government claimed to have done its full duty by the Jews. But the high hopes that were placed in him failed to materialize.

He was not a Zerubabel or an Ezra or a Nehemiah each of whom were appointed by Cyrus to govern. Instead, he set the example for the other high commissioners in thinking that by appeasement and concessions he would placate the Arabs. On the other hand, even had he been a stronger and more astute man than he was how could he discharge his duty to the Jews with both the governing and military officials in Palestine hostile to Zionism and to the Jews? "A hero at the Government House," Weizmann wrote in his unmailed letter to Churchill, "might perhaps have established equilibrium. But I cannot bring myself to censure Sir Herbert Samuel for not being a superman and carrying off the gates of Gaza on his own back. . . . They [the Arabs] were not discouraged in Palestine; they have even been encouraged by prominent men in England and in Palestine in their policy of opposition and obstruction."

The obstruction and opposition of the Arabs took the more sinister form of organized attacks and murder. From 1920 to 1929 there was not a year when the Arabs did not attempt to put an end to Zionism through terror. As the Russian authorities had done during the pogroms, the police and the military forces either feigned neutrality or looked the other way. In 1920, when Captain Jabotinsky appeared with a small group of young men to defend the Jewish quarter in Jerusalem during an unprovoked attack, he was promptly arrested and received the savage sentence of seven years at hard labor. He was later offered amnesty but refused it because the decree included Amin el Husseini, the infamous Mufti of Jerusalem, one of the chief instigators of the outrage. Leaping over the years and the intermittent Arab attacks on the Jews, the most atrocious assault was staged in August, 1929, when the leaders of the *Yishuv* were attending the Zionist Congress in Zurich and a group of young Jews were peacefully assembled before the wailing Wall in Jerusalem on the Ninth of Ab, as had been the custom of Jews for generations on the anniversary of the destruction of the Temple. The tension which had been whipped up by the Arabs for weeks erupted in an orgy of murder and pillage. From Jerusalem the atrocities spread to Hebron, where one hundred Jews were among the killed and wounded, who included young students of the Torah. In Safed, the classical home of the Kabbalah, forty-five Jewish men, women, and children were done to death. It was the Haganah, the Jewish Self-Defense Corps, that finally checked and routed the murderers. Despite long tension and ample warning, the Administration exonerated itself that it did not have sufficient forces to protect the *Yishuv*. The usual Commission "investigation" followed, with the conclusion that the only guilty ones were the unfortunate victims who happened to be in the way of the Arab bandits. The Mufti was declared innocent of the outrage, the Arab Executive was absolved, and the Palestine Administration was cleared of responsibility. By implication, the Jews alone were at fault. The combined effect of the Shaw Commission and the Passfield White Paper was sympathy for the "evicted Arab peasant," the suspension of immigration and the sale of land to Jews, and the general overhauling of Anglo-Zionist relations. But the intended bribe to the Arabs did not work. The Jews were deeply hurt and injured by the White Paper, but, at the same time, not a single Arab nationalist in Palestine regarded it as in any way satisfactory except as a blow to Zionism and an implied license for further depredations against the Jews.

The contrast between the Persian monarch and the English pledge to facilitate the establishment of the Jews in Palestine is too glaring to be overlooked. Cyrus not only permitted the Jews to return to their country and rebuild the Temple but handed back to the exiles the sacred vessels taken by Nebuchadnezzar and provided them with means from his own treasury for the journey and a garrison to repel marauders on the way. England, on the other hand, provided the Jews with nothing except her empty pledges and left them helpless against the attacking Arabs.

Weizmann was the most tragic figure of the Zionist fiasco. He never dreamed it would come to such an end. He had great faith in England and loved and admired her. He had faith in her ruling classes and trusted their sincerity. He believed in the mutual value of the Anglo-Jewish association he was building up, and it never occurred to him it would one day be betrayed. England was the only country in which Weizmann felt at home. She was to him the ideal nation. He would not listen to the doubts that arose in the minds of some of his colleagues concerning England's intentions, and counseled patience and forebearance when there proved to be reason for criticism and anxiety. His unchanging attitude was that the Jews would not have fared any better under any other government.

Dr. Weizmann was the most widely traveled Zionist leader of his generation and was rarely allowed the luxury of his home and family. Besides London, his home, and Palestine, frequently his temporary abode, his travels covered almost every substantial Jewish community in the world. He was as familiar a figure in Paris, Rome, Vienna, and Johannesburg as he was in Washington, New York, Chicago, and Cleveland. After his first visit to this country in 1922 he returned to the United States almost every year. He was one of the triumvirate, with Nahum Sokolow and Shmaryah Levin, who may be said to have introduced Zionism to this country in its active form.

Dr. Weizmann had his battles and triumphs in the United States. He came to further the cause of the Keren Hayesod (Palestine Foundation Fund), to awaken American interest in the Hebrew University and in the founding of the Jewish Agency for Palestine ——all three important instruments for building up the Homeland. But he soon became involved in a controversy with Louis Brandeis and his group, who had their own ideas how to help Palestine. Brandeis insisted upon private investment and individual initiative, while Weizmann, sensitive to the corporate strength and national capacity of the Jews, held to the Keren Hayesod and the Jewish National Fund as the only appropriate agencies for the re-creation of the Jewish Homeland. The stormy controversy lasted for a considerable time, with the partisans aligning themselves on the respective sides under the slogan "Washington vs. Pinsk"—an allusion to Brandeis and Weizmann. It was an unhappy situation and it threatened to disrupt the American Zionist Organization until the masses of American Zionists upheld Weizmann's view in a formal trial of strength at the famous Cleveland Convention.

The Zionist Congress of 1931 was a stormy assembly—almost as turbulent as was the "Uganda Congress," which twenty-six years earlier had threatened to disrupt the Zionist Organization. It met in Basel, the classical home of Zionist Congresses, over the first of which Herzl had presided. It convened under the shadow of the gory Arab slaughter in Hebron, the sinister specter of Hitler, and the business depression in the United States, which seriously affected the *Yishuv*. With Jews slaughtered by the Arabs and their homes destroyed, Weizmann was the target of long and bitter debate. Everything conspired to bring the wisdom of his leadership into question. His blind faith and belief in England had undermined his judgment, it was argued. When the vote was taken, a resolution of non-confidence in his policy was passed. At the time of his defeat Weizmann was fifty-six years old—an age at which repudiation is deeply felt. The Revisionists, led by the young and brilliant Vladimir Jabotinsky, with whom he was always at odds, demanded his resignation, and were joined by the *Mizrachi,* the religious Zionists, and even by friends in the other factions of the movement.

Weizmann went back to chemistry and to his long-neglected laboratory. But Zionism and the Jewish Homeland were not for a moment out of his mind. The times were heavy with threats and disaster, and it was no time for him to throw in the sponge. Nor had his love for England been completely destroyed. Hitler was on the rise, the frightful phase of his diabolical career had just begun, and it took but little imagination to anticipate the horrors to come. Weizmann did not lessen his pressure on the English government. Streams of German refugees fleeing the Hitler terror, among them gifted young Jewish scientists expelled from their country, were almost daily flocking to Palestine. It was a great opportunity for the country, and Weizmann had his hands full, trying to help. His efforts were divided between the Youth Aliyah, in collaboration with Henrietta Szold, a most remarkable figure in Jewish history, and building up of the Scientific Institute at Rehovot, at which the brilliant scientific talents exiled by Hitler were given a chance to continue their work. It also fell to his responsibility to provide the means for realizing his ambitious plans for the Institute.

In 1935 Dr. Weizmann was recalled to the Presidency of the World Zionist Organization. He replaced Nahum Sokolow, a many-faceted genius in his own right but not Weizmann's equal as a leader and negotiator. Though respected by the British as a man of learning and dignity, the famous editor of *Hazefirah,* a veritable encyclopedia of knowledge, had not gotten along well with the authorities. But although Weizmann's return to office was a personal satisfaction, it did not resolve his differences with some of his leading opponents in the Zionist Movement. His classic forensic duels with Vladimir Jabotinsky and Pinhas Rutenberg were among the historic scenes of the Congress sessions. Jabotinsky and Rutenberg were both dedicated Zionists and men of extraordinary genius. The former was equally brilliant as soldier, poet, novelist and linguist. Rutenberg was a man of immense energy, tact, and ability. During the Russian Revolution, he was repeatedly in and out of prison, until he finally found his way to the Jews, from whom he had long been estranged; it was he who conceived the idea of the electrification of the Jordan. The creation and extension of the Jewish Agency to include Jews who were not prepared to declare themselves as Zionists but were anxious to assist in the building up of Palestine was resented and opposed by many European and some American Zionists who were not willing to give the "rich Jews" an equal voice in the affairs of the Zionist Movement. But Weizmann "was not a loyalist disturbed by phraseology or the mechanics of organization or the dialectics of partisanship," writes Louis Lipsky. Thus, in spite of the bitter struggle that raged about the Agency, he not only succeeded in establishing it firmly but gained the support of men who turned out to be of material assistance in the development both of Palestine and the Zionist Movement.

Dr. Weizmann's return to office did not bring him the happiness he had known during his former term as Zionist leader. He was past middle age and he had many disappointments and disillusionments to look back upon. The Zionist situation had greatly deteriorated. There were renewed anti-Jewish Arab outbreaks in Palestine with accompanying murder, destruction of homes and fields and up-rooting of trees over the whole country, with the Administration reluctant to take any decisive action to stop the outrages. With the Hitler catastrophe increasing in intensity, boatloads of fleeing Jews were denied admission to Palestine. Some of these vessels—derelict freighters fit only for the junkyard but clung to by the desperate victims of the German terror—were fired upon by British coast guards and their human cargo captured, interned, and finally deported as illegal immigrants. Weizmann had lost his grip on the British ruling class; his charm no longer worked. His personality, which was so influential at the time of the Balfour Declaration, carried no weight with the crude, vulgar Ernest Bevin, the Foreign Secretary of the Labor Government. Indeed, Bevin gave the *coup de grâce* to the Balfour Declaration, the British Mandate for Palestine, the Jewish National Home, and everything that Zionism stood for. When six million Jews were being done to death by scientific methods and Weizmann pleaded with him for certificates for refugees, Bevin, without a feeling of shame, writes Weizmann, declared at a news conference: "If the Jews, with all their sufferings, want to get too much at the head of the queue, you have the danger of another anti-Semitic reaction through it all." Weizmann adds: "The British Government would have the Jews stay on and contribute their talents toward the upbuilding of Germany, so that the Germans might have another chance of destroying the last remnants of the Jewish people."

It was now a question of life and death for the Jews of Palestine, and the Haganah took over the defense of the *Yishuv*. The Haganah defensive work was carried on so effectively that Bevin became frightened and produced plan after plan for enlarged Jewish immigration, but so cunningly worded that they would leave the *Yishuv* at the mercy of the Arabs without British protection. It is impossible to close this phase of the Anglo-Jewish relations in Palestine without mention of Brigadier Orde Wingate, a legendary figure of the Jewish groups organized against the terrorist activities of the Arabs. He was a fanatical Zionist, and that not because of Zionist literature but due to his spiritual outlook and his study of the Bible. He was of great help to the *Yishuv* in its desperate struggle against their terrorist enemies. His death in a plane accident was an irreparable loss to the Jewish cause in Palestine.

Weizmann abhorred violence, but he rejoiced in the work of the Haganah. His conscience was clear and he had no apologies for the British mess in Palestine. He had his hurts and wounds, but the warm spot in his heart for England had not cooled. Despite all that had happened, he still hoped for a Jewish Homeland as a British protectorate. When talk of partition of Palestine developed, Weizmann was living in London, ignored and neglected by his former friends and associates in the government. He never admitted to himself that he had failed as, indeed, he had not. It was the insane moral and political age in which he lived that had failed. Not even he, with all the grace and magic of his personality, could talk the British out of their political stupidity and national selfishness. Despite the numerous controversies the Jews did not disown him when the *Yishuv* was strong enough to fend for itself and organize a government. For on February 14, 1949, when the First Knesset met in Jerusalem, Chaim Weizmann was elected the first President of the Israeli Republic. It was, of course, a purely honorary office, and Dr. Weizmann knew it. But at seventy-nine, the actual leadership of so complex a state as the Israeli Republic had become would have been beyond his strength. The ruling power was passed on to younger men who had no faith in the policy of co-existence with England, so dear to the heart of Weizmann, but who, instead, drove out the British and achieved one of the most remarkable feats by a democracy in modern times.

Today, after fifteen years of the new State, the spirit of Dr. Chaim Weizmann finds expression in what are perhaps the greatest monuments to his life—the Hebrew University and the Weizmann Institute at Rehovot. In these two institutions of higher learning and scientific research Dr. Weizmann realized his dream of scientific achievement for the Holy Land. They serve today as a standard for all the underdeveloped countries of Asia and Africa. "It is true," said Weizmann, "that we are moved by instincts of national self-preservation, but rarely has the right of existence of a people been asserted with such attendant benefits to others."

Almost with his last breath he pleaded for his beloved Institute. "Tell them [the Jews]," he said to a friend, "not to permit the destruction of the thing we have labored to build. We Jews can do something which can be an honor to us and to all mankind. But we mustn't spoil it." It is heartening to recall the words of his friend and admirer, Richard Crossman: "I believe that if he could look at what has grown and what has been built since his death . . . he would be proud, and he would say, 'They haven't spoilt it. This is the Jewish state I dreamt of . . .'"

Dr. Chaim Weizmann died November 9, 1952.

Bibliography

EZRA

The Holy Scriptures: Books of Ezra and Nehemiah

Albright, William Powell, *The Jews, Their History, Culture and Religion*, vol. 1, ed. Louis Finkelstein (Philadelphia; JPS,* 1949)

Kittel, Rudolf, *Great Men and Movements in Israel* (New York: The Macmillan Co., 1929)

Moore, George Foot, *Judaism*, vol. 1 (Cambridge: Harvard University Press, 1927)

Schurer, Emil, *A History of the Jewish People*, vol. 1 (Edinburgh: T. & T. Clark)

HILLEL

Finkelstein, Louis, *The Pharisees* (Philadelphia: JPS, 1938)

Geiger, Abraham, *Judaism and Its History* (New York: The Bloch Publishing Co.)

Goldin, Judah, *The Jews, Their History, Culture, and Religion*, vol. 1, ed. Louis Finkelstein (Philadelphia: JPS, 1944)

Moor, George Foot, *Judaism*, vol. 1 (Cambridge: Harvard University Press, 1927)

PHILO

Bentwich, Norman, *Philo Judaeus of Alexandria* (Philadelphia: JPS, 1910)

Goodenough, Erwin R., *The Politics of Philo Judaeus* (New Haven: Yale University Press, 1938)

Klausner, Joseph, *From Jesus to Paul* (New York: The Macmillan Co., 1943)

Wolfson, Harry, *Philo* (Cambridge: Harvard University Press, 1947)

* Jewish Publication Society of America

SAADIA GAON

The Book of Beliefs and Opinions, trans. Samuel Rosenblatt (New Haven: Yale University Press, 1948)

Husik, Isaac, *A History of Medieval Jewish Philosophy* (New York: The Macmillan Co., 1918)

Malter, Henry, *Saadia Gaon* (Philadelphia: JPS, 1921)

Mart, Alexander, *Essays in Jewish Biography* (Philadelphia: JPS, 1947)

Simon, Leon, *Saadia in Aspects of the Hebrew Genius* (London: George Routledge & Sons, 1910)

RASHI

Rashi, ed. Dr. Simon Federbush (New York: World Jewish Congress, 1958)

Rashi Anniversary Volume, American Academy for Jewish Research (Philadelphia: JPS, 1941)

Blumenfield, Samuel M., *Master of Troyes* (New York: Behrman House, 1946)

Liber, Maurice, *Rashi,* trans. Adele Szold (Philadelphia: JPS, 1906)

JUDAH HALEVI

Kitab Al Khazari, trans, with an intro. by Hartwig Hershfeld (London: George Routledge & Sons, 1906)

Selected Poems of Jehudah Halevi, trans. Nina Salaman (Philadelphia: JPS, 1928)

Husik, Isaac, *A History of Medieval Jewish Philosophy* (New York: The Macmillan Co., 1918)

MOSES MAIMONIDES

The Code of Maimonides, Yale Judaica Series (New Haven: Yale University Press)

The Eight Chapters by Maimonides on Ethics, trans. Joseph Gorfinkle (New York: Columbia University Press, 1912)

The Guide for the Perplexed, trans. M. Friedlander (London, 1881)

Friedlander, Israel, *Past and Present* (Cincinnati: Ark Publishing Co., 1919)

Husik, Isaac, *History of Medieval Jewish Philosophy* (New York: The Macmillan Co., 1918)

Hyamson, Moses, *The Mishnah Torah by Maimonides*

Minkin, Jacob S., *The World of Moses Maimonides* (New York: Thomas Yoseloff, 1957)

Rabin, Chaim, *Maimonides. The Guide for the Perplexed* (London: East and West Library, 1952)

Roth, Leon, *The Guide for the Perplexed* (London: Hutchins University Library, 1947)

Yellin, David, and Abraham, Israel, *Maimonides* (Philadelphia: JPS, 1946)

Zeitlin, Solomon, *Maimonides: A Biography* (New York: Bloch Publishing Co., 1955)

JOSEPH ALBO

Sefer ha-Ikkarim, trans, with an intro. by Isaac Husik (Philadelphia: JPS)

Husik, Isaac, *A History of Medieval Jewish Philosophy* (New York: The Macmillan Co., 1918)

DON ISAAC ABRAYANEL

Minkin, Jacob S., *Abarbanel and the Expulsion of the Jews from Spain* (New York: Behrman's Jewish Book House, 1938)

Minkin, Jacob S., "Don Isaac Abravanel" in *Great Jewish Personalities,* ed. Simon Noveck, the B'nai B'rith Great Books Series (New York: Farrar, Strauss & Cudahy, 1959)

Netanyahu, B., *Don Isaac Abravanel* (Philadelphia: JPS, 1953)

Sarachek, Joseph, *Don Isaac Abravanel* (New York: Bloch Publishing Co., 1938)

RABBI MEIR OF ROTHENBURG

Agus, Irving, *Rabbi Meir of Rothenburg,* two vols. (Philadelphia: The Dropsie College, 1947)

Ginzberg, Louis, *Jewish Encyclopedia,* vol. XIII

Kisch, Guido, *The Jews in Medieval Germany* (Chicago: University of Chicago Press, 1948)

Lowenthal, Marvin, *The Jews of Germany* (Philadelphia: JPS, 1944)

ISRAEL BAAL SHEM TOV

Tales of the Hasidim (The Early Masters and the Later Masters), comp. Martin Buber (New York: Schocken Books, 1947-48)

Buber, Martin, *Hasidism and Modern Man*, ed. and trans. by Maurice S. Friedman (New York: Horizon Press, 1958)

Buber, Martin, *The Legend of the Baal Shem*, trans. Maurice S. Friedman (New York: Harper & Brothers, 1948)

Minkin, Jacob S., *The Romance of Hassidism* (New York: The Macmillan Co., 1935; New York: Thomas Yoseloff, 1958)

Newman, Louis I., and Spitz, Samuel, *The Hasidic Anthology* (New York: Charles Scribner's Sons, 1934; New York: Bloch Publishing Co., 1944)

RABBI ELIJAH GAON

Great Jewish Personalities, ed. Simon Noveck, the B'nai B'rith Great Books Series (New York: Farrar, Straus & Cudahy, 1959)

Cohen, Israel, *Vilna* (Philadelphia: JPS, 1943)

Ginzberg, Louis, *Students, Scholars, and Saints* (Philadelphia: JPS, 1928)

Schechter, Solomon, *Studies in Judaism*, first series (Philadelphia: JPS, 1918)

MOSES MENDELSSOHN

Lady Magnus, *Jewish Portraits* (London: Meyers & Co., 1905)

Roback, A. A., *Jewish Influence in Modern Thought* (Cambridge: Sci-Art Publishers, 1929)

Walter, H., *Moses Mendelssohn* (New York: Bloch Publishing Co., 1930)

SOLOMON SCHECHTER

Adler, Cyrus, *Lectures, Selected Papers, Addresses* (Philadelphia: JPS, 1933)

Bentwich, Norman, *Solomon Schechter: A Biography* (Philadelphia: JPS, 1938)

Ginzberg, Louis, *Students, Scholars, and Saints* (Philadelphia: JPS, 1928)

Marx, Alexander, *Studies in Jewish History and Booklore* (New York: The Jewish Theological Seminary of America, 1944)

I. L. PERETZ

Peretz, trans. and ed. Sol Liptzin (YIVO: 1947)

Peretz, I. L., *In This World and the Next,* trans. Moshe Spiegel (New York: Thomas Yoseloff, 1958)

Roback, A. A., *I. L. Peretz, Psychologist of Literature* (Cambridge: Sci-Art Publishers, 1935)

Samuel, Maurice, *Prince of the Ghetto* (Philadelphia: JPS, 1948)

SOLOMON JACOB ABRAMOVICH (MENDELE MOKHER SEFARIM)

Roback, A. A., *The Story of Yiddish Literature* (New York, 1940)

Sefarim, Mendele Mokher, *The Nag,* trans. Moshe Spiegel (New York: The Beechhurst Press, 1955)

Sefarim, Mendele Mokher, *The Parasite,* trans. Gerald Stillman (New York: Thomas Yoseloff, 1956)

Wiener, Leo, *The History of Yiddish Literature in the Nineteenth Century* (New York: Charles Scribner's Sons, 1899)

SAUL TCHERNICHOVSKI

Raisin, Max, *Great Jews I Have Known* (New York: Philosophical Library)

Spiegel, Shalom, *Hebrew Reborn* (New York: The Macmillan Co., 1930)

ASHER GINZBERG (AHAD HA'AM)

Gottheil, Richard, *Zionism* (Philadelphia: JPS, 1914)

Learsi, Rufus, *Fulfillment: The Epic Story of Zionism* (Cleveland and New York: The World Publishing Co., 1951)

Simon, Leon, *Selected Essays by Ahad Ha'am* (Philadelphia: JPS, 1912, 1960)

Spiegel, Shalom, *Hebrew Reborn* (New York: The Macmillan Co., 1930)

SIMON M. DUBNOW

Nationalism and History: Essay on Old and New Judaism, ed. Koppel Pinson (Philadelphia: JPS, 1958)

Dubnow, Simon, *Jewish History: An Essay in the Philosophy of History,* trans. H. S. (Philadelphia: JPS, 1903)

Friedlander, Israel, *Past and Present* (Cincinnati: Ark Publishing Co., 1919)

LOUIS GINZBERG

Finkelstein, Louis, *Louis Ginzberg*, American Jewish Year Book, vol. 56, 1955

Goldman, Solomon, *Ginzberg Jubilee Volumes*, American Academy for Jewish Research (Philadelphia: JPS, 1943)

Waxman, Meyer, *History of Jewish Literature*, vol. IV (New York: Thomas Yoseloff, 1960)

CHAIM WEIZMANN

Crossman, Richard, *A Nation Reborn* (New York: Atheneum, 1960)

Learsi, Rufus, *Fulfillment* (Cleveland and New York: The World Publishing Co., 1951)

Weizmann, Chaim, *Trial and Error* (New York: Harper & Brothers, 1940)

To Rabbi Rieden –

To my rabbi, because he
chose to be a rabbi, and mine.

H Jay Sharp
1/1/64